COMPENSATION

EFFECTIVE REWARD MANAGEMENT

SECOND EDITION

COMPENSATION
EFFECTIVE REWARD MANAGEMENT
SECOND EDITION

Rabindra N. Kanungo
Manuel Mendonca

McGill University

John Wiley and Sons

Toronto • New York • Chichester • Brisbane • Singapore • Weinheim

Canadian Cataloguing in Publication Data
Kanungo, Rabindra N., 1935-
Compensation: effective reward management

2nd ed.
Includes bibliographic references and index.
ISBN 0-471-64143-X

1. Compensation management.
2. Incentives in industry.
I. Mendonca, Manuel
II. Title

HF5549.5.C67K35 1997   658.3142   C96-931414-0

Acquisitions Editor: John Horne
Developmental Editor: Michael Schellenberg
Publishing Services Director: Karen Bryan
Cover and Interior Design: JAQ
Graphic Artist/Electronic Assembly: JAQ
Co-ordinating/Developmental Editors: Karen Bryan and Michael Schellenberg
Printing and Binding: Tri-Graphic Printing Limited

Printed and Bound in Canada
10 9 8 7 6 5 4 3 2 1

To our parents for the invaluable lesson that
"it is more blessed to give than to receive".

To Minati and Rita for their enduring patience, encouragement,
and warm and generous support.

To managers committed
to the full development of the human potential.

Brief Table of Contents

Contents

Chapter 8: Promoting Organizational Membership Behaviours, 155

Chapter 9: Performance-Based Pay: Personal Equity 1, 177

Preface

The globalization of business in the early 1990's has put increased pressure on Canadian corporations, both public and private, to remain highly productive and competitive in the world market. This competitive pressure poses many challenges for Canadian human resource management practice. One major challenge facing Canada's organizations today is how to design and manage employee compensation. As we head towards the new millennium, motivating employees for high performance by establishing appropriate linkages between performance, satisfaction, and compensation will be the key issue for human resource management.

The average amount that an organization invests in compensation can range as high as 75% of its total expenditures. In order for this huge investment to pay off, there needs to be a closer link between the compensation package and the desired performance level. In order for compensation—monetary and non-monetary—to be effective, rewards must be managed in a coherent manner. The writing of this book was prompted by the above considerations and one other major consideration: the absence of a Canadian textbook that adequately addresses the issue of managing rewards within organizations in a coherent and comprehensive manner.

In the second edition of *Compensation: Effective Reward Management*, we have continued to provide an approach to the design and management of organizational rewards that is both practical and consistent with the findings of research into work attitudes and behaviour. We strive to integrate motivational theories with management practices.

THE FOCUS OF THIS BOOK

This book is different from other existing textbooks in three ways. First, the book achieves an integration of theory and practice through a unifying model. The model will force students and practicing managers alike to take a good look at reward systems from a motivational perspective and to determine if there is a rational basis for the techniques and practices that prevail in an organization.

Second, the book advocates the use of our innovative diagnostic procedure for evaluating the effectiveness of each reward item of an organization's compensation system. This procedure will enable an organization to determine if it is, indeed, achieving the intended motivational effectiveness from its enormous compensation expenditures. If it is not, the diagnostic procedure has the capability of identifying the specific reward item, policy, practice, or technique that needs to be addressed, and proposing concrete and practical remedial interventions.

Finally, the book deals with unique and newsworthy Canadian topics, legislation, and practices related to compensation management, including such topical issues as how the Canadian labour movement affects compensation, the compensation packages of Canadian Members of Parliament, and a look at pay equity and where it now stands in provincial jurisdictions.

New Features to the Second Edition

The second edition has been thoroughly updated and includes new material that is both topical and practical including:

- a new chapter which considers **the influence of unions on compensation**.
- a new section focusing on new and emerging issues in the field of compensation, including:

  - **person-based pay**—a consideration of the design and role of pay-for-skills and pay-for-knowledge systems

  - **executive compensation**—one of the "hottest" issues in the media today

  - **the impact of culture on compensation**—the influence of the sociocultural environment on compensation design and management in organizations in the emerging economies of developing countries

  - **the diagnostic tool**—one of the major features of this book—has been enhanced and improved.

As a text both at the undergraduate and graduate levels, this structured and logical guide to compensation theory and practice will provoke students to experiment and to test the conclusions of the model. The book thus serves to promote deductive and inductive approaches to learning that are invaluable to the educational experience of both students and researchers in the field. Furthermore, practicing managers, compensation specialists, and management consultants will find the textbook to be a valuable resource in their effort to understand the reward-motivation phenomenon and to design and administer reward policies and systems. In this connection, the discussion of how existing compensation approaches can be extended to assess their own organizations will provide particularly useful insights.

ACKNOWLEDGEMENTS FOR THE SECOND EDITION

We thank the many individuals who contributed to the book through their comments and constructive criticism. Special thanks to the primary reviewers of our manuscript:

Naresh Agarwal, McMaster University
Nina Cole, University of Toronto
J.R. Edmonds, University of Saskatchewan
Steve Harvey, Bishop's University
Lissa McRae, Bishop's University
Ross Plater, Brandon University
Hermann F. Schwind, St. Mary's University
William J. Wood, Conestoga College
Phillip C. Wright, University of New Brunswick

We would like to thank the Jaico Publishing House, Bombay, for permission to reprint an excerpt from the *Panchantantra*.

We would like to express our appreciation to all those who have helped us during the preparation of this book. We are thankful to our students and management trainees whose skepticism went a long way in persuading us to prepare the original volume, and whose input into the new edition has been invaluable. Thanks to Ann O'Neill of Henson College at Dalhousie University.

Finally, we wish to acknowledge the help and support of staff at John Wiley and Sons Canada, Limited. We are grateful to Karen Bryan and Michael Schellenberg whose perceptive editorial queries and comments helped to clarify many an unclear thought and example. As well, thanks must go to John Horne for his support at every stage of the project.

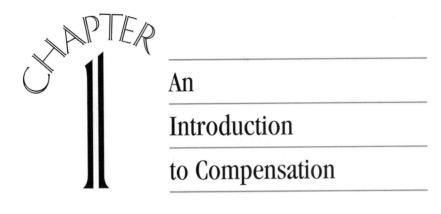

An Introduction to Compensation

OVERVIEW

This chapter introduces the subject of compensation and explores the components and objectives of the reward system. The chapter develops the model of effective reward management, which provides an integrative and comprehensive framework for the concepts, techniques, and processes discussed in the various chapters. The model provides both a perspective of, and a structure for, the text.

LEARNING OBJECTIVES

▶ To understand the nature of compensation and how it affects individuals, organizations, and society at large.

▶ To identify the components of the compensation system and to understand the rationale for the classification of compensation.

▶ To become aware of the goals of the compensation system.

▶ To acquire a coherent perspective of compensation theories, techniques, and processes.

THE NATURE OF COMPENSATION

"Wine gladdens life, and money answers everything." (Ecclesiastes 10:19)

"The laborer deserves his wages." (Luke 10:7)

Conduct, patience, purity,
Manners, loving-kindness, birth,
After money disappears,
Cease to have the slightest worth.

Wisdom, sense and social charm,
Honest pride and self-esteem,
After money disappears,
All at once become a dream.

Money gets you anything,
Gets it in a flash;
Therefore let the prudent get
Cash, cash, cash.   (Panchatantra)

The idea of compensation is deeply rooted in every culture and society. Traditionally the term compensation has meant economic or monetary reward in a work context, but in this text the term will be used in its broadest sense to include all forms of rewards: monetary, payments in kind, and non-economic (for example, praise or recognition). In this broad sense, compensation is one of the most important aspects of human relationships. A relationship between two individuals is often perceived as a reciprocal exchange. People learn to say "Thank you" for any object, service, or compliment received. In some circumstances, the thank-you is an adequate recompense. In different circumstances, the thank-you needs to take on a substantial form, like a payment in kind or money. In work relationships, compensation takes the form of salary or wages, a variety of benefits, and non-economic rewards such as challenging assignments and praise from the supervisor.

The following news items underscore the critical nature of compensation for society, individuals, and organizations:

- "Are civil servants getting fair a layoff deal?...Ontario officials estimate their more modest downsizing plan will cost the province $150 million to $200 million, versus about $1.5 billion for union buyout proposals. The $1.3 billion gap is an extra $100,000 per position or more than two years' pay" (Daw, 1996, p.A1).

- "Law graduates starving for work...many are still searching for work or have settled for the bare minimum, scrabbling for a foothold in a profession that once guaranteed a healthy income and elevated station in life" (Makin, 1996, p.A1).

- "At least 5,100 auto workers at Big Three assembly and parts plants in Canada will be off the job next week because of stagnant auto sales...Workers at all three plants will receive 65 to 70 per cent of their wages" (Keenan, 1996, p. B5).

We will briefly explore the reasons for the interest and concerns of society, individuals, and organizations with regard to compensation in the following pages.

Societal Concerns

Compensation in the form of monetary rewards has always been a societal concern because of its effect on justice, and taxes and the health of the economy.

Effects on justice Different religions have ordained that the principles of justice should govern compensation. After the industrial revolution, the concept of a just wage was extended to include a living wage. Progressive gains in collective agreements brought unionized workers closer to the realization a just, living wage. Minimum wage legislation provided some safeguards for non-unionized workers. All workers have benefited from social security legislation that provides for medicare, unemployment insurance, worker's compensation, and old age pensions.

In recent times, societal concerns for justice have focused on the issue of "pay equity" for women—known as "equal pay for work of equal value" or the issue of "comparable worth". The principle underlying pay equity is that jobs which hold the same value for the employer should be paid at the same rate, regardless of whether these jobs are held by men or women. Pay equity was first legislated at the federal level in 1977, and since then has been adopted, in varying forms, by the provinces. However, its implementation has been neither smooth nor swift. For example, the *Toronto Sun* of February 18, 1996 reported that the $1.5 billion pay equity dispute of 80,000 federal government employees, started in 1984, was still not settled.

Effects on taxes and economy Societal concerns about economic compensation also arise because of the effects of compensation on taxes and the health of the economy. For example, increases in compensation to government and municipal employees ordinarily lead to tax increases, which are not popular with taxpayers. Furthermore, the reduction of government deficits necessary for a healthy economy may require such actions as pay reductions, pay freezes, or budget cuts that lead to massive layoffs of government employees—refer to news report on Ontario civil servants on page 2. Also, wage increases without corresponding increases in productivity can lead to inflationary pressures that could adversely affect the competitiveness of business and industry.

Individual Concerns

For individuals, compensation is their source of income, a return on their investment in education and skills development, a return on their work contributions, and an important element of job satisfaction.

Source of income For the vast majority of people, monetary compensation is the primary, if not the only, source of the income that determines their social status and standard of living. Compensation enables the individual to put food on the table, pay the rent, buy clothes, and send the children to school. The pay cheque is a crucial determinant of the individual's socioeconomic well-being.

Return on education investment The pay cheque also represents a return on the individual's investment in education and skills training. The time spent in school or in a profession constitutes the individual's investment of time, effort, and expense. An organization will ordinarily benefit from such investments by its employees. Hence, it is not unreasonable for individuals to expect that their compensation will adequately reflect this investment. Hence, one can understand the disappointment of the law graduates in the news item on page 2.

Feedback on performance Individuals also expect that their compensation will provide an adequate feedback on their work contributions. Steve Gordon and Rachel Kiwanuka joined the Toronto Trading Company on the same day as personnel officers, on salaries that adequately reflected their education, training, and experience. For their first year of service, the performance assessment report showed that Rachel performed much better than Steve. Assuming that the performance assessment was conducted properly and fairly, the higher merit pay to Rachel relative to Steve serves as a feedback on performance. If this differentiation is not made and both receive the same merit pay, the organization has not provided the correct feedback on their work contributions.

Element of job satisfaction The concerns and expectations of individuals about their monetary compensation are inextricably linked with job satisfaction. If Rachel does not receive an equitable merit pay, she will experience considerable job dissatisfaction. While monetary compensation is only one component of job satisfaction (other components include satisfaction with job tasks, co-workers and supervisors, working conditions, and job security), satisfaction with financial compensation has been found to be a major contributor to job satisfaction (Judge, 1993).

Organizational Concerns

From the point of view of organizations, financial compensation is a concern because it is a major component of operating costs, it impacts on the success of business strategies, and it is a key motivational tool. Also, organizations need to comply with pay laws.

Component of operating costs In manufacturing organizations, the compensation package constitutes as much as 50 to 60 per cent of the total operating costs; in service organizations and in the government and its agencies, the compensation package can go as high as 80 per cent of the total costs. Hence, cost control strategies such as the layoffs of auto workers are used— refer to the news item on page 2. However, organizations that focus only on compensation costs might overlook that employees are a valuable resource. For this reason, successful organizations view the compensation package in strategic terms—as an investment in people.

Impact on business strategies Organizations that view compensation as an investment in their employees develop compensation programmes that are consistent with, and support, their business strategies. For example, organizations with relatively stable products, markets, and technology generally prefer to acquire employees from outside the company for entry-level positions and develop them internally. Such organizations are more likely to emphasize internal pay relationships, maintaining the proper differentials between job values. On the other hand, organizations with a broad, changing product line and changing markets are successful with a compensation strategy that focuses on external pay relationships, which ensure that the organization can attract the talent, skills, and abilities needed to constantly meet the challenges of shifting market demands.

Key motivational tool A compensation package that includes both economic and non-economic elements serves as a key motivational tool to attract, retain, and motivate employees to perform the organizationally desired behaviours. For example, absenteeism is a serious problem in Canadian organizations. The total cost of absenteeism to the Canadian economy is estimated at 15 billion dollars (Booth, 1993), or 10 to 11 times the costs resulting from strikes! Compensation can be an effective strategy to address absenteeism. Compensation is equally effective to motivate employees to grow on the job, to accept challenge, responsibility, and self-direction. Lawler's (1971, 1981) seminal work on pay and organizational effectiveness has demonstrated that a properly designed compensation programme constitutes an important element of the strategies used to mobilize and manage human resources.

Compliance with pay laws Until recently, unions were the major source of organizational concerns about compensation issues. With the advent of pay equity legislation, organizations are now forced to look at compensation programmes not in paternalistic terms, but in terms of fairness and equity.

To summarize: The issue of compensation is fraught with conflict and tension among employees, between employees and their employer, between voters and civil servants, between legislators and employers, and among employers—as can be seen from the bulleted news items. It is beyond the scope of this text to address all the issues related to such conflicts. The focus in this text is primarily on economic and non-economic compensation issues in work relationships in an organizational context.

CLASSIFICATION OF COMPENSATION: ECONOMIC AND NON-ECONOMIC REWARDS

Unlike small-scale business enterprises in traditional societies which compensated their employees through wages only, modern organizations offer a wide variety of rewards to employees in order to remain competitive. An extensive list of such rewards (Table 1.1) has been compiled by Kanungo and Hartwick (1987). The type and the number of reward items in a compensation package of an organization depend upon the organization's needs and its ingenuity in creating appropriate items to meet those needs. The reward system can be defined as constituting all the economic compensation and non-economic compensation items that an employee is entitled to by virtue of the employment contract or relationship—refer Figure 1.1. We briefly review the major elements of: (a) the economic compensation system; and (b) the non-economic compensation system.

TABLE 1.1 A List of Work Rewards Offered by Organizations (in Alphabetical Order)

Accident and sickness insurance	Paid parking space
Achieving the organization's goals	Paid personal time off
Authority	Participation in decision making
Awards for long service	Pay
Awards for superior performance	Personal challenge
Cafeteria subsidies	Personal growth and development
Coffee breaks	Praise from co-workers
Company-sponsored life insurance	Praise from supervisor
Company-sponsored professional services	Prestige
Company-sponsored recreational activities	Pride in success of company
Cost-of-living increase	Pride in work
Dental plan	Profit-sharing plan
Discounts on purchase of company products	Promotion
Expense account	Recognition
Extended lunch periods	Responsibility
Feelings of worthwhile accomplishment	Retirement benefits
Holiday bonus	Sense of belonging
Interesting work	Sick leaves
Job security	Sick pay
Mortgage financing	Social status
Opportunity for creativity	Uniform/clothes allowance
Opportunity to make friends	Use of company car
Opportunity to use special abilities	Vacation
Paid absence for study	Variety of job

FIGURE 1.1. The Reward System

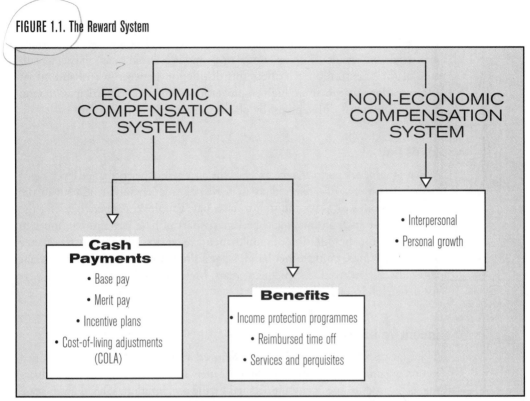

Source: Adapted from Milkovich and Newman (1990).

THE ECONOMIC COMPENSATION SYSTEM

Cash Payments

This category comprises: base pay, merit pay, incentive plans, and cost-of-living adjustments (COLA).

Base Pay

Employees expect their base pay to reflect the value of the inputs (education, skills, experience) that they bring to the job. The employer expects the base pay to reflect the value of the job's contribution to achieving the organization's goals. Thus, base pay represents a quid pro quo relationship between the employee (a return for services perceived to be rendered) and the employer (a payment for contribution perceived to be received). The base pay of a job is determined by a combination of the job's value to the employer, and the pay rate for such a job in the labour market. The job's value is computed by a job evaluation system; the market pay rate is obtained through wage surveys.

The base pay of unionized employees is expressed in an hourly rate and is referred to as wages. The base pay of non-unionized employees is generally expressed and calculated on an annual basis and is referred to as salary. The culture of the organization can affect this distinction between wages and salary. Organizations that focus on high employee involvement and participation tend to eliminate status differentials, by placing all employees on a salary basis.

Merit Pay

When employee's performance exceeds the acceptable performance level, he or she expects a reward—referred to as *merit pay*—which might be paid in the form of a bonus or as an addition to base pay. Employees generally prefer the latter because such an increment becomes a part of base pay and continues to be received for the duration of employment, regardless of future performance levels. The bonus, on the other hand, is for a single time period only and is not automatically received in subsequent years. Merit bonus is paid only when performance levels justify it.

Incentive Plans

These are cash payments available to employees when they exceed predetermined job or organizational goals—usually the latter. Incentive plans serve as inducements to produce specific results desired by the organization, such as an increase in the volume of output, revenue, profits, or return on investment; or a reduction in costs or reject rate. The plans are designed to allow employees a share in the specific gains that result. Employee motivation and involvement are considerably enhanced when organizations give employees a "piece of the action."

Incentive plans are based on the performance of individual employees, departmental units, or the organization as a whole. If the total operating results of the organization on a specific measure exceed the predetermined standard, then the resulting gain is shared among the departmental units according to an established performance measure, and is distributed among the employees of that unit, also according to the individual measures of performance.

Often a distinction is made between merit pay and incentive plans. The former is viewed as a reward for past performance and the latter as an incentive for future performance. In practice, the distinction gets blurred, especially when a merit pay programme is equitably designed and managed. In such a situation, employees are known to look forward to merit pay. Employee expectation of merit pay can serve as an inducement or incentive to future performance.

Cost-of-Living Adjustment

Also known as COLA, this cash payment is intended to compensate employees for the loss of the purchasing power of their compensation package usually resulting from inflation. Adjustments are made to the base pay when the cost of living increases as determined by the rise in the Consumer Price Index beyond a certain number of points.

BENEFITS

The multitude of employee benefits (and perquisites) programmes can be grouped into three categories: income protection programmes, reimbursed time off, and services and perquisites. These programmes, most of which were started during World War II, have increased both in variety and cost. In 1950 these programmes cost organizations an average of $515 per year—less than 15 per cent of gross payroll costs. In 1992, benefits averaged 26.9% of the gross payroll costs (Carlyle, 1995). Tax considerations (tax credit or allowable tax deduction) have often influenced the introduction of these programmes.

Income Protection Programmes

Employment insurance, worker's compensation, medical insurance, disability insurance, and pensions are examples of programmes designed to provide a continuation of income in a variety of circumstances and situations. Also included in this category are programmes that provide income continuation for the spouse and the family on the death of the employee. Some examples would be life insurance and pension plans whose features provide income for the family.

Reimbursed Time Off

Organizations pay for time not worked for a variety of reasons, for example, vacations, sick leave, maternity and paternity leave. Such reimbursed time off recognizes employees' needs for recreation and their obligations to attend to their family needs. Reimbursed time off is also given for jury duty, acknowledging that organizations, as good corporate citizens, should enable employees to fulfil their civic responsibilities.

Services and Perquisites

This miscellaneous category covers a wide range of services and perquisites that do not fall into the previous two categories, for example, dental plans, employee assistance plans (which provide for counselling for stress, burn-out, drug and alcohol addiction, etc.), use of a company automobile, a discount on company products, and professional memberships.

THE NON-ECONOMIC COMPENSATION SYSTEM

The non-economic compensation system includes all non-monetary rewards which can be grouped into two broad categories: interpersonal rewards and personal growth rewards. Examples of each category are:

- Interpersonal rewards:
  - good interpersonal social relationships with co-workers and supervisors;
  - social status in the workplace resulting from job position and performance;
  - social approval and social recognition for job activities; and
  - sense of belonging.
- Personal growth rewards:
  - job variety;
  - enhanced self-esteem for achieving organizational goals;
  - personal sense of achievement;
  - personal growth and development;
  - pride in work;
  - participation in decision making; and
  - autonomy and control in job-related matters.

Interpersonal rewards promote constructive social relationships and enhance emotional maturity. Personal growth rewards provide opportunities for developing skills and competencies. These are particularly suitable for employees with high growth need, that is, the need to develop one's capabilities through the exercise of job-related responsibilities. The growth-related rewards are also referred to as intrinsic rewards in the sense that they are derived directly from job performance.

OBJECTIVES OF THE REWARD SYSTEM

Rewards must be earned. The specific behaviours that employees must perform, and/or results they must achieve to earn the rewards, must be clearly stipulated and communicated to all employees. The statement of what behaviours are to be performed in order to earn which reward is termed as the "behaviour-reward contingency". If the behaviour-reward contingency is to be meaningful and effective in producing the organizationally desired behaviours, then it must be spelt out for each reward item in specific terms. For example, it is not sufficient to say: "Employees will get merit pay if they perform well." The behaviours and/or results that constitute performing well—for example, sales of so many dollars, meeting report deadlines—must be stated.

An organization can choose from a variety of objectives for its reward system as a whole and for the reward items in particular. The appropriateness of the objectives, a critical consideration, can best be determined by this test: Do the compensation objectives support and direct the efforts of employees towards the realization of the organization's business goals and objectives?

Organizations frequently choose from among the following major behavioural objectives:

- to attract individuals with the knowledge, ability, and talents demanded by specific organizational tasks;
- to retain valued and productive employees;
- to promote specific job behaviours conducive to higher levels of job performance;
- to promote attitudes conducive to loyalty and commitment to the organization, high job involvement, and job satisfaction;
- to stimulate employee growth that enables the employee to accept more challenging positions;
- to comply with the requirements of pay equity and related laws.

These specified performance objectives should contribute to the control of labour costs and organizational effectiveness.

EFFECTIVE REWARD MANAGEMENT: A COMPENSATION MODEL

This introductory chapter has discussed the nature of compensation or rewards, identified the components of the reward system, established a set of dimensions or classification categories to help make sense of the array of reward items, and explored the major objectives or goals of the reward system. We now present the model of effective reward management (Figure 1.2). It provides a perspective of the text, and a comprehensive, logical, and coherent framework to graphically show the factors, concepts, processes, and techniques that impact the reward system. The model can be looked at in terms of the following five major questions a compensation specialist would need to address to ensure an effective reward system:

1. What are the various factors, events, and institutions that influence the composition and goals of the reward system?

2. What does the effectiveness of the reward system depend upon? Or, can the effectiveness of the reward system be predicted?

3. What are the critical methods—processes and techniques—that must be adopted in designing and implementing the reward system?

4. What are the key managerial issues and concerns in the design, administration, and evaluation of the reward system?

5. What are the new, emerging issues in reward system management?

The responses to these questions constitute the five major parts of the book.

Figure 1.2: Effective Reward Management: A Model

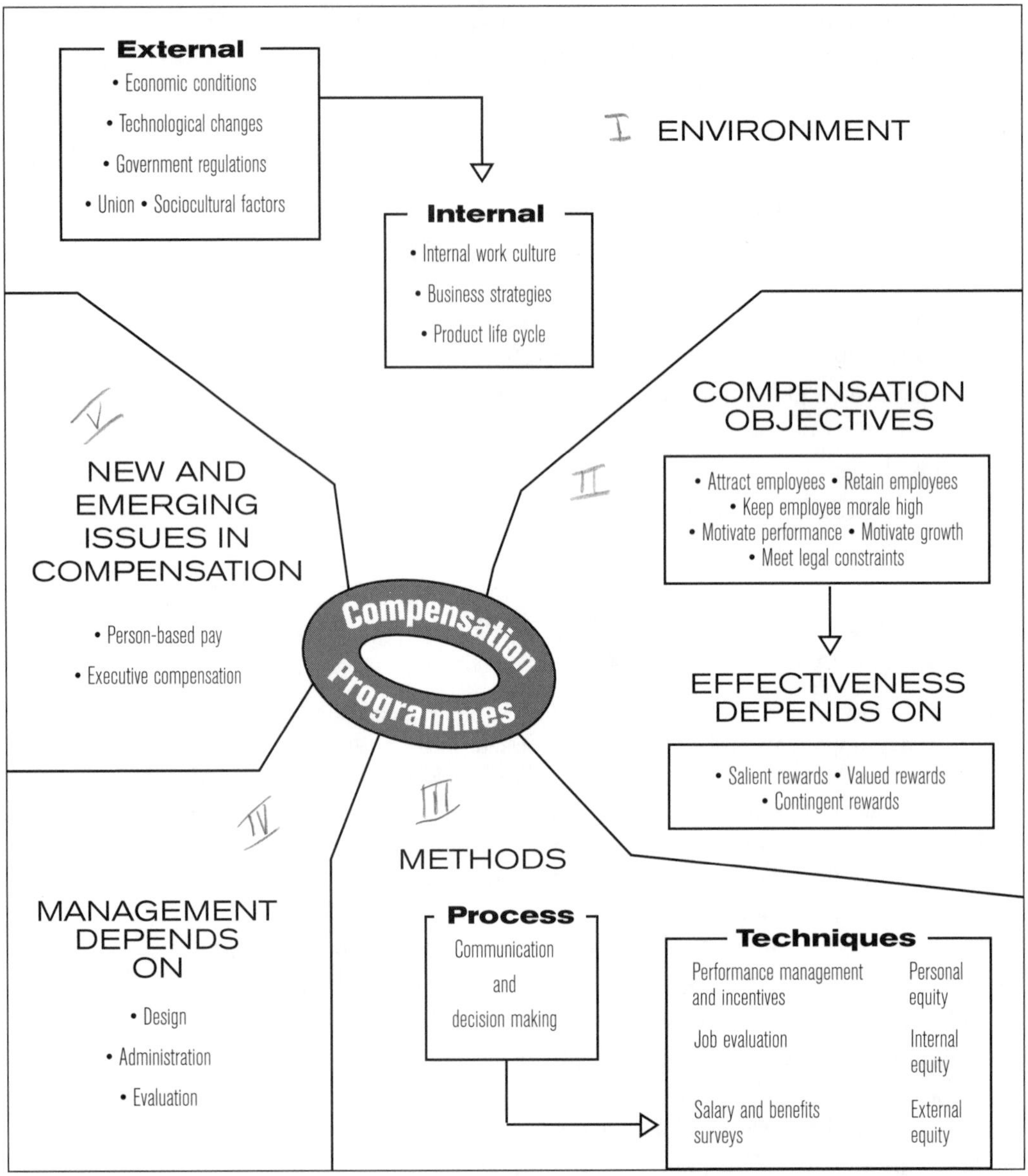

Part I explores the strategic influence that the environment, external and internal, has on the composition and goals of the compensation programme. The important determinants of the external environment are economic conditions (e.g., state of the economy, the Canada-U.S. Free Trade Agreement, goods and services tax, product markets), technological changes (e.g., rapid advances in computerization), government regulations (e.g., pay equity laws), unions (the impact of collective agreements, the state of union-management relations), and sociocultural factors (which shape the beliefs, attitudes, and action preferences of employees). The internal environment is the organization's business strategies, product life cycle, and work culture, which are developed or which evolve within the context of the external environment. Chapter 2 discusses these environmental factors, events, and issues, and their impact on the compensation programme. Chapter 3 examines in more detail the influence of unions on the organization's compensation system.

Part II considers the various theoretical approaches put forward to guide policies and procedures of the compensation programme. Chapter 4 critically examines the content theories of work motivation, which have contributed much to current practices in compensation. However, the intrinsic-extrinsic reward classification, which has dominated the content theories, has been found to be inadequate in providing clear, practical guidelines for the effective design and administration of the reward system. Chapter 5 explores the process theories of work motivation, and presents a model that is conceptually sound, has strong empirical support, and is immensely practical in the design and evaluation of a compensation programme. This model, founded on the constructs of expectancy theory, is also consistent with the intuitively accepted view that a reward item is effective in motivating employees towards performing the desired behaviours only if the reward is salient (i.e., it is uppermost in the employee's mind), valued (i.e., it is perceived to satisfy important needs and to be equitable), and contingent (i.e., it is given only on performance of the organizationally desired behaviours).

Satisfaction with pay and non-monetary outcomes has a considerable impact on employee motivation. Chapter 6 considers the determinants of pay satisfaction as well as the consequences of pay dissatisfaction. Job content factors, as determined by job design, are an important source of nonmonetary outcomes, which also play a critical role in determining pay satisfaction and in moderating the consequences of pay dissatisfaction. Therefore, Chapter 6 will also consider the theory and process of job design and its implications for reward management.

Part III addresses the methods—process and techniques—that contribute to making the rewards salient, valued, and contingent. Chapter 7 considers the strategic and process issues in compensation. These issues are related to and flow from the business objectives and the organizational culture. For example, if the business objectives include cost control, the appropriate compensation strategy would be either to lag behind or to be equal to the labour market in pricing the pay structure. Again, if the organizational culture is participative and favours high employee involvement, then the appropriate communication process in compensation will be open rather than secret, and a participative rather than a top-down approach. The strategic and process issues discussed in

Chapter 7 together with the conceptual framework developed in the previous chapters, provide the fundamental rationale for the compensation programmes, techniques, and processes presented in the chapters that follow.

Chapter 8 develops reward programmes and practices that promote organizational membership behaviours such as regular attendance and employee retention. Chapter 9 explores performance-based pay issues and their relation to personal equity. Personal equity is experienced by employees when they see that their work contribution (i.e., job performance) is fairly rewarded. When employees experience personal equity, the reward's valence (i.e., the reward's value to the employees) is increased. This chapter shows how a properly developed performance-based pay programme enhances employee motivation by making rewards contingent on performance and by increasing reward valence (or importance) through an equitable performance appraisal programme.

Chapter 10 explores issues in the design and development of individual and organization-wide incentive plans including: gain-sharing, profit sharing, and stock-based plans. These performance-based approaches have a tremendous potential for motivating employee behaviours towards the attainment of organizational objectives. Employee involvement in the design and implementation of these plans will be considered because such involvement has been known to considerably enhance employee perceptions of reward saliency, valence, and contingency.

Chapter 11 examines the methods and techniques of job analysis and job evaluation. Job evaluation is critical to assessing the similarities and differences in job values. When the similarities and differences among the jobs in the organization is fairly identified and recognized, then employees will experience internal equity. Since the pay structure reflects job values, the decisions made in this process have a considerable impact on internal equity, which in turn affects employees' perception of reward valence and their motivation. Of course, the mechanics of the methods alone do not determine equity. The process that is adopted is an equally important determinant of equity. Therefore, both mechanics and process issues will be considered.

Chapter 12 examines pay equity legislation and the related jurisprudence with the objective of developing practical guidelines for the design and implementation of reward systems that comply with the provisions of the law. The appendix to Chapter 12 briefly reviews the issue of "comparable worth" in the United States.

Chapter 13 focuses on external equity, which also impacts on the valence or importance of rewards and eventually on employee motivation. Employees experience external equity when they believe that their compensation is fair when compared with that of the external market. Hence, it is important to examine the scope and process of salary surveys of the relevant market, and the use of data in developing the organization's pay line. Also critical are the design of pay ranges and the formulation of a sound rationale for individual salary adjustments, which frequently become necessary after salary surveys.

Chapter 14 considers issues in the development of employee benefit programmes. Because it is not always possible to tie benefit programmes to the employee's performance, the contingency effect on employee motivation is limited. However, these programmes can still have an impact on employee motivation if employees are involved in their implementation and are perceived by employees to be salient and valuable.

The major focus of Part IV (Chapter 15) *Managing the Compensation System* is the evaluation of the compensation system. Is the organization getting the intended motivational effects from its compensation expenditures? To respond to this question, a managerial action plan is proposed to assess the effectiveness of each reward item and to introduce specific remedial interventions.

Part V (Chapter 16) examines new and emerging issues in the design of compensation systems. The issues dealt with are: person-based pay; issues in executive compensation; and reward system design and management in developing countries. It describes the features and design mechanics of different forms of person-based pay, and also discusses its advantages and disadvantages. It also examines the issues in executive compensation and, briefly, the issues related to the compensation of Canadian members of parliament. In addition, Chapter 16 discusses at length the design and management of reward systems, with practical strategies to fit the reward system to cultural contexts different from that of North America.

Each of the five parts of this model (in fact, each chapter in the book) can be studied as a topic separately and in isolation from the other parts. The perspective of this book, however, is to emphasize that if rewards are to contribute to organizational effectiveness, they must be viewed as a whole. Both the techniques and the processes involved in the reward system and its subsystems are crucial. As shown in the model, they have an impact on reward effectiveness. The model also demonstrates that the compensation programme—its components, techniques, and processes—gains legitimacy only to the extent that it contributes to organizational effectiveness and employee satisfaction. The model thus provides coherence, logic, and conceptual support to the effective management of rewards.

SUMMARY

This chapter explored the nature of compensation or rewards from the point of view of society, individuals, and organizations. Each point of view has its own interests and concerns. However, the perspective of the text, as depicted in the model, is the effective management of rewards to contribute both to organizational effectiveness and to employee satisfaction. These two considerations should be kept in mind when compensation decisions are being made. These decisions may concern the components and goals of a compensation programme;

the methods to be used in job analysis and evaluation, salary surveys, and performance assessment; the development of salary ranges; adjustments to an employee's salary; or the type of incentives, benefits, and services.

In order to address compensation needs of the future, the new and emerging issues are explored in Part V. In the ultimate analysis, the *raison d'être* of a compensation programme is organizational effectiveness and employee satisfaction. To ensure this, the key managerial activity and concern will be the managerial action plan (Chapter 15), which appropriately appears as the foundation upon which the model rests.

KEY TERMS

compensation objectives	*compensation theories*
compensation processes	*economic compensation system*
compensation techniques	*non-economic compensation system*

REVIEW AND DISCUSSION QUESTIONS

1. "The issue of compensation is fraught with conflict and tension among employees, between employees and their employer, between voters and civil servants, between legislators and employees, and among employers." Do you agree with this statement? Cite specific examples from your personal experience and/or observations to support your position.

2. Using the classification system proposed in Figure 1.1, classify the reward items listed in Table 1.1.

3. Refer to the six major behavioural objectives identified in the chapter, and give examples of reward items likely to attain these objectives. Try to think of different reward items for each behavioural objective.

The Nature and Purpose of the Compensation System

Objective

To reflect on your experiences as "recipients" of compensation in order to understand its nature and purpose from the point of view of both employees and the organization.

Procedure

1. Individual reflection: Each individual reflects on the compensation system of his or her organization in terms of the following questions:

   a) What types of rewards are offered by the organization? What are the criteria for each reward type?

   b) Is the base pay the same for all job categories? If different: why? what system is used to differentiate between job categories?

   c) Is the total pay the same for employees in the same job category? If different: why? what system is used to differentiate between employees in the same job category?

   d) Should the total pay for your job be the same, more, or less than a similar job in other organizations? Why? What system is used to make decisions on this issue?

   e) Why are rewards important for you? for the organization?

   f) Should the organization get a fair return on the compensation it pays employees? Why?

   g) How does the organization know that it does or does not get a fair return on its compensation program?

2. Group discussion: Groups of about four or five participants are formed, and each group appoints a spokesperson. Group members first share their reflections on the above questions. The group then explores the reasons for the similarities and differences in the reponses.

3. Plenary discussion: Group spokespersons present group findings, and a class discussion follows.

P A R T

II

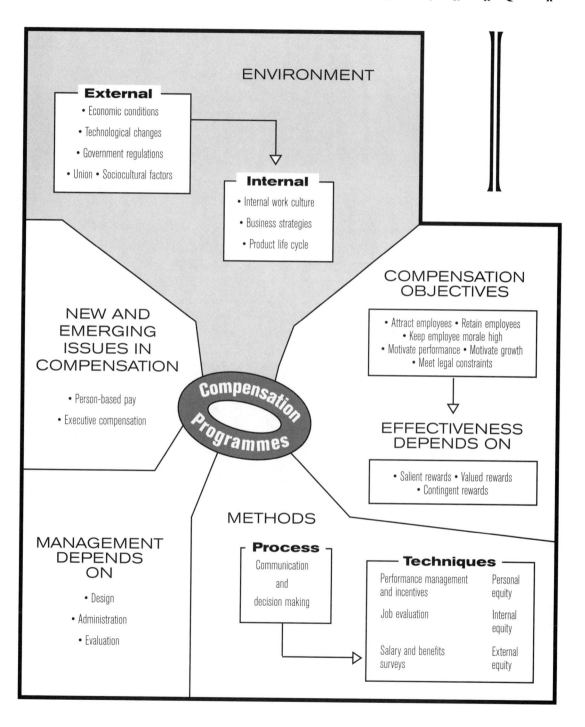

ENVIRONMENT

External
- Economic conditions
- Technological changes
- Government regulations
- Union • Sociocultural factors

Internal
- Internal work culture
- Business strategies
- Product life cycle

COMPENSATION OBJECTIVES

- Attract employees • Retain employees
- Keep employee morale high
- Motivate performance • Motivate growth
- Meet legal constraints

NEW AND EMERGING ISSUES IN COMPENSATION

- Person-based pay
- Executive compensation

Compensation Programmes

EFFECTIVENESS DEPENDS ON

- Salient rewards • Valued rewards
- Contingent rewards

METHODS

MANAGEMENT DEPENDS ON

- Design
- Administration
- Evaluation

Process
Communication
and
decision making

Techniques

Performance management and incentives	Personal equity
Job evaluation	Internal equity
Salary and benefits surveys	External equity

The External
and Internal
Environments

OVERVIEW

This chapter provides an overview of the organization's environment—internal and external, and examines its influence on the design and management of effective compensation systems.

LEARNING OBJECTIVES

▶ To identify the significant forces of the external environment within which an organization operates.

▶ To identify the significant forces of the internal environment of an organization that shape its policies and strategies in relation to people and products.

▶ To understand how internal and external environmental forces influence the compensation system.

THE ENVIRONMENT AND THE COMPENSATION SYSTEM

Today's world of globalization and rapid technological change creates a dynamic environment that brings unexpected challenges to organizations. For example, since approximately 75 per cent of Canada's exports go to the United States, the North American Free Trade Agreement (NAFTA) has opened a window of opportunity for some industries and posed considerable challenges for others. Such events impact on the design and management of the reward system. Hence, there is a need to consider the sources of environmental influence on organizations; these are:

External sources	Internal sources
– economic conditions	– internal work culture
– technological changes	– business strategies
– government regulations	– product life cycle
– union expectations	
– sociocultural climate.	

Figure 2.1 depicts the interaction of the external and internal environments as these combine to influence the compensation programme of an organization.

THE EXTERNAL ENVIRONMENT

Economic Conditions

The economic conditions of any country are in a constant state of flux. Canada and its provinces are no exception. Out of a multitude of economic conditions whose impact can be considered, our focus will be on two, namely, the rate of inflation and the rate of productivity.

Inflation Inflation has a detrimental effect on corporate budgets and the purchasing power of the employee's pay cheque. Government measures to fight inflation, such as high interest rates, aggravate matters, at least in the short run. High interest rates discourage home sales and discretionary purchases. As markets slacken, plans for plant expansion and increases in research and development activities are either cancelled or postponed.

Productivity Productivity is the ratio of outputs (value of products and services) to inputs (price paid for human, physical, and financial resources). Gains in productivity enhance the organization's competitive edge and also its capacity to provide a better compensation program. In Canada, the productivity rate has been on the decline (Statistics Canada, 1994). The increase of workers' output per hour in the 1980s was 18 percent in Canada compared to 33.3 percent in the US (Mathias, 1992).

Both inflation and a sluggish growth in productivity have a direct impact on the competitiveness of organizations and their business strategies. For example, organizations prefer conservative investment programmes to high-risk ventures, and focus on the short run where outcomes appear to be more controllable. Business strategies with a short-run perspective logically lead to compensation policies that emphasize short-term goals, often to the detriment of the economic health of the organization. With the increasing trend towards globalization, the ties between economic conditions and business strategies assume a greater complexity.

Figure 2.1: The Impact of the External and Internal Environments on the Compensation Programme

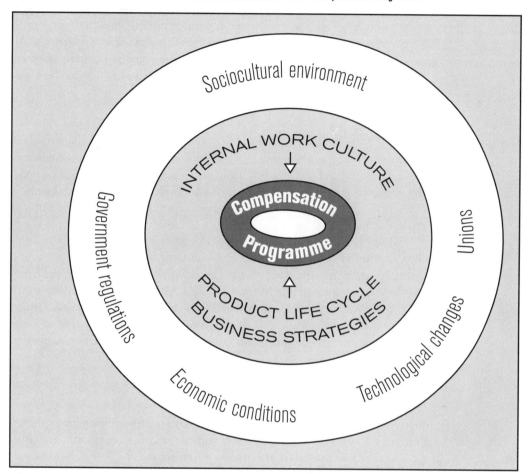

Technological Changes

Technology in particular, computerization and automation—has been found to increase the organization's competitiveness through improved productivity and quality (McMullen, Leckie, and Caron, 1993). In addition to decreased labour costs, technology can also impact on the design of the reward system as seen in the following cases:

- Increased computerization facilitates decentralization, which enriches jobs, tending to make the jobs psychologically more rewarding to the employees (Dean and Snell, 1991; Kiechel, 1993).

- Computerization also increases the organization's capability to generate performance measures that contribute to a more equitable administration of compensation programmes (Monsalve and Triplett, 1990).

- When General Motors (GM) opened its plant using robotics for the Saturn car project, the company formed a unique partnership with its employees not only through improved relations with the union but also through radical compensation practices such as the abolition of status differentials. All employees are on salary and are eligible for productivity bonuses; executive bonuses are similarly linked to the project's profits and not, as has been traditional, to the profits of GM's subsidiaries.

Government Regulations

The impact of economic conditions and technological changes on compensation is primarily indirect, flowing from the organization's strategic decisions. The impact of government regulations is direct. The objective of regulations is to ensure social justice and to address societal concerns involved in the employer-employee relationship.

Laws that regulated the employer-employee relationship are traditionally limited to areas such as: wages, overtime and vacation pay; working conditions; and financial protection in the event of loss of employment, work accidents, and retirement. Some examples are the Minimum Wages Act, the Employment Insurance Act, the Worker's Compensation Act, and the Canada (Quebec) Pension Plan.

The existence of a multitude of government regulations relating to compensation make legal compliance an important objective of the reward system.

Union Expectations

Although not to the same degree as government regulations, unions have a direct impact on an organization's compensation policies and programmes. Unionized companies are compelled to follow the collective agreement, which spells out the compensation programme for unionized employees. Non-unionized companies are also influenced by the wage and benefits settlements of the unionized firms in a region or industry. The critical influence of unions on organizations and their compensation programmes is examined in greater detail in Chapter 3.

Sociocultural Environment

Societal culture can be viewed as a system of shared ideas, beliefs, values, and behaviour patterns in a given society. It plays a crucial role in influencing and shaping the beliefs, attitudes, and action preferences of societal members, and constitutes the sociocultural environment of organizations which operate in that society. Employees bring to the workplace their cultural values and norms, which are instrumental in the formation of their expectations of, and responses to, reward systems. The sociocultural environment can thus profoundly influence the effectiveness of reward systems.

According to Hofstede (1980b) the cultures of different countries can be differentiated by the following four dimensions:

- *Power distance* – that is, the extent to which society accepts unequal distribution of power in organizations.

- *Uncertainty avoidance* – that is, the extent to which people avoid ambiguous situations because they feel threatened by them.

- *Individualism/Collectivism* – Individualism implies that people are supposed to take care of themselves and their immediate families only; collectivism implies that members of in-groups (family, relatives, clan, organizations) have a mutual obligation to look after and be loyal to each other.

- *Masculinity/Femininity* – Masculinity implies that people value assertiveness and the acquisition of money and things; femininity implies that people value caring for others and the quality of life.

In terms of these cultural dimensions, the sociocultural environment of developed countries like Canada can be characterized by high individualism and masculinity and low power distance and uncertainty avoidance (Jaeger and Kanungo, 1990). The way in which these characteristics are manifested in organizations, and their influence on rewards choice is outlined below:

Dimension	Manifestation
High individualism	Employees prefer independence, self-reliance, individual responsibility.
High masculinity	Performance orientation.
Low power distance	Subordinate-superior participation to achieve organizational objectives.
Low uncertainty avoidance	Employees willing to take risks in achieving organizational objectives.

Employees socialized in a sociocultural environment dominated by these characteristics will likely expect their reward system to focus primarily on material rewards that reflect individual, rather than group performance, and are commensurate with the job risk and responsibilities.

THE INTERNAL ENVIRONMENT

Internal Work Culture

An organization, deliberately or by default, develops its own unique work culture, which soon becomes the philosophical frame of reference for developing, understanding, and evaluating the company's mission objectives, policies, and programmes. The compensation programme is an important means of socializing employees in the organization's values and norms.

The internal work culture of an organization can be understood in terms of the following three-level model proposed by Schein (1985):

- *Level 1*: artifacts such as:
    - degree of automation, mechanization;
    - authority hierarchy, top-down and lateral communication.

- *Level 2*: values—as expressed in strategies, goals, and philosophy—explain and justify the behaviours, artifacts, and structures of the first level.

- *Level 3*: the basic managerial assumptions which explain the organization's activities, creations, and behaviours of the first and second levels.

Impact of Sociocultural Environment on Internal Work Culture

As seen in Schein's 3-level model, the underlying assumptions of the internal work culture of an organization are largely the product of the conscious or unconscious efforts of the founder or top management. These beliefs and ideas, however, are also influenced by the prevailing sociocultural environment. What are these culture-determined assumptions? Elaborating upon Schein's (1988) notion of organizational culture, Jaeger and Kanungo (1990) have categorized culture-determined values and climate of beliefs and assumptions under two

Figure 2.2: The Influence of the Sociocultural Environment on the Internal Work Culture

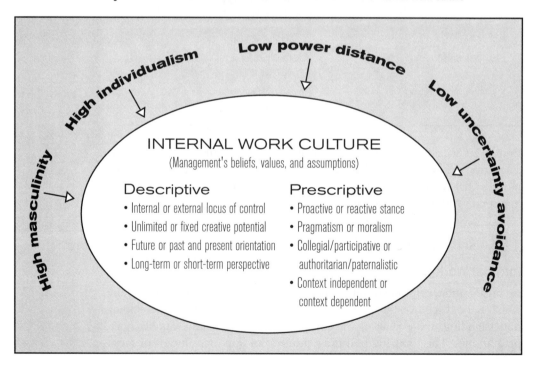

Figure 2.3: Impact of Managerial Assumptions on Reward System

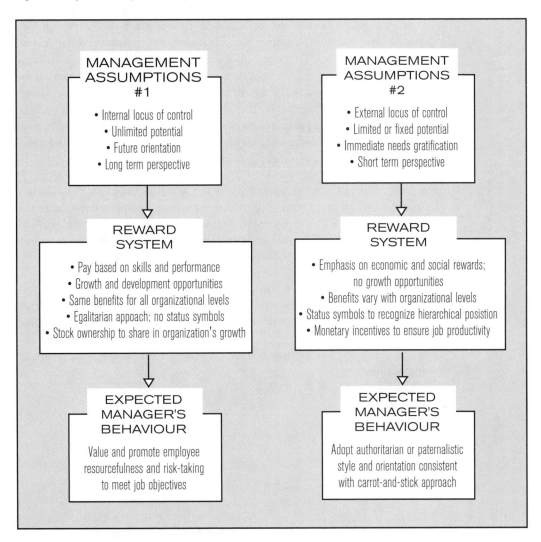

broad headings: (1) descriptive assumptions about human nature, and (2) prescriptive assumptions about the guiding principles of human conduct.

The descriptive category describes management's assumptions about human nature. Essentially, these are management's beliefs about their employees' attitude and behaviour. The prescriptive category spells out management's normative assumptions—that is, what managers' behaviour ought to be. According to Jaeger and Kanungo (1990), there is a consistent pattern between the sociocultural dimensions and management's descriptive and prescriptive assumptions, as depicted in Figure 2.2. Furthermore, as this figure shows, a set of prescriptive assumptions about the guiding principles of human conduct logically flows from a set of management's descriptive assumptions about human nature.

For example, consider the sociocultural environment of North America characterized by high masculinity, high individualism, low power distance, low uncertainty avoidance. Managers socialized in this environment will likely assume that employees have a high level of control, an unlimited potential for growth, an orientation toward the future, and a long-term perspective. Given these assumptions, managers will then be expected to adopt a proactive stance in task performance, to judge success on a pragmatic basis, to be guided by predetermined principles and procedures, and to promote a collegial/participative management style or orientation.

Internal Work Culture and Reward System Design   The impact on the design and management of the organizational reward system under the descriptive and prescriptive assumptions that underlie the internal work culture is depicted in Figure 2.3, which summarizes the impact under diametrically opposite sets of management assumptions.

Rewards and People vs. Performance Emphasis in Work Cultures
The relationship between rewards and the organization's internal work culture has also been viewed in terms of whether the reward system serves to reinforce "people" values or "organizational performance" values. Based on these dimensions, Sethia and Von Glinow (1985) proposed the following four types of work cultures:

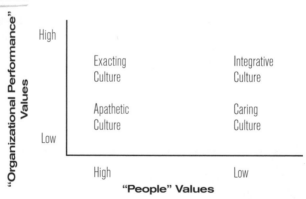

Drawing on Sethia and Von Glinow (1985) and Murphy (1983), Figure 2.4 summarizes the reward system in these work cultures.

The four work culture-types and their corresponding reward systems and strategies help us to understand how the reward system can contribute to the maintenance of a work culture. Thus, when we examine the organization's reward system, we can infer the work culture that is likely to exist in that organization. However, one can legitimately ask: Does the reward system create the

Figure 2.4: Impact of Four Types of Work Culture on Reward System

CULTURE TYPE	REWARD TYPE	REWARD STRUCTURE	EFFECTS
Apathetic	Job security and status	Based on custom and patronage	High job security and low performance expectations induce employee retention
Caring	Job security and pay based on: status, seniority; Retirement benefits	Based not on performance but on employee: loyalty, cooperation, organizational "fit"; benevolent paternalism	Emphasis on employee satisfaction programs motivate retention and adherence to organizational norms
Exacting	Performance bonus, profit-sharing, enriched job and career growth opportunities	Strictly performance-contingent rewards	Entrepreneurial, risk-taking with minimal organizational support
Integrative	Pay for skills, profit-sharing, stock options, enriched job	Contingent on individual and group performance; manager functions as coach and mentor	Strong performance orientation; organizational support fosters growth and development

work culture, or is it the work culture that creates the reward system? The four work-culture typologies do not address this significant issue of the relationship between the organization's internal work culture and reward system. Its practical significance becomes apparent when the organization finds it necessary to shift from a "caring" to an "integrative" work culture. Would a change to the reward system, bring about the desired shift? Clearly we cannot answer this question unless we know why or what created the existing work culture.

The reward system does not create the work culture. It is merely an important tool to reinforce the desired work culture. For example, Shell's lubricants plant in Brockville, Ontario, uses pay-for-skills to support a self-managed team environment (Information Booklet, 1991). The work culture is the creation of the organization's founder or senior management (Schein, 1985). Through the socialization process, which is helped by the reward system, management's beliefs and values are transmitted to employees who, it is hoped, will share and internalize these beliefs and values. At this point, we need to recognize that long before employees join an organization, they have been exposed to, and have likely incorporated, the cultural beliefs and values of the society into which they were born and raised. Therefore, the employee's internalization process is facilitated or hindered by the degree to which management's beliefs and values are congruent with those of its employee. This is an important consideration because with the increasing cultural diversity of today's workforce in North America, we simply cannot assume that management's and employees' values will be the same.

For this reason, it is critical to first understand the employees' sociocultural environment which provides some indication of their beliefs and values they bring to the workplace. The previous section, "Sociocultural Environment", provides a basic framework. The first part of the current section builds on that framework, and the next part extends it, in order to understand how it influences reward system design and management. Once the internal work culture is identified, to the extent it is feasible to do so, the four-work culture typology is a useful schema to illustrate how the reward system can be designed to reinforce people versus performance values in the prevailing work culture.

The preceding discussion described how the reward system flows from and reflects the internal work culture of the organization. The next section explores the direct impact of business strategies on the reward system.

Business Strategies

A strategy is "the pattern or plan that integrates an organization's major goals, policies, and action sequences into a cohesive whole" (Quinn, 1988, 3). The reward system of an organization must be congruent with and supportive of the organization's business strategy. It does so principally in two ways: (1) by attracting and retaining the people with the knowledge, abilities, skills, and willingness to support the business strategy; and (2) it motivates the employees to manifest behaviours (e.g., job performance and the acquisition of needed abilities and skills) that are conducive to the successful formulation and implementation of the business strategy. For example, organizations that operate in a highly entrepreneurial and/or innovative context need people who seek and enjoy challenging opportunities that involve considerable risk taking. Such people, in turn, expect rewards that truly reflect the risks and the challenges of the job. They will not be attracted by a fixed income, however stable that might be. They will want "a piece of the action"—a share in the gains generated by their performance. Consequently, the reward mix of organizations in the entrepreneurial context will emphasize variable rewards, with incentives forming a major component of the compensation package.

How does the reward system serve the business strategies of an organization? The research findings of Miles and Snow (1984) suggest that the variety of different business strategies can be grouped into three basic types, the Defender, the Prospector, and the Analyzer. This typology can be used to illustrate the compensation programme that is uniquely supportive of each type of strategy.

According to Miles and Snow, the characteristics of the business strategy types are:

The Defender strategy	A limited product line; single, capital-intensive technology; a functional structure; and skills in production efficiency, process engineering, and cost control. (1984, 37)
The Prospector strategy	A diverse product line; multiple technologies; a product or divisionalized structure; and skills in product research and development, market research, and development engineering. (1984, 38)
The Analyzer strategy	A limited basic product line; search for a small number of related product and/or market opportunities; cost-efficient technology for stable products and project technologies for new products; mixed (frequently matrix) structure; and skills in production efficiency, process engineering, and marketing. (1984, 38).

In the Defender-type organization, the products, markets, and technology are all relatively stable. This stability gives the tremendous advantage of accumulating expertise and know-how within the organization, which permits the organization to acquire human resources from outside at the entry level and then to develop them internally. The consequence for compensation management is that internal equity, rather than external equity, becomes the major preoccupation. The emphasis on efficiency and rigorous cost control requires a close monitoring of the performance-reward tie-up, with frequent performance evaluations using quantitative measures. It is quite common to use gain-sharing plans. The high degree of centralization in the control process also causes the compensation structure to reflect the organization's hierarchical levels. The orientation towards the organizational hierarchy is also derived from the fact that the incentive for long-term personal development inevitable in the Defender-type organization is through internal promotion. These characteristics of the compensation system are found in the Lincoln Electric Company, which is regarded as a classic Defender.

The impact of the Prospector strategy on compensation is just the opposite of that of the Defender strategy. Performance-based compensation is the primary consideration. The Prospector-type organization needs to acquire human resources from outside the organization not just at the entry level but at all levels. The external labour market tends to heavily influence the compensation structure, which now needs to focus much more on external equity, and is often based on a pay level higher than that of the market. Furthermore, the innovative people required by the organization can only be attracted by a compensation programme that is performance based and allows creative individuals to share in the gains generated by their innovations. Hewlett-Packard and Texas Instruments are examples of firms that follow the Prospector strategy.

The Analyzer-type organization combines the features of the Defender and Prospector strategies. Although the Analyzer organization operates in both the stable and changing markets, its operations are characterized by a balanced approach that seeks to minimize risk and at the same time to explore profitable opportunities. Consequently, the compensation philosophy programme of the Analyzer organization will be characterized by a similar balance—between internal and external equity, between fixed and variable rewards, and between rewards that emphasize performance and those that reflect the position in the hierarchical levels and their relative differentials. Canadian Pacific is a good example of the Analyzer-type organization.

Figure 2.5 summarizes the business strategies and reward system appropriate to each type of organization. Pay practices derived from the Miles and Snow strategy framework have been found to be quite effective (Gerhart, Minkoff, and Olsen, 1996).

Product Life Cycle

The preceding review underscores the fact that the organization's compensation programme must be congruent with and supportive of the organization's business strategies if it is to succeed in achieving its objectives. However, the effectiveness of the business strategies is also affected by the life cycle of its products. Therefore the compensation system—particularly the mix of base pay, incentives, and benefits—should also be appropriate to the business needs of each stage of the product life cycle (Gerhart, Minkoff, and Olsen, 1996).

What then is the appropriate pay mix for each stage of the product life cycle? What is the rationale for such a mix? To address these questions we explore the conditions in which the organization finds itself in each stage of the product life cycle—start-up, growth, maturity, stability, decline, and renewal.

In the **start-up** or introduction stage of a product, the organization's resources and efforts are devoted to entering the market. With high expenditures and low revenues, the organization's ability to generate cash flow is extremely limited, and so is its ability to include high base pay and benefits in its pay mix. The organization, nevertheless, needs to attract employees who will bring a high level of innovation and creative energy, and will expect a variable income plan. These expectations can be met by making incentives a major component of the pay mix, the other elements of the mix being low base pay and benefits. High incentives are also compatible with the organization's financial condition in this stage in the life cycle because incentives are paid only after the employees' efforts generate the predetermined financial resources.

The pay mix in the **growth stage** is competitive base pay, high incentives, and low benefits. The growth stage places the organization in a stronger financial position relative to the start-up stage, and the organization is then able to offer the competitive base pay that may be necessitated by shortages in the labour market. The major drawing card to attract and retain the creative and innovative employees continues to be high incentives, as was the case in the start-up stage. The organization still needs to invest its resources in activities

Figure 2.5: Impact of Business Strategy on Reward System

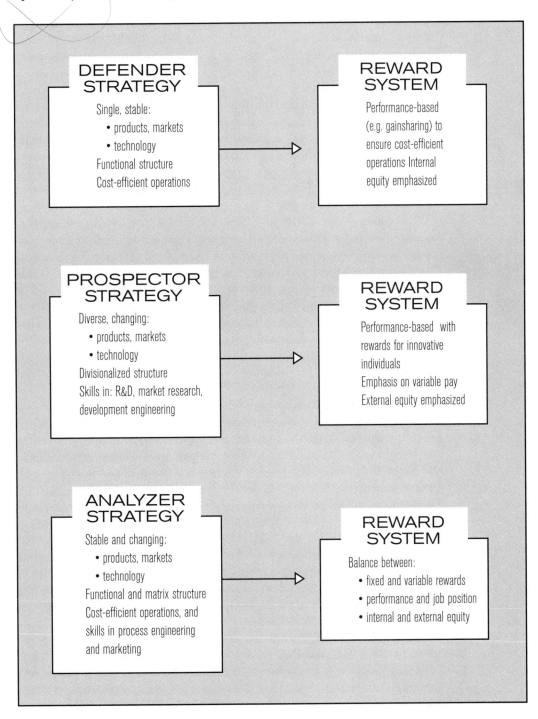

DEFENDER STRATEGY

Single, stable:
- products, markets
- technology

Functional structure
Cost-efficient operations

REWARD SYSTEM

Performance-based (e.g. gainsharing) to ensure cost-efficient operations Internal equity emphasized

PROSPECTOR STRATEGY

Diverse, changing:
- products, markets
- technology

Divisionalized structure
Skills in: R&D, market research, development engineering

REWARD SYSTEM

Performance-based with rewards for innovative individuals
Emphasis on variable pay
External equity emphasized

ANALYZER STRATEGY

Stable and changing:
- products, markets
- technology

Functional and matrix structure
Cost-efficient operations, and skills in process engineering and marketing

REWARD SYSTEM

Balance between:
- fixed and variable rewards
- performance and job position
- internal and external equity

that will provide a continuing impetus to growth. The mechanics of high incentives give the organization the flexibility it needs to channel its resources into growth and at the same time to meet the expectations of its high-performing employees.

In the **maturity stage**, the organization has carved out a relatively stable market niche for itself, and environmental uncertainty has been considerably reduced. Cash flow is now more predictable and generally reflects the higher revenues and earnings that result from economies of scale and a stable market share. The pay mix in this stage is competitive base pay, incentives, and benefits. The reduced emphasis on incentives reflects (a) the organization's capacity to pay a relatively higher base pay and benefits than before, and (b) the changing business environment of the organization, which now does not require that employees be motivated to be entrepreneurial and risk takers to the same extent as in the previous two stages.

The **stability stage**, of the product life cycle is a natural sequel to the maturity stage. The old products, with some model changes and improvements, continue. But there is no heavy investment in research and development. The market share is maintained, and sometimes increased, by competitive pricing made possible by a greater emphasis on cost-efficient operations. The pay mix will be high base pay and benefits, for the same reasons as in the maturity stage. Although incentives form part of the mix, they play a relatively limited role. They are used mainly to improve productivity and ensure cost-efficient operations.

In the **decline stage**, the pay mix is really not one of the organization's choosing. To retain its present employees, the organization may be compelled to pay a high base pay and benefits. In a declining market, it would be anachronistic to offer incentives to improve productivity and output that the market is unable to absorb. Hence, incentives do not form part of the pay mix.

In the **renewal stage**, the organization adopts strategies and actions similar to those in the growth stage. Therefore, the pay mix at the renewal stage will be identical to that of the growth stage, that is, competitive base pay, high incentives, and low benefits, and for the same reasons.

Research findings generally support the product life cycle approach to developing the pay mix—in particular, the dominance of incentives at the growth stage of the product life cycle (Elig, 1981; Gomez-Mejia and Balkin, 1992). However, we need to recognize the limitations of the product-life-cycle approach. First, not all the products of an organization are at the same stage in the product life cycle. Second, the conditions of shortages and surpluses in the labour market can, and often do, compel the organization towards a pay mix different from that dictated solely by considerations of the stages in the product life cycle. Third, it is not too clear in which direction the life cycle stage-pay mix effect operates, that is, whether the stage in the product life cycle affects the pay mix or vice versa. Finally, because the issues of the organization's business strategy and product life cycle stages are macro-level issues, they are nebulous and do not easily lend themselves to empirical testing.

Figure 2.6: The Influence of the Sociocultural and Internal Environments on the Compensation Mix

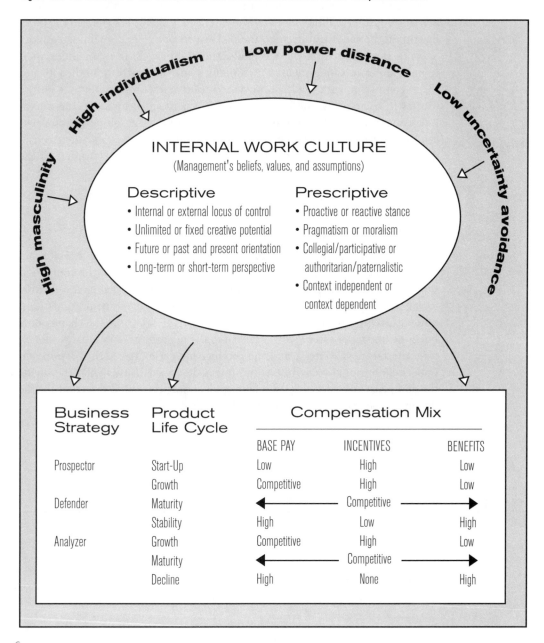

The business strategies and the product life cycle stages are useful, and even necessary, starting points in reward design. They provide the compensation specialist with an overall sense of direction, information on the likely availability of resources, and a guide to the optimal allocation of these resources. The compensation analyst will incorporate these factors in the process of reward design and management. In the ultimate analysis, the effectiveness of a compensation system will be judged by the extent to which it has enabled the organization to be successful in three areas: (1) in attracting and retaining employees with the required knowledge, skills, and abilities; (2) in maintaining their morale, and motivating them to high performance and growth on the job; and (3) in complying with the legal provisions relative to compensation. To ensure success in these areas, the compensation specialist must focus on the micro-level issues that lead to a sound understanding of how the compensation package influences the motivational dynamics within employees and their consequent behaviour. Such a focus is the thrust of the remaining chapters of the book.

SUMMARY

The environmental forces that affect an organization's capacity to operate successfully have an impact on the design and the management of the compensation system. This chapter explored the impact of five external environmental forces: economic conditions, technological changes, government regulations, union expectations, and the sociocultural climate. In addition, the chapter outlined the impact of three factors internal to the organization: internal work culture, the business strategy, and the product life-cycle. The identification and understanding of the environmental forces described in this chapter provide the compensation specialist with an overall strategic sense of direction for the design and management of the reward system.

KEY TERMS

business strategies

compensation mix

external environment

internal environment

internal work culture

product life cycle

sociocultural environment

REVIEW AND DISCUSSION QUESTIONS _____ ℛ___

1. Discuss the impact of each of the following elements of the external environment on the compensation policies and programmes of an organization:
   - economic conditions
   - technological changes
   - government regulations
   - union expectations
   - sociocultural environment

2. Explain how the sociocultural environment affects the internal work culture of the organization.

3. Discuss the impact of the internal work culture on the design and management of the rewards system.

4. Explain why it is important to tailor the compensation system to support the business strategies of the organization.

5. Identify the appropriate compensation mix for each stage of the product life cycle, and explain the rationale for such a mix.

6. Discuss the limitations of the product life cycle approach to developing a compensation mix.

CASE

Roasted Duck Delicacies Limited

Expo 84 was a memorable event in the history of British Columbia. It also marked the beginning of young Shengli Wang's love affair with Canada. He was brought to Vancouver from his native Beijing to work as a cook in a Beijing Chinese restaurant that specialized in Beijing roasted duck, a rage with British Columbians and the hordes of visitors to the fair that summer. Shengli recognized a tremendous business opportunity and was determined to bring the culinary delights of roasted duck to all of Canada. In 1986, Shengli and his wife opened Wang's Roasted Duck, his first restaurant in Vancouver. It was an instant success. By 1988, almost every major city in British Columbia and the prairie provinces had a Wang's Roasted Duck.

Although popular, the restaurants were not profitable. The quality of management was poor, labour costs were high, and the food had deteriorated largely because most of the cooks were recruited locally and did not have the expertise of a roasted duck chef. By 1990, with the exception of the Vancouver restaurant, all Wang's Roasted Duck restaurants were experiencing severe losses. In 1992, Jeff Robertson acquired a controlling interest in Wang's Roasted Duck. Jeff's fascination with Chinese cuisine developed during his stay in China as a CUSO volunteer. His graduate work in business administration gave him the business and management skills to recognize a business opportunity as well as to assess realistically the challenges of making Wang's Roasted Duck succeed.

Jeff shared in Shengli's vision of popularizing roasted duck delicacies but decided on a different strategy—a fast-food operation. His winning formula would be a combination of speedy service, cleanliness, and quality food with the exotic Chinese flavour and taste. Recognizing the increasingly popular desire for tasty nutritious foods, Jeff saw the skinless roasted duck as the perfect answer. He changed the name to Roasted Duck Delicacies Limited (RDDL) and decided to set up licensed franchises along with company-owned outlets. Each of the existing Wang's Roasted Duck restaurants was converted into a company-owned outlet of RDDL. The RDDL outlet, company-owned or franchised, is a fairly self-contained operation with a kitchen and a seating area. All the food is cooked in a specially designed oven and process which brings forth the exquisite flavor and taste of roasted duck.

Jeff was aware of the problems usually associated with fast-food operations—shortages of crew labour and competent and trustworthy store managers, high turnover of staff, need for continuous training and motivation of employees, and rising labour costs. He also recognized that critical to the success of the operation were quality products, which in turn required specialist chefs. Such chefs are not home-grown in Canada. He considered training chefs, but eventually decided on hiring them directly from China.

The growth of franchises outpaced that of company-owned outlets, but by 1995, the number of company-owned outlets had increased dramatically and is expected to eventually constitute about 40 per cent of the total outlets by the year 2000. Quality, cleanliness, and customer service are the main ingredients that translate into sales and profitability. Operating processes and equipment have been standardized and no changes are expected in this area. Jeff is concerned, however, about some developments that may adversely affect RDDL. First, the immigration department is reluctant to grant visas to chefs from China unless RDDL can demonstrate that catering graduates from the community colleges are not suitable. Second, RDDL's corporate office and warehouse, located in Ontario, is required to comply with Ontario's pay equity laws. Third, some attempts have been made to unionize RDDL's workforce.

The success of the company-owned outlet depends to a considerable extent upon its manager, who has responsibility for operations, employee training, customer relations, and cost effectiveness. Last year, RDDL experienced sales growth of 11 per cent, and expects the same rate this year. Cost effectiveness is particularly critical to RDDL's success in the context of its major competitors—McDonald's, Burger King, Kentucky Fried Chicken, Wendy's, and similar fast-food operations. Jeff is rather ambivalent in his attitude to NAFTA. He recognizes the potential for increased competition from Mexican-American fast-food outlets, as well as the opportunity for RDDL to expand in the United States.

Discussion Questions

Using the concepts discussed in this chapter:

1. Identify the external environmental challenges faced by RDDL.

2. Identify the internal environment of RDDL, in particular, the business strategies and the internal work culture.

3. Recommend a compensation mix that will support RDDL's business strategies and at the same time be consistent with RDDL's internal work culture.

Union Management
Relations: Impact
on Compensation

OVERVIEW

In the previous chapter, we touched on the issue of union expectations as a significant influence on organization's compensation programs. This chapter examines in some detail the nature and extent of this influence, and discusses its implications for compensation design and management.

LEARNING OBJECTIVES

► To become aware of the perspectives on union-management relations that influence the compensation objectives which each seeks to achieve.

► To understand the factors and the issues which are critical to unions, and the trade-offs involved.

► To understand the union impact on wages and benefits and the conditions under which it occurs.

► To understand the implications of the union role for the effective design and management of compensation systems.

INTRODUCTION

The industrial relations system in a country can be viewed in terms of its three major constituents or parties: the workers, the employers, and the government. These parties operate within the economic, legal, and sociocultural environments that define and determine the norms, rules and regulations that govern their relationships with each other, and influence the outcomes which each seeks to achieve (Craig, 1988; Gunderson and Ponak, 1995). In terms of a specific organization, management's relations with its employees would be influenced by the organization's internal and external environment. Chapter 2 explored the impact of the organization's environment on employee relations—as these relate to the design and management of the compensation system.

We now examine the influence of unions, a significant element of the external environment, on the organization's compensation system. This becomes necessary for two reasons. First, 37.5 per cent of Canada's non-agricultural workers, about 4 million, are represented by unions (Gray, 1996), which underscores the fact that the compensation system of a sizable portion of the workforce is influenced by unions' actions and decisions. Second, union initiatives also influence the compensation package of non-unionized organizations. For example, the nonunion Dofasco Steel in Hamilton, Ontario "... closely monitors the collective agreements at Stelco, its unionized crosstown competitor, to ensure that its employees receive equal or better wages, hours, and conditions" (Gunderson and Ponak, 1995, p.3).

Our discussion will first examine some of the perspectives from which union-management relations might be viewed in order to better understand the reasons for the compensation objectives which each seeks to achieve. We then examine the union's role and impact on the organization's compensation structure, techniques and processes. Finally, we explore the implications for compensation design and management in the perspective of the reward management model proposed in the text.

DIFFERING PERSPECTIVES ON UNION-MANAGEMENT RELATIONS

The study of unions has been approached from several perspectives (Gunderson and Ponak, 1995). Our focus is on two perspectives: institutional perspective, and strategic choice perspective.

Institutional perspective

Throughout the eighteenth and nineteenth centuries, the formation of trade unions—be it in the UK, the US, or Canada, was viewed as a criminal conspiracy designed to disrupt the operation of free trade and commerce. However, the oppressive, treatment of workers almost from the inception of the industrial revolution led many to question how "free" and "fair" the exchange contract was between workers and the employer. They argued that in the exchange situation between the workers and an enormous, resource-rich organization, the workers do not have much power as individuals to assert and obtain a fair price for their labour. Hence, they need unions to restore some balance in the relationship between workers and management. The institutional perspective recognizes and accepts an inherent conflict of interest between workers and management.

The strategic choice perspective

According to the strategic choice perspective, both management and unions make strategic decisions or choices to achieve their goals, in response to economic, social, political, and technological pressures (Gunderson and Ponak, 1995). For example, an organization that pursues a "defender" strategy would want to focus on being cost-efficient and, for this purpose, could choose from several options: a new technology, relocation in areas in order to take advantage of tax incentives, improved infrastructure, or reduced labour costs. The option that the organization might be compelled to pursue could limit the options available to the union. Suppose that the only viable option for the organization is new technology which makes layoffs inevitable. In this circumstance, union's bargaining efforts would focus on issues such as generous severance packages. As Gunderson and Ponak have observed: "...despite its focus on management as the initiator of change in the industrial relations system, the strategic choice perspective...recognizes that inherent conflicts of interest exist between employees and employers and accepts unions and collective bargaining as legitimate and valuable mechanisms through which employees may pursue their interests" (p.13).

ROLE OF THE UNION IN COMPENSATION DESIGN AND MANAGEMENT

The primary purpose of unions is to meet their members' workplace objectives in three areas: compensation, job security, and due process in decisions affecting the conditions and tenure of employment. Therefore, the collective agreement which results from union-management negotiations generally covers issues in these areas. Thus:

- the following compensation issues: wage rates and pay grades that provide for differentials, usually based on seniority; incentive systems; overtime pay; shift differentials; hours of work; vacations and sickness, parental, bereavement leaves; allowances for clothing, tools, etc; income protection benefits such as pensions, disability, health, and life insurance;

- the following job security issues: lay-off rules based on seniority; severance pay; provisions relating to contracting out union jobs, new technology and relating training issues;

- the following due process issues: grievance and arbitration procedures, joint worker-management committees.

The collective agreement also embodies management's recognition of the union as the bargaining agent for the workers, because such recognition is critical to the union's effectiveness. In addition, it is important to note that the union's effectiveness depends upon several other factors: the organization's ability to pay and to remain competitive, and trade-offs imposed by the demographic mix of union membership.

Organization's ability to pay

As discussed in Chapter 2, the organization's business strategies and product life-cycle stages are useful starting points in reward design. They provide information on the organization's overall direction and resource availability, and guide the optimal allocation of these resources. Critical to resource availability is the issue of worker productivity. In unionized organizations, the collective agreement might tend to impose limits on management's freedom to design work, to modernize, and to contract out union jobs. These limits reduce worker productivity and, as a result, operate to weaken the organization's competitive ability. This state is further aggravated when the collective agreement includes a cost of living (COLA) provision for the full term of the agreement. The COLA provision, negotiated during an inflationary period, becomes a severe burden when prices fall and the organization's COLA obligation still continues.

The low productivity and resulting increase in labour costs might not impair the organization's competitive ability in the domestic market if the following conditions prevail: (a) the entire industry is unionized, or the labour market economics compel non-union firms to adopt similar labour cost increases; and (b) the organization is in a position to satisfy the other stakeholders—that is, reasonable return to investors, and acceptable prices to consumers. However, with increasing globalization, the assumed conditions might not prevail. For example, the relatively lower-priced imports weaken the organization's ability to compete in the domestic market. Also, the organization's ability to compete in international markets might be impaired by its increased labour costs. These factors can lead to union concessions in the form of wage cuts or reductions in benefits. Some collective agreements might include clauses which provide for reopening the contract in certain circumstances.

Trade-offs due to membership mix

One of the critical factors which influence the union's pursuit of certain goals is the composition of its membership: workers with more seniority versus the new workers; older versus younger workers; male versus femal workers. For example, suppose the union is faced with a choice between higher wages with lay-offs, or lower wages with job security. If the resulting layoffs affect mainly the new employees who constitute a relatively small percentage of the membership, the union will pursue higher wages with layoffs. The union might also pursue higher wages with layoffs if the union finds that concession bargaining such as accepting lower wages, would not guarantee job security. The principal reason for this might be that "...the cost of layoffs may be mitigated by unemployment insurance, while wage concessions or hours reductions are not supported by such insurance" (Gunderson and Hyatt, 1995, p.313).

On the other hand, if increased wages are to result in massive layoffs, the union will likely forego the higher wages in favour of job security. Alternatively, it may accept layoffs on condition that the workers receive reasonable severance packages—as in the dispute between the Ontario Public Service Employees Union and the Ontario government (Gray, 1996). The Ontario Public Service Employees Union strike, the largest strike in Ontario's history, was eventually settled when the union gained "successor" and "seniority for bumping" rights (Rusk and Mittelstaedt, 1996). The effect of successor rights is that laid-off union members whose work is outsourced by the government have employment priority with the organizations which take over that work. The seniority-for-bumping rights give laid-off senior employees priority over their junior colleagues. Both rights provide a form of job security.

The demographic mix of union membership also play a critical role in the union's emphasis on benefits. For example, older rather than younger workers tend to prefer pensions; women rather than men workers tend to opt for flexible job schedules. In these situations, the union's decisions might be influenced by the voting power of the groups.

The Impact of Unions on Compensation

It is universally admitted that union actions impact on the organization's compensation structure. This impact is found to vary for different worker groups, in different industries, and with economic conditions (Freeman and Medoff, 1984). The major difficulties in estimating the nature and the extent of this impact relate to (a) causality; and (b) quality differences between union and nonunion workers (Gunderson and Ponak, 1995).

It is a fact that, in general, wages in the unionized sector are high. Since one of the major goals of unions is to improve the wages of its members, it seems obvious to attribute the high wages to actions by the union. But, is unionization the cause of the higher wages? We do not have a definitive response to this question because reasonable explanations have been proposed to suggest the opposite: unions are more likely to be formed when high wages already exist. In a free market, one can choose to stay and compete, or leave the field. When business needs cause employers to offer lucrative compensation packages to attract and retain workers, workers feel the pressure to stay even if they are not satisfied with other aspects or conditions of their employment. This pressure is intensified when prospects of alternative employment are bleak. In these situations, workers are hesitant to leave the organization. They, however, need a channel to communicate their dissatisfaction with their jobs and related matters. Thus, unionization becomes the channel or medium to ensure due process at the workplace (Freeman and Medoff, 1984).

The second difficulty in estimating union impact on compensation relates to the issue of quality differences between the union and nonunion workers. Unionized organizations with higher wages will tend to attract the more qualified applicants, because the more qualified and more flexible the workers, the greater the value added to the organization's resources. This raises the question whether the higher wages in the organization are the result of union initiatives and actions or whether the organizations offered the high wages to attract the better quality, more flexible workers.

Based on a review of empirical studies, Gunderson and Hyatt (1995) found that unions have had considerable impact on union and nonunion wages and employee benefits. The discussion that follows is based on these findings.

Union impact on wages

- Union wages tend to be higher than non-union wages—the differential varies from 10 to 30 percent depending upon the method used. However, more recent estimates place these differentials at 10 percent.

- The union impact is greater in recessions due to long-term union contracts. The wage rates and wage structures agreed to in collective agreements during the recovery or growth period of the business cycle remain unchanged during the recession.

- When the wage profiles of less skilled workers are compared with those of more skilled workers, the wage profile of the former is higher because of union influence, mainly due to the seniority-based progression built into the wage structure. This difference is offset when we consider the higher rate of increase for the non-unionized, more highly skilled workers for reasons such as productivity, experience, and qualifications.

- Unions impact wages in nonunion organizations in several ways. First, when a non-union organization decides not to have a union, it is inclined to incorporate the union wage rates. Second, when the higher union wage rates weakens the competitive ability of the union organization, it introduces remedial measures. For example, the unionized organization adopts labour cost control strategies such as contracting out or shifting production to a non-union plant. Both strategies lead to an increase in demand for the relatively lower wage non-union labour. However, the impact of wage rates will depend upon the corresponding supply of non-union labour. Third, the union movement's initiatives and support for minimum wage laws and working conditions directly affect non-union labour because the union wage rates and working conditions are better than those that are legislated.

Although unions have an impact on wages, it would be useful to consider some aspects of this impact. First, unions tend to reduce the variation in wages both within the organization as a whole and within the bargaining unit (Freeman, 1982). Second, although the empirical evidence suggests that union's impact has lowered the wages of non-union workers by a small amount, "...it is not possible to state theoretically the expected impact of unions on the wages of non-union workers" (Gunderson and Hyatt, 1995, p.327).

Union impact on employee benefits

Unionization has a much greater impact on increasing employee benefits than wages for several reasons. To begin with, as will be discussed in greater detail in Chapter 14, the wage controls during World War II compelled a shift of focus from cash compensation to that of deferred compensation. Benefits such as pensions, life insurance, and health insurance were ideal forms of deferred compensation that suited the workers and the employers. Such benefits provided some form of tax advantages to both worker and employer. The average union member can be characterized as a worker who is older, more senior and with dependents to support (Gunderson and Ponak, 1995). Such workers need these benefits and, because of their voting strength, the union is more likely to include these benefits in the collective agreement.

Coincidentally, employee benefits, are also in the employer's interest as they are deferred compensation. Employees receive this compensation after certain conditions are fulfilled. The pension plan is an example of deferred compensation. It is usually designed to ensure the employer's contribution transfers to the worker only after a certain period of continuous service. In addition to the tax advantages which may exist, deferred compensation can serve as a motivational tool to retain employees. Furthermore, the capacity of such plans to generate adequate benefits is often dependent on the economic viability of the business. This fact provides the motivation for workers to be involved in the organization and contribute to its effectiveness.

Implications for Compensation Design and Management

As we have established in previous chapters, the design and management of the compensation system should support the organization's mission, business strategies and objectives which have been developed in the context of the prevailing external environments. One of the important external environments is the union and its expectations. The fact of whether the organization is unionized does not have a significant or substantive bearing upon the fundamental issue of what makes a compensation system effective. Viewed in its quintessential form, an item of compensation is effective when it is designed and managed in a manner which permits the recipient to perceive it as **salient**, **valued**, and **contingent** on the desired behaviour. Therefore, in this section, we discuss some of the major implications for compensation system design and management in an unionized organization to ensure that the compensation system preserves its critical, essential characteristics of saliency, valence, and contingency.

The strength and existence of the three characteristics of "saliency", "valence", and "contingency" are inevitably affected by the content of the compensation system but, even more so, by the process of design and management. Hence, the strategic and process issues in compensation, discussed in later chapters, need to be seriously considered. In an unionized organization, the process issues ought to be relatively straightforward because of the ready availability of communication mechanisms offered by the union structure. In practice, the process issues become complex and problematic because of the adversarial relations that might exist between management and union. For this reason, the issue of compensation cannot be divorced from the bigger, overarching issue of management-union relations. Efforts to promote a cooperative or integrative, problem-solving approach are imperative and cannot be overemphasized in management-union relations.

Related to the issue of trust building and openness is the need to share with the union information about the business such as: business economics, technology, nature of the product, market conditions and related factors which affect their bargaining power. Thus, the more competitive the market, the greater is the pressure on the organization to maintain a lid on wages in order to be cost-efficient. This is especially so in labour-intensive operations where labour costs constitute a relatively major portion of production costs. Similarly, the more feasible it is for labour to be replaced by technology or by contracting out strategies, the more likely it is that demand for labour is low which can weaken the union's bargaining power.

Examples abound of initiatives to turn negative, competitive, and adversarial relationships into positive, cooperative, and integrative ones. One example, briefly mentioned in chapter 2, is the Cardinal River Coals Ltd in Alberta. From 1969 to 1984, the hostile and confrontational relationship between the company and its union, Local 1656 of the United Mine Workers of America, produced three lengthy strikes, 12 months of lost production and lost wages, 700 grievances, and $117,000 annual arbitration fees. In 1983, they changed their approach to a proactive labour-management relationship characterized by a cooperative conflict resolution process. As a result, from 1984 to 1989, they have had three collective agreements, fewer grievances a significantly reduced industrial accident rate, and a jointly-sponsored financial plan for all employees. The Cardinal River Coal Mine has been called a "model of labour-management cooperation in North America" (Canadian Council on Working Life, 1990).

In preparation for negotiations, both the union and management do their own, separate research on compensation systems design and, both invest considerable time, effort, and money. However, when this effort is done separately, the process is not conducive to problem solving but rather to developing strategies of how each can get a better deal from the other. Therefore, a specific recommendation in the design process would be to involve the union in the design of compensation systems, techniques and procedures such as: job evaluation systems, performance appraisal processes, salary surveys, incentive systems and gainsharing programs, and benefits programs. Appropriate joint committees can be set up for this purpose together with mechanisms for an appeal process where appropriate. The process is time-consuming and involves costs such as time away from normal job duties and administrative costs for both union and management. But, as fully discussed in Chapter 7, the payoffs are immense in terms of organizational effectiveness and employee satisfaction.

A closer examination of the primary purpose of unions would reveal that workers join unions for compensation, job security, and due process at the workplace. In the area of compensation, unions accept pay rate differentials but only when these are based on criteria which do not need to be interpreted by management. An example of this is progression in pay grade based on seniority rather than on performance. Similarly, in the area of job security, decisions on lay-offs based on seniority are acceptable, whereas lay-offs based on worker performance are not acceptable. Clearly, the underlying rationale for these union preferences is that unions have a deep-seated scepticism about managers being objective in their decisions. Unions seem concerned that decisions on compensation might be used to serve the manager's personal agenda or to victimize employees who are union activists. In other words, unions are apprehensive that employees might be deprived of due process at the workplace on issues of significant consequence to them.

The underlying issue is the absence of trust. It is beyond the scope of this discussion to determine whether unions or management, or both are responsible for this state of affairs. We do believe that the proactive managerial strategies proposed in this section, particularly with regard to the process issues, provide opportunities for joint problem solving on an ongoing basis, building a climate of trust and openness. These strategies contribute not only to the effectiveness of the compensation system, but also permit management to demonstrate to the union that its goals of fair compensation and due process for its members can be met in a manner that is satisfactory to both management and union. The eventual outcomes can only be improved union-management relations which are conducive to cooperation in collective bargaining and conflict resolution.

The Effect of American Strategies on Canadian Companies

The positive effect of trust-building strategies is supported by a study of four US companies—GM's Saturn plant, Southern Pacific Rail Corporation, AT&T Power Systems, and Xerox. These innovative companies are unionized, but relations with their unions are characterized by a great deal of openness and consultation in decision making. According to this study, both management and union in these companies operate on the belief that: (a) both management and union are concerned about the organization's success; (b) union-management relationship should be based on "mutual trust, respect, and shared goals"; and (c) the organization's success and innovativeness depends upon "continuous improvement" at all levels and in all areas.

In Canada, data from one study suggests that very few organizations have adopted the union-management partnership approach or shared decision making (Gibb-Clark, 1996). However, Canadian organizations which have adopted the union-management partnership approach have found it to be a positive experience in terms of organizational effectiveness and employee satisfaction. Some examples of such organizations are Saskatoon Chemicals; SaskEnergy; Canadian Forces Base Shearwater, Nova Scotia; and Algoma Steel (Newman and Chase, 1993; McFarland, 1996). According to a Conference Board of Canada study, the priority in 83 percent of respondent organizations was to improve relations with unions—more specifically, to cooperate on contracting out, reduced job classification, and job security (Carlyle, 1994).

SUMMARY

The chapter explored the impact of union-management relation on compensation. For this purpose, we reviewed the perspectives on union-management relations and considered compensation issues of interest and concern to unions in the context of their role and objectives. We concluded with an examination of the strategic implication of union expectations for compensation design and management.

KEY TERMS

compensation issues
due process issues
job security issues

REVIEW AND DISCUSSION QUESTIONS

1. State and explain the different perspectives on union-management relations.

2. Describe the primary interest and concern of unions in the area of compensation.

3. Discuss the factors which influence an union's effectiveness in meeting their compensation objectives.

4. Describe some of the problems in determining or estimating union's impact on the organization's compensation structure.

5. Explain the nature of union impact on employee wages and benefits.

6. Discuss the major implications for compensation system design and management in an unionized organization.

The Union's Influence on Compensation

EXERCISE
3.1

Objective

To consider the factors which enhance or reduce the influence of unions on compensation issues.

Situation One

With the opening of the creative graphics department at *The Montreal Gazette*, the job of the the traditional typographer became superfluous resulting in the possible layoffs of 62 typographers. The dispute over this issue led to a 15-month lockout which ended with an agreement in August 1994. The agreement offered the typographers separation packages of $80,000 to $150,000 per employee.

51 typographers accepted the buyout offer and 11 rejected it. The latter employees were guaranteed job security until the age of 65 and retraining and reassignment to other available positions. Consequently, the 11 employees received full salary until May 1996 when the August 1994 agreement expired. With the expiry of the agreement, management offered three of the 11 employees positions in the creative graphics department and decided to discontinue payment to the 8 other employees; these eight employees still have priority for new job openings. The salary of the new positions in the creative graphics department is about 50% of that of the typographers. The union has not accepted management's decision and filed a grievance against it. The 8 typographers are also suing the *Gazette* for lost wages during the 15-month lockout. (King, 1996)

Situation 2:

In the Ontario Public Service Employees Union strike in 1996, the lay-off plan for the 13,000-plus workers became a major issue. According to the union, it was unfavourable compared to that offered by the Federal government to reduce its 45,000 employees, and to the one which Bell Canada used to reduce about 10,000 employees. Details of severance pay and job security plans are as follows (Daws, 1996):

	Ontario government	Federal government	Bell Canada
Severance Pay	2 weeks for each year of service up to 26 years, plus one for each year over 26 years.	39 weeks to a maximum 90 weeks—depending on years of service	26 to 69 weeks depending on age & years of service
Job Security	No guarantee of job security, benefits, or representation by union in outsourced jobs.	Temporary wages or lump-sum payments when salaries are lower in outsourced jobs	3 month training and consideration when opening exists.

Discussion:

In the light of the above information, discuss the factors which enhance or reduce the union's influence on compensation.

PART

II

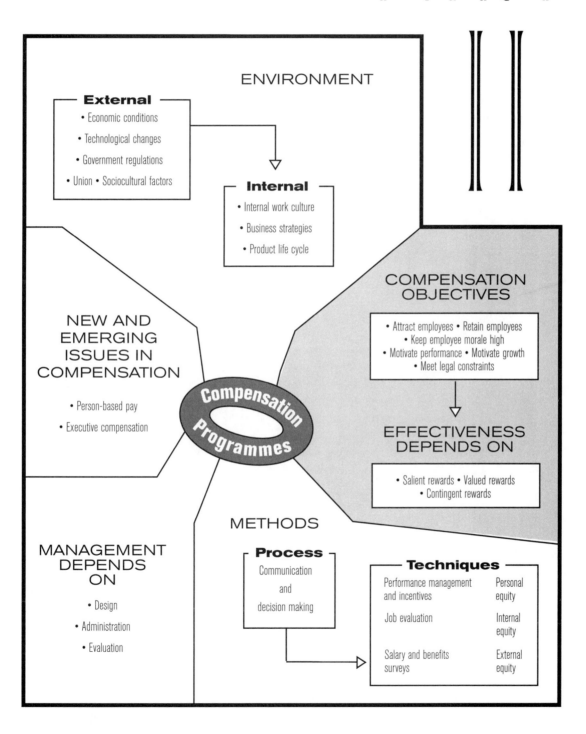

ENVIRONMENT

External
• Economic conditions
• Technological changes
• Government regulations
• Union • Sociocultural factors

Internal
• Internal work culture
• Business strategies
• Product life cycle

COMPENSATION OBJECTIVES

• Attract employees • Retain employees
• Keep employee morale high
• Motivate performance • Motivate growth
• Meet legal constraints

NEW AND EMERGING ISSUES IN COMPENSATION

• Person-based pay
• Executive compensation

Compensation Programmes

EFFECTIVENESS DEPENDS ON

• Salient rewards • Valued rewards
• Contingent rewards

METHODS

MANAGEMENT DEPENDS ON

• Design
• Administration
• Evaluation

Process
Communication
and
decision making

Techniques

Performance management and incentives	Personal equity
Job evaluation	Internal equity
Salary and benefits surveys	External equity

Theoretical Foundations:
Content Theories
Approach

OVERVIEW

This chapter examines the content theories of work motivation in order to understand how the reward practices derived from these theories can help in the design and management of an effective compensation system.

LEARNING OBJECTIVES

► To distinguish between motives and motivation as explanations for human behaviour.

► To distinguish between *content* and *process* theories of motivation.

► To explain the content approach to motivation.

► To understand how many current compensation practices have been influenced by the scientific management and human relations movements.

► To explain Herzberg's two-factor theory.

► To understand how Maslow's hierarchy of needs has influenced Herzberg's two-factor theory.

► To understand how Herzberg's two-factor theory worked its way into contemporary thinking on motivation and what impact the theory has had on reward classification.

► To evaluate critically the intrinsic-extrinsic dichotomy in rewards management.

INTRODUCTION

The discussion on the external and internal environments in Chapter 2 concluded with the recognition that the real test of the effectiveness of a compensation system is whether it enables the organization to attract and retain employees, to motivate them to high performance in their present jobs, to induce them to want to prepare themselves to seek and accept additional responsibilities and challenges, and to promote commitment and loyalty to the organization. How does an organization design and reward a compensation system that will successfully meet this test? In order to address this critical question, it is essential to explore the motivational dynamics inherent in reward-behaviour relationships.

MOTIVATION AND MOTIVES

The topic of motivation is of interest to any observer of human behaviour—especially to both the practising manager and the behavioural scientist. Most people have met individuals who are not particularly gifted, but who achieve a great deal by dint of sheer hard work confirming Edison's observation: "Genius is one per cent inspiration and ninety-nine per cent perspiration." And most people have come across capable and talented individuals who are allergic to the very thought of work. What is it that causes some individuals to exert much more effort than others in what they do—their studies, jobs, or personal and social development?

Consider, for instance, the case of Howard, the fudge sales manager's dream sales person. He is diligent, industrious, and persevering in his efforts to exceed the assigned sales targets. Why does Howard work so hard? To most people, the obvious explanation would be that he works hard to make money. This explanation supplies the motive for Howard's behaviour, but leaves several questions unanswered. Why does Howard not adopt some other behaviour to make money, for example, starting his own fudge business, buying a lottery ticket, or marrying a rich widow? Why does Howard prefer money to some other outcome such as the thrill of goal achievement or the exhilaration of overcoming challenges? Answers to these questions would explain not only the motive for the behaviour, but also the motivational process underlying the behaviour. A theory of motives provides a limited explanation for human behaviour. A theory of motivation explains the reasons why individuals pursue certain goals, as well as the conditions which influence the behaviors they adopt in pursuit of these goals. A comprehensive theory of motivation, then, will seek to explain how behaviour is initiated and the different factors and influences that contribute to energizing, maintaining, and directing that behaviour. Such a definition of motivation goes beyond the question of motive, and establishes a set of behavioural characteristics manifested in the process of motivation.

THEORIES OF MOTIVATION

Motivation is a basic psychological process that has been subjected to considerable investigation in the domain of psychology—clinical, physiological, child, social, educational, industrial, organizational. The literature of psychology is filled with theories of motivation (Kanfer, 1990). This chapter will consider only those theories that help provide an understanding of how a compensation item can influence an individual to start and to persevere in a desired behaviour in the work context. Such an understanding will directly facilitate the effective design and management of the compensation system. The focus, therefore, will be on work motivation theories that have been traditionally categorized in the literature as the *content* and *process* models of work motivation (Kanungo and Mendonca, 1994).

- *Content theories* explain human behaviour as an attempt to satisfy a need and, therefore, seek to identify what need prompts the behaviour.
- *Process theories* explain human behaviour in terms of the cognitive process the individual goes through before and during the behaviour. These theories seek to identify *how* an individual starts, directs, and stops a behaviour.

The approach of the content theories to compensation system design are discussed in this chapter, the process theories in Chapter 5.

CONTENT THEORIES OF WORK MOTIVATION

The content theorists postulate that when an individual's need is not met or satisfied, the individual experiences tension that motivates her or him towards a behaviour to satisfy that need, and thereby to reduce or relieve the tension. The content theorists explain human behaviour as being started and sustained by a deprived need, and stopped when that need is satisfied. Of the several content theories, Maslow's hierarchy of needs and Herzberg's two-factor theory are of greater relevance in that they have spawned a variety of approaches to compensation design that are still current in North American organizations.

A discussion of the content theories begins with the two major movements in the evolution of management thought, namely, the scientific management and the human relations movements. Although these are not theories of work motivation *per se*, the concept of need satisfaction has characterized their thinking on work motivation and their corresponding prescriptions for compensation practices. For example, the need for money was assumed by the scientific management movement to be the primary motivator of work behaviour, and the need for belonging and social recognition was assumed by the human relations movement to be the critical motivator of work behaviour. Luthans (1992) traces the content models to these two movements and suggests that with Maslow and Herzberg the emphasis of the content theories shifted to higher-level or growth needs. Understanding these movements will provide a historical perspective of developments in compensation practices.

The Scientific Management Movement

Approach to compensation Around 1900, Frederick Taylor, known as the father of the scientific management movement, introduced the first systematized approach to compensation. Prior to Taylor, management established incentive systems with production standards and wage rates that were based on an inadequate knowledge of the reasonable and fair time necessary to complete a job. When workers met or exceeded these standards, management reduced the wage rates to keep costs down. Workers responded by restricting output. To resolve this continuing antagonism between labour and management, Taylor linked wage rates to work standards established rationally through time and motion study and related techniques. Taylor's programme produced benefits for workers as well as employers. It enabled workers to earn high wages based on work standards seen to be fair because the standards were rationally determined. The employer benefited from reduced labour costs that resulted from increased productivity.

Major features of compensation system The scientific management movement operated on the "economic man" concept, which assumed that the worker's work behaviour is motivated primarily by a need for money. The compensation system of an organization that subscribes to the assumptions of the scientific management movement emphasizes economic rewards, predominantly money. These rewards are conditional upon performance, with appropriate penalties for failure to meet minimum performance standards. Implicit in the concept of contingent rewards is a performance appraisal process to ascertain if the predetermined job standards have been met. Thus, the scientific management approach to compensation came to be known as the "carrot and stick" approach.

The scientific management approach to motivation does not qualify as a "pure" content theory because it includes elements of both content and process theories. By assuming that the worker's need for money motivates work behaviour, it focuses on the *what* of the motivation process. But it also makes the satisfaction of the need for money dependent or contingent upon a certain work behaviour. By so doing, the scientific management movement also makes a statement on *how* behaviour can be started, energized, directed, and sustained.

The Human Relations Movement

Approach to compensation system This movement, which began in the late 1920s, viewed the workplace as a social system with the potential for satisfying workers' social needs. The individual's work behaviour is motivated by a desire to satisfy his/her need for belonging and social recognition. The movement was sparked by the Hawthorne experiments—refer to Roethlisberger and Dickson's (1939) classic book. The results of these experiments, although inconclusive, led to other studies. The findings of these later studies reported that factors such as interpersonal and intergroup relationships and attitudes were important contributors to job satisfaction and productivity.

Major features of compensation system   The human relations movement operated on the "social man" concept. The compensation system in an organization that subscribes to the assumptions of this movement emphasizes non-financial rewards in addition to reward items that satisfy physical and financial needs. Examples of non-financial rewards are opportunities to work in groups, social recognition, improved communication, pleasant supervisors and co-workers, company-sponsored recreational and social activities, and so forth. Unlike the scientific management movement, the human relations movement emphasized unconditional rewards, which meant that the worker's needs—physical, financial, social—had to be satisfied before the worker could be expected to perform the required job behaviours.

The rationale underlying unconditional rewards is the implicit assumption that need satisfaction would cause the worker to develop a positive attitude, loyalty, and commitment to the organization. Unconditional need satisfaction was believed to strengthen the worker's membership affiliation to the organization, and this strengthened affiliation would lead to high performance. Stated differently, the human relations movement advocated the view that a happy worker would be a productive worker. The compensation system under the human relations movement is often described as the "carrot" approach, because of the apprehension among its proponents that the use of the "stick" would be too traumatic for employee morale and satisfaction and, as a result, would adversely affect performance.

Compensation Approaches under Scientific Management and Human Relations Movements

Both the scientific management and human relations movements have had an enormous influence on the design and management of reward systems and practices. The fundamental differences in their approach to compensation systems are outlined in the following table:

Differences between Scientific Management and Human Relations Movements

	Scientific Management	Human Relations
Worker motivation assumptions	Need for money	Need for belonging and recognition
Type of rewards	Economic (mainly, money)	Non-economic (social recognition, pleasant supervisors & coworkers)
Basis of rewards	Conditional on performance	Not conditional on performance
Objective of reward system	Promote performance behaviour	Promote membership behaviour

One of the objectives of the compensation system is to motivate employees to manifest both membership and performance behaviours. Membership behaviour is attained through ensuring employee retention; performance behaviour, through the desired job behaviours. Through its emphasis on performance-contingent rewards, the scientific management movement focused on performance behaviour to the total exclusion of the social needs of workers. Such an overemphasis on productivity proved to be counter-productive, as was evident from employee dissatisfaction, sabotage of the production process, unionization, and resulting increases in the cost of production.

The failure of the human relations movement, on the other hand, was its overemphasis on unconditional rewards that ensured membership behaviour to the total exclusion of performance behaviour. Organizations following this approach were successful in retaining their employees, keeping them happy, and even eliciting their loyalty and commitment. But membership and high employee morale and commitment do not by themselves lead to high job performance and productivity. In fact, many organizations were disillusioned with the human relations movement when they discovered that productivity had decreased, and that the adversarial role of the unions had intensified, probably because the unions saw in the paternalistic approach of the movement an attempt to alienate employees from their union affiliation.

Against this brief summary of the influence of the scientific management and human relation movements on compensation systems, the next content model—Herzberg's two-factor theory—can be discussed. This theory advocates the inclusion in the reward system of items that could satisfy physical, financial, social, and growth needs. In this way, the theory seeks to address not only the membership and performance behaviours, but also the growth behaviours, of the worker, with a major emphasis on the latter. Herzberg's theory also provides the background for the contemporary approach to rewards classification in terms of intrinsic and extrinsic rewards.

Herzberg's Two-Factor Theory of Reward Classification

Maslow's Hierarchy: Influence on Herzberg's Two-Factor Theory
In the early 1960s, Frederick Herzberg developed a content theory of motivation that postulated two categories of rewards or job factors to explain *what* it is that motivates work behaviour. Herzberg's approach was based on Maslow's hierarchy of needs and considerably influenced by its humanistic orientation, namely, that people do not work mainly for money but for ego-need gratification and self-fulfilment. Maslow's theory is a content model of human motivation in general, but not of work motivation *per se*. A brief exploration of Maslow's hierarchy of needs will help to place Herzberg's theory in its proper perspective.

Maslow's Need Hierarchy   According to Abraham Maslow (1954), an individual's behaviour can be explained as an attempt to satisfy an unsatisfied need; a satisfied or satiated need is not a motivator of behaviour. Maslow grouped needs into five categories, which he arranged in a hierarchical order of strength, from most prominent to least prominent, as follows:

self-actualization ego-status	"growth needs"
belongingness safety and security physiological and survival	"deficiency needs"

He postulated a specific sequence in which the individual will progress through the hierarchy. Thus, starting at the lowest level (the strongest), the individual will move to the next higher level only when the immediately pre-ceding level need is largely satisfied. The first three lower level need categories —physiological and survival, safety and security, belongingness—are viewed as "deficiency needs", which means that when they are satisfied, the deficiency is removed and these will no longer operate to motivate behaviour.

The self-actualization need level, and to a large extent the ego-status need level, function as higher level or "growth needs," which operate differently from deficiency needs. As growth needs are satisfied, their intensity may increase rather than decrease, particularly in the case of individuals with strong growth needs. This is so because the very process of self-actualization is both a challenging and gratifying experience, giving the individual a sense of accom-plishment and achievement. Maslow did not develop his theory specifically to explain work motivation, but its influence is at the very core of Herzberg's two-factor theory.

Herzberg's Two-Factor Theory—basic features   Herzberg's two-factor theory is the typical and most popular of the content theories. It has direct implications for compensation design because it makes concrete and spe-cific pronouncements and predictions on which reward items will motivate and which will not. According to this theory (Herzberg, 1966), rewards affect work behaviour in substantially different ways depending on whether they are intrin-sic rewards (the motivators) or extrinsic rewards (hygiene factors). Thus:

- *Intrinsic rewards* are inherent in the job; for example: responsibility, autono-my, feelings of accomplishment. Employees experience these rewards direct-ly as they perform the job tasks.
- *Extrinsic rewards* are external to the job, for example: pay, benefits, praise, pleasant working conditions, job security.

Effects of Intrinsic Rewards Intrinsic rewards generate in employees a level of satisfaction with what they do on the job, and consequently these rewards induce a high level of performance. For this reason, intrinsic rewards are regarded as the real motivators. On the other hand, extrinsic rewards do not generate satisfaction with job activities and therefore do not motivate performance. However, if the extrinsic rewards surrounding one's job are not present up to a certain level, then such absence or deficiency causes dissatisfaction, which nullifies the positive effects of the intrinsic rewards.

Effects of Extrinsic Rewards Extrinsic rewards are called hygiene factors, because just as hygienic conditions are necessary for, but do not by themselves cause, good health, so extrinsic rewards are necessary for, but do not motivate, performance. For example, an employee with autonomy and responsibility in a challenging job receives intrinsic rewards that generate a considerable degree of satisfaction; as a result, the employee will be motivated to put in a high level of performance. If at the same time this employee receives a low salary that is not commensurate with the job, the dissatisfaction caused by the low salary will prevent the employee from performing at the high level induced by the intrinsic rewards. Hence, Herzberg postulates that extrinsic rewards function as hygiene factors that must exist in the right amount and be of the right type before the intrinsic rewards, the motivators, can begin to operate.

Hygiene/Motivator Factors Parallel Deficiency/Growth Needs
The distinction between hygiene factors and motivators closely parallels the distinction between deficiency and growth needs in Maslow's hierarchy of needs. Just as deficiency needs when satisfied do not operate to motivate behaviour, so hygiene factors when provided do not operate to motivate job performance. On the other hand, just as growth needs continue to operate even when satisfied, so Herzberg's motivators continue to provide the impetus for improved job performance. In fact, a correspondence between hygiene factors/motivators and deficiency/growth need levels can be seen in the following table:
Examples of:

Hygiene Factors	Maslow's Need Levels
Pay, working conditions ⟶	physiological, survival needs level
Job security ⟶	safety and security needs level
Relations with co-workers ⟶	belongingness need level
Motivators	
Recognition from job performance ⟶	ego-status need level
Challenging assignments ⟶	self-actualization need level

The Intrinsic-Extrinsic Reward Classification

Main Features of intrinsic-extrinsic classification   The distinction between hygiene factors and motivators soon worked its way into contemporary thinking on motivation, with the result that the compensation system came to be looked at in terms of two categories:

1. extrinsic rewards that corresponded to hygiene factors: e.g., pay, working conditions, praise from supervisor, congenial co-workers and supervisors and so forth; and

2. intrinsic rewards that corresponded to motivators: e.g., challenging assignments, autonomy, participation in decision making, and so forth.

Impact of intrinsic-extrinsic classification   The distinction between intrinsic and extrinsic rewards became popular among motivation theorists in explaining the contents of human motives. The impact of the intrinsic-extrinsic distinction on management practice was even more profound. It became an integral part of the manager's thought, vocabulary, and practice (Robins, 1996). The reason for this is easy to see. The intrinsic-extrinsic distinction provided a relatively direct, unambiguous answer to the practical question managers faced each work day: "What rewards do I give my employees to get them to be productive?" The programmed response was: provide intrinsic rewards by job redesign to include more variety, more responsibility, more autonomy, and more control.

Not only was the answer new, it was specific and its implementation seemed possible with relatively little expense and effort. It also seemed to provide a method to prevent or redress worker alienation, which Karl Marx had predicted would result when workers were denied control of and participation in matters relating to their jobs. This panacea for employees' motivational ills included an assortment of programmes: job rotation, job enrichment, flexible scheduling, semi-autonomous work groups, and quality circles.

Obsessed with the idea of intrinsic rewards as the only motivators of performance, academic researchers and practitioners alike relegated the role of extrinsic rewards to the background (Staw, 1984). They were too preoccupied with job and work design to ask whether the organization was getting its money's worth from its expenditures on pay and benefits. Indeed, the manager would deny that this issue of a return on compensation expenditures was relevant to effective management because, according to the intrinsic-extrinsic approach, monetary rewards are least likely to induce productivity.

When a theory causes a results-oriented manager to be apathetic to such an enormous item of expenditure as pay and benefits, the inference is that a vital aspect of reality has been overlooked in the formulation of that theory. The fact is that the intrinsic-extrinsic dichotomy, which has dominated the compensation management literature for over three decades, is inadequate in providing clear, practical guidelines for the effective design and administration of the reward system. Much less does the concept lend itself to analytical investigations of whether the organization is maximizing the returns on its investment in the reward programme. The intrinsic-extrinsic dichotomy approach is again becoming popular in management circles (Kohn, 1994). For this reason, the next section critically examines the meaning and the effectiveness of the intrinsic-extrinsic dichotomy approach to rewards management. The discussion cites empirical studies of the mid-70s onwards which pointedly addressed the claims of this approach.

A Critique of the Intrinsic-Extrinsic Dichotomy in Rewards Management

Advocates of the intrinsic-extrinsic dichotomy approach claim that it is built on sound theory that provides the foundation for its techniques and practices. This section explores the myths surrounding this claim.

Myth 1 The intrinsic-extrinsic dichotomy assumes that people seek and need work that is meaningful and in which they are free to function on an independent basis. Implicit in this assumption is the belief that the work role is central to one's life and provides the best opportunity for the realization of the human potential for growth. This assumption is the fundamental rationale for giving intrinsic rewards a unique role. As McGregor observed: "Unless there are opportunities at work to satisfy these high level needs (esteem and self-actualization), people will be deprived, and their behaviour will reflect this deprivation" (McGregor, 1966, 12-13). Intrinsic rewards, therefore, provide people with the opportunity to satisfy their need to find self-fulfilment in work.

Fact The relevant research contradicts these motivational assumptions.

- A study of blue-collar and white-collar motivation concluded that only about 15 to 20 per cent of the blue-collar workforce look for challenging jobs in order to satisfy their growth needs at work (Fein, 1976).

- For many people growth needs are not important and the work role is not their central life interest (Dubin, 1956; Kanungo & Misra, 1988).

Myth 2 The concepts of intrinsic and extrinsic rewards provide a simple, straightforward, and unambiguous basis for rewards management.

Fact The following studies show that intrinsic and extrinsic rewards concepts are ambiguous.

- A survey of industrial psychologists found that only 7 out of 21 rewards were classified as either intrinsic or extrinsic by more than 75 per cent of the respondents (Dyer and Parker, 1976).

- A survey of Canadian managers found that they had difficulty in classifying rewards as intrinsic or extrinsic (Kanungo and Hartwick, 1987).

A persistent and fundamental problem relates to the criteria by which a reward is identified as intrinsic or extrinsic. Of the wide range of conflicting criteria that is used, the most popular are: the *task criterion* and the *mediation of reward* criterion. According to the task criterion, intrinsic rewards are those that derive directly from or are inherently connected with job tasks (Herzberg, Mausner, and Synderman, 1959); all other rewards are extrinsic rewards. In the mediation criterion, the focus is on the persons who administer the reward (Deci, 1972). Thus, intrinsic rewards are those which employees administer to themselves—that is, self-mediated rewards; extrinsic rewards are those received from others—that is, other-mediated.

The definition of each criterion appears to be clear by itself. Now, if the two criteria, task and mediation of reward, refer to the same intrinsic-extrinsic dimension of reward classification, then a set of rewards classified as intrinsic or extrinsic using the task criterion should be similarly classified using the mediation of reward criterion.

In the Kanungo and Hartwick (1987) study referred to earlier, 13 out of the 48 rewards were differentially classified as intrinsic or extrinsic under the two criteria. For example, promotion, authority, participation, praise from supervisor and from co-worker, recognition, awards for superior performance were all classified as intrinsic rewards using the task criterion. These same rewards were also classified as extrinsic using the mediation of reward criterion. Another noteworthy finding from this study was that "pride in the success of the company" and "opportunity to make friends" were classified as extrinsic rewards using the task criterion. But when the mediation of reward criterion was used, these rewards were classified as intrinsic.

Thus, the concepts of intrinsic and extrinsic rewards do not provide managers with a clear, unambiguous basis for rewards identification and, consequently, for rewards management. Furthermore, the inability to classify rewards consistently as intrinsic or extrinsic, as reported by these studies, brings into question whether the intrinsic-extrinsic dichotomy has a similar meaning for all managers. The conclusion is that the intrinsic-extrinsic dichotomy is conceptually flawed. After reviewing four methods typically employed to dichotomize intrinsic and extrinsic rewards, Guzzo concluded: "… if a further understanding of work motivation is to be gained, it is imperative that characteristics of work rewards be conceived of in other than intrinsic-extrinsic terms …" (Guzzo, 1979, 82).

Myth 3 Even if the intrinsic-extrinsic dichotomy is conceptually flawed, one must nevertheless accept the overall motivational value of designing jobs through job enrichment programmes that flow from the theories of motivation based on this dichotomy. It is assumed that job enrichment programmes provide motivators or intrinsic rewards to all employees and thereby enhance their job performance.

Fact Job enrichment programmes have not fared any better than the theory from which they were derived (Beer, Eisenstat, and Biggadike, 1996). The reader is also referred to the following specific studies which support this fact:

- Some researchers have reported that these programmes are for the most part successful (Davis and Cherns, 1975), others have questioned the data on which such conclusions are based (Fein, 1974).

- Job enrichment programmes are applicable to only a narrow spectrum of jobs; productivity gains from such programmes are, if any, minimal and workers frequently prefer jobs that are not enriched (Luthans and Reif, 1973).

- Some workers prefer highly routine, repetitive jobs that are devoid of any challenge (Luthans and Reif, 1972); for these workers, job security and the relative independence and the freedom to socialize at work are more important.

- Workers will respond positively to enriched jobs only in the presence of certain conditions: worker's knowledge and skill, growth need strength, and satisfaction with the work context, for example, pay, working conditions, supervisory practices, and co-workers (Hackman and Oldham, 1980).

To conclude It is not surprising that the experience with the intrinsic-extrinsic approach to rewards management has been disappointing. This approach looks at only one aspect of the behaviour-reward relationship, namely, the assumed inherent potency of the reward to produce the desired behaviour. It ignores the fact that a reward, whether intrinsic or extrinsic, will influence behaviour only when it is valued by the recipient and received as a consequence of that behaviour. Hence, any effective approach to rewards management must take into account the perceptions and expectations of the recipient. The process theories of work motivation discussed in the next chapter meet this requirement.

SUMMARY

Compensation plays a fundamental role in employee work motivation. In order to use compensation programmes successfully, the compensation specialist needs to understand what it is about the reward item that prompts employees to start and maintain a desired behaviour, or to stop an undesired work behaviour.

This chapter explored the content models or approaches to work motivation that explain human behaviour as an attempt to satisfy a need. The chapter began with a discussion of the scientific management movement and the human relations movement, two major movements that viewed employees' work behaviour as a means to satisfy a need. The scientific management movement, which operated on the "economic man" concept and assumed that employees' work behaviour is motivated primarily by a need for money, emphasized economic rewards that were made contingent on performance.

The human relations movement, which operated on the "social man" concept and assumed that employees' work behaviour is motivated primarily by the desire to satisfy social needs, emphasized non-financial rewards in addition to reward items that satisfy physical and financial needs. The human relations movement emphasized unconditional rewards because of the belief that need satisfaction would promote loyalty and commitment and eventually lead to high performance. In reality, however, the reward system only contributed to retaining the employees and keeping them happy.

Herzberg's two-factor theory, the typical and most popular of the content approaches to work motivation, was considered next. Based on Maslow's hierarchy of needs and influenced by its humanistic orientation, the two-factor theory included in the reward system items that could satisfy physical, financial, and social, as well as growth, needs. It addressed not only membership and performance behaviours, but also growth behaviours, which had been neglected by both the scientific management and human relations movements.

However, it proposed that rewards affect work behaviour in substantially different ways, depending on whether they are intrinsic rewards (the motivators) or extrinsic rewards (hygiene factors). Herzberg claimed that intrinsic rewards—responsibility, autonomy, feelings of accomplishment, and so forth—are the real and only motivators of job performance. Extrinsic rewards—pay, benefits, praise, job security, and so forth—do not motivate employees to high job performance; their absence generates dissatisfaction. The extrinsic rewards, however, must be present before the intrinsic rewards, the motivators, can begin to operate.

Although the two-factor theory appears to have been popular with both practitioners and academic researchers, an examination of the intrinsic-extrinsic dichotomy reveals that (a) the empirical findings contradict its motivational assumptions; (b) it does not provide managers with a clear, unambiguous basis for rewards identification and management; (c) and its job enrichment programmes do not have universal applicability. Essentially, its approach to rewards management ignores the fact that a reward, whether it is intrinsic or extrinsic, will influence behaviour only when it is valued by the recipient and received as a consequence of that behaviour.

KEY TERMS

content theories   *motivation*
extrinsic rewards   *motives*
hierarchy of needs   *process theories*
human relations movement   *scientific management movement*
intrinsic rewards   *two-factor theory*

ᔕ REVIEW AND DISCUSSION QUESTIONS

1. Explain why a theory of motives is not adequate to explain human behaviour.

2. Distinguish between the content and process theories of work motivation.

3. From the late nineteenth century until today, compensation practices have been profoundly influenced by the scientific management and human relations movements. Compare and contrast these movements with specific reference to:

   a) their assumptions about employee work motivation in so far as compensation is concerned;

   b) the reward items emphasized;

   c) the basis of giving rewards; and

   d) the types of behaviours promoted by the rewards.

4. How does Maslow's hierarchy of needs explain an individual's behaviour?

5. What are the salient features of Herzberg's two-factor theory? Explain in what way it has been influenced by Maslow's hierarchy of needs.

6. What are the reasons for the popularity of the intrinsic-extrinsic reward classification among motivation theorists and managers?

7. The advocates of the intrinsic-extrinsic dichotomy approach claim that it is built on sound theory that provides the foundation for its techniques and practices. Critically examine this claim with reference to:

   a) the assumptions underlying the intrinsic-extrinsic dichotomy;

   b) the validity of the constructs intrinsic and extrinsic;

   c) the effectiveness of job enrichment programmes derived from this approach; and

   d) the inherent potency of the reward implied in this approach.

8. What are the similarities between Maslow's hierarchy of needs and the scientific management movement, the human relations movement, and Herzberg's two-factor theory?

Preferences for Pay and Other Job Outcomes

Objective

This exercise will give you an opportunity to develop some insights into why different groups of employees prefer different job outcomes.

Procedure

1. After reading all the job outcomes listed in Table 4.1, decide which outcome you think is most preferred by factory workers; by managers/professionals.

2. In the blank column under Factory Workers, rank the outcomes in order from 1 to 15, using 1 for the most preferred outcome and 15 for the least preferred. Repeat for Managers/Professionals.

3. Share your individual decisions with your group. As a group, decide on the rankings. Make sure your spokesperson records the consensus of the group together with the rationale for the ranking decisions.

4. Each group reports its decisions.

5. Discussion will follow each presentation. The discussion could consider the following questions:

   - Using Maslow's hierarchy of needs, explain the outcome preferences of the two groups.

   - In view of your findings of differences in the outcome preferences of these employee groups, do you think that there might also be differences in the outcome preferences of:

     a) male and female employees?

     b) anglophone and francophone employees?

     Think of some reasons why this might be so.

   - What are the managerial implications of such outcome preferences for the design of the compensation system?

TABLE 4.1: Preferences for Pay and Other Job Outcomes

Job Outcomes (Things people look for in their jobs/careers)	Factory Workers	Managers/ Professionals
Security (Permanent job, steady work)		
Earnings (for a better standard of living)		
Merit pay (for high job performance)		
Benefits (vacations, bonus, pension, insurance, profit-sharing, medical benefits, disability, dental benefits, etc.)		
Working conditions (pleasant surroundings, good lighting, air-conditioning, adequate office space)		
Opportunity for future promotion		
Sound company policies and procedures (reasonable and non-discriminatory)		
Good peer relations (a job that gives you the opportunity to work with others whom you like)		
Considerate and sympathetic superior		
Technically competent superior		
Respect and recognition (from superiors and peers for your work)		
Interesting work (a job that you very much enjoy)		
Responsibility and independence (to work in your own way)		
Achievement (opportunity to achieve excellence in your work)		
Opportunity for growth (professionally; to become more skilled and competent on the job)		

The Intrinsic-Extrinsic Approach to Rewards Classification

Objective

To understand the basis for classifying rewards.

Procedure

1. Refer to Table 1.1 in Chapter 1, and classify each item as either intrinsic or extrinsic.

2. Share your decision with your group. As a group, attempt to arrive at a consensus on each item. If the group is unable to reach a consensus on an item, make sure that your spokesperson records the reasons for the different points of view.

3. Each group reports its decisions and differences.

4. Discussion will follow each presentation. It may be instructive to consider the relevance of the Kanungo and Hartwick (1987) findings with regard to the ambiguity of the intrinsic-extrinsic basis of classifying rewards.

CHAPTER 5

Theoretical Foundations: Process Theories Approach

OVERVIEW

Continuing the search for a suitable theoretical approach to guide the design and management of a compensation system, this chapter provides an extensive consideration of the process theories of work motivation. It reviews equity theory, its elements and process, and then presents a comprehensive motivational model for reward management. Founded on the basic framework and process of expectancy theory, the model incorporates the essence of equity theory and some of the more appropriate concepts of need theories. The chapter concludes with a discussion of the practical managerial implications of the model for the effective design, implementation, and evaluation of a compensation system.

LEARNING OBJECTIVES

▶ To understand how the process theories explain work motivation.

▶ To understand the elements and the process of equity theory and its explanation of the behaviour-reward relationship.

▶ To understand the elements and the process of the expectancy theory model for reward management.

▶ To identify and explain the determinants of each element of the expectancy theory model.

▶ To identify and explain the moderators of the process of the expectancy theory model.

▶ To explain the research findings that provide empirical support for the expectancy theory model.

▶ To understand the direct impact and the concrete, practical guidelines
that the expectancy theory model offers with regard to the strategies,
processes, and techniques used in the design and management of the
compensation system.

PROCESS THEORIES OF WORK MOTIVATION

Process theories attempt to explain the *how* of an individual's work motivation,
that is, how the individual's work behaviour is started, sustained, and stopped.
These theories look at the cognitive processes involved in motivation, how an
individual makes conscious choices that lead to a specific work behaviour. The
process theories that have profound implications for the design, management,
and administration of compensation programmes are equity theory and
expectancy theory.

EQUITY THEORY

Elements and process 205

This theory, formulated by J. Stacy Adams (1965), attempts to explain the process
of how an individual comes to be satisfied or dissatisfied with a reward. In the event
the individual is dissatisfied, equity theory predicts the behaviours to which the individual might have recourse in order to eliminate or to reduce the dissatisfaction.

Equity theory is based on the notion of the equity or fairness that individuals expect in the numerous exchanges of the work situation. An employee
brings to the job what he/she perceives are his/her *inputs*—knowledge, skills,
abilities, experience, diligence, and industriousness. For these inputs the
employee receives *outcomes*—pay, praise from the supervisor, promotion, interesting assignments. According to equity theory, the employee will determine
the equity or fairness of the outcomes by comparing the ratio of his/her outcomes
to inputs with the ratio of the outcomes to inputs of a relevant other person. If
such a comparison shows that the employee's perceived ratio of outcomes to
inputs is equal to his/her perceived ratio of the other person's outcomes to
inputs, then the employee will experience equity. If the employee perceives the
two ratios to be unequal, then he/she will experience inequity.

Effects of inequity 26

The nature of the inequity could generate feelings of guilt or anger. If the
employee perceives his/her ratio of outcomes to inputs to be greater than that
of the relevant other, then the employee will perceive that he/she is overpaid
and will likely experience feelings of guilt. If the employee perceives his/her
ratio of outcomes to inputs to be less than that of the other, then the employee
will perceive that he/she is underpaid and will likely experience feelings of

anger. The feelings of guilt or anger resulting from the perceptions of inequity will motivate the employee to behaviours that the employee believes will restore equity or reduce inequity (Gerhart, Minkoff, and Olsen, 1996).

The behaviours that the employee adopts can include increasing his/her own inputs (working harder) or outcomes (success in persuading the supervisor that a raise is justified); decreasing his/her own inputs (tardiness, absenteeism) or outcomes (if compensation is on a piece-rate basis, focusing on quality rather than on quantity); cognitively distorting his/her own or the other's inputs or outcomes (through reevaluation of perceptions); acting on the other (sabotage, vandalism); changing the other (comparing self with a different worker); leaving the field (transfer or resignation).

The elements and process of equity theory is summarized in Figure 5.1.

Figure 5.1: Elements and process of equity theory

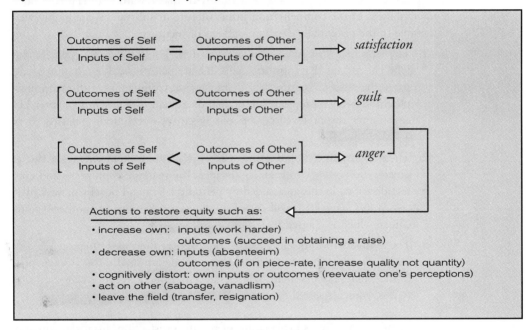

Equity and the principles of justice

The desire for equity flows from the fundamental principles of justice discussed later in Chapter 12. In the context of exchange relationships in organizations, the two relevant principles of justice are: distributive justice and procedural justice. Distributive justice, relates to the outcomes received in the exchange relationship. It explores the question: Are the outcomes fair or equitable? Procedural justice, is concerned with the fairness of the procedures or process in the determination of the outcomes. Studies (Greenberg, 1986) have found that employees' beliefs of the fairness of outcomes are based on:

a) the perceived outcomes/inputs ratio of self relative to that of the comparison other—that is, the distributive justice perspective; and

b) the perception of the process used to determine the outcomes—that is, the procedural justice perspective.

Hence, to ensure equity in an exchange relationship, it is critical to ensure that decisions are consistent with both the distributive and procedural principles of justice.

Importance of equity to compensation system

Feelings of equity or inequity lead the employee to form judgements on the value (or valence) of a reward. When an employee perceives the reward item to be inequitable, either in its content (the distributive justice perspective) or in the methods by which it is determined (the procedural justice perspective), the employee will not experience satisfaction with that reward item. Three fundamental areas of the compensation infrastructure or subsystems are highly vulnerable to the potentially damaging effects of inequity:

1. The basic pay structure of the organization should reflect the value of the job. This means that jobs of equal value are paid the same and appropriate pay differentials recognize job dissimilarities. Compliance with this principle through an appropriate job evaluation system (discussed in Chapter 11) contributes to employee perceptions of equity—technically referred to as *internal equity*.

2. The pay structure should reflect market wage rates, in accordance with the organization's policy to lead, lag, or meet the market. Appropriate and correct decisions in this area, aided by periodic salary and benefit surveys (discussed in Chapter 13) will ensure employee perceptions of another type of equity, which is referred to as *external equity*.

3. The compensation of employees should reflect their performances. Performance-based pay (discussed in Chapter 9), determined through a fair performance appraisal system, will ensure employee perceptions of the third type of equity, referred to as either *personal equity* or *individual equity*.

To conclude: By its explanation of reward satisfaction/dissatisfaction and its impact on work motivation, equity theory makes a substantial contribution to the behaviour-reward relationship. A fuller understanding of this relationship is provided by Lawler's expectancy motivation model.

EXPECTANCY THEORY

Expectancy theory is a cognitively oriented model of human behaviour. It recognizes that the individual's behaviours are the product of rational, conscious choices from alternative courses of action. These choices are based on the individual's perceptions and beliefs. The first formulations of expectancy theory are found in the works of psychologists Kurt Lewin (1935) and Edward Tolman (1932). Since then, several theorists have used the expectancy framework to develop their own theories on general human motivation. It was Victor Vroom, in his *Work and Motivation* (1964), who first applied expectancy theory to explain motivation in the work environment. His book received considerable theoretical and empirical attention, which led to several refinements of his model.

In essence, it postulates that the motivational force to perform in a specified manner will depend on the individual's belief that he/she has the ability to perform the specified behaviours and that such performance will satisfactorily lead to the outcomes associated with the performance. (Lawler and Jenkins, 1992; Gerhart, Minkoff, and Olsen, 1996). Expectancy theory, then, has three basic elements:

1. the effort-performance expectancy (E⇨P).
2. the performance-outcome expectancy (P⇨O).
3. the valence or attractiveness of the outcomes (V).

Lawler (1971) developed his motivation model on these basic elements, but incorporated into the model the determinants of each element to provide a more comprehensive explanation of both the what and how of the motivational process. The remainder of the chapter considers this model and the implications it has for the design and management of the compensation system.

THE ELEMENTS OF EXPECTANCY THEORY Q7

The Effort-Performance Expectancy (E⇨P)

This is the individual's belief or probability estimate that in a given situation his/her expenditure of effort will lead to the intended level of performance. The probability can vary from 0, which is the certainty that the effort will not result in the required performance, to 1, which is the certainty that the effort will result in the required performance.

> For example, John, a machinist, is assigned to machine 500 widgets a week, an increase from 300 widgets a week. If John is certain that he can produce the 500 widgets as required, then his (E⇨P) expectancy will be 1. If John is certain that he cannot produce the 500 widgets as required, then his (E⇨P) expectancy will be 0. On the other hand, if John is uncertain of successful performance, then his (E⇨P) expectancy will be between 0 and 1, depending on his assessment of the chances of doing the assignment successfully.

Later in the chapter, some of the factors that determine the (E⇨P) expectancy will be examined.

The Performance-Outcome Expectancy (P⇨O)

This expectancy represents the individual's belief, or estimate of probability, that a given performance level will result in a certain outcome. The (P⇨O) expectancy can range from 0 (this performance level definitely would not lead to this outcome) through 1 (this performance level definitely would lead to this outcome). Since performance generally leads to several outcomes, the individual will develop probability estimates for each outcome.

> Consider again the case of John, the machinist. Suppose John perceives that the outcomes associated with producing the 500 widgets will be either a bonus, a promotion, or a lay-off. He estimates that the probability of each outcome following successful performance is .7 for the bonus, .3 for promotion, and .6 for lay-off.

The (P⇨O) expectancy, then, must be viewed as a subjective probability estimate for each outcome associated with a performance level. The determinants of (P⇨O) expectancy will be discussed in a later section.

Valence, or the Attractiveness of the Outcome (V)

Valence expresses the individual's preference for the outcome, or the value or importance of the outcome to the individual. It is the anticipated satisfaction (positive valence) or dissatisfaction (negative valence) that an individual associates with an outcome. The valence for an outcome can range from -1 (the outcome is extremely unattractive or undesirable) through 0 (the outcome is neither attractive nor unattractive), to +1 (the outcome is extremely attractive or desirable).

> Returning to the case of John, the machinist: his probability estimates of each outcome following successful performance were .7 for the bonus, .3 for promotion, and .6 for lay-off. John may value each outcome either positively or negatively. Thus, his valence for each outcome might be +.7 for the bonus, +.5 for the promotion, and -.8 for lay-off.

It is known that the attractiveness or the value of an outcome differs considerably from person to person. In fact, even for the same person, the value of an outcome will differ over time. The determinants of valence are discussed in the next section.

THE DETERMINANTS OF THE ELEMENTS OF EXPECTANCY THEORY

The (E⇨P) Expectancy

The major determinants of (E⇨P) expectancy are the actual situation, communications from others, and past experiences in similar situations. These can be seen in the left-hand segment of Figure 5.2 as impacting on (E⇨P).

Figure 5.2: The Expectancy Theory Model

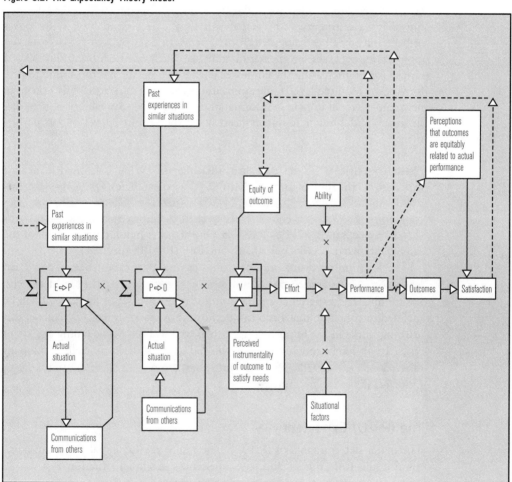

Source: Adapted from Lawler (1971, 1973)

Actual situation   In the organizational context, a major determinant is the performance of job tasks at a required level. The individual's appraisal of the facts and circumstances of the actual situation leads him/her to assess the chances that his/her effort will lead to the required performance. Initially the individual can misread the situation and develop unrealistic expectancies that the effort expended may or may not lead to the required level of performance. In most organizations, however, these unrealistic expectancies are not held for an extensive period of time because the employee gets direct feedback from the job and also from his/her peers and supervisor and adjusts his/her expectancies to a more realistic level.

Communications from others   This determinant operates in two ways to influence $(E \Rightarrow P)$ expectancies. The first way is the indirect impact on $(E \Rightarrow P)$ expectancies discussed above, when a corrective is provided for the unrealistic assessment of the actual situation. The second way is the direct impact on $(E \Rightarrow P)$ expectancies that happens, for example, when a peer and/or a supervisor provides direction and guidance. Such on-the-job training plays a crucial role in increasing the employee's belief that he/she has the ability to perform at the required level. Communications from others, particularly crucial to new employees, also include information relating to the availability of material, financial, and human resources needed for the required level of job performance.

Past experiences in similar situations   What is learned from past experiences contributes immensely to $(E \Rightarrow P)$ expectancies. If a person has had a series of failures at one or more job tasks, then the belief in his/her abilities to perform those tasks is considerably weakened, and to that extent the person's $(E \Rightarrow P)$ expectancies will be quite low. On the other hand, past successes at the same or similar job tasks will greatly increase $(E \Rightarrow P)$ expectancies.

The learning need not only be from personal past experiences. People can learn from their observations of others in similar situations. If I see Marie who has training and experience similar to mine perform a set of job tasks, I will be inclined to conclude that I too can perform those tasks as well. Of course, this learning works in the opposite direction as well. If I see Marie failing at a set of tasks, I will likely conclude that I will fail at those tasks as well. Thus, past observations of relevant others in similar situations also have the potential to influence $(E \Rightarrow P)$ expectancies.

The $(P \Rightarrow O)$ Expectancy

The major determinants of $(P \Rightarrow O)$ expectancy are the actual situation, communications from others, and past experiences in similar situations.

Actual situation   This determinant refers to the individual's assessment of the outcomes following the performance, as in the case of the performance pay relationship. For the new employee, the assessment is generally based on his/her acceptance of the information, including the documentation, given at the time of hiring.

Communications from others   Included in this determinant is the information one receives from one's peers and supervisor on issues relating to pay and other job outcomes. It is not uncommon for workers to maintain low productivity because of information from their peers that management invariably reduces the pay rate when productivity is high. They also fear being ostracized by other workers.

When organizations keep their reward systems secret, they unwittingly foster speculative gossip that does not promote realistic (P$\Rightarrow$O) expectancies.

Past experiences in similar situations   This refers to the experience in relation to outcomes. Suppose, for example, the organization introduces an incentive plan that is performance based. Suppose further that the organization also operates at the present time a merit pay plan with a performance appraisal system which employees perceive to be unfairly administered. With this experience, what is the likelihood of the employees' believing that the incentive plan will be truly performance based? Since the past experience showed that the merit plan is not truly based on performance, will influence the employees' (P$\Rightarrow$O) expectancies for the proposed incentive plan will be influenced.

Valence or the Attractiveness of Outcomes

There are basically two determinants of valence. These are the perceived instrumentality of the outcome to satisfy needs, and the perceived equity or fairness of the outcome (see Figure 5.2).

Instrumentality of outcome to satisfy needs   Individuals value an outcome when it is perceived to satisfy an important or salient need. As discussed in the previous chapter, the needs that outcomes can satisfy could be categorized as physiological and survival, safety and security, belongingness, ego-status, and self-actualization. Which outcome will an individual use to satisfy which need? This depends on the way the individual has been socialized. Most people learn that money can satisfy physiological, security, and ego-status needs. The more needs that an outcome will satisfy, the more positively that outcome will be valued.

It is necessary to recognize that the valence or importance attributed to pay depends upon the salient needs of the individual and the extent to which other outcomes can satisfy those needs more effectively than pay. For example, it is not uncommon to find an individual turning down an attractive job offer for a job in another organization that pays less but offers opportunities for challenging and interesting work assignments. Likewise, certain people who are attracted to careers in government and hospitals tend to value pay less than people who are attracted to careers in business. This is so because people tend to work for the type of organization they believe will satisfy salient and important needs.

The equity or fairness of the outcome This is the second and equally important determinant of valence. As equity theory suggests, the individual's perception of the equity is based on a comparison of his/her outcome-input ratio with the outcome-input ratio of a relevant other. If the two ratios are perceived to be equal, then equity exists and the outcome's valence increases. If the two ratios are not perceived to be equal, then the outcome is inequitable, and to that extent there is a drop in valence.

Combined effect of instrumentality & equity of outcome To illustrate the effects of instrumentality to satisfy need and equity on the valence of outcomes, consider that Tom expects the outcome associated with his performance to be a merit bonus of $3,000. He values this outcome because it will meet his important need to pay his house tax bill. Therefore the valence of this outcome will be high. But Tom is also aware that the structure of the merit bonus system will not adequately reflect his performance *vis-à-vis* his colleague. This inequity will cause him to reduce the high valence of the $3,000. If Tom had perceived the merit bonus system to be fair, then the equity would have contributed towards an even greater increase in valence of the $3,000 bonus.

THE PROCESS OF EXPECTANCY THEORY

The preceding discussion has covered the three elements of expectancy theory model and the major determinants of each element. We now discuss the process of the model, Figure 5.2, in terms of its critical stages: the initial motivational force generation stage; the effort-to-performance stage; the performance-to-outcomes stage. We conclude this section on the process of the model with a discussion on the dynamic nature of the process.

The initial motivational force generation stage

Computation of motivational force The three elements combine to generate the individual's motivational force to exert the effort to achieve the desired performance level—thus:

$(E \Rightarrow P) \times [(P \Rightarrow O) \times (V)]$ = Motivational Force—as illustrated below:

John, a machinist, is required to produce 500 widgets. His expected outcomes for this level of performance are: a bonus, a promotion, or a lay-off possibility. Assume that his:

  – $(E \Rightarrow P)$ expectancy is 1,0;
  – $(P \Rightarrow O)$ expectancy is: bonus =.7, promotion =.3, lay-off =.6;
  – (V) is: bonus = +.7, promotion = +.5, lay-off = -.8

The motivational force in this example will be computed as follows:

$$\{(E \Rightarrow P) \times \Sigma[(P \Rightarrow O) \times (V)]\} = \text{Motivational Force}$$

Step 1 $\Sigma[(P \Rightarrow O) \times (V)]$

$$[(0.7) \quad \times (+.7)] = 0.49 \quad \text{(due to bonus)}$$
$$[(0.3) \quad \times (+.5)] = 0.15 \quad \text{(due to promotion)}$$
$$[(0.6) \quad \times (-.8)] = \underline{-0.48} \quad \text{(due to lay-off)}$$
$$\Sigma[(P \Rightarrow O) \times (V)] = 0.16$$

Step 2 $\{(E \Rightarrow P) \times \Sigma[(P \Rightarrow O) \times (V)]\}$ = Motivational Force
$$\{(1.0) \quad \times \quad [0.16] \quad = +0.16$$

In this example, since there are three outcomes, the range of the motivational force is a minimum of -3 to a maximum of +3. Therefore, the total motivational force of +.16 shows that John is motivated to put in the effort to perform, but that his motivation is extremely weak. The computation shows the depressing effect of a negative valence, without which John's motivational force would have been +.64. The higher, positive expectancy values of each term contribute eventually to a stronger motivational force.

Motivational Force: Multiplicative Function The equation incorporates a multiplicative function rather than an additive function. There is no firm empirical basis for hypothesizing a multiplicative relationship between the three elements. However, in extreme situations, when either $(E \Rightarrow P)$ or $(P \Rightarrow O)$ is 0, or when (V) is -1, one can logically reason that the multiplicative function is most appropriate.

For instance, if you believe that $(E \Rightarrow P)$ is 0, namely, that your effort will not lead to successful performance, then you will not be motivated to put in the effort, even though you believe that the required performance would definitely lead to outcomes [i.e., $(P \Rightarrow O) = 1$], and you find the outcomes to be extremely desirable [i.e., $(V) = +1$]. Likewise, if you believe that $(P \Rightarrow O)$ is 0, namely, that your performance will definitely not lead to the outcomes associated with the required performance level, then you will not be motivated to make the effort, even though you believe that you can perform at the required level [i.e., $(E \Rightarrow P) = 1$], and you find the outcomes associated with the required performance to be extremely desirable [i.e., $(V) = +1$]. Finally, if you expect that (V) is -1, namely, that the outcomes associated with the required performance are extremely undesirable, then you will not be motivated to make the effort, even though you believe that you can perform at the required level [i.e., $(E \Rightarrow P) = 1$], and that performance will lead to the associated outcomes [i.e., $(P \Rightarrow O) = 1$].

Do individuals explore all possible alternatives? The assumption in the illustration is that John's $(E \Rightarrow P)$ expectancy for 500 widgets was 1.0. In reality, an individual might consider several (E⇨P) expectancies for different performance levels, and for each performance level, a corresponding set of (P⇨O) expectancies and valence values. The motivational force to exert the effort to perform would then be computed for each alternative. The performance level with the strongest motivational force would be the likely decision of the individual.

This discussion raises the question whether an individual does in fact explore all the possible alternative behaviours and compute the expectancies and valences of each before arriving at a decision. Theoretically, there is no limit to the number of alternatives that can be considered. The "economic man" view takes the approach that an individual has the capacity to consider, and in fact does consider, all possible alternatives, the corresponding outcomes of each alternative, and his/her preference for each outcome in order to arrive at an optimal decision that will optimize his/her satisfaction.

Simon (1957) has argued against this "economic man" view, saying that an individual operates as more of a "satisfier" than as an "optimizer." In reality, when individuals decide on a course of action, they do not consider all the outcomes, but only those valued outcomes that are salient to them. Therefore, as Lawler observes: "In using the present model to predict an individual's behaviour, consideration must be limited to only those cognitions that the person is using as a basis for decision" (1973, 60).

The effort-to-performance stage

The model, Figure 5.2, recognizes that although an individual is motivated to put in the effort to perform, the effort that is exerted will result in performance only if the two factors—ability and situational factors—that moderate the process are present. If the employee does not have the ability to perform the given tasks, then however eager and well-intentioned the employee is, the effort will not result in performance. Similarly, the effort will not result in the required performance level, despite the motivation and ability of the employee, if situational factors—the lack of essential material, technological, or financial resources—hinder performance. For example, the efforts of the most able and motivated truck driver to deliver the shipment on time could be frustrated if the driver has to cope with a poorly maintained vehicle.

The performance-to-outcomes stage

In the model, performance is connected to outcomes by a wavy line to signify that the expected outcomes do not always result from performance. The employee's satisfaction with the outcomes depends upon his/her perceptions that the outcomes are, in fact, received and are equitably related to the actual level of performance.

The dynamic nature of the process

The dynamic nature of the process can be seen in Figure 5.2 from the loops formed by the dotted lines that emanate from "performance," "performance outcomes," and "satisfaction". The actual performance that results is a feedback that becomes a part of his/her "past experiences in similar situations"; both factors will serve to confirm or revise the individual's (E⇨P) expectancies.

Likewise, the actual outcomes that follow performance will revise the individual's (P⇨O) expectancy, inasmuch as this experience becomes a part of the individual's "past experience in similar situations". Finally, the satisfaction generated by the outcomes has the potential, through the individual's perceptions of the equity of each outcome, to modify his/her valences of the outcomes. The dynamic process underlying the model provides the rationale for varied managerial strategies in effective reward management to improve employee motivation and performance.

EMPIRICAL SUPPORT FOR THE EXPECTANCY THEORY MODEL

Unlike the content theories, expectancy theory does not take a simplistic approach to human motivation. Its logical and rigorous conceptual framework with strong empirical support enables the manager to better understand the components of motivation and, more importantly, how they relate to one another in the motivational process. The model provides a solid foundation upon which to erect an effective compensation structure. Before considering its practical implications, we briefly recall the inferences from the model as far as the compensation system is concerned, and examine whether these inferences have empirical validity.

Critical reward attributes derived from expectancy theory 2008

According to expectancy theory, employees will be motivated to perform at a given level if they believe that a series of conditions exists.

1. Employees believe that they have the *skill* or *ability* to perform at the required level.

2. Employees believe that the reward is *contingent upon performance*—that is, directly linked to a given level of performance.

3. Employees *value* the reward—that is, it satisfies one or more needs, and is fairly administered.

4. Finally, the reward must be *salient* in the sense that the reward is uppermost in the minds of employees. The notion of saliency is implicit in the "communication from others" and "actual situation" determinants of the (P⇨O) expectancy. It is also implicit in the "instrumentality" and "equity or fair-

ness" determinants of valence. Unless one gets the proper information and feedback on the qualifying conditions, one is unable to make a judgement with regard to the instrumentality of the outcome to satisfy needs and to the fairness of the reward.

Thus, expectancy theory suggests that the critical attributes (properties) of organizational rewards are *contingency*, *valence*, and *saliency*. If the rewards are seen by employees in terms of these attributes, then expectancy theory postulates that the rewards will, to the extent of such perceptions, have a significant influence on work motivation. The crucial questions are: Do employees, in fact, see the rewards offered by their organization in terms of these attributes? What kind of influence does each of these attributes have on work motivation?

Empirical findings on reward attributes

In an attempt to answer these questions, Kanungo and Hartwick (1987) investigated employees' perceptions of rewards typically offered by organizations. Their study used the following ten attributes:

1. Is the reward intrinsic (i.e., related to or derived from the task) or extrinsic (i.e., not related to, or not derived from, the task) according to the task criterion?

2. Is the reward intrinsic (i.e., self-administered or self-mediated) or extrinsic (i.e., other-administered or mediated) according to the mediation criterion?

3. Saliency: is the reward salient?

4. Valence: is the reward valued?

5. Is the reward contingent on high performance?

6. Is the reward contingent on low performance?

7. Is the reward considered to be concrete or abstract?

8. The time of administration of the reward: how soon after one's performance is it administered or received (immediate or delayed)?

9. Is the reward given for the mere completion of task activities (desirable task behaviour) or for the successful outcomes of task activities (profit, productivity, etc.)?

10. The frequency of administration: how often is the reward typically used by organizations?

These ten particular attributes were chosen because both researchers and practitioners alike have used one or more of these attributes to study and manage rewards. An apparent rational basis exists for each of these attributes. Thus, the first two attributes correspond to the most popular criteria, task and mediation, for defining intrinsic and extrinsic rewards. The next four attributes correspond to the expectancy theory constructs of saliency, valence, and contingency. The next three attributes (concreteness, timing, and purpose of the

Figure 5.3 : How employees perceive work rewards

First Dimension: Performance Contingency

Attribute Cluster	Contingent on High Performance Most Valued Most Salient	Non-Contingent on High Performance Least Valued Least Salient
Examples of Rewards	Pay Promotion Interesting Work Feelings of Accomplishment	Paid Parking Space Cafeteria Subsidies Discounts on Company Products

Second Dimension: Intrinsic-Extrinsic Mediation

Attribute Cluster	Intrinsic – Self-Administered Abstract Received During or Soon After Performance	Extrinsic – Administered by Others Concrete Received Long After Performance
Examples of Rewards	Personal Challenge Feelings of Accomplishment Pride in Work Personal Growth & Development	Profit-Sharing Promotions Awards for Long Service Retirement Benefits

Third Dimension: Reward Generality

Attribute Cluster	Performance Non-Contingent and
	   Given to All Employees (and
	   not connected to job tasks)
	Most Frequently Given
		Performance Non-Contingent and
		   but Given to a Few Employees
		   (connected to job tasks)
		Least Frequently Given

Examples of Rewards	Vacations Coffee Breaks Accident/Sickness Insurance Retirement Benefitis	Expense Accounts Company Car Uniform Allowance

Source: Kanungo & Hartwick, 1987

compensation) were included because these have in the past been linked with the intrinsic-extrinsic dichotomy. The last attribute, frequency of administration, captures an important aspect of work rewards not found in the other attributes.

Kanungo and Hartwick (1987) found that rewards are perceived by employees in terms of three distinct dimensions (or clusters of attributes), or that there are three important meaningful ways in which rewards are perceived by employees. Of these, the first and most important dimension was "performance contingency"—refer to Figure 5.3. Hence, rewards are meaningful to employees when they perceive them to be performance-contingent, valued and salient.

The ten attributes used in the Kanungo and Hartwick study provided the possibility of three ways to characterize compensation elements. These represent the ways in which employees do, in fact, perceive rewards. However, only one cluster of three attributes of rewards emerged to offer an incontrovertible explanation of the way that employees are motivated by rewards to perform in their jobs. It is significant that these attributes represent the expectancy theory constructs of contingency, saliency, and valence. Therefore, these findings provide a compelling reason to focus on the expectancy theory constructs in the management of employee compensation.

Rewards can, of course, be classified in terms of the other two clusters of attributes—the intrinsic-extrinsic mediation dimension, and the reward generality dimension. But the findings show that these clusters "... seem to be unrelated to motivational effectiveness, and therefore have minimum practical utility" (Kanungo and Hartwick, 1987, p. 765). From the practical perspective of compensation management, it is of very little consequence in the motivation of work behaviour whether a reward is mediated by oneself or by the other (the second dimension), or whether a reward is received frequently or infrequently (the third dimension). What is of consequence and is therefore critical to work motivation is that the reward be salient, valued, and contingent on a desired work behaviour.

IMPLICATIONS OF THE EXPECTANCY THEORY MODEL FOR REWARD MANAGEMENT

Under expectancy theory, the motivating power of rewards does not reside in the rewards themselves but in a process that reflects employee perceptions and expectations of these rewards, and the connection or tie-up of the rewards with performance. This process is crucial if the reward system is to be effective in motivating behaviour—job performance, organizational tenure or retention, job attendance, personal growth, or skill development. There are four fundamental conditions that management ought to initiate and manage. These conditions have a direct impact on the compensation system, and offer concrete, practical guidelines for developing the strategies, process, and techniques of the compensation system.

Ensure that employees have the ability to perform

To ensure that employees can perform at levels established by the organization, the obvious and logical action would be to select employees who have the knowledge, skills, and abilities for the job. Alternatively, appropriate training should be provided for potential job incumbents. The objective here is to increase the $(E \Rightarrow P)$ expectancy of the employees, an objective that can also be achieved through the performance management process to be discussed in Chapter 9. In this process supervisors clarify job responsibilities and procedures, provide necessary resources, and act as coaches and mentors to empower the subordinate, that is, to increase the employee's belief in his/her capabilities.

Design and administer valued rewards

Individuals value outcomes that help to satisfy their salient needs. But different people have different needs at different times. An outcome such as a promotion that is positively valued by one employee may have a negative valence for another if that promotion involves a transfer to another city. When managers recognize this fact, they will be more sensitive to employee needs and will provide, where possible, the most highly valued outcomes. Some companies have adopted a cafeteria-style approach to benefit plans to cater to the specific needs of employees.

However, perceptions of inequity either in the design or administration of a reward play a considerable role in the individual's valence of the reward. There are three types of inequities: individual (or personal), internal, and external. Individual inequity occurs when an employee perceives that his/her compensation does not adequately reflect his/her job performance. This usually happens when no distinction is made between mediocre and outstanding performers in the administration of rewards. Internal inequity arises when employees perceive that the company's pay rates for jobs do not reflect the relative internal value of each job. External inequity results when employees perceive that the company's pay rates do not correspond to those prevailing in the external job market.

These inequities can be prevented by sound policies and procedures that are consistently and fairly administered. For example, proper performance appraisals accompanied by a fair merit increase system (Chapter 9) will ensure individual equity; a sound job evaluation programme with employee involvement in its mechanics as well as its process (Chapter 11) will contribute to internal equity; finally, salary surveys in the right job markets (Chapter 13) will help prevent external inequity.

Make rewards contingent on desired behaviours

This is achieved by directly linking the rewards to the specific behaviour, for example, commission on sales, performance-based pay increments, or promotions. The objective here is to increase the (P⇨O) expectancy, which, like the increase in valence, can be achieved primarily through the reward system. The compensation philosophy (Chapter 7) and, in particular, performance-based pay (Chapter 9) and incentive system and gain-sharing plans (Chapter 10) are specific vehicles to make rewards contingent.

Make the reward salient

For saliency to be achieved, the conditions for earning the reward, that is, the performance of specific behaviours, must be clearly spelt out and frequently communicated. A policy statement will help, but deeds speak louder than words. The things that management does affect saliency as much as, if not more than, the things it says. For example, if the organization's merit pay policy states that it is to be performance based, but in practice no significant differentiation is made between poor and outstanding performers, saliency will not be ensured.

To conclude   Expectancy theory is no longer "primarily a theory for the scholar and the scientist rather than for the practitioner ... It is becoming increasingly evident, though, that applications are possible and that they might well prove very fruitful" (Miner, 1980, 160-61). In addition to providing a basis for reward design, the elements of expectancy theory—in particular, the saliency, valence, and contingency of outcomes—also provide management with the means of evaluating the effectiveness of each item of the compensation programme.

The process approach in the expectancy theory of motivation has the potential to provide sound guidelines for developing effective compensation programmes. This approach is at the very core of the effective reward management model presented in the first chapter. Therefore, every strategy, technique, practice, and process of the compensation system design and its evaluation that will be discussed in the text will flow from, and be judged in the light of, the principles and predictions of this model.

SUMMARY

The process theories provide a more comprehensive explanation of how an individual starts, sustains, directs, and stops work behaviour. The discussion in this chapter focused on equity theory and expectancy theory because of their direct relevance to understanding the role of compensation in the motivational process.

Equity theory explains motivation as an individual's attempt to restore equity or reduce the inequity the individual experiences in the numerous exchanges of the work situation.

Expectancy theory postulates that individuals will exert the effort to perform if they believe that their efforts will lead to the required level of performance [(E⇨P) expectancy], that the performance will result in outcomes [(P⇨O) expectancy], and that they positively value the outcomes [Valence of outcomes]. The expectancy theory model for reward management presented in this chapter incorporates the basic elements of expectancy theory as well as the determinants of each element, including equity theory's explanation of the satisfaction/dissatisfaction with outcomes. The model thus provides a more comprehensive explanation of both the what and the how of the motivational process.

The chapter examined effort-performance, performance-outcomes, and valence expectancies; it explored the dynamic process underlying the model and demonstrated how its different stages contribute to the individual's repertoire of expectancies and valence of outcomes; and it showed the impact this contribution has on the individual's motivation to put in the effort to perform.

KEY TERMS

(E⇨P) expectancy   *inputs-outcomes ratio*
(P⇨O) expectancy   *internal equity*
contingency   *personal or individual equity*
equity theory   *relevant other person*
expectancy theory   *saliency*
external equity   *valence*

REVIEW AND DISCUSSION QUESTIONS

1. Carole Shaw was quite excited about her new job. After working for about a year, however, she discovered the following about her job and base pay:

   a) The base pay of her job is less than the base pay of the other jobs in the company that she has reason to believe are similar to hers.

   b) The base pay of her job is less than the base pay of the other jobs in the company that she has reason to believe are identical to hers.

   c) The base pay of her job is less than the base pay of the identical job in other companies.

In which of these scenarios will Carole experience (i) the *most* dissatisfaction and (ii) the *least* dissatisfaction? Explain your responses with reference to the elements and the process of equity theory.

2. Recall a part-time or full-time job and answer the following questions with reference to that job:

   a) What motivated you to accept the job, that is, to put in the effort to perform on the job?

      Respond to this question by examining your $(E \Rightarrow P)$, $(P \Rightarrow O)$, and (V) expectancies while you were considering whether you should accept the job. Specifically, explore the determinant of each expectancy:

      • Was $(E \Rightarrow P)$ high because of past experiences, actual situation, communications from others, self-esteem?

      • Was $(P \Rightarrow O)$ high because of past experiences, actual situation, communications from others, and so forth?

      • Was (V) high because of a belief that outcomes will satisfy needs, and will be equitable?

   b) Assume you performed well on the job. What contributed to the high level of performance resulting from your effort? Respond to this question by exploring the moderators of ability and situational factors. Perhaps you had the ability, or the ability was enhanced by training; perhaps the situational factors were positive, that is, there were no obstacles to impede your performance.

   c) Assume that at the end of some period you received outcomes with which you were satisfied. What contributed to your satisfaction with the outcomes? Respond to this question by exploring the moderator of equity.

3. Refer to the experience you reflected upon in question 2. In the context of the implications of the expectancy theory model for reward management discussed in the chapter, think of specific actions the manager might have taken to increase your motivation to perform.

4. What are the key findings of the Kanungo and Hartwick (1987) study? Explain how these findings provide empirical support for the expectancy theory model.

The Practical Implications of Expectancy Theory

Objective

To experience the process of expectancy theory. The exercise will enable you to determine how motivated you are to put in the effort to pursue a career (job) that is assigned to you.

Procedure

1. Divide the class into groups of about four or five participants.

2. Assign to each group one of the following jobs/careers:
   - high school teacher
   - assembly-line operator
   - travelling salesperson
   - computer programmer
   - truck driver
   - administrative assistant
   - human resource specialist/generalist
   - independent business entrepreneur

3. Keeping the assigned job/career in mind, each participant, working individually, responds to questions 1, 2, and 3 on the worksheet below and then completes the score-sheet to obtain his/her motivational force to put in the effort to pursue the assigned job/career.

4. Group discussion: The objective of the discussion is to understand the determinants of the expectancies of individuals in respect of the assigned job/career. The discussion could include:

   a) the identification of similarities/differences in the motivational force score (MFS) of the group members.

   b) an exploration of the reasons for the similarities/differences. Consider the following issues:

   Re: Question 1:
   Why do some more than others believe that they can do the assigned job/career? Is this because of

   ____ good grades in school?

   ____ success in past jobs? success in voluntary service projects?

   ____ specialized education and training?

   ____ role model in the family? in the community?

   ____ any other factor that enhanced the individual's self-efficacy belief?

Re: Question 2:

Why do different individuals place different values on the listed outcomes? Is this because of

_____ a difference in needs?

_____ a difference in the sense or standard of equity or fairness?

Re: Question 3:

Why do some more than others believe that if they perform the assigned job/career they will receive all or some of the listed outcomes? Is this because of

_____ past experiences? Did they always receive the expected outcomes/rewards?

_____ the assumption that such outcomes/rewards are naturally associated with the assigned job/career?

_____ the observed or narrated experiences of others? Did they see or were they told that such outcomes/rewards were associated with the assigned job/career? Did the knowledge of these experiences enhance their general belief that organizations honour their reward commitments to their employees?

5. Class discussion: Some areas to focus on include

   • the determinants of the expectancies.

   • the relationship between the MFS and actual performance. Assuming an individual has a high MFS, does this mean that the effort he/she puts in will, in fact, result in the expected level of performance? This question will uncover the role of the moderators in the expectancy theory model.

   • Whether performance always lead to satisfaction with the outcomes received from that performance. Why or why not?

   • Whether a person can have a high valence for a given outcome and a low feeling of equity for that outcome. Why?

Table 5.1.1: Expectancy Theory Worksheet

Question 1
Do you think that your hard work now as a student, your past jobs, life experiences, and so forth, will lead you to believe that you are likely to be successful in the assigned job/career? In other words, do you believe that if you put in the effort in the assigned job/career, that effort will likely lead to performance?

No chance at all					Possible					Absolutely certain
0	.1	.2	.3	.4	.5	.6	.7	.8	.9	1

Question 2
Below is a list of outcomes that may accompany or may be received in jobs/careers. How likely is it that each of these outcomes will be realized (received) in the assigned job/career? In other words, how likely is it that performance in the assigned job/career will lead to each outcome?

	No chance at all									Absolutely certain

a) Security (permanent job, steady work)

    0 .1 .2 .3 .4 .5 .6 .7 .8 .9 1

b) Earnings (for a better standard of living)

    0 .1 .2 .3 .4 .5 .6 .7 .8 .9 1

c) Merit pay (for high job performance)

    0 .1 .2 .3 .4 .5 .6 .7 .8 .9 1

d) Benefits (vacations, pension, insurance, dental
   and medical benefits, etc.)

    0 .1 .2 .3 .4 .5 .6 .7 .8 .9 1

e) Working conditions (pleasant surroundings, adequate
   and air-conditioned office space)

    0 .1 .2 .3 .4 .5 .6 .7 .8 .9 1

f) Long working hours and frequent and extensive
   business trips, leaving no time for family/social life

    0 .1 .2 .3 .4 .5 .6 .7 .8 .9 1

g) A high level of personal stress and/or financial risk

    0 .1 .2 .3 .4 .5 .6 .7 .8 .9 1

h) Responsibility and independence (to work in your own way)

     0   .1   .2   .3   .4   .5   .6   .7   .8   .9   1

i) Achievement (opportunity to achieve excellence in your work)

     0   .1   .2   .3   .4   .5   .6   .7   .8   .9   1

j) Opportunity for growth (professionally; to
become more skilled and competent on the job)

     0   .1   .2   .3   .4   .5   .6   .7   .8   .9   1

Question 3

Below is a list of possible outcomes that can accompany or be received in jobs/careers. How favourable or unfavourable is each of the following outcomes to you personally? In other words, what kind of value do you place on each?

     Very Unfavourable   **Very Favourable**

a) Security (permanent job, steady work)

     -1   -.8   -.6   -.4   -.2   0   .2   .4   .6   .8   1

b) Earnings (for a better standard of living)

     -1   -.8   -.6   -.4   -.2   0   .2   .4   .6   .8   1

c) Merit pay (for high job performance)

     -1   -.8   -.6   -.4   -.2   0   .2   .4   .6   .8   1

d) Benefits (vacations, pension, insurance,
dental and medical benefits, etc.)

     -1   -.8   -.6   -.4   -.2   0   .2   .4   .6   .8   1

e) Working conditions (pleasant surroundings,
adequate and air-conditioned office space)

     -1   -.8   -.6   -.4   -.2   0   .2   .4   .6   .8   1

f) Long working hours and frequent and extensive
business trips, leaving no time for family/social life

     -1   -.8   -.6   -.4   -.2   0   .2   .4   .6   .8   1

g) A high level of personal stress and/or financial risk

     -1   -.8   -.6   -.4   -.2   0   .2   .4   .6   .8   1

h) Responsibility and independence (to work in your own way)

     -1   -.8   -.6   -.4   -.2   0   .2   .4   .6   .8   1

i) Achievement (opportunity to achieve excellence in your work)

     -1   -.8   -.6   -.4   -.2   0   .2   .4   .6   .8   1

j) Opportunity for growth (professionally; to become more skilled and competent on the job)

$$-1 \quad -.8 \quad -.6 \quad -.4 \quad -.2 \quad 0 \quad .2 \quad .4 \quad .6 \quad .8 \quad 1$$

Motivational Force Score (MFS) Scoring Instructions and Score-Sheet

To compute your motivational force score (MFS), proceed as follows:

Step 1:
Refer to your response to question 1. Your response to this question provides an indication of your effort performance expectancy for your assigned job. Suppose your response was .3. This measure is your belief that if you work at that job (i.e., put in the effort today), it is most unlikely that you will succeed in that job (i.e., reach the required performance level). Your response is a statement that says: "Yes, I think I can perform that job," or "No, I do not think I can perform that job," or any other belief level in between these two extremes.

Enter your response as the (E⇨P) score in the score-sheet.

Step 2:
Refer to your response to question 2. Your response provides an indication of your performance outcome expectancy for a given set of outcomes in the assigned job. The response for each outcome represents your belief that you will receive or not receive the outcome when you perform in the assigned job. In reality there may be more or a different set of outcomes to consider. Only a few have been chosen for this exercise.

Enter your response for each outcome (a to j) in the (P⇨O) column of the score-sheet.

Step 3:
Refer to your responses to question 3. Your responses indicate the value you place on each outcome. It is your measure of the valence of each outcome. You could place a positive, neutral, or negative value for each outcome.

Enter your response for each outcome (a to j) in the Valence column of the score-sheet.

Step 4:
According to expectancy theory, the motivational force score is obtained by the following formula:

$$(E \Rightarrow P) \times [(P \Rightarrow O) \times (V)]$$

You will multiply the (P⇨O) expectancy for each outcome by its corresponding valence. The sum of the products is then multiplied by the (E⇨P) expectancy. Complete the arithmetic in the manner laid out in the score-sheet to obtain the motivational force score. This score tells you how motivated you are *at this time* to put in the effort to pursue or accept the job assigned to you in the context of the outcomes spelt out for you. The value of the MFS is out of a possible value range of 0 to 10, with 0 = a low motivational force, and 10 a high motivational force.

Score-Sheet

(E⇨P) expectancy, that is, score of Q. 1 _____ (A)

	(P⇨O) expectancy Q. 2 Scores		Valence Q. 3 Scores		Product of (P⇨O) (V)
a)	_____	X	_____	=	_____
b)	_____	X	_____	=	_____
c)	_____	X	_____	=	_____
d)	_____	X	_____	=	_____
e)	_____	X	_____	=	_____
f)	_____	X	_____	=	_____
g)	_____	X	_____	=	_____
h)	_____	X	_____	=	_____
i)	_____	X	_____	=	_____
j)	_____	X	_____	=	_____

Sum of products of [(P⇨O) (V)]   = _____ (B)

Motivational force score (MFS)   = { (E⇨P)   X   Σ [(P⇨O)(V)]}

= (A)   x (B)

= _____   X _____

= _____

Satisfaction With Pay and Non-Economic Issues

OVERVIEW

An employee's satisfaction or dissatisfaction with a reward item can greatly enhance or impair the motivational effectiveness of that item. This chapter probes the satisfaction issue in some detail through a focus on pay, the major item of an organization's compensation system. Specifically, the chapter addresses the determinants and consequences to the organization of the employee's dissatisfaction with his/her pay. The chapter also examines the theory and the process of job design, which the organization can use to increase the non-economic outcomes component of the compensation system.

 LEARNING OBJECTIVES

► To understand the meaning of *satisfaction*, which is derived from a combination of notions from equity theory and discrepancy theory.

► To understand the elements and the process of the determinants of the pay satisfaction model, with a special emphasis on the critical notion of social comparison.

► To identify the components of person-related, job-related, referent-other-related, and context-related factors, and to learn how these factors influence an individual's satisfaction with his/her pay.

► To understand the process of the consequences of the pay dissatisfaction model.

► To identify the components of job context factors, job content factors, and external environmental factors, and to explain how these factors moderate the consequences of pay dissatisfaction.

► To learn how to use the practical guidelines for increasing pay satisfaction that flow from the determinants of pay satisfaction and the consequences of pay dissatisfaction models.

► To understand the nature, objective, and consequences of the classical approach to job design.

► To understand the nature and objective of the approach of the growth theories of Herzberg and Maslow to job design.

► To distinguish between the classical and growth theory approaches to job design.

► To understand the elements and the process of Hackman and Oldham's (1980) job characteristics model.

► To learn how the job characteristics model can be used to generate non-economic outcomes.

INTRODUCTION

At the present time the only systematic approach to reward satisfaction and dissatisfaction relevant to management practice is Lawler's (1971) model on the determinants of pay satisfaction and the consequences of pay dissatisfaction. This models focuses exclusively on pay and does not consider the other compensation items. Nevertheless, it is useful for two reasons. First, pay is the largest component of the reward system and constitutes from 50 to 75 per cent of the total operating costs of an organization. Second, the model illustrates the fact that satisfaction or dissatisfaction with a compensation item, and the resulting consequences, can be anticipated and incorporated in the design and administration of that compensation item.

SATISFACTION WITH PAY

Approaches to satisfaction

The psychological phenomenon of satisfaction has been dealt with by fulfillment theory, discrepancy theory, and equity theory (Gerhart and Milkovich, 1992).

Fulfillment theory & "satisfaction"

According to fulfillment theory, satisfaction results when one's needs are fulfilled. In the work context, fulfillment theory predicts that an employee who receives a greater amount of positively valued outcomes will fulfil his/her needs to a relatively greater extent and will therefore be more satisfied than an employee who receives a lesser quantity of the positively valued outcomes. It has been found that this proposition does not reflect the reality. For example, it is common to see an employee perfectly contented with an annual salary of

$50,000 and another employee in the same organization totally dissatisfied with a salary of $100,000.

Discrepancy theory & "satisfaction"

An insight into this anomaly is provided by a version of discrepancy theory (Rice, Philips, and McFarlin, 1990) that defines satisfaction as the perceived discrepancy between what one has received and what one believes one should receive. Thus, the employee with an annual salary of $50,000 is contented because that employee does not perceive any discrepancy between the amount received and the amount that should have been received. On the other hand, the employee with an annual salary of $100,000 might be dissatisfied because he/she perceives the discrepancy between the amount received and the amount to which he/she was entitled to be inequitable. But how does an individual determine what is fair and equitable? This question is addressed by equity theory.

Equity theory & "satisfaction"

Equity theory, discussed in the previous chapter, provides an understanding of the pay satisfaction of the employee earning the $50,000 and the pay dissatisfaction of the employee earning $100,000. The satisfied employee perceives his/her own and the relevant other's outcomes-inputs ratios to be equal; the dissatisfied employee perceives these ratios to be unequal. Unlike discrepancy theory, equity theory explains satisfaction through the use of *social comparison* and the individual's perceptions of the outcomes-inputs ratios. Discrepancy theory explains satisfaction through the *difference* in perceptions between what the outcome is and what it should be.

Combining notions from equity & discrepancy theories

When we combine the notion of social comparison (from equity theory) and the notion of difference in perceptions of what is and what should be (from discrepancy theory), we can conclude that an employee's satisfaction with pay is the difference between his/her perceptions of the *amount of pay received* and of the *amount of pay that should be received*. (Gerhart and Milkovich, 1992; Lawler and Jenkins, 1992; Lawler, 1971). When the two perceptions are equal, the employee experiences pay satisfaction; when they are unequal, the employee experiences pay dissatisfaction. Fundamental to this process are the principles of justice—distributive and procedural justice—referred to in the previous chapter. In the case of pay satisfaction, the principle of distributive justice seems to be particularly salient. When employees received high pay, they perceived it to be fair and equitable regardless of the procedure used. However, when they received low pay, there was a greater tendency to perceive it as equitable if it was based on a fair procedure (Greenberg, 1987).

The next two sections explores the specific, practical questions with regard to pay satisfaction. What are the determinants of the employee perceptions that promote pay satisfaction? What are the consequences of pay dissatisfaction?

DETERMINANTS OF PAY SATISFACTION

According to the model (Figure 6.1), the two sets of employee perceptions, the amount of pay received, and the amount of pay that should be received can be explained by a combination of four categories of variables: person-related, job-related, referent-other-related, and context-related. A proper understanding of the component elements of each category of variables and their impact on pay satisfaction is essential for the successful management of the many design and administrative issues in compensation.

Person-related Variables

This category can include a variety of inputs that an employee brings to the job: knowledge, skills, and abilities; specialized training; work experience; job performance; age and length of service; gender and ethnic origin; and loyalty and commitment to the organization.

Knowledge, skills and abilities, and job performance   The research evidence (Gerhart and Milkovich, 1992; Lawler and Jenkins, 1992; Lawler, 1971) suggests that education, skills and abilities, and job performance are significant variables that must be recognized in the determination of the level of pay. It would seem logical and in accord with the norms of natural justice that employees would expect their pay to reflect these personal inputs. For example, an employee with a higher educational level or a recognized competence in a skill will expect to be paid more than another employee with a lower educational level or a lower level of competence in the required job skill.

Similarly, employees who perceive that their job performance is superior to that of their peers will expect to receive a merit pay higher than that of a mediocre employee. If pay does not reflect the qualitative and quantitative inputs that an employee brings to a job, then the employee will inevitably tend to experience greater pay dissatisfaction. Of course, it must be recognized that the actual pay dissatisfaction experienced by an employee will depend on the importance that the employee attributes to a particular input.

Age & length of service   There is no conclusive evidence that age and length of service (i.e., seniority) are significant input variables, in the sense that they would cause employees to be dissatisfied with their pay if pay did not reflect these inputs. It must be recognized, however, that age and seniority may be culture-bound factors; in certain cultures, age and seniority may be considered to be significant input variables. In such cultures employees will be dissatisfied with their pay if it does not reflect age and seniority.

Figure 6.1: Determinants of Pay Satisfaction

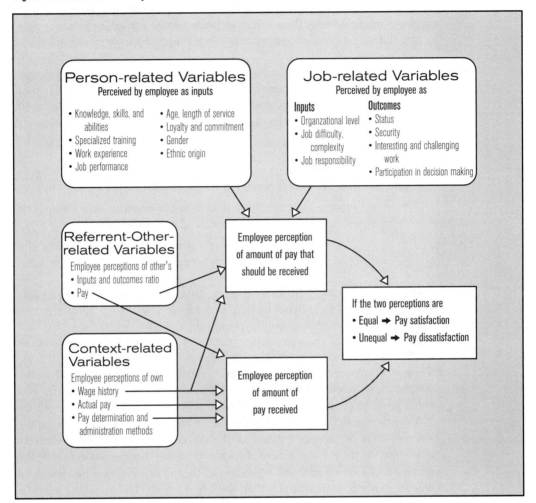

Source: Adapted from Hawler (1971).

Gender & ethnic origin   The employee's gender and ethnic origin can moderate the influence of the variables known to determine pay satisfaction. For example, Kanungo (1975) found that women employees in Quebec were more satisfied with their pay then men employees; similarly francophone employees in Quebec were more satisfied with their pay than anglophone employees. Perhaps both groups of employees, women and francophones, had lower expectations of pay. The experience of highly qualified new immigrants who are satisfied with their relatively lower level of pay could also be cited. Their euphoria at having been accepted in the country of their adoption tends to lower the expected pay level for their high qualifications.

Loyalty & commitment   No specific studies linking these factors to pay have been reported. However, it would not be unreasonable to speculate that an employee might perceive these inputs to be important enough to justify a higher pay, and might experience dissatisfaction if this expectation is unfulfilled.

To conclude: Employees who bring more to a job in terms of knowledge, skills, and experience, and perform better than their peers perceive that they contribute more inputs and, therefore, expect to receive more pay. When their pay fails to reflect these inputs, they will experience pay dissatisfaction.

Job-related Variables

This category includes factors perceived by the employee:

- *as job inputs*—for example: job level in the organization's hierarchical structure; job difficulty, complexity, and responsibility.
- *as job outcomes*—for example: job status and security, interesting and challenging work, and opportunity for participation in decision making.

Job level, difficulty, and complexity, and its relation to employee responsibility   Employees in jobs at a higher level in the hierarchy will expect to be paid more than employees in jobs at a lower level of the organization's hierarchy. For example, senior managers expect to be paid more than middle managers, who in turn expect to be paid more than first-line supervisors. Likewise, employees in jobs that involve a relatively greater level of difficulty, complexity, or responsibility expect to be paid more than employees in jobs with a lower level of difficulty, complexity, or responsibility.

A situation is *difficult* if the job incumbent is required to function with insufficient resources or support systems, or the job tasks themselves place relatively more stress on the job incumbent. *Complexity* means that the job demands the utilization of a variety of skills. For example, the job of a manager in a fast-food outlet is relatively more complex than the job of a cook. The manager's job calls for the exercise of conceptual, interpersonal, and leadership skills.

To conclude   Employees in higher-level jobs, and in jobs of greater difficulty, complexity, and responsibility perceive that they contribute more in terms of inputs and, therefore, expect more pay. They will experience pay dissatisfaction when their pay does not reflect these inputs.

Job status & job security

These are job-related variables that function as outcomes. If the need for self-esteem is high in an employee, he or she will likely value any outcome—pay, status, or promotion—that satisfies that need. If the self-esteem need is met by a job perceived by the employee to be of high status, the employee will not seek pay to satisfy this need. Consequently, the employee will likely not expect more pay. The underlying rationale is that pay is one of the many outcomes received by employees.

When employees perceive outcomes other than pay to be more instrumental in satisfying a need, then employees will value the other outcomes. Such employees will not be dissatisfied with a lower pay when the other more valued outcomes are provided. For example, in periods of severe unemployment, employees tend to prefer job security to higher pay.

Interesting & challenging work: Participation in decision-making

It is not uncommon to find employees with high growth needs accepting jobs in an organization with relatively lower pay, because the jobs offer opportunities for challenging and interesting work, or greater participation in decision making.

To conclude When employees perceive that non-economic outcomes satisfy their important and salient needs better than pay, employees will not be dissatisfied with pay. Their perceptions of the amount of pay that should be received will tend to be low. Other things being equal, the noneconomic outcomes, when they are regarded as a substitute for pay, will promote pay satisfaction.

Referent-Other-related Variables

The term *referent-other* has the same meaning as the term *relevant other person* discussed under equity theory. This category includes employee perceptions of relevant other persons' inputs and outcomes, and employee perceptions of pay received by relevant other persons.

Perceptions of other's inputs-outcomes ratio

It will be recalled that in equity theory the employee's determination of equity or inequity is based on the comparison of the employee's perceptions of his/her own inputs-outcomes ratio with his/her perceptions of the inputs-outcomes ratio of the relevant other person. When equity theory is applied to pay, the employee's perception of the amount of pay that should be received will be influenced by his/her perceptions of the outcomes the relevant other person will likely receive relative to that person's inputs.

For example, Elijah perceives that his colleague Melanie is likely to receive the following set of outcomes: a pay raise of $4,000, special recognition from the department head, and preferential treatment in the choice of assignments. Elijah recognizes that Melanie has specialized training, but that he has substantially more work experience and has put in a consistently superior job performance. Based on this assessment of Melanie's inputs-outcomes ratio relative to his own, Elijah develops an expectation of a pay raise of $4,500. It can thus be seen how an employee's perceptions of the relevant other person's inputs-outcomes ratio relative to his/her own will influence the amount of pay that should be received.

Perceptions of other's pay   Employee perceptions of the pay received by the relevant other person has a direct impact on the employee's perception of the amount of pay received. Elijah believed that a pay raise of $4,500 would be equitable. Assume that Elijah receives the expected $4,500. Assume also that Elijah perceives that the actual pay raise received by Melanie is not the $4,000 that Elijah had earlier believed that Melanie would receive, but $4,200. Before Elijah formed any perceptions of Melanie's actual pay raise, Elijah had attributed a certain value to his actual pay raise of $4,500.

As discussed in the previous paragraph, this value or valence resulted from, among other factors, a comparison of Elijah's perceptions of his inputs-outcomes ratio and his perception of Melanie's inputs-outcomes ratio. The valence was also based on what Elijah believed the $4,500 would fetch him in terms of the goods and services he needed. The reference here is to the instrumentality-of-the-outcome determinant of valence as postulated by expectancy theory.

After Elijah discovers that Melanie's actual pay raise is $4,200, the value or valence he attributes to his $4,500 undergoes a change. The $4,500 will now have a relatively lower value or valence for Elijah. True, Elijah's $4,500 can and will still buy the same quantity of goods and services, regardless of what Melanie actually receives. In other words, the potential instrumentality of the $4,500 to satisfy certain needs is undiminished. What, then, is the reason for Elijah's lower valence of the $4,500? The answer is to be found in the expectancy theory model. As will be recalled from the model, valence is determined by both the instrumentality to satisfy needs and the equity of outcomes. The inequity of outcomes, which he perceives relative to Melanie, explains why Elijah now values the $4,500 much less than he did before his perceptions of Melanie's actual pay raise.

The discussion of the referent-other-related variables strongly underscores the significant and powerful effect of the notion of social comparison as a determinant of pay satisfaction, and the profound practical implications that flow from it.

Context-related Variables

These variables concern the outcomes the employee receives from the job context. The critical factors that affect pay satisfaction in this category are employee perceptions of the pay received in the past (wage history), the actual pay now received, and the methods of pay determination and administration.

Wage history   The employee's perceptions of his/her wage history affect pay satisfaction by influencing employee perceptions of the amount of pay that should be received, and also of the amount of pay received. For example, employees who have had a record of high salaries and pay raises will generally expect their present pay to be consistent with that record of high salaries and pay raises. In other words, their high wage history leads to higher expectations, which influence their perceptions of the amount of pay that should be received.

The high wage history also affects employee perceptions of the amount of pay received. Employees who have had a high pay history tend to perceive their present pay as low. The magnitude of the dollars involved is viewed through the perspective of past pay history. Therefore, for the reasons discussed here, the higher the past pay level, the greater the pay dissatisfaction will be unless the amount of pay now received is also high, consistent with the expectations generated by the high wage history.

Actual pay received & method of pay determination　The actual pay received is, of course, the direct source of the employee's perception of the amount of pay received. The larger the amount of current pay, the greater is the pay satisfaction. Consistent with the principle of procedural justice, the methods of pay determination and administration also affect pay satisfaction (Greenberg, 1986). For example, performance-based pay will be perceived as equitable if it is determined by a fair performance appraisal system, and administered by a process that is open rather than secret, and involves the employees concerned. In other words, pay ought to be determined and administered in a manner that permits the employee to see a linkage between pay and performance, that is, the $(P \Rightarrow O)$ relationship of expectancy theory. When pay determination and administration methods enable employees to see clearly the performance-outcomes linkage, then employees are found to experience greater pay satisfaction (Lawler and Jenkins, 1992; Gerhart and Milkovich, 1992).

Determinants of Pay Satisfaction—Figure 6.1　Figure 6.1 depicts the influence of each of the four sets of variables on employee perceptions of either the amount of pay that should be received or the amount of pay received. If the two perceptions are equal, then the employee experiences pay satisfaction. If these are unequal, then the employee experiences pay dissatisfaction.

This section concludes with two observations that have already been mentioned but need to be reiterated. First, the elements of the model and its underlying process are essentially based on the perceptions of the employee. Second, the notion of social comparison is absolutely critical to the model (Gerhart and Milkovich, 1992). In a study by Shapiro and Wahba (1978), social comparison, actual pay, and wage history were the significant factors that explained the variance in pay satisfaction. From these observations flow several implications of practical interest to the compensation specialist and to managers, which will be considered in later chapters.

CONSEQUENCES OF PAY DISSATISFACTION

What are the consequences of pay dissatisfaction? If this question were posed to ten managers, more than ten different answers might result: low productivity; poor quality of products and service; high reject rates and wastage; unnecessary overtime; tighter supervisory controls; low morale and unmotivated employees; strikes; attempts to unionize; high grievance rates; job dissatisfaction; pilferage and vandalism; tardiness, absenteeism, and turnover; psychological withdrawal and poor mental health.

Organizations need to address the issue of pay dissatisfaction because it renders futile its enormous expenditures on pay. It is ironical indeed that pay, intended to motivate employee work behaviours towards organizational objectives, can itself become the cause of work behaviours that frustrate these objectives.

How is pay dissatisfaction related to the consequences attributed to it? Lawler (1971) proposed a model of the consequences of pay dissatisfaction (see box A and box B in Figure 6.2). According to this model, when employees experience pay dissatisfaction, the numerous consequences attributed to pay dissatisfaction do not automatically follow. Instead, the model posits that (1) employees experience a desire for more pay, or (2) employees find the job to be less attractive. The possible effects of each is discussed.

Employees experience a desire for more pay (box 1)

In this scenario, employees will be motivated to increase their performance, rather than lower it, *if* the compensation system is designed to pay for performance (box 2). If pay is not performance based, employees will not be able to satisfy their desire for more pay by increasing or improving their performance. In such an event, employees will pursue other options to obtain more pay. Such options include union pressures on management, which if unsuccessful may eventually result in a strike (box 3); grievances filed by employees in an attempt to demonstrate their dissatisfaction (box 4); or a search for a higher-paying job (box 5).

This last action would, according to the model, lead to absenteeism (box 6) and possibly turnover (box 7). The reason for the absenteeism is that the employee must be absent as he/she explores job opportunities and attends interviews with placement agencies or prospective employers. If the search efforts prove successful, there will be turnover. Thus, in the first scenario, turnover would appear to be a measure of last resort.

Employees find the job to be less attractive (box 8):

The lower rewards attached to the job do not make it attractive any more. The employee's efforts in this situation are directed towards looking elsewhere for a job. The search efforts lead to absenteeism (box 9) and, if successful, to turnover (box 7). The employee could also use absenteeism as a strategy (i.e., reducing inputs) to restore equity, provided the absence does not result in a loss of pay. If the job search efforts are not successful, then the employee continues in the present job. At the same time, the employee's dissatisfaction with the job (box 10) also continues. If not addressed, this dissatisfaction will likely lead to illness (box 11), poor mental health (box 12), or psychological withdrawal (box 13).

Figure 6.2: Consequences of Pay Dissatisfaction

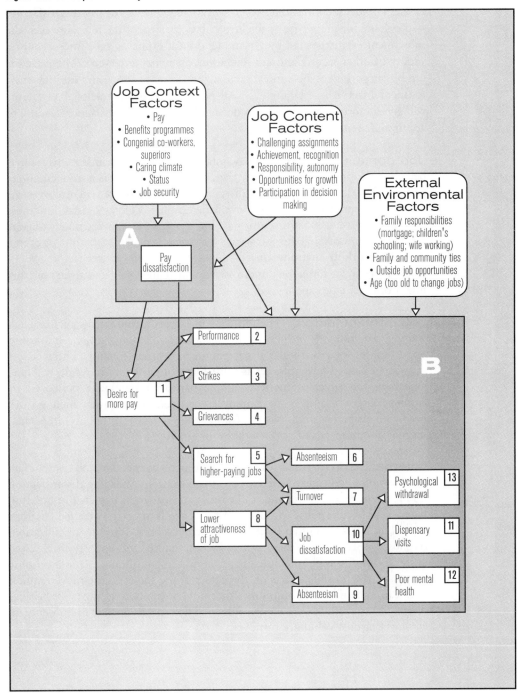

Source: Adapted from Lawler (1971).

Other factors moderating pay dissatisfaction consequences

Lawler's model identifies the psychological consequences of pay dissatisfaction —the desire for more pay, or the lower attractiveness of the job. However, the subsequent events posited by the model do not explicitly take into account a variety of other factors and considerations that may intervene. These factors can be categorized as job context factors, job content factors, and external environmental factors (see Figure 6.2). An examination of the role of these factors will give a more comprehensive understanding of pay dissatisfaction leading to appropriate remedial strategies.

Job context   In addition to pay, job context factors include items such as benefits programmes, job security, status, congenial co-workers and superiors, and a caring climate that reflects the company's concern for its employees. As was noted in an earlier discussion on the determinants of pay satisfaction, these factors can serve as substitutes for pay. For example, employees might tolerate a lower pay in exchange for job security or some benefit programme or even a congenial working environment. To the extent that job context factors compensate for a lower pay, these items will reduce pay dissatisfaction that might otherwise be experienced.

Job content factors   The job content factors include items such as challenging assignments, achievement, recognition, responsibility, autonomy, opportunities for growth and participation in decision making. These factors can also be viewed by employees as substitutes for pay and, as a result, will likewise have the effect of moderating the pay dissatisfaction experienced by employees. For example, an employee, particularly one with high growth needs, might accept a job with a relatively lower salary if the job offers challenging assignments and opportunities for growth.

External Environment   Suppose that the job context and job content factors do not significantly weaken pay dissatisfaction. Will pay dissatisfaction lead inevitably to turnover and to the other consequences depicted in box B in Figure 6.2? The response to this question depends upon the external environmental factors which often intervene in the decision to leave the organization. As shown in Figure 6.2, these factors include limited job opportunities, especially in times of high unemployment; family responsibilities such as a house mortgage; the possible effects on the career of the spouse if the move requires a relocation; family and community ties; and reluctance to change jobs because of age. One or more external environmental factors can operate to influence an employee against voluntary turnover.

PRACTICAL GUIDELINES FOR ENHANCING PAY SATISFACTION

There is no doubt that the consequences of pay dissatisfaction are debilitating both for the organization and for the employees. It is not surprising that organizations are concerned to ensure that their employees are satisfied with their pay. What concrete measures can an organization take to meet this concern? The guidelines, proposed here, are stated in general terms because the specifics follow in later chapters which discuss in detail the various compensation strategies and techniques.

Offer high pay to all employees

This action would result in a high average level of pay satisfaction. However, it can be costly to the organization, and induce a feeling of inequity if no differentiation were made among the poor, mediocre, and superior performers (Lawler and Jenkins, 1992). Hence, the pay level must take into account the organization's business strategies as well as the principles of internal, external, and individual equity. To ensure internal equity, the organization will need to institute and implement a job evaluation system that fairly reflects the job's value to the organization. External equity will be ensured by periodic salary surveys in the right labour markets. Individual equity calls for a performance appraisal system that enables the organization to properly differentiate between the performances of employees in the granting of merit raises.

Monitor pay satisfaction levels

The second guideline will be to monitor pay satisfaction levels through periodic surveys. If the level of pay satisfaction is found to be low, it does not automatically follow that pay should be increased. The organization must analyze the benefits it will likely derive from increased pay and the costs of the consequences (absenteeism, turnover, etc.) of a low level of pay satisfaction. If, on the other hand, the pay satisfaction level is high and the organization still experiences high turnover, the remedy will not be to increase pay but rather to explore other job outcomes that the employees are likely not receiving.

Pay satisfaction is moderated by job content factors and job context factors (other than pay). Managers can consider a mix of pay, benefits, and non-economic outcomes that are valued by the employees. The organization might also consider *cafeteria-style* plans, which enable employees to pick and choose items of pay and benefits that they value. Giving employees the choice will greatly enhance their pay satisfaction.

Communication and employee involvement

The third guideline relates to the important process issue of communication and employee involvement in pay determination and administration. Should the pay system be secret or open? Social comparison is a crucial determinant of pay satisfaction. When the pay system is secret, social comparison, based on rumour and speculation, inevitably produces distortions with detrimental effects to pay satisfaction. An open system, on the other hand, allows for a more realistic social comparison and to that extent enhances pay satisfaction, provided that the employee perceives fairness and equity in pay decisions.

Employee involvement in pay determination and administration contributes to more accurate employee perceptions of one's own and the relevant other's inputs and outcomes. Employee involvement in pay determination and administration allows for a more realistic social comparison and generally promotes employee perceptions of fairness and equity, thus enhancing pay satisfaction.

SATISFACTION WITH NON-ECONOMIC OUTCOMES

The non-economic outcomes generated by all of the job content factors and some of the job context factors play a critical role in determining pay satisfaction, and also in moderating the consequences of pay dissatisfaction. The almost endless variety of non-economic outcomes include items from:

- the job context category: job status, job security, congenial co-workers and supervisors, and a caring organizational climate;
- the job content category: challenging assignments, exercise of autonomy and responsibility, participation in decision making and opportunities for growth.

Of the two categories, the non-monetary outcomes generated by job content factors, through the process of job design, have been found to be significantly effective in employee motivation. For this reason, we consider, in some detail, the job characteristics theory and its implementing concepts (Hackman and Oldham, 1980).

The Job Characteristics model – elements & process

This model provides a specific and more comprehensive treatment of why job design works and how it can be used as a compensation strategy to provide effective non-economic outcomes to employees. According to Hackman and Oldham (1980), a job can be structured in such a manner that its good performance gives employees a sense of accomplishment that makes them feel good about themselves and their work. Poor performance, on the other hand, produces the opposite effect. Employees will strive to perform well in order to experience good feelings and avoid unpleasant outcomes. Good performance becomes "an occasion for self-reward, which serves as an incentive for continuing to do well" (Hackman and Oldham, 1980, 72). Hence, job design, through its potential for self-reward for good performance, is an effective vehicle for creating internal work motivation.

The core job characteristics   According to the job characteristics model, the job should have five core characteristics: skill variety, task identity, task significance, autonomy, job feedback. Hackman and Oldham's (1980) description of these characteristics is shown in Table 6.1.

Table 6.1 : Core Job Characteristics

Skill variety

The degree to which a job requires a variety of different activities in carrying out the work, involving the use of a number of different skills and talents of the person.

Task identity

The degree to which a job requires completion of a "whole" and identifiable piece of work, that is, doing a job from beginning to end with a visible outcome.

Task significance

The degree to which the job has a substantial impact on the lives of other people, whether those people are in the immediate organization or in the world at large.

Autonomy

The degree to which the job provides substantial freedom, independence, and discretion to the individual in scheduling the work and in determining the procedures to be used in carrying it out.

Job feedback

The degree to which carrying out the work activities required by the job provides the individual with direct and clear information about the effectiveness of his or her performance.

Source: Hackman & Oldham, 1980, pp.78-80.

Effect of the core job characteristics   An individual performing a job that is high in the first three characteristics (skill variety, task identity, and task significance) will experience the work as meaningful. When the job is high in autonomy, the job holder will experience responsibility for the outcomes of the work, since these now flow from the exercise of his/her discretion and initiative. Finally, when the job is high in job feedback, the job holder will have direct knowledge of the results of his/her performance. The model postulates that when the job enables the employee to experience the work as meaningful, to feel responsible for the work outcomes, and to have knowledge of the work results, the employee will have high internal work motivation.

Role of moderators It is necessary to recognize that the enriched job only makes it possible for the individual who has performed well to experience the internal work rewards that will then motivate the individual to continue to perform well. Will all employees perform well in an enriched job? This question requires that individual differences be taken into account. The job characteristics model recognizes individual differences in three areas: (1) knowledge and skill, (2) growth-need strength, and (3) context satisfactions such as satisfaction with compensation, job security, co-workers, and superiors.

An individual who has neither the knowledge and skill nor the competence demanded by an enriched job will not be able to perform well. Likewise, an individual who does not have strong growth-needs will not recognize or fully appreciate the opportunities for the exercise of autonomy and discretion, and for the growth or mastery of varied skills presented by an enriched job. In fact, such an individual might even feel threatened by the demands of such a job. On the other hand, suppose an individual has the knowledge and skill, and even high growth-needs, but is dissatisfied with one or more aspects of the job context, for example, the pay of the enriched job or the lack of job security. This individual will be much too preoccupied with rectifying the perceived deficiencies in the job context to perform well on the job.

Thus, the job-relevant knowledge and skill, growth need strength, and context satisfaction of an individual moderate his/her performance in an enriched job and, in turn, his/her internal work motivation. The more of these moderators (knowledge and skill, growth-needs strength, and context satisfaction) the individual has, the greater the likelihood of high internal work motivation in an enriched job.

To conclude The job characteristics model provides a coherent and comprehensive approach to job design. It fully explains the process of how job design leads to the internal rewards that flow from good performance. It identifies the conditions that must exist if the job holder is to experience the internal rewards of an enriched job (Kanfer, 1990). The model also prescribes a set of specific, practical guidelines for job design, which will be treated in the next section.

THE PROCESS OF JOB DESIGN

The process of job design answers the question: How are the core characteristics of a job enhanced? In other words, how can skill variety, task identity, task significance, autonomy, and job feedback be increased? The job characteristics model proposes a set of five implementing principles: combining tasks, forming natural work units, establishing client relationships, vertically loading the job, and opening feedback channels. Each principle will be discussed, as well as how that principle contributes to improving one or more of the core characteristics of the job. A summary of the discussion is shown in Table 6.2.

TABLE 6.2: The Process of Job Redesign

To increase the job characteristic of	Managerial Action
SKILL VARIETY	*Combine Tasks:* As the employee performs many more tasks than before, more of the employee's skills and abilities will be used.
	Establish Client Relationships: This additional set of tasks will call for a greater use of the employee's interpersonal and communication skills.
TASK IDENTITY	*Combine Tasks:* Employees are now able to see themselves contributing to more of the finished product.
	Forming Natural Work Units: Employees develop a sense of ownership as they identify with a customer group.
TASK SIGNIFICANCE	*Forming Natural Work Units:* Employees' close association with their customer group enables them to see the impact of their work.
AUTONOMY	*Vertically Loading the Job:* Control in areas such as developing work schedule, methods, procedures, etc., enables employees to experience autonomy and responsibility for their work.
	Establish Client Relationships: The exercise of discretion and decision making in managing client relationships inevitably increases autonomy.
JOB FEEDBACK	*Opening Feedback Channels:* When employees are given responsibility for quality control checks, for example, they are able to see fairly immediately the results of their work.
	Establish Client Relationships: Direct client contact allows employees to receive information on the quality of the goods/services they provide.

Combining Tasks

This principle suggests the putting together of "existing, fractionalized, tasks to form new and larger modules of work" (Hackman and Oldham, 1980, 135).

This principle can be applied in the assembly-line operation for a small appliance. In such an operation, the entire task of assembling the appliance is broken down into several smaller operations, which are performed as the appliance moves from one point of the assembly line to the next. When the combining-tasks principle is implemented, the entire assembling operation is done by one person or a team of workers.

Restructuring the work in this manner enables the individual to do the job from the beginning to end, and take ownership of the visible outcome. Hence, task identity is improved. As the individual now has to perform many more tasks and activities than before, more of his/her skills, abilities, and talents are being used, and skill variety is increased. Thus, redesigning the job by combining tasks enhances the core job characteristics of task identity and skill variety.

Forming Natural Work Units

According to this implementing principle, the items of work are "arranged into logical or inherently meaningful groups" (Hackman and Oldham, 1980, 136). The staff of a travel agency might be randomly assigned to the customers, or the staff might be assigned to particular groups of customers, for example, government, business, or individual accounts. The redesign to form natural work units allows the staff to develop a sense of ownership of the tasks and outcomes in respect to a customer group, thereby increasing task identity.

The close association of the staff with their customer group will also enable them to see for themselves the impact of their work on their customers, thus contributing to task significance. The task identify and the task significance characteristics of the job are greatly enhanced when the job is redesigned to form natural work units.

Establishing Client Relationships

This principle prescribes that, as far as possible, the employee deal directly with the clients and be responsible for managing client relationships. This prescription also involves the establishment of the criteria that the client will use in providing feedback to the employee. Suppose that the job of the travel agency staff in the previous example is redesigned to form natural work units. This redesign could be taken a step further by allowing the employees to establish relationships with their clients and to manage these relationships.

Such a redesign will increase the job's core characteristics of skill variety, autonomy, and job feedback. The increase in skill variety comes about because client relationships call for a greater use of interpersonal and communication skills. The exercise of discretion and decision making in the management of client relationships will increase the degree of autonomy in the job. The increase in feedback comes from the fact that dealing directly with the clients places the staff in a position to receive information on the quality of service they provide.

Vertically Loading the Job

This principle gives workers "increased control over the work by 'pushing down' responsibility and authority that were formerly reserved for higher levels of management" (Hackman and Oldham, 1980, 138). This control could be in a variety of areas, for example, developing the work schedule, methods, and procedures; decision making (even if it is limited) in budget and financial matters related to the job; and involvement in planning. Redesigning the job by vertical loading will increase the employee autonomy.

Opening Feedback Channels

This principle prescribes that job redesign enables employees to receive feedback directly from the job, preferably immediately upon performance rather than later from the supervisor. Establishing client relationships is one way to ensure feedback. Other ways are giving workers responsibility for quality control checks, and for maintaining performance records such as production data and budget reports that are sent to both the employee and the supervisor. With computerization, direct feedback from job performance tends to be more feasible. Opening feedback channels increases the job feedback characteristics of a job.

To summarize

The implementing principles or concepts proposed by the job characteristics model provide practical prescriptions for job enrichment. These prescriptions operate to specifically increase the core job characteristics of skill variety, task identity, task significance, autonomy, and job feedback. As discussed in the previous section, the greater the degree of these characteristics in a job, the more the job holder who performs well will experience internal work rewards. The process is, however, moderated by the individual's job-relevant knowledge and skills, growth-needs strength, and satisfaction with the context—all of which will considerably influence his/her job performance.

IMPLICATIONS FOR REWARD MANAGEMENT

The job diagnostics survey developed by Hackman and Oldham (1980) provides a job profile that identifies the core characteristics needing improvement. The implementing concepts can then be applied to improve these job characteristics. Thus, the job characteristics model makes it possible for job design to be integrated into the compensation system to provide non-economic outcomes.

SUMMARY

The issue of satisfaction with a compensation item is critical to the effectiveness of a compensation system. Combining notions from equity and discrepancy theories, this chapter has discussed satisfaction in terms of the difference between an individual's perceptions of what should be received and what is received. In dealing with the issue of satisfaction with pay, the determinants of pay satisfaction model identified four factors—person-related, job-related, referent-other-related, and context-related—that contribute to the employee's perceptions of the amount that should be received and the amount that is received. The difference between these perceptions causes employees to be satisfied or dissatisfied with their pay.

The two major consequences of pay dissatisfaction, are the desire for more pay, and the reduced attractiveness of the job. Each consequence has its own set of employee reactions. The desire for more pay leads to a higher level of job performance if pay is performance-based; otherwise, the non-fulfilment of this desire leads to a variety of employee reactions ranging from absenteeism and turnover to the filing of grievances and union pressures.

Employees reactions to the reduced attractiveness of the job have found to vary from absenteeism and turnover to job dissatisfaction, which might result in poor mental health or psychological withdrawal. It is, necessary to recognize that the very fact of employees' pay dissatisfaction, whether it will occur and what its nature will be as well as employees' reactions to it, are moderated not only by the content and the context of the job but also by the external environmental factors in which employees find themselves.

Both models, the determinants of pay satisfaction and the consequences of pay dissatisfaction, provide a firm conceptual basis on which to develop a repertoire of strategies for ensuring pay satisfaction and for coping with the consequences of pay dissatisfaction. One such strategy is the use of job design to generate non-economic outcomes. Of the several approaches to job design, the job characteristics model offers an empirically proven technology that allows an organization to adopt job design as a practical compensation strategy to provide non-economic outcomes for its employees.

KEY TERMS

classical approaches to job design

core job characteristics

discrepancy theory

growth theories approaches to job design

implementing principles of job design

job characteristics model

job content factors

job context factors

job design

satisfaction

REVIEW AND DISCUSSION QUESTIONS _____ ℛ__

1. Consider the following cases of dissatisfaction with pay:

   Case 1

   Robert is not satisfied with his pay as a bank teller because it does not enable him to maintain the standard of living he was accustomed to before he married a widow with three children. He concedes that the pay fairly reflects the job's value relative to the other jobs in the bank, and that the pay reflects his performance.

   Case 2

   Richelle is not satisfied with her pay as a bank teller because she believes that, although her job title is the same as Robert's, her job has additional responsibilities. These responsibilities require her to work extra hours for which she is not paid. She also believes that the pay does not adequately reward her superior performance. Richelle is single and lives with her parents. Her only dependants are her pets, a cat named Fluffy and a dog named Fido.

   Which case corresponds with the notion of dissatisfaction in equity theory? Why?

2. Identify and explain the factors that influence an individual's satisfaction with his/her pay.

3. It is not uncommon to find that individuals who are dissatisfied with their pay still

   a) stay on with the organization;

   b) maintain a high level of performance.

   How would you explain these situations, which seem to be inconsistent with the predictions of the consequences of pay dissatisfaction model?

4. Discuss some practical guidelines for increasing pay satisfaction.

5. Distinguish between the classical and growth theories approaches to job design.

6. Using examples, discuss the potential of Hackman and Oldham's job characteristics model as an effective compensation tool.

Star Wars

When Ted Sharp joined the Space Age Technology Company (SATCO) as a design engineer, he brought to the job an exceptionally strong academic record and three years of related work experience. SATCO was a relatively small and unknown company in suburban Winnipeg, but its association with Star Wars technology offered Ted an unusual opportunity for professional growth.

Ted was pleased with his decision to join SATCO. It had certainly come up to his expectations: challenging assignments and opportunities for creativity and innovation as well as professional growth and development and signals from top management that he was being considered for a management position. Of course, Ted's career progress had its costs— hard work, long hours, and frequent travel. The last two were especially hard on his wife and their teenage daughter. A tragic automobile accident had rendered his wife a paraplegic requiring constant attention. The daughter had to assume the responsibility of tending to the mother, in addition to the household chores and school work. However, Ted's career received strong encouragement from his wife and daughter. They loved Winnipeg and had become very attached to their neighbours, who were very friendly and provided them with support and assistance.

As Ted looked out of his office window, the bright sunshine, typical of Winnipeg in February, seemed to reflect his optimism about his future in SATCO. He had just finished talking to his boss, Jeremy Harper, and was delighted to learn of his merit raise, the largest in the design engineering department. Recognition was not new to Ted; he had received prizes and honours in school and university, and in his previous job he had received above-average raises. The fact that he had been awarded the highest raise for each of the last five years he had been at SATCO made him look forward to a satisfying and productive association with the company.

His cheery, upbeat mood was cut short when George burst into his office with a printout of the salaries and merit raises of the department. George was a competent engineer but in his weaker moments he regressed to being a computer hacker, a bad habit he had picked up as an undergraduate. In one of these moments he had come across the salary information that Ted was staring at in disbelief. It confirmed that he had the highest merit raise, but he was totally flabbergasted to see the almost negligible difference between his salary and that of Ron Brown. When Ron Brown was hired two years back, there was considerable opposition for two reasons. First, he was hired in preference to several other applicants who were better qualified. The major consideration seemed to be that he was the nephew of a senior vice-president of SATCO. Second, his starting salary was about $2,500 more than the salary of most engineers who were equally, if not more, qualified and had been with SATCO for over two years.

At that time, Ted had reconciled himself to receiving almost the same salary as Ron because he was hopeful that his merit raises would eventually remedy the situation. To his utter disappointment, he now found that his merit raises had not put him very much ahead of Ron. At the first opportunity, he met Jeremy Harper and demanded an explanation, saying, "I'm tired of working for just the joys of engineering. My salary should fairly reflect my competence and contribution to SATCO." Jeremy tried to explain the merit system, "Our performance rating system consists of three categories: outstanding, acceptable, unacceptable. Each year your performance was assessed as outstanding, which entitled you to 6.5 per cent increase. Ron's performance was assessed as acceptable, which entitled him to a 5.5 per cent increase. You must not forget that the merit increase includes a COLA of 5 per cent for everyone." Expressing his disappointment that SATCO did not think very highly of him, Ted stormed out of the office.

Discussion Questions

1. What are the reasons for the inequity that Ted experienced?
2. Explore all the possible actions that Ted can take. Which of these actions do you think Ted might actually take? Why?
3. As a compensation specialist, what are your recommendations for resolving this situation?
4. Assume that instead of Ron Brown, the person who was hired belonged to one of the "protected groups" (i.e., women, visible minorities, aboriginal peoples, persons with disabilities) and had qualifications identical with Ron Brown's. Assume further that this person was hired as part of SATCO's affirmative action programme. In this scenario, explore the possible impact of the programme on the employees' perceptions of equity, and the strategy that SATCO might adopt to address such an impact.

PART

III

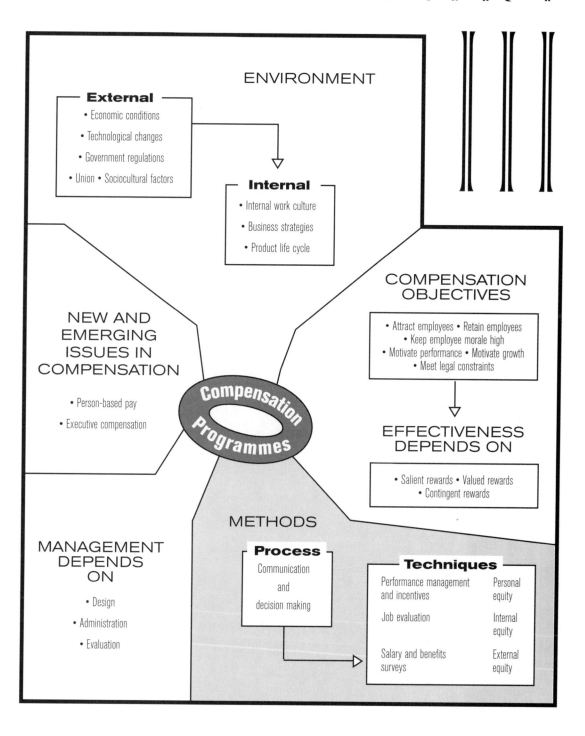

ENVIRONMENT

External
- Economic conditions
- Technological changes
- Government regulations
- Union • Sociocultural factors

Internal
- Internal work culture
- Business strategies
- Product life cycle

COMPENSATION OBJECTIVES
- Attract employees • Retain employees
- Keep employee morale high
- Motivate performance • Motivate growth
- Meet legal constraints

NEW AND EMERGING ISSUES IN COMPENSATION
- Person-based pay
- Executive compensation

Compensation Programmes

EFFECTIVENESS DEPENDS ON
- Salient rewards • Valued rewards
- Contingent rewards

MANAGEMENT DEPENDS ON
- Design
- Administration
- Evaluation

METHODS

Process
Communication and decision making

Techniques

Performance management and incentives	Personal equity
Job evaluation	Internal equity
Salary and benefits surveys	External equity

CHAPTER 7

The Strategic and Process Issues in Compensation

OVERVIEW

This chapter identifies and examines the nature and the contents of the strategic and process issues in compensation, and the critical options that are contained in each issue. The chapter also considers the criteria for an organization's options as it seeks a compensation system that is supportive of its business objectives and congruent with its internal work culture.

 LEARNING OBJECTIVES

- ▶ To identify the major strategic and process issues and explain why they are critical in designing a total compensation system.

- ▶ To distinguish between the strategic and process issues.

- ▶ To identify and explain the criteria for the choice of the critical alternative options contained in the strategic and process issues.

- ▶ To understand the strategic and process issues and, for each issue, to discuss the conditions under which its alternative options would be most appropriate.

- ▶ To explain how the decisions on the strategic and process issues can enhance or impair the effectiveness of the compensation system.

THE CASE OF THE BEWILDERED COMPENSATION SPECIALIST

On his flight back to his division from a visit to the corporate office, Ed Fairpay, a compensation specialist, found himself sitting next to Ann Dumont, a friend from university days who now operated her own consulting firm in human resource management. After the usual social chatter, Ed poured out his woes. At his company, despite an elaborate pay structure based on a complex and mathematically precise job evaluation programme, there was considerable dissatisfaction with the compensation programme, resulting in the loss of good people. The conversation went as follows:

Ann: You're not alone, Ed. Compensation activity has caused many a human resource person to nurse an ulcer. Let's begin at the beginning. Do you have a compensation philosophy in your organization?

Ed: Sure, we do. Our company is known to pay well.

Ann: Do your employees know of your philosophy?

Ed: That's what the theorists say. Our employees are interested in money, and we have a first-rate job evaluation programme that guarantees our employees are paid the right salary. Our expertise in this respect is the envy of the competition. Isn't this more important?

Ann: It depends upon whether you want to base the total compensation on the job or on the person. The former produces one set of consequences; the latter, quite a different set.

Ed: There you go again—theorizing!

Ann: Ed, do you see your compensation system as an end in itself or as a means to an end?

Ed: I forgot your forte in college was the Socratic method. But, really, Ann, means and ends are okay for an academic discussion. I don't see the relevance. As I told you already, my concern is why we're losing people like Leo when his compensation was determined fairly *vis-à-vis* the other jobs in the company.

Ann: Your concern raises another question: Are you striving for internal equity?

Ed: You bet we are. We have to be fair and equitable.

Ann: At the risk of external inequity?

Ed: Every time I mention the need for salary surveys, the treasurer screams: "Costs!"

Ann: Poor Ed, you seem caught between the devil and the deep blue sea.

Ed: You'd better believe it. Although our division is a profit centre, major compensation decisions are made in the corporate office. I'm now carrying back one of those decisions.

Ann:	Perhaps I can address your concern from a different angle. What role does your organization assign to performance in determining the compensation of an individual?
Ed:	Isn't it obvious that pay should be related to performance? Don't all organizations relate pay to performance?
Ann:	It depends. Some organizations focus on seniority rather than performance, just as they vary widely on the compensation mix.
Ed:	Why should organizations differ on the compensation mix?
Ann:	Touché! You sure pick up the Socratic method fast.
Ed:	Thanks. Let me move to a really academic issue. What do you think of the practice of secrecy in compensation?
Ann:	How can a discussion about a practice be academic?
Ed:	Because one Dr. Lawler wrote about secrecy in compensation while sitting in his academic ivory tower.
Ann:	Dr. Lawler's work on pay secrecy is based on empirical research. So is his work on employee participation in pay decision making.
Ed:	Openness in pay is bad enough. Employee participation in pay decisions? That's ludicrous!

This conversation makes clear that a compensation system is more than a collection of compensation practices and techniques hastily put together in an attempt to ward off crises as they occur. Instead, the component elements of compensation programmes and processes are blended into a meaningful pattern to serve the interests of both employees and the organization. A coherent and purposeful compensation system requires that management carefully think through the strategic and process issues—refer to Table 7.1—that are critical in the design of a total compensation system (Lawler and Jenkins, 1992). It would be more appropriate to describe them as cardinal, or fundamental issues because the effectiveness of the compensation system itself depends upon the decisions on these issues.

THE CRITICAL NATURE OF STRATEGIC AND PROCESS ISSUES Qu 1.

As can be seen from Table 7.1, strategic and process issues call for a set of mutually exclusive approaches. Decisions on the strategic issues will provide the direction for the compensation system for an extended period of time. The right direction will result in an effective use of the compensation dollar; the wrong direction will lead to an ineffective deployment of organizational resources. It is more than a question of compensation dollars. Employee dissatisfaction with compensation can have adverse consequences for the organization's effectiveness.

Process issues are equally critical; these determine *how* the decisions on the strategic issues are implemented. The mode of implementation is just as crucial to

Table 7.1: Critical Strategic & Process Issues in Compensation

Strategic Issues	Decision required
Compensation philosophy	Should the organization have a compensation philosophy?
Mechanistic and Process	What should the balance be between the two?
Job Evaluation System	Job-content-based? or Person-based?
Compensation System Objective	An end? or A means to an end?
Internal and External equity	Which is emphasized?
Relevant Labour Market	Local? Regional? National? International?
System Design and Administration	Centralized? Decentralized?
Performance, Membership, or Seniority	Which is rewarded?
Cash & Benefits	What is the mix of cash & benefits?

Process Issues	Decision required
Communicating Compensation System	What aspects are open? secret?
Employee Involvement in Compensation	Should employees be involved in compensation system design? in administration?

Source: Based on Lawler, 1981

the effectiveness of the compensation system as the strategies chosen. Often it may be more crucial because the beneficial effects of a right choice on a strategic issue may be completely eliminated by a wrong choice on a process issue.

Criteria for decision on strategic and process issues

It will be recalled from Chapter 2 that the reward system of an organization must be supportive of the organization's business strategy. When the choice of the compensation strategy is consistent with and supports the business strategy, the compensation system will contribute to the accomplishment of the organization's mission. The next section examines each of the strategic and process issues in terms of its contents, alternative approaches, and the specific conditions or criteria that favour one approach over another.

STRATEGIC ISSUES

Compensation philosophy

Considerations in formulating the compensation philosophy
In formulating the compensation philosophy, the following four considerations are paramount:

1. Compensation is a major expenditure of the organization.

2. Compensation is a major motivational tool.

3. The compensation system must support the organization's business strategy.

4. Compensation is extremely important to employees.

These considerations prompt the organization to think seriously and systematically about its compensation system:

- What are the objectives of the compensation system?
- Does the compensation system support the business strategies?
- Is it compatible with the work culture of the organization?
- How is the compensation mix determined?
- How can the organization ensure that the compensation mix is fair and equitable?
- Should employees be involved in the design and the administration of the compensation system?

Answers to these and related questions will crystallize the organization's thinking on compensation and contribute to the formulation of a coherent compensation philosophy.

The beneficial effects of a compensation philosophy

A well-thought-out compensation philosophy produces several beneficial effects. First, it fosters the credibility of the compensation system in two ways. By its clear and unambiguous statement of the objectives of the compensation system, it serves as a guide for managerial decisions in compensation. When all managers in an organization use the same frame of reference for their compensation decisions, there is a greater likelihood of consistency and equity, which increases the credibility of the compensation system.

The other way the compensation philosophy fosters credibility is by stating the circumstances under which compensation changes will occur. Consequently, unless the stipulated circumstances come about, employees will not expect changes in compensation, regardless of how much they may desire a change. If the compensation philosophy stipulates that pay will be performance-based, then employees will not be disappointed or dissatisfied if seniority is not rewarded by a pay increase.

The compensation philosophy enhances employee motivation. The effects of consistency, equity, and credibility contribute to increasing employees' valence of the compensation items; leading to higher employee motivation. Employee motivation is also improved when the clearly articulated contents of the compensation philosophy communicate the performance-outcomes linkage, which increases the employee's (P⇨O) expectancy.

Contents of a compensation philosophy statement

There is no one exhaustive list of contents. The organization's compensation philosophy should reflect its culture and business strategies, and the decisions on the strategic and process issues (Lawler and Jenkins, 1992). Some examples of contents are:

- Objectives of the compensation system: What specific returns does the organization expect? What specific employee behaviours does the organization intend to promote?

- Market position: Does the organization intend to meet, lead, or lag behind the market in determining its package of pay and benefits?

- Compensation-system fit with the internal work culture of the organization. Does it emphasize skill-based or performance-based pay and non-economic rewards? Does the system offer non-contingent pay and social rewards? If the former, then the compensation system promotes a performance-orientation culture if the latter, a people-orientation culture.

Table 7.2 is an example of a compensation philosophy statement of a major Canadian corporation in the transportation industry.

Table 7.2: Extracts from a Compensation Philosophy Statement Relating to Objectives, Market Position, and Performance-Based Pay

Objectives

The Cash Compensation Program's primary objectives are:
- to attract and retain qualified employees;
- to reward effective performance;
- to provide incentives to further improve performance; and
- to accomplish the above objectives in a manner that will ensure fair and equitable treatment of all employees.

Market Position

We pay particular attention to the salary practices of large national organizations representative of major and primarily unionized employers in Canada.

The market surveys we use allow us to:
- look at specific types of jobs throughout many companies;
- select industries;
- select companies within those industries;
- select companies by geographic location;
- select specific jobs by numerical value; or
- combinations of the above.

Performance-based Pay

The objectives are:
- to improve on-the-job performance;
- to provide linkages to other plans through
- identification of individual potential and support for career development;
- to increase the overall effectiveness of the organization.

Based on your assessed performance your superiors will establish an appropriate salary level within your salary range. Progress towards the salary range maximum will be dependent upon your performance level.

An employee should progress through the salary range based on achievement of objectives and continued performance improvement. Once the employee has reached the fully competent level, that employee should normally be paid the full value of the job.

Any reward beyond the fully competent level is for superior performance and is provided for by our Performance Incentive Plan.

These are the features of the Performance Incentive Plan:
- recognizes superior performance;
- provides reward beyond the salary range maximum;
- is delivered in an annual lump sum payment;
- must be earned annually.

It is important to remember that awards made under the Performance Incentive Plan, as well as salary increases, are based on the performance rating given in the last Assessment of Performance.

An individual may receive compensation for superior performance in one of three forms:
- all salary
- part salary and part incentive
- all incentive.

BALANCING THE MECHANISTIC AND PROCESS ISSUES

What is meant by "mechanistic"? by "process"?

Mechanistic means the mechanics of the techniques, which are the "tools" or "decision mechanisms" used in compensation; *process* means how the techniques are implemented and interpreted. To explore the need for balance between mechanistic and process issues, let us suppose we are engaged in evaluating job—an activity that is necessary before a job's wage rate is established. Let us also suppose that we have decided to use a technique called the point factor method of job evaluation.

Effects of mechanistic approach

A purely mechanistic approach to job evaluation presupposes that the point factor method has the capacity to come up with job values that are valid—the job values accurately reflect job differentials in the organization. Using the point factor method to rate a job, however, involves considerable subjectivity. The use of quantitative techniques to overcome subjectivity "...usually have the effect of masking the soft and subjective side of their assumptions and creating a false sense of objectivity" (Korukonda, 1996, p.81). Besides, each employee has his/her own perception of a fair and equitable job value, which will frequently differ from that determined by the job evaluation technique, however advanced and sophisticated it might be.

In the final analysis, it is the employee's perception that determines whether the job value is equitable or not. And this has been found to be the case with almost every other technique of salary design and administration— salary surveys, performance appraisals, incentive and gain-sharing plans, salary structure, and so forth (Gerhart and Milkovich, 1992; Lawler and Jenkins, 1992).

Effects of process approach

The issue of differing perceptions can only be addressed by greater attention to the process approach or issues—how the techniques are implemented. Let us return to our example of job evaluation using the point factor method. Attention to the process issue in implementing the point factor method of job evaluation would be to involve employees, directly or through their representatives on the job evaluation committee, in the various stages of the evaluation process. Such an involvement would increase employee participation and hence contribute to a better understanding of the technique. Involving employees in design and implementation also leads to a greater sense of "ownership".

Effects of process predicted by expectancy theory

In terms of the expectancy theory model, taking care of the process issues will clarify the effort-performance and the performance-outcomes relationships in the case of techniques where these relationships are relevant. A good example where these relationships are relevant is in the technique of performance appraisal used in performance-based pay programmes. A clarification of these relationships will greatly increase employees' $(E \Rightarrow P)$ and $(P \Rightarrow O)$ expectancies. Furthermore, employee involvement will contribute to a more realistic perception of the equity of outcomes, and this perception will have a significant positive impact on the employees' valence of the outcomes. It can, therefore, be concluded that proper attention to the process issues will improve the motivational efficacy of the technique.

The point of raising the issue of balance between mechanics and process in compensation is to draw attention to an overemphasis on techniques and technology. This overemphasis on techniques can be traced to the assumptions and practices of the scientific management movement, which assumed that workers would produce only if they received economic rewards. Hence, compensation design efforts were concentrated on developing techniques to tie pay with performance. The process issues in pay effectiveness were completely neglected. Managers need to be aware of the scientific management movement's legacy and its total mechanistic approach. They should recognize the necessity of a judicious balance of the mechanics and process issues; in other words, organizations should ensure that techniques are implemented with the appropriate degree of communication and employee involvement.

THE CHOICE OF A JOB-CONTENT-BASED OR A PERSON-BASED EVALUATION SYSTEM

What is a "job-content-based" evaluation system?

A job-content-based evaluation system is a mechanism to determine the pay grade. Traditionally, it has achieved this objective by developing a job structure (hierarchy) that reflects the differential in a job's value or worth to the organization. This differentiation also achieves internal equity if the pay reflects the relative value of various jobs within the organization. The focus of the evaluation effort is on the value (or contribution) of the *job alone* to the organization. The qualifications of the individual are disregarded in determining the job's worth and the corresponding pay grade attached to it.

How a system develops its sources of job value depends on the method used. As will be discussed in Chapter 11, some methods (ranking, for example) are entirely subjective and use vague criteria for job evaluation; others (point factor and factor comparison methods,) evaluate jobs on the basis of compensable factors. *Compensable factors* are judgements about the specific aspects of jobs that the organization values to the extent that it is willing to pay for them. Examples of compensable factors are skills, effort, responsibility, and work conditions. It must be noted, that the factors are not the skills possessed by the job incumbent but rather the skills required by the job. If the job incumbent possesses more skills than those required by the job, the job will not be worth more; it will still be valued on the basis of the skills that are judged to be necessary for the job. The focus of the system is on the job content, not the person holding the job.

The job-content-based evaluation system has often been subjected to severe criticism (Lawler, 1986b), which will be reviewed in Chapter 15. For now, it is sufficient to note some of its unintended adverse effects.

Weighting compensable factors

For example, a heavy weight is usually assigned to the factor of responsibility; jobs high on this factor will fetch a higher dollar value. Most managerial jobs rate high on this factor. Consequently, employees will seek these jobs in order to earn a higher salary. The problem with this is that employees who have neither the competence nor the inclination for managerial jobs may, and often do, get those jobs. For example, in a school the only way for a teacher to earn a higher salary is to move into a principal's position. Many a school superintendent has ruefully witnessed the dysfunctional consequences of such a move. Often, the classroom loses an exceptionally gifted teacher, and the school gains an incompetent principal.

Budget inflation and resistance to change

The other dysfunctional effects are inflated job responsibilities and budgets, and resistance to needed reorganization plans (Lawler and Jenkins, 1992). When compensable factors include responsibility for people and budgets, managers may be needlessly tempted to increase the size of their staff and budgets in order that their job may qualify for a higher job value and a higher salary. The job-content-based evaluation system is also known to have become an obstacle to a company's reorganization plans. When a job is redefined in a reorganization, its position in the hierarchy as established by the evaluation system is threatened. To preserve such vested interests, efforts are soon initiated to discard the reorganization plans.

What is a "person-based" job evaluation system?

The person-based job evaluation system is often proposed as an alternative to the job-content-based evaluation system. Under the person-based approach, the base pay is designed to reflect the knowledge and the skills of the job holder, even though the individual's job might require the use of only some of the knowledge and skills. The mechanics and processes of person-based job evaluation system, also known as "pay-for-skills" and "pay-for-knowledge", is discussed in detail in Chapter 15. Here, we provide some illustrations of person-based job evaluation system, and briefly note its merits and demerits.

In the Montreal Catholic School Commission, teachers are paid on the basis of their *scolarité*, that is, their number of years of university schooling. A teacher with an M.A. in history and a teacher with a B.A. in history may be assigned to teach Canadian history in Grade 9. Both teachers are responsible for teaching the same curriculum, both have classes of identical size, and both prepare students for the identical provincial examinations. Yet the teacher with the M.A. earns a higher base pay.

In the Shell Canada Chemical Company plant in Sarnia, the person-based approach takes the form of multi-skilling. The base pay is computed according to the number of skill modules in which the worker is proficient. The greater the number of skill modules in which the worker has acquired proficiency, the greater is the base pay—even though the assigned job may not require the worker to use all the acquired skills.

Person-based job evaluation system: merits and demerits

There are several advantages to a person-based evaluation system. It encourages the employees to acquire additional skills and expertise which makes for a more flexible and capable workforce (Gerhart, Minkoff, and Olsen, 1996). It permits the development of "career ladders", which enable employees to earn higher salaries as they acquire professional or technical expertise; these employees need not seek managerial jobs in order to earn higher pay. The person-based approach eliminates the dysfunctional effects of the job-content-based approach.

The motivational effectiveness of the person-based approach is also greater because of the impact on the employees' $(E \Rightarrow P)$ expectancy and the valence of outcomes. The acquisition of knowledge and skills also increases the $(E \Rightarrow P)$ expectancy. The visible, direct linkage between knowledge and skills acquisition and pay improves the perceptions of equity and thus increases the valence of pay.

However, the person-based approach is not widely used, and as will be discussed in Chapter 15, it requires a fairly drastic reorientation of the internal work culture for successful implementation. Nevertheless, the person-based approach is suitable where technical expertise is critical, and in organizations that operate employee involvement programmes and autonomous work teams. Job-content-based evaluation is more suitable where responsibility for human, financial, and material resources is the critical compensable factor.

THE COMPENSATION SYSTEM AS AN END OR AS A MEANS TO AN END

Compensation system – a means to an end

The compensation system is a means to an end. Compensable programmes are designed to serve the needs of the organization—to attract and retain qualified employees and to motivate them to perform work behaviours that help to attain organizational objectives. If compensation programmes fail to attract and retain qualified employees or are unsuccessful in motivating employees to perform the desired work behaviours, they must be modified.

Dysfunctional effects of means-end displacement

The reality, however, is often very different. Traditionally, the most important consideration in developing a compensation system has been an overwhelming concern for internal equity. To ensure internal equity, organizations have taken great care to create a hierarchy of jobs that adequately reflects the differential in job values to the organization. This objective is worthwhile as long as job and salary structures serve organizational needs and objectives.

The problem arises when this structure is treated as if it were immutable. Most organizations today operate in a turbulent environment. A Canadian crown corporation that once operated in a regulated industry now finds itself privatized, in a deregulated industry, and in a fiercely competitive free trade market. To cope with the new environment and to respond to its changing dynamics, the corporation might need to reorganize. Redefined jobs necessitate a shift to external equity to attract qualified employees, decentralization, and performance-based programmes rather than the automatic seniority-based pay increase. A compensation system that cannot readily respond to the required changes has become an end in itself.

Remedy for the means-end displacement of compensation system

In companies that have been in existence for a long time, systems and practices, if not regularly reviewed, tend to become rigid and resistant to change. Longevity itself becomes an argument for continuing with the status quo. This is acceptable as long as the organization's needs are well served. In today's changing business environment, an organization is better served if it takes specific steps that will allow it to modify the compensation system. The most important step is to incorporate the organization's intentions in the compensation philosophy. An explicit statement that compensation is a means to meet the needs of the organization will serve as a clear message to all employees to expect changes if the organization's conditions so require.

In terms of the expectancy theory model, such a statement will give employees a better understanding of the performance-outcomes relationship and will help towards a more realistic $(P \Rightarrow O)$ expectancy. It will also prevent an adverse effect on employees' valence of outcomes should business conditions necessitate modifications to the compensation system, assuming that such modifications are done in an equitable manner and that such process issues as communication and employee involvement are prudently managed. If the modifications are managed properly, employee motivation should not suffer.

THE CHOICE OF INTERNAL OR EXTERNAL EQUITY Q3
What is internal equity? external equity?

Internal equity means that the pay rates of jobs in an organization reflect the relative value of those jobs or their relative contribution to organizational objectives. External equity means that the pay rates of jobs in an organization correspond to the rates of those jobs in the external labour market. Consider the following data about five jobs in the ABC Company. Since the internal pay rates of these jobs reflect their job value as indicated by their job evaluation points, it can be concluded that internal equity exists in the organization. There is external equity for all jobs except for job 3, which is underpaid relative to the external labour market.

Job	Job Evaluation Points	Option C Organization's Pay/Year Based on Internal Equity only $	Pay Rate/ Year in External Labour Market $	Option A Maintain Internal and External Equity $	Option B Maintain External Equity only $
1	1,100	77,000	77,000	88,000	77,000
2	1,000	70,000	70,000	80,000	70,000
3	800	56,000	64,000	64,000	64,000
4	500	35,000	35,000	40,000	35,000
5	300	21,000	21,000	24,000	21,000

Internal/external equity: illustration of some options   Q 4

The ABC Company has three basic options: option A, to maintain both internal and external equity; option B, to maintain external equity only; and option C, to maintain internal equity only. If the company chooses option A, job 3 must be paid the market rate of $64,000 to ensure external equity. The pay of the other jobs would have to be increased proportionately to maintain the differentials of job value in order to ensure internal equity. The costs of this option are prohibitive. If the company chooses option B, job 3 is paid the market rate of $64,000 to ensure external equity. No other changes are made, because this option does not seek to maintain internal equity. If the company chooses option C, to maintain internal equity alone, it decides in favour of the status quo.

Internal/external equity: consequences of different options

What are the consequences of these options? The consequence of maintaining the status quo is, other things being equal, a relatively higher rate of turnover among employees in job 3. Most likely a shortage in the external labour market of the skills of job 3 is driving up the pay rates. The consequence of option A is higher costs, which can only be justified if the organizational needs can be better served by maintaining both internal and external equity. An organization whose business strategies call for a policy of leading in the external market might choose option A.

The consequences of option B are controlled costs, the elimination of pay as a cause of turnover among employees in job 3, but dissatisfaction among employees in the other jobs because these employees will now experience internal inequity. The last consequence of option B need not arise if ABC Company's compensation philosophy has explicitly provided for such a situation, by stating that although the compensation system strives to pursue the objective of internal equity. External equity will apply in determining the pay rates of jobs that are in short supply.

As discussed in the means-ends issue, such a statement will contribute to a more realistic $(P \Rightarrow O)$ expectancy and prevent any adverse impact on the employees' valence of outcomes. Therefore, the preferred option will be option B, external equity alone, if there is a shortage in the external labour market of people with job 3 knowledge, skills, and abilities.

THE CHOICE OF EXTERNAL LABOUR MARKETS FOR SALARY SURVEYS

Almost every organization collects data on wages and salaries. The issues, methods, and techniques for salary surveys are fully discussed in Chapter 13. This section briefly explores some basic strategic and policy questions: What are the right market data? Is one survey for all jobs in the organization adequate? Should employees be involved? (Lawler and Jenkins, 1992; Gerhart and Milkovich, 1992).

The relevant labour market

What are the right market data? This question arises because several labour markets exist: the local labour market, the national labour market, and the international labour market. In addition, the companies in the same industry which compete for industry-specific skills and know-how can also be considered to form a labour market for these skills and know-how. The choice of the data source is influenced by two major considerations: (a) the relevance of the labour markets; and (b) the cost competitiveness of the organization.

In general, the relevant guideline should be to survey those organizations at the local, regional, national or international level to which employees are likely to move. Employees in clerical and low level skilled jobs are more likely to move to organizations in the local area; employees in managerial, professional, and high-tech jobs are more mobile and, therefore, more likely to seek jobs nationwide and sometimes worldwide.

One cannot ignore the issue of labour costs which affect an organization's ability to be competitive. For this reason, organizations are likely to collect data from comparable companies in the same industry. An organization's cost competitiveness becomes a major consideration when it has to compete for people with industry specific skills and know-how. An organization aims to be competitive to attract and retain employees, as well as to manage its costs in order to maintain its competitive edge. Relevance of labour markets and the organization's cost competitiveness are discussed in more detail in Chapter 13 in the context of the organization's need to ensure external equity.

Data collection; employee involvement

Is one survey for all jobs in the organization adequate? In view of what has just been said, the organization needs more than one survey, each survey covering a set of jobs that have the same labour market. Should employees be involved? The organization should allow employees to contribute any data they might have and also make it possible for them or their representatives to review the data collected by the surveys.

Employee involvement increases trust in the process. Involvement improves employees' perceptions of external equity; these perceptions contribute to increasing the valence and satisfaction of pay. Besides improved employee motivation, the organization benefits from the surveys because the data enable it to develop a more rational approach to managing payroll costs.

CENTRALIZATION VERSUS DECENTRALIZATION

Centralized and decentralized compensation systems

In a centralized compensation system, all decisions relating to the pay and benefits structure and the policies, used in the design and administration of the system are made by one unit, for the entire organization. In a decentralized compensation system, the different divisions of the organization have the autonomy to design and administer the system to suit the specific needs of their business operations.

Centralized compensation system – merits and demerits

A centralized compensation system ensures internal equity throughout the organization, facilitates the movements of people across the organization, and ensures the uniform and consistent treatment of compensation issues. Centralization also allows the organization to control compensation costs effectively.

There are disadvantages to centralization. Centralization does not allow the organizational units that are substantially different to design a system that better suits their local needs and conditions. A unit might find that it has to raise the company's pay rates in order to compete with the local labour market to attract and retain a qualified workforce. A centralized compensation system will not give the required autonomy to the unit for reasons of internal equity and cost control. When a compensation system permits different pay structures, policies, and procedures for different organizational units, the system loses the advantages of internal equity. The absence of autonomy in a centralized system also prevents the different parts of the organization from experiencing the motivational benefits that come from employee participation and involvement in the compensation system.

When is a centralized compensation system more appropriate?

A centralized compensation system is more suitable for a small organization where it is feasible to get a clear understanding of the needs of all the parts of the organization and to reflect these needs in the compensation system. A large organization that operates a single business and is located in one place can similarly get a clear understanding of the needs of the business and the conditions of the one local labour market. If the organization also pays attention to employee involvement issues, it should succeed in operating a centralized compensation system.

When is a decentralized compensation system more appropriate?

Large organizations with multiple businesses operating in multiple locations are better served by a decentralized compensation system that adequately addresses the often conflicting needs of the different businesses and locations. The divisional autonomy made possible in a decentralized system is conducive to employee involvement and participation in the design and administration of the system.

PERFORMANCE VERSUS SENIORITY

Effects of performance-based pay

Compensation can be based on performance, on membership, on seniority, or on the whims of the supervisor. When compensation is based on performance, there is a clear distinction in pay outcomes between outstanding and mediocre performers, with the former receiving higher pay than the latter. Such a distinction promotes employee perceptions of individual or personal equity, which is the recognition of the individual's performance inputs. Compensation based on performance can have a powerful impact on employee motivation (Gerhart and Milkovich, 1992) because it is fair and equitable and increases the employee's valence of pay and contributes to satisfaction. It also reinforces the performance-outcomes relationship, and thus increases the employee's ($P \Rightarrow O$) expectancy.

Effects of pay that is not based on performance

If compensation is not based on performance, outstanding performers will experience inequity. This experience of inequity will lower their valence of pay and contribute to dissatisfaction, with such consequences as absenteeism and turnover. It will also weaken the performance-outcome relationship and thus decrease employees' ($P \Rightarrow O$) expectancy. For these reasons, pay will neither be effective in motivating the good performers to continue performing well, nor be effective in retaining them in the organization. They will likely leave. The organization will also experience difficulty in attracting good, innovative employees who expect that their performance will be rewarded.

When pay is not contingent on performance, it is contingent on some other behaviour or consideration such as membership behaviour, length of service, or the supervisor's caprices. Pay that is not contingent on performance will promote behaviours that are not conducive to making the organization effective. Nor will the poor performers leave because they receive pay regardless of their performance.

The critical nature and the strategic importance of performance-based pay cannot be overemphasized. Decisions on this issue strike at the very core of managing human resources in a manner that contributes both to organizational effectiveness and to employee satisfaction. For these reasons, Chapters 9 and 10 examine this issue in greater detail.

THE CHOICE OF THE COMPENSATION MIX

Major elements of the compensation mix

Historically, the compensation package in industry consisted mainly of cash—base pay, incentives, merit pay. The benefits component became significant during World War II when wage and price controls to support the war effort placed a freeze on wages and salaries. Conscription to the army, navy, and air force produced acute shortages of available workers for business and industry, compelling organizations to take extraordinary measures to retain their workforce and compete for a smaller labour pool. Prevented from offering higher wages, organizations offered deferred benefits such as life insurance.

After the war, favourable tax treatment for employers and employees, along with the demands of the labour unions, led to the introduction of a plethora of benefits. In 1953-54, benefits in Canadian organizations constituted 15 percent of the gross annual payroll. In 1992, this figure ranged from 26.9 percent to 52 percent of the gross annual payroll (Carlyle, 1994).

Factors influencing compensation mix

What is an ideal mix of cash and benefits in a compensation package? The answer depends on the organization's business strategies and the stage of the life cycle of its products. As was discussed in Chapter 2, the different stages of the product life cycle make differing mixes of cash (pay and incentives) and benefits possible. The other determinants are employee preferences, union demands, legal obligations, and preferential tax treatment as applicable both to employers and employees. Chapter 14 considers the critical issues in the development and implementation of a benefits programme.

Role of benefits in employee motivation

It is important to note two aspects of the role of benefits in employee motivation. First, performance-based benefits programmes are difficult to develop. A dental plan stipulating that the entitlement of cavity fillings or root canal work depended upon an employee's performance appraisal—unrestricted fillings or root canals for an outstanding rating, two fillings and one root canal for a superior rating, and so on—would not be practical. Therefore, it is difficult to assess the potential of some benefits to motivate performance behaviours. Benefits programmes can be developed to motivate membership behaviours. Providing transportation can reduce tardiness and absenteeism. Second, benefits cater to individual need satisfaction and thus contribute to maximizing the total satisfaction of the individual.

THE PROCESS ISSUES

COMMUNICATING THE COMPENSATION SYSTEM 05

This issue can also be framed as secrecy versus openness with regard to pay information. There has been a long-standing practice in the area of compensation administration that pay information is personal and confidential and secrecy should prevail. Is this practice sanctioned by cultural norms? Do organizations keep pay information secret in deference to the wishes of their employees? Or is it in the interest of the organization to keep pay information secret?

Some reasons for pay secrecy (a)

Many managers choose to hide behind the veil of pay secrecy lest they be called upon to explain or defend their pay decisions. If an organization's pay administration practices are indefensible, openness in that organization will have disastrous consequences for employee pay satisfaction as the inequities are disclosed. Do employees wish to keep their pay secret? Studies suggest that employees generally favour secrecy about the individual's salary but favour disclosure of pay ranges and pay administration policies; employees do not mind openness once it has been introduced, provided the pay is fairly and equitably administered (Lawler, 1990). In the management category, the manager who is paid the lowest in each management level has been found to resist openness, probably out of fear that such disclosure would reveal his/her identity (Lawler, 1972). Pay scales and related information of unionized employees have always been made public.

Effects of pay secrecy

Research findings (Lawler, 1972, 1981; Lawler and Jenkins, 1992) suggest that secrecy has two major effects: (1) a lowering of the pay satisfaction of the employee, and (2) a reduction of the employee's motivation to perform.

Employee's pay satisfaction is lowered A strong argument for pay secrecy is that it protects low-paid employees from being dissatisfied with their pay. According to this argument, when low-paid employees do not know that others are being paid more, they will not make unfavourable comparisons and will not be dissatisfied with their pay. This argument does not seem to recognize the reality: employees compare their pay with that of others all the time. In the absence of the actual pay information, employees base their comparisons on speculation and on information generated by the grapevine. As one manager observed: "I don't like to do it, but I can't help but look at other managers' houses, cars, and things and wonder if they are making more money than I do" (Lawler, 1972, 461). Chapter 6 revealed that social comparison is one of the key determinants of pay satisfaction. When employees make comparisons based on inadequate, inaccurate, or grossly exaggerated information, they tend to overestimate the pay of their peers and subordinates and underestimate the pay of their superiors.

The same erroneous perceptions have been found where the size and the frequency of merit raises have been kept secret. On the basis of speculation and rumours, employees overestimated the merit raises of their peers and subordinates and underestimated the merit raises of their superiors. The consequence of misperceptions stemming from secrecy is the employee's belief that his/her pay or merit raise relative to that of his/her peers (the relevant other persons) is unfair and inequitable, a belief that causes him/her to be dissatisfied with the pay or merit raise. In actuality, the employee's pay or merit raise might have been more than that of his/her peers. But in a secret system employees have no way of making the comparison except by speculation and rumour.

Employee's motivation to perform is reduced Secrecy reduces the employee's motivation to perform in three ways: (a) by failing to engender trust, (b) by causing misperceptions of the performance-outcome linkage, and (c) by causing misperceptions of feedback.

Secrecy cannot engender trust In terms of the expectancy theory model, motivation to perform is generated by the employee's beliefs about the performance-outcomes relationship—the $(P \Rightarrow O)$ expectancy—and the equity of outcomes (valence). Beliefs are based on trust. But secrecy cannot engender trust. Therefore, the employee will not have the basis on which to develop the expectancies of $(P \Rightarrow O)$ and valence. Without these expectancies, the employee will not be motivated to perform.

Secrecy distorts the performance-outcomes linkage The merit raise, which is a sign or a score that provides feedback on performance, depends for its effectiveness on employee perceptions that merit raises differentiate between employees according to their performance. In an open system, employee pay perceptions are formed by direct knowledge of the actual situation. If the open pay system is fairly and equitably administered, employees will have access to the reality and will be able to conclude for themselves that the merit raises are equitably administered.

Suppose, however, that the pay system is equitably administered, but there is secrecy in the system. The only source of information is speculation which leads to an overestimation of the size and the frequency of the merit raises of one's peers. When an employee overestimates, his/her own merit raise appears low relative to that of his/her peers. This perception of a low merit raise causes the employee to feel that he/she has been inequitably rewarded for his/her performance. The reality, however, is that the merit raise equitably reflects his/her performance. Only the misperception brought about by secrecy create the feelings of inequity and obliterate the motivational effects of a fairly administered merit pay plan.

A study (Lawler, 1972) of the merit plan of managers in one organization illustrates this phenomenon. The average merit raise, six per cent, was not disclosed to the managers because of a pay secrecy policy. Most managers, overestimating their peers' pay raises, speculated that the average merit raise was eight per cent. Any manager who received an eight per cent raise concluded that it was merely average. Such a conclusion demotivated the manager who believed that his/her performance was above average and deserved an above-average raise. Only the secrecy policy prevented the manager from experiencing the motivational force of the merit raise which was more than the average recognizing an above-average performance, and therefore equitable and fair.

Secrecy does not give clear feedback on performance The job characteristics model discussed in Chapter 6 demonstrates how feedback contributes to the job holder's experiencing internal work motivation. Job performance feedback has a significant impact on the employee's $(E \Rightarrow P)$ and $(P \Rightarrow O)$ expectancies, as well as on the employee's valence of outcomes.

Among the many forms of feedback an employee receives in the course of performance, pay is direct, visible, and concrete. When an individual receives high pay relative to his/her peers, that pay is a positive feedback to signify that his/her performance is outstanding or superior relative to that of his/her peers. A low pay relative to one's peers is a negative feedback, indicating that the performance relative to one's peers is unsatisfactory.

An open pay system allows individuals to make realistic and factual pay comparisons that give individuals accurate feedback, either positive or negative. A secret pay system prevents factual pay comparisons. The overestimation of a peer's pay relative to one's own pay causes the individual to perceive his/her pay to be low and automatically provides negative feedback. Such negative feedback reduces the motivational effects of pay. Furthermore, such feedback is a message to the individual that his/her performance needs to be improved—a perplexing message, because the individual is performing well. Pay secrecy has the insidious effect of providing negative feedback not warranted by the actual situation.

Conditions for and extent of pay disclosure

Pay secrecy seriously inhibits the motivational effects of pay, causing employees to be dissatisfied with pay and reducing their motivation to perform. Should all organizations make their pay system public? An organization whose pay history is riddled with inequitable pay practices should first strive to make improvements in this area before going public. When an organization is ready to make pay public, it is usually advised to disclose the pay range gradually, revealing the minimum, the midpoint, and the maximum of the different pay grades.

The organization should also involve employees in implementing compensation techniques such as performance appraisals, job evaluations, and salary surveys. A good practice is to involve employees in the design of the merit pay programme. As employees develop confidence that the programme is operating in a fair manner, information on the size, the frequency, and the recipients of merit raises can be made public. The pay level of individuals is the last information to be made public (Lawler, 1990).

INVOLVING EMPLOYEES IN DECISION MAKING (b)

There are two aspects to employee involvement in decision making: (1) involvement in the design of the compensation system, and (2) involvement in the administration of the compensation system. A complete discussion of these two aspects should include a consideration of *why* employees should be involved and *how* employees should be involved in decision making.

Why should employees be involved in decision making?

Employee involvement in decision making means that management does not unilaterally impose a particular compensation programme or technique but actively seeks and genuinely considers the employees' views and concerns about making the programme fair and equitable. Why should employees be involved in decision making? In general, employee involvement leads to increased organizational effectiveness and employee satisfaction.

Employee involvement in compensation system design

In this section the question of why employees should be involved in decision making is addressed with regard to employee involvement in the design of a compensation system. Examples of such programmes and techniques are performance-based pay and performance appraisals, incentive systems and gainsharing plans, job evaluation techniques, development of job and salary structures, salary surveys, and benefits programmes (box A of Figure 7.1).

Involvement increases system information and commitment

As shown in Figure 7.1, when employees are involved in designing programmes and techniques, they receive information from the other participants in the design effort. In addition, as equal partners, they feel inclined to provide their own insights and to raise the questions and concerns of the constituency they represent, thus increasing the information pool about the programme or technique (box 1). The unrestricted flow of information and participation produces two effects. First, it gives employees a better and fuller understanding of the programme or technique. Second, it makes them experience the feeling of ownership of the programme, which they no longer view as just another management programme; rather, they feel that they share the responsibility for its development (box 2).

Involvement increases trust of system

The expertise they have now acquired makes them confident that they control the programme. Responsibility and control are critical elements of ownership. When employees feel they control a programme, they are more open to change and to new ideas because they have the responsibility and the competence to propose appropriate modifications that will achieve fairness and equity. Ownership of a programme naturally leads to commitment to it. Involvement and participation in programme design increase the employees' understanding of the relevant issues of the programme and also make employees responsible and committed to it (box 2).

In other words, the programme is theirs. Not surprisingly, employees trust the system (box 3). They can gain a proper understanding of the programme and because they are an integral part of the structure and process, they have the capability and the mandate to exercise whatever controls are necessary to ensure that the programme contributes to fairness and equity. In this way, employee

Figure 7.1: The Effects of Employee Involvement in Decision Making

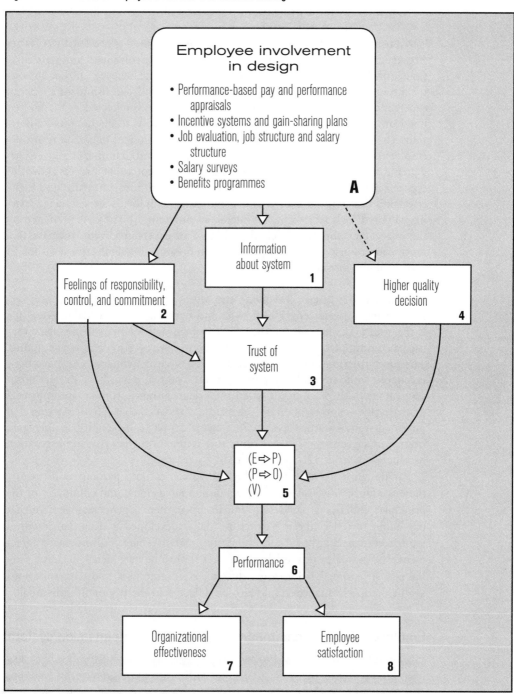

Source: Adapted from Lawler (1981).

involvement enables employees to satisfy themselves that the system procedures are consistent with the principle of procedural justice.

Involvement: quality decisions, employee satisfaction and organizational effectiveness Do employee involvement and participation contribute to decisions of a higher quality? Some believe that they so contribute only when employees are knowledgeable and can bring some special expertise to the process. This is not always the case as is reflected by the broken line from the Employee involvement in design (box A) to Higher quality decisions (box 4). However, if a higher quality decision is one that improves employee perceptions of the fairness and equity of a programme, employee participation should always lead to higher quality decisions. The process shown in Figure 7.1 reveals that employee ownership and commitment, trust, and higher quality decisions all contribute to enhancing employees' expectancies relating to $(E \Leftrightarrow P)$, $(P \Leftrightarrow O)$, and the valence of outcomes (box 5). As predicted by the expectancy theory model, the increase in expectancies will increase the, motivation to perform (box 6), resulting in organizational effectiveness (box 7) and employee satisfaction (box 8).

Research findings Involving employees in designing compensation system enhances it (Lawler, 1990; Lawler and Jenkins, 1992). A striking example is the study (Lawler and Jenkins, 1976) of a small manufacturing plant that used a committee of workers and managers to develop a job and pay structure. The new structure resulted in increased salary costs, which would have been inevitable without employee participation. The real pay-off for the organization came within six months when the organization's turnover rate improved dramatically. A survey of employee attitudes revealed that job satisfaction had increased from 44.4 per cent to 72.2 per cent, pay satisfaction had increased from 7.1 per cent to 37.5 per cent, and satisfaction with pay administration had increased from 12.7 per cent to 54.5 per cent.

Pay design lends itself to employee involvement and participation because there is a fairly universal acceptance among management and employees of the principles underlying pay design. For instance, there is general agreement that pay ought to reflect the job structure that is developed in accordance with a job-based or person-based job evaluation system. There is also general agreement that pay rates in the labour market should be considered in developing the pay structure. Barring some differences in emphasis, most organizations accept that performance should also be reflected in the pay of an individual.

Employee Involvement in administering the compensation system (d)

High employee satisfaction and increased organziational effectiveness have also been found when employees participate in the administration of the compensation system by making decisions that set their own pay or that of their peers.

Employee decisions on peer's pay Employee decisions on the pay of one's peers are quite common in organizations that have adopted the practice of multi-skilling or skill-based pay and have structured the work into autonomous work teams. For example, in the Shell Canada Chemical Company plant in Sarnia, Ontario, members of the work team evaluate each other's performance and make decisions on the merit pay of their peers. In other organizations with similar Quality of Working Life programmes, employees also decide whether their peers have acquired the needed proficiency level in a skill. These decisions determine whether employees will move to the next higher pay level. The experience of organizations that let employees set their peers' pay is that the employees can be trusted to make responsible decisions. Furthermore, the pay satisfaction of these employees is quite high (Lawler and Jenkins, 1992).

Conditions favouring employee decisions on peers' pay The participation of employees in decisions on peers' pay is more feasible provided an appropriate procedure exists to ensure that these decisions are made in groups. Group decisions are fair and equitable when based on predetermined performance standards that are developed by the group itself (Lawler and Jenkins, 1992). This procedure leads to an effective pay decision, engenders trust, promotes autonomy and responsibility, and provides opportunities for employee growth and development.

Employee decisions on own pay Not as widespread as the practice of allowing employees to set the pay of their peers is the practice of allowing employees to set their own pay, possibly because organizations have difficulty trusting their employees to make unbiased decisions. Allowing employees to set their own pay works best under certain conditions. First, the organization should be small and the relationship between management and employees characterized by openness and trust. In a small company, employees can see and evaluate one another's contributions to the attainment of the company's objectives and, thereby, satisfy themselves that the pay raises do indeed reflect performance.

Second, employees should know and understand the nature and the economics of the business. Such knowledge and understanding give employees a better appreciation of the impact of their pay decisions on the costs and margins of the business. Third, the pay decision should be made public. The realization that pay is made public operates as a restraining mechanism on employees who might be tempted to set salaries that adversely affect the continued operations of the business.

In large organizations these conditions do not generally exist, and employees have difficulty recognizing that their interests are closely linked with the interests of the organization. In the absence of such a recognition, an employee's pay decision in setting his/her own pay might be guided only by self-interest to the detriment of the interest of the organization.

THE ROLE OF STRATEGIC AND PROCESS ISSUES IN COMPENSATION DESIGN AND ADMINISTRATION

Table 7.3 summarizes the role of strategic and process issues in the design and administration of the compensation system.

The choices in the three groups of issues contribute to the effective design and administration of the total compensation system. It cannot be overemphasized that the test for a correct choice of the options involved is to determine whether, as a result of the choice, the reward item is perceived by employees to be salient, valued, and contingent on the desired work behaviours.

Table 7.3: Strategic & Process Issues: Role in Compensation System

Issue	Role in Compensation System
Strategic macro-level issues	
• Compensation Philosophy	Decisions on this category of
• Process versus Mechanics	issues provide the compensation
• Job-content-based versus	system its rationale, purpose,
Person-based Job evaluation	and direction.
Strategic micro-level issues	
• Internal versus External Equity	Deriving their meaning from the decisions
• Relevant Market Data	on the strategic macro-level issues in this
• Centralization versus Decentralization	category, the choices have a significant
• Performance versus Seniority	impact on employee motivation, pay
• Compensation Mix	satisfaction, and job satisfaction.
Process issues	
• Communicating the Compensation	Determine the effectiveness of the
System	strategic issues—in particular,
• Employee Participation in Compensation	the implementation of decisions
System Design and Administration	on the micro-level issues.

SUMMARY

This chapter has discussed the strategic and process issues in compensation. These issues provide a set of critical alternative options that an organization must choose when it designs a total compensation system. Decisions on these issues will provide the direction for, and determine the effectiveness of, the compensation system. In general, the organization's business strategies and internal work culture are the criteria for decisions on the alternative options contained in these issues.

The compensation philosophy, together with the other macro-level strategic issues (process vs. mechanics, job-based vs. person-based job evaluation, and means vs. end), provides the rationale, purpose, and direction for the compensation system. Decisions on the micro-level strategic issues (internal vs. external equity, choice of labour markets and market position, performance vs. seniority, and compensation mix) have an impact on employee motivation. Choices in the process issues (communication and employee participation in decision making) influence the effectiveness of the strategic decisions, particularly in regard to the micro-level strategic issues. Thus, the strategic and process issues taken together play a pivotal role in the effective design and administration of the total compensation system.

KEY TERMS

centralized compensation system

compensation philosophy

decentralized compensation system

job-content-based evaluation system

pay secrecy

person-based evaluation system

process issues in compensation

strategic issues in compensation

REVIEW AND DISCUSSION QUESTIONS

1. What are the major strategic and process issues? Explain why these issues are critical in compensation system design.

2. Distinguish between the strategic and process issues.

3. Identify and explain the criteria that must be borne in mind when deciding on the options inherent in strategic and process issues.

4. What useful purpose does a compensation philosophy serve in an organization? What are some of the items that should be included in a compensation philosophy?

5. "An effective compensation system should include a judicious balance of mechanics and process issues." Why?

6. Distinguish between the job-content-based and the person-based job evaluation system. What are the dysfunctional effects of the job-content-based job evaluation system?

7. How can an organization ensure that its compensation system does not become an end in itself?

8. An organization has three basic options: to maintain both internal and external equity; to maintain internal equity only; to maintain external equity only. Discuss the consequences of each option.

9. With regard to salary surveys, what are the right market data? Is one survey for all jobs in the organization adequate? Should employees be involved?

10. Explain the conditions under which

    • a centralized compensation system is more appropriate.

    • a decentralized compensation system is more appropriate.

11. Discuss the consequences of using seniority rather than performance as a basis for compensation decisions.

12. What are some of the conditions that determine the mix of cash and benefits in a compensation package?

13. Discuss the effects of pay secrecy. What are the advantages and risks in an open policy as opposed to a secret pay policy?

14. Employee involvement in decision making has been found to contribute to both organizational effectiveness and employee satisfaction. Discuss why this is so.

Deciding on Strategic and Process Issues in Compensation System Design

Objective

To identify and make decisions on the strategic and process issues that contribute to the effectiveness of the organization's compensation system.

Procedure

Note: The case analysis of Roasted Duck Delicacies Limited of Chapter 2 is a prerequisite for this exercise. First, do activities 1 to 4 individually. Then discuss your decisions in your work group, and arrive at a group consensus, keeping note of the major differences.

1. Refer to the case Roasted Duck Delicacies Limited (RDDL) in Chapter 2.

2. Identify the strategic and process issues that should be considered in designing a total compensation system for RDDL.

3. Examine the alternative options under each strategy and each process issue you have identified, and decide on the option that will enable RDDL to craft a coherent and purposeful compensation system.

4. Write up a compensation philosophy for RDDL.

5. Each group reports its decisions to the class. The class discussion could include a consideration of the reasons for the recommendations. Specifically:

   • Do the choices on the strategic and process issues support the business strategies of RDDL that were identified when you analysed the case in Chapter 2?

   • Are the choices consistent with the internal work culture of RDDL as it was identified when you analysed the case in Chapter 2?

CHAPTER 8

Promoting

Organizational

Membership Behaviours

OVERVIEW

The conceptual framework, developed in previous chapters, is now utilized to design reward programmes and practices that promote organizational membership behaviours such as regular attendance and staying with the organization.

LEARNING OBJECTIVES

► To identify some of the effects of employee absenteeism on the Canadian economy and organizations.

► To recognize the personal and job factors related to absenteeism.

► To explain the reasons for absenteeism, using the expectancy theory model of motivation.

► To develop practical proposals for controlling absenteeism and tardiness, with an emphasis on the use of positive rewards to motivate regular attendance.

► To explain the reasons for employee turnover, using the expectancy theory model of motivation.

► To develop practical proposals for controlling turnover, with an emphasis on the role of the equity of the compensation system.

INTRODUCTION

No organization is satisfied with merely attracting qualified and competent individuals. It also endeavours to retain them and wants them to report to work regularly. Stated differently, the organization's major preoccupation is to reduce absenteeism and turnover among its workforce. The questions this chapter addresses are: How can rewards be used to reduce absenteeism? and How can rewards be used to reduce turnover? The responses to these questions will explore the variety of factors that are related to these questions, and propose practical strategies whose effectiveness is predicted by the conceptual framework discussed in the previous chapters.

HOW CAN REWARDS BE USED TO REDUCE ABSENTEEISM?

This issue will be examined by considering the problem and the effects of absenteeism, reasons for absenteeism, and the methods of controlling absenteeism, with a focus on the role of the compensation programme in the control effort.

PROBLEM AND EFFECTS OF ABSENTEEISM

- A 1980 report suggested that absenteeism cost the Canadian economy an estimated $7.7 billion a year (*The Gazette*, 1980); thirteen years later, this figure is placed at $15 billion (*The Financial Post*, 1993);

- Absenteeism has been estimated to lower the aggregate productivity levels by 1 to 2 percentage points (Booth, 1993);

- A survey of 400 organizations found (Booth, 1993) that absenteeism:

    – had increased in 30 percent of the organizations;

    – was considered to be a problem in 32 percent of the organizations;

    – in one company averaged 9.6 absent days per employee per year which resulted in direct costs of $15.4 million;

- A more recent survey (Carlyle, 1994) found that 62 percent of the 396 Canadian companies that responded did not have a formal attendance management program.

- Absenteeism is a significant issue as these statistics attest. They do not fully reveal all the effects of the problem. These do not portray a host of other detrimental effects to organizations such as:

    – idle machinery and unused plant capacity;

    – lower productivity;

    – disrupted work schedules;

    – increased cost in finding and substituting untrained labour;

    – increased spoilage and poor product quality;

    – increased overtime costs of carrying a higher inventory to offset production foul-ups brought about by absenteeism; and

    – the inability to maintain contracted delivery schedules.

To put these effects on productivity into proper perspective, it is useful to note that according to the Organization for Economic Cooperation and Development surveys of productivity growth in the 24 OECD countries, Canada was very lowly ranked (Booth, 1993).

REASONS FOR ABSENTEEISM

Understanding Absenteeism: The Expectancy Theory Approach

The phenomenon of absenteeism illustrates a rupture of the bonds that tie the employee to an organization and motivate him/her to attend. Understanding absenteeism means understanding an employee's attendance motivation. The expectancy theory model provides a useful conceptual framework for explaining attendance motivation.

As can be seen in Figure 8.1, employees will be motivated to put in the effort to attend work when:

(a) they believe that they can attend;

(b) they believe that when they attend they will receive outcomes; and

(c) they value these outcomes.

In other words, their attendance motivation is a function of their effort⇨ attendance and attendance⇨outcomes expectancies, and the valence of the outcomes. The terms are added and multiplied as discussed in the expectancy theory model in Chapter 5. This section considers the determinants of the expectancies and how they influence the attendance motivation process.

The Effort⇨Attendance Expectancy

Actual situation Employees' effort⇨attendance expectancy is determined primarily by their perceptions of the *actual situation*. Several factors or circumstances in the actual situation can prevent or make attendance difficult, such as the employees' health, family obligations, and the availability of transportation. These factors can reduce the employees' belief that their effort will enable them to attend work.

Employee illness and accidents are a frequent cause of absenteeism, particularly as the employee advances in age. Most illnesses are the result of natural causes but can sometimes be the result of drug and alcohol abuse. If such abuse is related to the monotonous and repetitive nature of the work or the stressful conditions under which the work is done, the illness becomes the special concern and responsibility of the organization. Illnesses and accidents that render an employee unable to attend work can be categorized as involuntary absence. Not included as illness is the voluntary absence that masquerades as illness. Some years ago a newsletter, the *Morgan Guaranty Survey* (n.d.), reported that a company experienced a 43 per cent rise in absence due to sickness within a

Figure 8.1: Expectancy Theory Model for Explaining Attendance Motivation

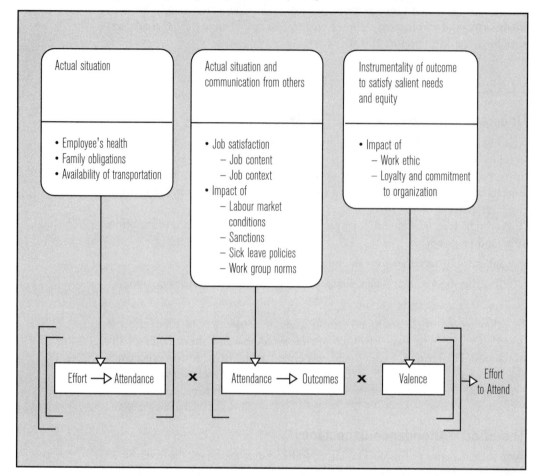

five-year period. A close examination revealed that a substantial improvement in sick leave benefits during that period had apparently provided employees who were faking illness with positive incentives. This form of absence will be discussed further in considering the impact of sick leave and benefits.

Family obligations often work as an impediment to regular attendance at work (Booth, 1993). This appears to be so more in the case of married women who, regardless of the job held, are traditionally expected to attend to the care of their sick children. With husbands now increasingly involved in the raising of their children through such benefits as paternity leave, the absenteeism of married females will likely decrease. Absenteeism due to family obligations can be classified as involuntary or unavoidable absence.

Availability of transportation can also make attending work difficult. This is especially true when transport services are disrupted by bad weather or by the strikes of public transportation employees. Absence from work because of transportation problems is often unavoidable and involuntary.

The Attendance⇨Outcomes Expectancy

The critical determinants of this expectancy are the *actual situation* and *communication from others*.

Actual situation Examples of factors which constitute the actual situation are: the prospects of satisfaction with the job content and the job context resulting from work attendance; the impact of labour market conditions; sanctions when one is absent; and sick leave policies. These factors affect the employee's expectancy of the type of outcomes which will follow when he or she attends work.

The job content influences an individual's expectancy of personal work outcomes when he or she attends work. As discussed in Chapter 6, internal work motivation, including the motivation to attend work, is influenced by core job characteristics. Employees with high growth needs and the requisite knowledge and skill will be motivated by an enriched job. Such a job makes employees want to go to work, because it provides them with an opportunity to experience challenge and feelings of being needed in the job. If the core characteristics of an enriched job are missing, however, the employee's attendance motivation will be severely affected, and the likelihood of voluntary absence will greatly increase. If dissatisfaction from the unfulfilling job is intolerable, the individual may engage in a job search that will cause absence from work.

Dissatisfaction with the **job context**—working conditions, pay, co-workers, supervisors—weakens the employee's motivation to attend work. Absenteeism under these conditions can also be considered voluntary and is generally a device to redress the inequity experienced by the employee, particularly pay inequity. Voluntary absenteeism and job dissatisfaction are closely associated. When employees are satisfied with both the content and context of the job, regular work attendance becomes an occasion for experiencing outcomes that are attractive and desirable. But, when attendance becomes an occasion for experiencing dissatisfaction, as is usually the case when employees are not satisfied with the job content or the job context, absenteeism is usually the result.

The labour market conditions can operate to alleviate or worsen the absenteeism that results from job dissatisfaction. For instance, when unemployment is high, job search activities will be reduced and the rate of absenteeism will be lower; on the other hand, low unemployment could increase absenteeism.

Sanctions for absenteeism can also serve to reduce voluntary absences. Examples of sanctions for absenteeism are: the docking of pay, undesirable assignments, and depriving absentees the opportunity to earn overtime pay.

Sick leave policies sometimes control absenteeism and sometimes contribute to its increase. The experience of one Montreal organization provides a graphic illustration of how a sick leave policy can have the unintended effect of increasing absenteeism. The policy granted employees 15 paid sick days per year, but the unused days could be accumulated and cashed on retirement. Despite this incentive, the average rate of absenteeism did not decrease and cost the organization $11 million (Johns, 1980). Younger employees preferred to use the sick days at the time for casual absences rather than benefit from them later on at retirement.

Communication from others   A major factor in this category is the norms in the work group. Employees' perceptions of these norms provide an indication of the type of outcome—that is, acceptance or rejection by group members when they attend.

Work group norms are a powerful factor but they function as a two-edged sword. If the norms of a highly cohesive work group are supportive of regular attendance, employee absence in that group will be low. But if group norms operate to socially ostracize members who attend regularly, absenteeism will be high.

The Valence of Outcomes

Before the valence of outcomes is discussed, it is important to recognize that the attendance-outcomes linkage and the absence-outcomes linkage are really two sides of the same phenomenon. The valence of outcomes, whether the outcomes are from attendance or from absenteeism, is determined by the instrumentality of outcomes to satisfy needs and the equity of outcomes.

Instrumentality to satisfy needs

When employees with high growth needs attend work, they anticipate that they will be working in an enriched job that will be instrumental in satisfying their growth needs. But if these same employees are required to attend work on a monotonous, repetitive job that is low on the core job characteristics, they will find their growth needs frustrated, and are likely to resort to absence from work in order to indulge in more autonomous activities. Absenteeism in such cases becomes instrumental in providing outcomes that they value. By remaining absent from work, they are also able to avoid outcomes that they find unattractive and do not value.

There are many occasions when, despite the negative valence of outcomes from attending work (unsatisfactory job content or job context), employees might not resort to absenteeism. Their work ethic, a compelling belief in the goodness of work itself, might induce in them a moral compulsion to attend work. Also, employees' loyalty and commitment to the organization's objectives might compel them to attend work even if they find the actual job tasks to be repulsive and unpleasant. Attending work for reasons of work ethic or organizational commitment generates outcomes that are valued because they are instrumental in satisfying salient needs born of the individual's personal value system. These positive valences far outweigh the negative valence of the outcomes of an unsatisfactory job content or job context.

Equity of Outcomes

Employees also resort to absenteeism in order to reduce the inequities they might experience in the job context, particularly in the area of compensation. This point was discussed at some length in Chapter 6, where we considered the determinants of pay satisfaction and the consequences of pay dissatisfaction.

METHODS OF CONTROLLING ABSENTEEISM

Control of involuntary absenteeism

The preceding analysis of the reasons for absenteeism provides a useful framework for developing practical proposals for controlling absenteeism. The discussion of the effort⇨attendance expectancy highlights the need to differentiate between involuntary and voluntary absences. The former are unavoidable, the latter are avoidable. Absences caused by illness and accidents, by the necessity to attend to family obligations, or by the unavailability of transportation are involuntary, unavoidable absences. Nevertheless, some organizational interventions in this area might help. For instance, drug or alcohol abuse and the resulting illnesses or accidents might be related to the nature of the work. An employee counselling or related programme, such as the now commonly used employee assistance programme (EAP), would be an appropriate way to address this kind of situation. Along with the EAP, efforts should be made to identify and eliminate the work-related sources of the problem.

Control of voluntary absenteeism

Controlling absenteeism, particularly where there is a high incidence of voluntary or avoidable absences, needs approaches that are specifically designed to address the cause of the absence. The approach that is adopted must be specific both to the organization and to the employee. A considerable burden is placed on the ingenuity of managers to develop strategies that are appropriate for their employees. The strategies that will be discussed in this section are: flex time, and a shorter work week; transportation facilities; job design; job context satisfaction; sick leave policies; the use of sanctions; and the use of positive rewards.

Flex Time, Shorter Work Week

Absences caused by the need to meet family obligations have been reduced to some extent by day-care centres situated in the workplace. Some organizations have introduced flex time and a four-day, 40-hour work week. Flex time gives employees the flexibility to attend to some of their family obligations. Flex time also eliminates the employee tendency to covert tardiness into a full day's absence. Attending to personal matters may cause an employee to be late for work by an hour or so. If the organization's attendance policy requires that employees' pay be docked for the period they are late, an employee might decide to be absent for the whole day since the additional loss of pay will not appear to be especially painful.

With a shorter work week, the organization still receives 40 hours of work, but the employee gets an additional day off for attending to personal and family obligations. Organizations must consider the possibility of fatigue that the extended work day might cause and the effects it might have on absenteeism or productivity.

Transportation Facilities

Attendance problems created by transportation difficulties are sometimes addressed by a company-organized shuttle bus, especially where the plant is not adequately served by public transportation. Some organizations encourage their employees to organize car pools and as an incentive provide special parking facilities to these employees. These measures, where feasible, should alleviate the problems of absenteeism and tardiness.

Job Design

A well-designed job contributes greatly to attendance. Hence, job redesign is appropriate when a job diagnostic survey reveals a job profile that is low on the core job characteristics. Special attention should also be paid to increasing an employee's commitment to the organization. Such commitment has a beneficial effect on attendance. The rationale and the implementing procedures for job redesign have been discussed in Chapter 6. Employee training and career development programmes should also be considered for promoting job satisfaction.

Job Context Satisfaction

Dissatisfaction with the job context requires several interventions, depending upon the aspect of the context that causes the dissatisfaction.

Pay inequities The most frequent cause is pay—more specifically, the perceived inequities of the compensation system—which could be in the area of personal, internal, or external equity. Specific recommendations to address such inequities will be discussed in later chapters when compensation programmes and techniques are considered for: performance-based pay to ensure personal equity (Chapter 9); job evaluation to address internal equity (Chapter 11); and salary and benefit surveys to ensure external equity (Chapter 13).

Organizational stressors   The more common of these, an oppressive supervision style, can have detrimental effects on employee attendance. Efforts to remove these stressors, possibly through appropriate training for supervisors and managers, will help to reduce absenteeism. Furthermore, employees are generally not satisfied with autocratic supervision. In an autocratic environment, control of absenteeism is obtained through incentive plans to promote attendance. In a democratic environment, employees experience relatively greater job satisfaction. Control of absenteeism can be accomplished through plans that involve the satisfaction of the higher-level needs. This point will be considered again when the use of positive rewards to promote attendance is discussed.

Working environment–physical conditions, work norms   Improving the physical working environment (e.g., by illumination, by building design) contributes to reducing absenteeism. Closely related to the work environment are work group norms, which can facilitate or punish regular attendance. An organizational culture should promote the development of work norms that support regular attendance. Autonomous work teams created by Quality of Working Life and related employee involvement programmes are usually successful in developing work norms that bring pressure on members to attend work regularly. Although the work team is given the freedom and resources to achieve its objectives, it is also held accountable for them. Any behaviour by a member that hinders the group's effectiveness is subjected to sanctions whose efficacy is ensured by the remarkably high degree of cohesiveness in the group.

Job security   Another aspect of the work context that affects work attendance is employee perception of job security. Open and honest communication on matters that threaten job security will tend to reduce the uncertainty that often causes employees to search for alternative job opportunities. The elimination of the need for job searches will contribute to reducing absenteeism.

Sick Leave Policies

Set guidelines   An organization's sick leave policies need to be carefully reviewed. A useful set of guidelines would be:

(a) clearly specify the exact entitlement of the paid sick leave (e.g., 7, 10, or 12 paid sick days per year);

(b) allow employees to accumulate or carry forward unused sick days;

(c) pay only from the second day of absence (Ng 1989).

(d) consider alternative benefits such as short-term disability plans.

Specify entitlement   When the entitlement is clearly specified, there is a greater likelihood that decisions on this issue will be consistent, and hence, fair and equitable. Also, a clearly specified entitlement can be better monitored.

Permit accumulation   Employees who are allowed to accumulate unused sick days are encouraged to utilize them for genuine illnesses, either now or in the future. An organization that does not permit such accumulation fosters an irresponsible use of sick days, for casual absences, particularly towards the end of the year when the entitlement lapses.

Pay only from the second day of absence   The rationale for not paying for the first day of absence is to discourage the use of sick days for casual absences. A casual absence is expensive, particularly if employees are on a four-day, 40-hour week. The organization also sends a message that sick days are for genuine illness and not for occasional indispositions.

Alternative plans   An organization might consider more generous long-term illness or disability benefits that employees can use when necessary in place of the fixed, annual entitlement of sick days, which tend to be used for casual absences. In one organization, the accumulation plan was replaced by an insured short-term disability plan with positive results (Booth, 1993).

Use of Sanctions

Many organizations use sanctions to control absenteeism. The objective of sanctions is primarily to control casual absences of a short duration.

Features of a sanctions program   A programme of sanctions requires that a detailed record of attendance be kept, and every absence is checked to ensure that the employee has complied with reporting procedures and produced the medical documentation required. Failure to comply with stringent reporting procedures exposes the employee to a host of measures ranging from docking of pay to disciplinary measures that in cases of chronic absenteeism might even lead to termination.

Are sanctions effective?   A programme that is well publicized, consistently and uniformly applied, and based on a rigorous monitoring of absences tends to be effective. Such a programme, however, controls only casual absences, because ingenious employees soon find creative ways around the system, such as staying absent for longer periods that fall outside the scope of the sanctions programme. Thus, sanctions reduce the frequency of absences, but the fewer absences are of a longer duration.

Problems with sanctions   There are two basic problems with sanctions: (1) the measurement problem; and (2) the side-effects, which are inevitable in any programme based on punitive measures.

The Measurement Problem   The following can be used to measure absenteeism: (1) the percentage time-lost index; (2) the frequency index; (3) the blue Monday index; (4) the worst-day index.

1. The percentage time-lost index is a measure of the absence level expressed as a percentage of time lost from the total available working time. The time lost includes both voluntary and involuntary absences and therefore covers long-term sicknesses as well as casual absences. The percentage time-lost index, which is weighted heavily in favour of long-term unavoidable absences, does not provide a realistic picture of voluntary absences which are usually the target of the sanctions programme. Nevertheless, the percentage time-lost is a good indicator of the total economic cost to the organization.

2. The frequency index is a count of the number of times an absence of a given length has occurred per employee. The length of absence could be one day, two days, three days, and so forth. For example, Victor has had 5 two-day absences in the last 12 months. The frequency index gives greater weight to shorter absences, which are more likely to be the target of the sanctions programme. Note that the organization must question which is preferable—10 one-day absences or 3 three-day absences.

3. The blue Monday index keeps track of absences that occur on Mondays and Fridays. Because this index emphasizes casual absences on predetermined weekdays, but ignores absences on the other days of the week, it does not provide a complete picture of all casual absences. Nevertheless, if the index serves to highlight a historical pattern in the organization, it might be worthwhile. For example, assembly-line workers in the auto industry have been known to have a high blue Monday index.

4. The worst-day index attempts to document which days of the week have the best and worst record of absences.

   Which measures are appropriate for a sanctions programme? No one answer is universally applicable to all organizations. Each organization must keep detailed absence records, from which absence patterns will emerge. An analysis of the emergent patterns relative to their economic and non-economic costs should help the organization to identify one or more absence patterns that need to be subjected to the control processes of the sanctions programme.

The Side-Effects of Sanctions   Punitive measures (docking of pay, stringent administrative controls) are effective in reducing absenteeism, but they also produce a variety of side-effects, for example, an increase in grievance rates, vandalism, the sabotage of operations, and stress on the managers and supervisors who are required to implement the programme. The poor climate produced by sanctions could lead to an increase in turnover. In any event, sanctions do not reduce the average rate of absenteeism; they only reduce the frequency of absences. For these reasons, the use of positive rewards is preferred to the use of sanctions.

Use of Positive Rewards

Designing rewards—contingency and valence In this approach, employees who put in the desired attendance at work receive rewards that reinforce the attendance behaviour. This reinforcement will be achieved only if the reward is designed in such a manner that it is directly linked to the desired level of attendance that is within the reach of the employees. In other words, the required attendance level to earn the reward must be capable of being achieved. For example, suppose the reward is set for perfect attendance for a 12-month period. If an employee happens to miss work in the first couple of months, he/she will not be eligible for the reward and the reward will cease to be an incentive for this employee. The qualifying attendance period needs to be short. "The best documented successful cases have used time periods of 13 weeks or less—usually much less, ranging down to a week" (Johns, 1980, 56).

The reward must be valued by the employees. Some employees prefer time off credited to their vacation; others prefer cash. Furthermore, employees should be involved in the design of the rewards. Such employees have a much better attendance record than employees who are not given the opportunity to participate (Lawler and Hackman, 1969).

Lotteries as rewards Rewards for perfect attendance can also take the form of lotteries. Employees who have perfect attendance for a predetermined period qualify to have their names drawn for a lottery prize.

Recognition The recognition of perfect attendance by one's peers and supervisors is also effective in promoting attendance.

Overtime policy The overtime policy of the organization should be carefully reviewed, since it has the potential to promote either absenteeism or perfect attendance. For example, a policy that allows employees who have had a paid casual absence to catch up with their work on overtime at the premium rate of pay encourages employees to be absent. If the opportunity to work overtime and to earn the premium pay is given only to perfect attenders, the overtime policy rewards attendance. However, overtime should not be an imposition on an employee who attends regularly if for some reason that employee is unwilling to work overtime.

Special assignments These assignments must be perceived by employees to be particularly attractive and should be given to those with an organizationally acceptable attendance record.

Conditions which favour effective control of absenteeism

A variety of proposals for controlling absenteeism have been reviewed. The effectiveness of the proposals is enhanced when superior-subordinate trust is high and when workers' initial experiences with the measures have been positive. In controlling absenteeism, the fundamental first step that managers should take is to recognize the severity of the problem and accept their responsibility for confronting and controlling it. Managers should be evaluated on their initiatives and efforts in controlling absenteeism.

HOW CAN REWARDS BE USED TO REDUCE TURNOVER?

Employee turnover—types and consequences

Employee turnover usually hurts the organization. The costs of turnover range from the cost of replacing the employee (costs of recruitment, selection, and training) to the costs resulting from loss of revenue or the inefficiency and ineffectiveness of operating an understaffed organization. Of course, not all turnover is undesirable. The departure of poor performers is a blessing, as is the departure of employees who can, without detriment to the organization's effectiveness, be replaced by low-paid employees. In practice, this last scenario is rare, and highly improbable in a well-managed organization where high pay is commensurate with the employee's contribution to attaining the organization's objectives. Most organizations strive to minimize the turnover rate because they cannot afford the luxury of an unstable and inexperienced workforce.

Why do employees stay with or leave an organization?

A frequent response to this question is job dissatisfaction (Hom, Caranikas-Walker, Prussia, and Griffeth, 1992). But some dissatisfied employees leave the organization while others stay. With what aspect of the job must an employee be dissatisfied before leaving the organization? As discussed in Chapter 6, pay dissatisfaction, an important element of job dissatisfaction, does not necessarily lead to turnover; on the contrary, it could lead to a desire for higher pay and in turn to higher performance if pay is performance based. Therefore, a more complete and satisfactory treatment of the issue of turnover must consider related factors, for example, job content, job context, and external environmental factors.

The expectancy theory approach to managing turnover

As can be seen in Figure 8.2, employees will be motivated to put in the effort to stay with an organization when

Figure 8.2: Expectancy Theory Model for Explaining Organization Tenure

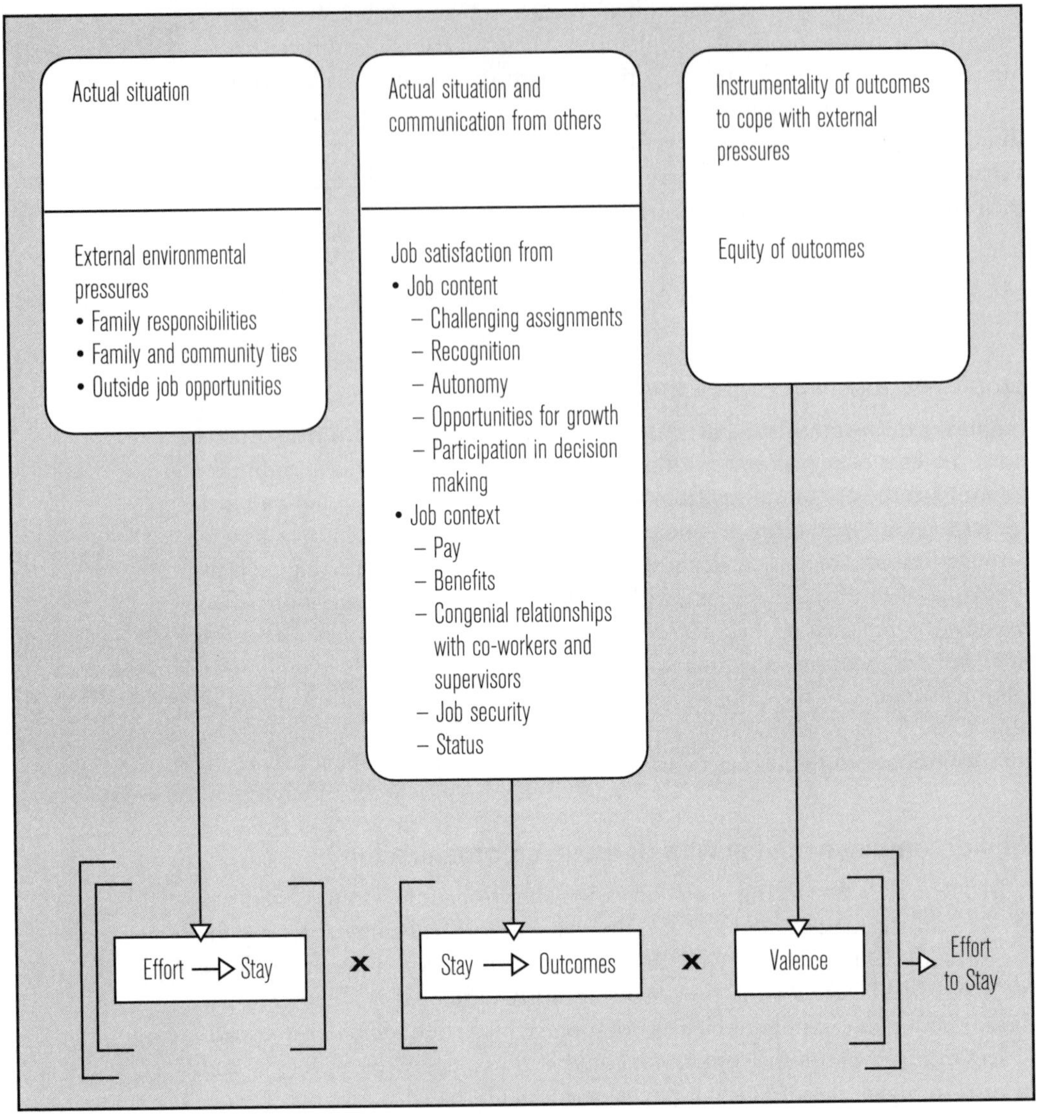

(a) they believe that they can stay;

(b) they believe that when they stay they will receive a set of outcomes; and

(c) they value these outcomes.

In other words, their motivation to stay is a function of their effort⇨stay and stay⇨outcomes expectancies, and the valence of the outcomes. The terms are added and multiplied, as discussed in the expectancy theory model in Chapter 5. The next sections consider the determinants of the expectancies and how they influence the individual's motivation to stay.

The Effort⇨Stay Expectancy

Actual situation Employees' effort⇨stay expectancy is determined primarily by their perceptions of the external environmental pressures experienced by employees, for example, family responsibilities, family and community ties, and available outside job opportunities.

Family responsibilities A variety of family responsibilities can determine employees' effort⇨stay expectancies. Employees who have financial obligations such as a mortgage or the cost of their children's university education are less able to bear the risks involved in a move to another organization unless the move enables them to cope better with these obligations. If the move involves relocation to another city and the spouse is also pursuing a career, whether the move will adversely affect the spouse's career must be considered. If the move will be detrimental to the spouse, the employee is compelled to stay on in the organization.

Family and community ties Strong family and community ties, including the undesirability of disrupting children's schooling, will increase the pressures to stay.

Outside job opportunities The lack of outside job opportunities in times of high unemployment or the individual's perception that he/she has few marketable skills will increase the pressure to stay.

The Stay⇨Outcomes Expectancy

Actual situation, Communication from others The critical determinants of this expectancy are the *actual situation* and *communication from others*. The outcomes in Figure 8.2 are derived primarily from the job content and the job context.

Job content Employees with high growth needs and the requisite knowledge and skill will experience the non-economic outcomes that flow from challenging assignments, achievement, recognition, responsibility, and opportunities for growth; these outcomes will influence employees to stay with the organization because they want to stay. On the other hand, if the core characteristics of the job are missing, the job content will not be a significant factor in employees' motivation to stay with the organization.

Job context As shown in Figure 8.2, outcomes from the job context are pay, benefits, job security, status, congenial co-workers, satisfactory supervision, and a generally good working environment. These outcomes serve as pressures from within the organization (internal environmental pressures) that make it attractive for employees to stay with the organization. When employees' expectancy of these outcomes is low, either in respect to the job content or the job context, then employees will be less inclined to stay with the organization.

The Valence of Outcomes

The determinants of the valence of outcomes are equity and the instrumentality of outcomes to satisfy needs.

Equity Generally, outcomes from the job content are within the employee's control because these are received or experienced by the employee as he/she performs the job. On the other hand, outcomes from the job context are administered by the organization. They are therefore more susceptible to being perceived by employees to be inequitable, either because of the size of the outcomes or because of inequity in the modality used to determine the outcomes. The perception of such inequity may decrease employee motivation to stay in the organization.

Instrumentality to satisfy needs Outcomes from the job content are the means of satisfying an employee's growth needs. Employees with high growth needs will regard these as essential to their satisfaction with the job and to their willingness to stay with the organization. Outcomes from the job context contribute to satisfying many of the employee's salient needs which are significant factors in the employee's decision to stay with the organization. The outcome of pay, which enables the employee to meet his/her financial obligations, may be the major reason why the employee stays with the organization. Similarly, a congenial working environment may be the factor that makes the organization attractive to the employee.

The preceding analysis, based on the expectancy theory model, predicts that the employee's decision to stay with or leave the organization will be determined by environmental pressures and by the employee's satisfaction with the job content. Environmental pressure takes two forms—the pressure from the external environment and the pressure from the internal environment. The job context is the source of the internal environmental pressure to stay with the organization. It follows that the external environmental pressure the internal environmental pressure (the job context), and job satisfaction (the job content) provide the basis for effective strategies to control turnover.

METHODS OF CONTROLLING TURNOVER

A systematic approach to controlling turnover must begin with efforts to assess the organization's annual turnover rate. The annual turnover rate is usually computed as a percentage, which is derived by dividing the total new hires in a one-year period by the average workforce in that same period. For example, the ABC Company hired 100 new employees in one year and its average workforce in that same period was 1,000 employees. The annual turnover rate of the ABC Company is 10 per cent, that is, 100/1,000. Although the annual turnover rate is frequently computed for the entire organization, it is more use-fully assessed for each work unit in order to identify the problem areas.

From the analysis in the preceding section it can be seen that the optimal sit-uation for the organization will be to have its employees stay because they are satisfied with both the job content and the job context, and because pressures from the external environment compel them to stay. In other words, employees will stay because they want to (the work attracts them) and also because they have to (pay and benefits are attractive and family responsibilities or family ties make it necessary for them to stay). An organization cannot control external environmental pressures, but it can closely monitor the job content and the job context. The practical guidelines discussed in Chapter 6 for managing the job content and pay are also relevant and effective in controlling turnover.

In addition, the organization should pay particular attention to the issue of the equity of the compensation system, namely, personal, internal, and exter-nal equity. Turnover is one of the means that employees adopt to remedy inequity. Employees expect personal or individual equity which is achieved when pay is based on performance. When merit pay does not significantly dif-ferentiate between mediocre and superior performers, superior performers are demotivated and may leave the organization. Specific action plans for address-ing personal equity are discussed in Chapters 9 and 10.

Employees also expect that internal equity exists when their base pay is determined. Through internal equity, the organization recognizes the knowl-edge, skills, and abilities required for the job, as well as the level of difficulty and complexity of the job. Internal equity is achieved through job evaluation systems. Chapter 11 examines the policies, techniques, and processes that make for effective job evaluation programmes. Turnover is often a warning signal that there are external equity problems in the organization's compensation system. External equity is achieved when the organization's pay and benefits level is comparable to that of the external labour market. Chapter 13 discusses the techniques of pay and benefit surveys and related processes that an organiza-tion can use in order to ensure that its compensation system is consistent with the conditions of the external labour market.

The policies, techniques, and processes used to achieve equity in the com-pensation system are some of the principal strategies used to combat turnover. However, the organization needs to be vigilant in detecting the signs of turnover. Many organizations maintain employee turnover statistics on a regu-lar basis and analyse them periodically to identify significant variations that might portend a high incidence of turnover. Exit interviews, systematically conducted, can also be useful in uncovering reasons for turnover. Finally, the diagnostic procedure discussed in Chapter 15 can be used in the turnover-con-trol programme. The procedure evaluates the effectiveness of each compensa-tion item and identifies equity problem areas.

ABSENTEEISM, TURNOVER—INDICATORS OF ORGANIZATIONAL COMMITMENT?

Absenteeism and turnover can be diagnosed using a trial-and-error approach suggested by researchers who have studied employee commitment to the organization. Employee commitment is defined as the "...psychological state that binds the individual to the organization" (Meyer, 1988, p.20). This psychological attachment has been viewed in terms of "affective commitment", "continuance commitment", and "normative commitment" (Allen and Meyer, 1990).

Employees develop affective commitment when they are satisfied with the content and context of the job. Employees' satisfaction with their work experiences make them want to attend work regularly and stay with the organization. Continuance commitment results when employees perceive that the cost of leaving is greater than staying with the organization. This would generally occur due to loss of benefits (such as vesting pension rights), limited job opportunities, family responsibilities, and a host of other environmental factors. Employees develop normative commitment when they believe and value the organization's vision, and internalize its norms. Although normative commitment may exist at the time of joining the organization, it is greatly reinforced by the organization's socialization practices.

Studies suggest that absenteeism and turnover are indicators that the employee's bond with or commitment to the organization has been ruptured (Becker, Billings, Eveleth, and Gilbert, 1996). The compensation system enables managers to be proactive in strengthening the employee's bond with the organization and, thereby, reduce absenteeism and turnover. As suggested in this and previous chapters, examples of some compensation strategies in this direction would be:

- provide valued economic and non-economic outcomes to enhance employee satisfaction with job content and context—to increase affective commitment; this strategy is consistent with the Mobley, Horner, and Hollingsworth's model which suggests that job satisfaction is negatively related to turnover (Hom, Caranikas–Walker, and Prussia, 1992);

- make some salient and valued rewards contingent on retention behaviour to promote continuance commitment;

- provide economic and non-economic rewards for innovative job performance which contributes to organizational objectives to enhance normative commitment.

SUMMARY

This chapter explored the phenomena of employee absenteeism, tardiness, and turnover, and developed practical proposals for controlling them. Employees' basic motivation to attend and to be punctual is affected by several personal and job-related factors. Health and family obligations, and lack of transportation to work are critical determinants of absenteeism and tardiness. Employees' motivation to attend is also affected by the content and the context of the job. Employees with high growth needs are frequently absent to avoid a monotonous and repetitive job. Dissatisfaction with the job context—pay, co-workers, or supervisors—also weakens employees' motivation to attend work. Absenteeism may also serve as a means of reducing the inequities that the employee perceives in the job context.

A wide variety of strategies exists to control absenteeism and tardiness. These range from flex time and a shorter work week to transportation facilities. In many cases, job design and career development programmes are effective in motivating attendance. Although sanctions are useful and have a role in the control of absenteeism and tardiness, positive rewards that are valued by the employees have been found to be more effective. The organization's sick leave policies need to be carefully reviewed to determine that these do not produce the unintended effect of promoting absenteeism.

Programmes to control employee turnover should recognize the impact of the job content and context factors as well as of external environmental factors. Although dissatisfaction with the outcomes from the job content or job context might cause employees to consider leaving the organization, the ultimate determinants of an employee's decision to leave are external environmental pressures from family responsibilities, family or community ties, or outside job opportunities. A programme to control turnover should include the practical guidelines discussed in Chapter 6 for managing job content and pay, the major item of job context. The other principal strategies in turnover control are the policies, techniques, and processes used to achieve personal equity (Chapters 9 and 10), internal equity (Chapters 11 and 12), and external equity (Chapter 13). The diagnostic procedure (Chapter 15) is also an invaluable tool for identifying equity problem areas in the compensation system.

KEY TERMS

blue Monday index

employee assistance programme

flex time

frequency index

organizational stressors

percentage time-lost index

worst-day index

℞ REVIEW AND DISCUSSION QUESTIONS

1. Why are some personal and job factors more related to absenteeism than others?

2. "The expectancy theory model provides a useful conceptual framework for explaining attendance motivation." In light of this model discuss the reasons for absenteeism.

3. Discuss some methods of controlling absenteeism. (Be sure to consider the conditions that contribute to their effectiveness.)

4. Lisa, an undergraduate student in business management, makes the following comments about her part-time sales job in a relatively fashionable, moderately priced retail clothing store in downtown Calgary:

   "It's a great place ... friendly co-workers and customers ... terrific discounts on clothes. The company is very successful but its human resource policies aren't! The wages of salespersons are individually negotiated with wide variations for no rhyme or reason; and all employees are asked not to discuss their pay rates. The supervisors run the store as feudal lords ..."

   Lisa and her co-workers are dissatisfied. Why then do they still continue to work there? Using the expectancy theory model, explore the conditions and circumstances that cause an employee to stay or leave the organization.

5. Discuss how compensation strategies can be used to control turnover.

Intexpro Inc. Meets Absenteeism Head-On

Intexpro Inc., a relatively small manufacturer of industrial textile products, was plagued by the problem of absenteeism and decided to do something about it. Intexpro introduced an attendance bonus plan (ABP) whose salient features were as follows:

- Rule 1: A bonus of $75 if the employee's total absence in one quarter was less than three hours.
- Rule 2: An additional bonus of $75 if the employee earned the attendance bonus stipulated in rule 1 in *each* of the four quarters.

Intexpro had a workforce of 213; about 90 per cent were women and 10 per cent were men. The average age was about 50 years and the average tenure in the company was about 12.4 years. The nature of the job tasks was moderately skilled. The cash compensation, made up of base rate and piece-work bonus, amounted to an average of $60 per day. The company was not unionized.

Source: Based on Schneller and Kopelman (1983).

Discussion Questions

1. Do you think the attendance bonus plan was successful in reducing absenteeism? Why or why not?

2. Do you think that the plan would provide the low-pay employee group with a relatively stronger incentive to attend compared to the high-pay employee group? Why or why not?

3. Do you think the marital status of the employees would have an impact on the effectiveness of the plan? In other words, would the plan provide the unmarried employee group with a relatively stronger incentive to attend compared to the married employee group? Why or why not?

4. Would the prior absence rate (i.e., absence rate prior to the introduction of the plan) moderate the effectiveness of the plan? To consider this question, think in terms of the following employee groups:
   - low prior absence rate group
   - moderate prior absence rate group
   - high prior absence rate group

   Which group(s) would likely respond most favourably to the plan? Why?

5. What are some of the changes you would make to the plan? Why?

CHAPTER 9

Performance-Based Pay: Personal Equity I

OVERVIEW

This chapter explores the concept of performance-based rewards, with a focus on performance-based pay, and considers the strategic and process issues in the design of a performance-based compensation system. In view of the critical role of performance appraisal in the effective administration of performance-based pay, the chapter concludes with a discussion of the performance appraisal process and practical guidelines for the successful conduct of the major activities in each step of the process.

 LEARNING OBJECTIVES

► To define *job performance* and distinguish it from *effort* and *productivity*

► To explain the objectives of performance-based rewards.

► To understand the conditions that must exist before pay can motivate employees to higher job performance.

► To understand the content of the strategic and process issues in performance-based pay.

► To develop appropriate criteria for strategic decisions that are critical to an effective performance-based pay plan.

► To describe the performance appraisal process.

► To develop practical guidelines for the major steps of the performance appraisal process in order to make it effective in the administration of performance-based pay.

▶ To understand the essential preconditions for an effective performance appraisal programme.

INTRODUCTION

- Job performance has replaced seniority and position in the organizational hierarchy as a basis for compensation increases in Canadian organizations (Booth, 1990).
- A survey of 405 Canadian organizations found that "performance management" was regarded as the top human resource management priority for 1995 (Carlyle, 1994).
- Organizations get from employees the behaviour they reward (Lawler & Jenkins, 1992).

These items succinctly underscore two points. Employees will perform what they are rewarded to perform. As a result, Canadian employers are placing greater value on performance-based pay. In principle, no reasonable employee would quarrel with the notion of performance-based pay. After all, the organization hires and retains employees to enable the organization to achieve its objectives through their job performance. It follows that the organization's compensation system should be designed to reward only those job behaviours that contribute to achieving the organization's objectives.

In practice, however, employees often have difficulty accepting this fact. Their objection is not to the concept of performance-based rewards *per se*, but rather to the inequity or unfairness of the methods and the processes through which the concept is implemented. This chapter addresses some fundamental questions relating to the concept of performance-based rewards, and the methods and processes of its implementation. These questions are: What are job performance behaviours? What are the objectives of performance-based rewards? What are the conditions under which rewards increase or improve job performance? What are the strategic and process issues that must be considered in designing an effective performance-based compensation system? What is the role of performance appraisal in the administration of performance-based rewards?

JOB PERFORMANCE BEHAVIOURS

Effort, Performance, Productivity

What are job performance behaviours? This is a simple but crucial question in the design and administration of performance-based rewards. If a manager intends to reward performance behaviours, both the manager and the subordinate must be of one mind about what constitutes performance behaviours. To arrive at this agreement, they must be able to distinguish between effort, performance, and productivity.

Consider the job of Sandra LaPierre, a salesperson, who is hired on a commission basis. She is assigned a sales target of $100,000 per month. By the third week of the month, she succeeds in closing a sale of $300,000, with the usual delivery period of two weeks. But a strike at her plant prevents adherence to the scheduled delivery date, and the customer cancels the order.

Has Sandra performed? Should she be rewarded? From the point of view of Sandra, she has performed the required job behaviours that resulted in the sale. From the point of view of the organization, the end result has not been achieved. But can Sandra be held responsible for this end result? These questions arise because the reward system has focused on the end result or productivity, rather than on performance.

Performance   Performance refers to an employee's actual behaviour at work. It is the set of behaviours that are organizationally required. These behaviours are usually spelt out as tasks or behaviours in the official description of the job for which the employee is being compensated. Performance depends on the employee's knowledge, skills, ability, and motivation. All these factors can be considered to be within the employee's control. Therefore, an employee can be held accountable for performance that is defined in this manner. The evaluation of the individual's performance in a performance appraisal will be a check to see if these behaviours were performed, and how well they were performed.

Productivity   Productivity, on the other hand, is the result of performance, that is, of the organizationally required behaviours. For productivity (i.e., output) to occur, the employee's performance must interact with the inputs of the socio-technical system and the environment of the organization. The other inputs of the social system are from co-workers, supervisors, and subordinates. The inputs of the technical system are materials, tools, machines, and the transforming or production process that occurs. The environmental inputs are from the market, the economy, the union, and government regulations.

Performance depends on an employee's inputs which are under the employee's control. But productivity depends upon the employee's performance and the inputs of the socio-technical system and the environment. These latter inputs are *not* under the control of the employee. Sandra LaPierre's performance made the sale, but the sale did not materialize in terms of output or end result (i.e., productivity) because of an environmental factor that was not under her control. Sandra will not be rewarded, because the reward is based on productivity (i.e., end result) and not on Sandra's performance. Sandra and other employees who operate under such a reward system will be justified in being demotivated.

Should rewards be tied to performance or productivity? This discussion is not intended to suggest that rewards should not be tied to productivity. Rather, the point is that rewards should be tied to a performance or an end result that is clearly and unmistakably under the control of the employee. In fact, if both the performance and the end result are under the employee's control, the rewards should be tied to both. Sandra's job as a salesperson includes the responsibility of deciding on her customers' credit applications, and her terms of compensation stipulate commission on sales that is subject to a charge back if the customer defaults on the payments. In this situation, Sandra's performance (her credit decisions) and sales (end result) are under her control. Therefore, the charge back is perfectly reasonable because it flows directly from Sandra's credit decision which was under her control.

Effort   How does effort differ from performance? Effort can be defined as the expenditure of time and energy incurred in preparation for performance. Of course, time and energy (i.e., effort) are also expended when one performs. In the context of this text, effort is viewed as a set of behaviours that are not organizationally required, but that the individual must engage in, in order to better perform the required job behaviours. Sandra's job requires her to make credit decisions about her customers, which constitute her performance. Prior to making these decisions, she researches the customer's background and related matters, and this work involves effort. This effort, however, is not performance, but behaviours preparatory to making the decision that is the performance. An organization would ordinarily not pay for effort, but only for performance or end results (productivity) or both. Rewards should not be based on effort as defined here.

If a compensation system rewards employees for productivity only, it risks demotivating employees if the expected end results are not within the employees' control. Such rewards will be ineffective. Organizations with such a compensation system should not be surprised if some of their employees expect to be rewarded only for the effort. A common stereotype of the work performance of government employees suggests that they appear to be paid primarily for coming to work, for membership behaviours only. A close probe might reveal that this type of compensation design also exists in private-sector organizations. It is a question of degree and not of kind. Hence, the distinction between effort, performance, and productivity behaviours needs to be kept in mind in designing effective performance-based reward programmes.

OBJECTIVES OF PERFORMANCE-BASED REWARDS

The use of performance-based rewards is an excellent strategy available to an organization to achieve a variety of objectives in the management of its human resources.

First, performance-based rewards have a significant influence on the type of personnel attracted to the organization. Employees who are achievement-oriented prefer and seek out organizations in which their work contributions will be recognized and suitably rewarded. Organizations that do not differentiate between mediocre and outstanding performers but simply treat them alike will not be able to attract qualified, high-performing individuals.

Second, even if an organization succeeds in hiring highly motivated performers, it may not be successful in retaining them unless it has an effective performance-based reward system in place. At selection time, either because of an unrealistic job preview, inadequate research, or lack of employment opportunities, these candidates might join an organization that does not believe in or implement performance-based rewards. Such high performers soon realize the total lack of fit between their concept of rewards and the company's. Employees socialized in North America's highly individualistic culture naturally expect a work culture in which they are held accountable for their performance and are correspondingly rewarded. If these expectations are not met, it is unlikely that the organization will be able to retain the employees for long. Performance-based rewards serve to retain high-performing employees.

The third objective of performance-based rewards is to motivate employees to attain organizational objectives. When employees perceive that their performance goes unrewarded, their perception of the performance-outcomes linkage is considerably weakened and their ($P \Leftrightarrow O$) expectancy is eventually lowered. Consequently, employees will not be motivated to perform and job objectives will not be achieved.

Fourth, performance-based rewards increase employee satisfaction. As has already been seen, the equity or fairness of a reward determines satisfaction. Rewards administered by a rational process that reflects employees' inputs will increase employees' perception of the fairness of the rewards. Performance-based rewards, supported by such a process, contribute to employee perceptions of equity, which in turn increase satisfaction. The resulting increase in satisfaction also contributes to reducing absenteeism and turnover. It is evident that performance-based rewards provide effective support to an organization's efforts to attract, retain, and motivate its employees to attain its goals and objectives.

THE ROLE OF PAY IN INCREASING JOB PERFORMANCE

One of the critical objectives of performance-based rewards is to increase job performance. The experience of many organizations is that the mere introduction of these rewards does not lead to increased performance. There are, however, underlying conditions that facilitate the effectiveness of these rewards. If these conditions are lacking, performance-based rewards often do not motivate the desired job behaviours, making the rewards futile. At other times the rewards produce dissatisfaction with all its adverse consequences. Hence it is important to explore the conditions that make performance-based rewards effective. The discussion in this section focuses on one type of performance-based rewards, namely, pay. Other forms of monetary rewards, such as incentives and gain-sharing plans, will be discussed in Chapter 10. In absolute and relative terms, pay lends itself to being tied to performance. In fact, most organizations intend and hope that pay, the largest reward item, will motivate employees to attain organizational goals and objectives. Historically, pay has invariably been based on performance, hence the expression: No work, no pay.

Facilitating conditions for performance-based pay

Performance-based pay is effective when employees value money, the pay is tied to performance, the negative consequences of performing well are minimized and positive consequences are ensured, and manager-subordinate trust is high.

Employees must value money   Money must be valued by employees. As the expectancy theory model shows, money is valued when it is instrumental in satisfying the salient needs of the employee *and* when it is perceived by employees to be fair and equitable. Hence, the amount of pay that rewards performance should be sufficiently large. Once the employee's salient needs have been satisfied, the amount of money that was required is no longer necessary. To that extent, pay tends to decrease in importance. Of course, pay also functions to satisfy esteem needs. If the self-esteem needs of the employee are salient, pay will continue to be instrumental in satisfying these needs and will continue to be valued by the employee. Employee perceptions of the fairness of the process by which the amount of merit pay is arrived at also influence the degree to which the merit pay will be valued.

Employee perception of performance-pay linkage   The second condition is that employees have an accurate perception of the performance-pay linkage, so that their (P$\Leftrightarrow$O) expectancy will be increased. The performance-pay linkage should be made visible through effective communication and the proper implementation of the performance-based pay policy. Such communication and implementation will promote the performance behaviours necessary to support the organization's objectives. In a situation where the organization's objectives require employee cooperation, it is important that the pay be linked to the performance of cooperative behaviours.

    A good example is the reward system for players in the National Hockey League, where the success of a team depends upon the teamwork of its players. In order to foster and encourage teamwork, the reward system recognizes not only the scorers of the goals but also the other players who have contributed through assists. Such recognition extends to the efforts of the defencemen and the goalie. The defencemen are rewarded for clearing the puck from their end as well as for offensive play. The goalie's contribution is recognized on the basis of both shut-outs and shots saved relative to shots on goal.

Minimize the negative consequences of performing well It can happen that good performance results in negative consequences for employees. For example, a performance-based pay programme becomes effective in increasing the organization's productivity and increased productivity eventually leads to lay-offs. The fear of such negative consequences could seriously jeopardize the effectiveness of performance-based pay. The third condition for ensuring that pay increases performance is that performance-based pay be designed and administered in such a way as to minimize the negative consequences of performing well.

Ensure positive consequences for performing well The fourth condition under which pay increases job performance relates to the administration of the performance-based pay programme. The process of design and administration should not only minimize the negative consequences of performing well but should also produce positive consequences: feedback on the specific aspect of performance that needs to be improved and how that improvement can be made, empowerment of employees leading to an increase in their self-efficacy beliefs, and removal of organizational obstacles to good performance.

Develop a climate of trust The relationship between managers and subordinates must be characterized by trust and openness. The previous four conditions would inevitably lead to such a relationship, but management must make a special effort to see that such a relationship precedes the design and installation of a performance-based pay programme. Hence, the establishment of trust and confidence in manager-subordinate relations is the fifth condition under which pay increases performance.

ISSUES IN PERFORMANCE-BASED PAY

The discussion so far, particularly the consideration of the conditions under which pay increases performance, provides the conceptual backdrop for the development of a performance-based pay plan. The actual structure and mechanics of such a plan for an organization require decisions on several other issues (Lawler, 1981; Lawler and Jenkins, 1992) summarized in Table 9.1.

The choices on these issues are largely dependent on the organizational structure and culture of the organization. The choices must also be consistent with the conditions which facilitate effective performance-based pay. What are the organizational and environmental factors that affect the choices? How does a given set of choices impact on the effectiveness of the merit pay programme? The following discussion (based on Lawler, 1981) examines these questions.

Table 9.1: Critical Issues in Performance-based Pay

Issues	Decision required
Aggregation Level	Should reward be based on the performance of the: • individual? • group? • organization?
Number of Plans	Should there be a separate plan for: • each organizational level? • each department or function? • short-term performance? • long-term performance?
Form of Merit Pay	As a salary increase? As a one-time bonus?
Amount of Merit Pay	Factors which influence size of merit pay?
Measures of Performance	Subjective? Objective?
Length of Payout Periods	Factors which influence payment frequency?
Employee Involvement	Should performance-based pay be secret? open? Should employees participate in merit pay design? merit pay administration?

REWARDING EMPLOYEES ON THE BASIS OF INDIVIDUAL, GROUP, OR ORGANIZATIONAL PERFORMANCE

The issue underlying this option is that of the *level of aggregation*, which is the basis for measuring and rewarding performance. In an organization, performance can be measured and rewarded at the level of the individual, of a predetermined work group or department, of the organization as a whole, or of a combination of one or more of these levels. Should the employee be rewarded for his/her outstanding performance even though the work group of which he/she is a member does not meet its objectives? Likewise, should the members of a work group be rewarded for their excellent performance even though the organization as a whole has not achieved its objectives?

Each case raises the fundamental questions of performance-outcomes linkage, and of equity. When an individual's deserving performance goes unrewarded because of factors beyond the individual's control, the individual's perceptions of the performance-outcomes linkage is weakened, if not completely ruptured. As a result, the individual's ($P \Rightarrow O$) expectancy is lowered and his/her motivation to perform is decreased. In addition, the individual will experience inequity which lowers his/her valence of the outcomes. The drop in valence will also contribute to decreasing motivation. Furthermore, if the policy of secrecy prevails, the employee will likely receive inadequate and inaccurate feedback on performance. Such feedback has been found to lower the individual's $(E \Rightarrow P)$ expectancy, adversely affecting the individual's performance motivation.

In addition to having a motivational impact, the level of aggregation permits the organization to promote both cooperation and competition among its employees, depending upon which is beneficial for the organization. If the organizational needs are better served by autonomous work teams, the level of aggregation will be the work team. By measuring and rewarding team performance, the organization will promote team cohesiveness and motivate team members to work cooperatively. This intrateam cohesiveness and cooperation might produce interteam competition, which will benefit the organization so long as the teams are not dependent on one another. If the teams are interdependent, then the organization will need to opt for a higher aggregation level that promotes cooperation rather than competition (Gerhart and Milkovich, 1992). This point will be reviewed in considering the factors that influence the level of aggregation.

By adjusting the level of aggregation of the performance-based pay programme, the organization can obtain more objective measures of performance. The performance of certain individuals or smaller work groups in the organization may not lend itself to objective measures. In this case, a higher level of aggregation—a division or a plant—will produce more objective measures of performance. Profit, is generally a more reliable indicator of the performance of a division rather than of a work group or even of a department. Likewise, the total number of finished products is a more objective measure of the performance of the plant as a whole than of a work unit.

Because the level of aggregation is a critical decision in the design of a performance-based pay system, the factors that an organization must consider in deciding on a level of aggregation are technology, information systems, size, trust, and union status (Lawler, 1981). The rest of this section will consider the separate impact of each factor on the determination of the level of aggregation and will then explore how the factors, as they exist in an organization, can be utilized to combine the aggregation levels to develop an effective performance-based pay plan.

Technology

The technological characteristics that are relevant to the level of aggregation are complexity and interdependence. In a job requiring relatively simple technological tasks, the individual's job output or job performance behaviours can be easily identified and attributed to the individual's performance. The individual can be held accountable and rewarded for his/her performance. Where the job tasks require a complex technology, the output of the job, or the individual's performance behaviours in that job, are likely to be influenced by the performance of other employees. That being so, it may be unfair to attribute success or failure in meeting the job's objectives *entirely* to the individual's performance. A more complete measure of the individual's performance will be obtained if the contribution of the other employees is adequately considered. Therefore, the performance of all the employees involved will need to be measured and rewarded.

Information System

The process of evaluating employee performance is usually a combination of the measure of the job output and the supervisor's judgements of the performance of the job tasks. The measures of the job output (e.g., units produced, customers served, reports completed, sales closed) are the objective criteria; the supervisor's judgements (how well the required job behaviours were performed) are the subjective criteria. Generally, objective measures of performance are more acceptable to employees than subjective measures. Therefore, the preferred level of aggregation will be one that provides objective measures of performance. If the performance of the job tasks results in output that is capable of objective measurement, the preferred aggregation level will be the individual.

On the other hand, if the evaluation of the individual's performance involves subjective judgements, an aggregation level higher than that of the individual should be used. The specific aggregation level will be one that permits the development of reasonably objective measures of performance; such a level might be the work group, a departmental unit, the plant, or the organization itself.

Size

The influence of organization size on the aggregation level is derived from the fact that the effectiveness of the performance-based pay system is dependent on employee perceptions that the predetermined performance measures (goals, targets, objectives) are under his/her control. If these measures are under the employee's control, the appropriate aggregation level will be the individual. If not, the appropriate aggregation level will be the work group or some larger entity whose members feel reasonably confident that they have the resources and the necessary organizational support to attain the established goals.

How does the size of the organization affect employee perceptions of influence and control of the measures of performance? In a large organization, individual employees will generally not be able to see any significant connection between their performance and the overall net results of the organization measured in terms of profit, return on investment, market share, and so forth. That being the case, establishing performance-based pay at the organizational level will be inappropriate. Performance-based pay will need to be established at the individual level and related to the individual's job objectives. This conclusion imposes a challenge and a responsibility on supervisors to come up with performance measures that truly reflect their employees' job tasks and objectives.

In a small organization, on the other hand, individual employees are in a relatively better position to see that their performance contributes to the realization of organizational objectives. Performance-based pay in a smaller organization can be established in terms of the overall results of the organization. It might happen that individuals are unable to see how their performance influences overall organizational objectives. Even so, in a smaller organization individuals are more likely to see the influence of their performance on their work group or department. Thus, performance-based pay can be established at an aggregation level higher than that of the individual.

Trust

The element of trust is an important determinant of the aggregation level, because trust is at the very heart of employee perceptions of equity or fairness. This is especially so in the case of the performance-based pay system, which relies for its effectiveness on the employee's perceptions that the system is designed to measure and reward performance fairly and equitably. The evaluation of employees' performance is rarely an exercise in complete objectivity.

Consider a performance-based pay system in which the performance target is 1,000 units per month. Such a measure could reasonably be considered as objective. However, one could always argue that a supervisor's subjectivity might be involved in determining which units conform to the organization's quality standards. In the vast majority of jobs in an organization, the evaluation of performance has a large component of subjectivity, making a climate of trust an absolute imperative. The greater the trust of the employees, the greater their perceptions of the equity of the decisions, even in situations where the element of a supervisor's subjectivity in performance evaluation is high. On the other hand, where the trust is low, employees will likely be less inclined to accept a supervisor's subjective judgement of their performance.

There are two aspects of this trust: the employee's trust of the supervisor and the employee's trust of the work group, department, or organization. Suppose the supervisor has developed good relations with his/her employees, engendering in them a high trust. This situation will be conducive to establishing performance-based pay at the individual level because the employee's perceptions of the equity of the supervisor's decisions of his/her performance will be high.

On the other hand, suppose that employee trust of the supervisor is low, but the culture of the department has been supportive of an open communication policy which has clearly spelt out the department's objectives and the expected standards of performance. In this situation, employees will develop considerable trust in the department which will become the appropriate aggregation level. Thus, where employee's trust of the supervisor is high, rewarding employees on the basis of their individual performance is likely to be more effective. However, when employees' trust of an organizational unit or of the organization itself is high, this higher aggregation level is more conducive to an effective performance-based pay.

Union Status

Unions generally shy away from individual performance-based pay systems, because these systems provide management with the mechanisms to compensate employees on a differential basis. Unions have traditionally been reluctant to embrace management's willingness and inclination to administer performance-based pay programmes in a fair and equitable manner. Individual performance-based pay programmes do not lend themselves to influence and control by the unions. In fact, unions often suspect that these programmes are utilized to reward employees who are opposed to unionization. Hence, the programmes are viewed by unions as a threat to their security. Unions are more inclined to accept performance-based pay programmes where the level of aggregation is the organization.

Illustration of the choice of the aggregation level

For many organizations, the choice of the aggregation level will probably involve a combination of aggregation levels.

> An illustration of one such combination is the case of a large, non-unionized corporation whose internal work culture has successfully fostered a climate of trust and has encouraged its supervisors to function as coach and mentor to their subordinates. The positive response of employees is demonstrated by their effort and commitment to the specific, measurable job objectives set jointly by the supervisor and the subordinate. The job tasks are interdependent, and it is strategically important for the company's operations to be cost-efficient. The company has therefore decided on a merit pay programme linked to an objective measure of its overall performance, which is available from the company's information system.

What would be the appropriate aggregation level for this corporation? The interdependent tasks and the availability of objective performance measures clearly suggests that the aggregation level be the total organization. However, the employees' trust of their supervisors, the availability of good measures of individual job performance (i.e., measurable job objectives), the large size of the organization, and the non-union status all favour an individual level of aggregation.

This apparent conflict can be resolved by a combination of the aggregation levels. Thus, the measures of organizational performance can be used to develop a fund for merit pay. The individual's merit pay, drawn from this fund, will be decided on the employee meeting the established job objectives. Because the combination plan is usually fraught with administrative difficulties, the critical factors in its success are trust and good supervisor-subordinate relations engendered by the internal work culture of the organization.

Table 9.2 summarizes the conditions which influence the aggregation level —that is, whether performance is measured and rewarded on the individual or group level.

Table 9.2: Conditions Favouring Individual or Group Performance-based Plans

Individual-based Performance Plan	Group-based Performance Plan
If:	If:
technology is less complex and permits independent job tasks	**technology** is complex and requires interdependent job tasks
information system provides objective measures of individual's performance	**information system** provides objective measures only at group level
organization size is too large for individual to influence or control organization's performance or results	**organization size** is small enough for individual to control or influence organization's performance or results
employee **trust** of supervisor's judgement about his or her performance is high	employees **trust** the organization because they understand work unit's objectives and accept the performance standards
organization is not **unionized**	organization is **unionized** and supports the performance-based pay plan

THE NUMBER OF PERFORMANCE-BASED PAY PLANS

Single versus multiple plans

Organizations often choose to have more than one performance-based pay plan. Sometimes, it may be that organizational conditions necessitate different aggregation levels and a plan to combine these levels is not feasible. At other times, conditions such as the nature of business operations, industry practices, and strategic considerations will induce the organization to explore the feasibility of installing more than one performance-based pay plan.

Conditions for effectiveness of multiple plans

What are the conditions under which an organization can effectively operate more than one plan? It will be recalled that the effectiveness of any plan depends on the employee's perception of the performance-outcomes linkage and the equity of the plan.

Now, suppose that the organization decides to have three different plans for three different work units. Each plan will be effective if the employees covered by it believe that the predetermined performance measures truly reflect their performance. Furthermore, the employees should also believe that the results of their performance, on which the reward is based, are within their control. For instance, if the job tasks of the employees in one plan are dependent on the job tasks of the employees in the other plan(s), this element of influence or control suffers. Having more than one plan when such interdependence exists is certain to prove counterproductive, because the several plans will more likely promote competition than cooperation. As long as these conditions are met, organizations can quite successfully operate more than one performance-based pay plan.

Basis for multiple plans

Some of the bases for establishing multiple plans in an organization are (a) a plan for each level of the organization, (b) a plan for each department or function in the organization, and (c) a plan for each time span of performance (Lawler and Jenkins, 1992).

A plan on the basis of the **organizational level** views the organization as a set of independent entities that exist horizontally in the organization, for example, senior-management, middle-management, first-line-management, professional, clerical, operations, and maintenance employees. Each of these horizontal levels has a separate plan to recognize the performance of the entity. Is such an approach, which virtually follows the organizational hierarchy, effective? Because of the homogeneous nature of the job tasks, it would be relatively easy to develop performance measures that are controllable by the employees. This approach, tends to assume that the horizontal levels are independent of each other. If, in fact, the interdependence of these levels and the need for cooperation among them is high, the separate plans may prove to be dysfunctional.

Another basis for multiple plans takes a vertical approach to the organization—as a set of **departments**, **functions**, or **projects**. Each of these entities encompasses all of management, and non-management employees, and the plan's intent is to recognize the performance of each entity. This approach is at the heart of the profit centre concept. Is this approach effective? The heterogeneity of the job tasks—management, professional, clerical, operations, and maintenance employees—in one entity will make it difficult to develop measures that adequately reflect the contribution of each employee category to achieving the targets established for the entity. This situation also makes it difficult for the individual employee to perceive that he/she can influence or control the net results of the entity on which the rewards are based. The positive aspect of this plan is that it recognizes the interdependence that usually exists within a department or function. To that extent, the plan promotes cooperation within the entity. However, the plan might not recognize the interdependence that may exist between and among departments or functions. Hence, the plan design should ensure that the plan facilitates the cooperation that is needed among the interdependent entities.

An organization can have multiple plans to recognize **the time span of performance**. In some jobs, the employees, left to themselves, can focus either on the short-term or long-term objectives of the organization. The multiple-plans design is an excellent means by which the organization can send the right signals to these employees. For example, one plan might focus on the short-term objectives, another on the long-term objectives. This point will be reviewed in the discussion of the length of payout periods. The time span of performance basis is usually incorporated into plans that use horizontal or vertical approaches. Its effectiveness can therefore be enhanced by the positive features of the horizontal or vertical approach; its effectiveness can also be hindered by the negative features of these approaches. Nevertheless, the time span of performance emphasizes the temporal dimension of organizational objectives that often tends to be neglected in the design of performance-based rewards.

MERIT PAY AS A SALARY INCREASE OR A ONE-TIME BONUS PAYMENT

In addressing this issue, the chief consideration is: Which form strengthens the employee perceptions of the performance-pay linkage?

The salary increase approach

Content and mechanics   Traditionally, a salary increase has come to symbolize good performance. However, few organizations appear to administer a "salary decrease" when performance is below the expected standard. Consequently, an employee whose performance merits a salary increase in one year will continue to receive this increase in perpetuity even though his/her performance might drop significantly in subsequent years. Furthermore, in order to maintain external equity, organizations often use the salary increase as a device to adjust their pay level following changes in the cost of living and/or market pay levels.

Effects of the salary increase approach This practice of combining the merit increase with salary adjustments has the unintended consequence of weakening the employee's perception of the performance-pay linkage in two ways. First, all employees receive the salary adjustment increase, which frequently is a substantial component of the individual's total salary increase. As a result, the total salary increase conceals the differentiation that might be made between superior and mediocre performers. The effects of such concealment are aggravated in a secret merit pay system. Some organizations attempt to minimize the effect of concealment by clearly spelling out the merit-increase component of the total salary increase. Second, the merit component of the total salary increase would need to be substantial in order to create the desired motivational impact. But cost considerations might not make this feasible, especially when salary adjustments are necessitated by a spiralling increase in the cost of living, such as was experienced in the 1970s. The next section returns to other aspects relating to the issue of the size of the merit increase.

The bonus payment approach

Content, mechanics and effects Merit pay in the form of a one-time bonus is a better alternative to salary increase because it enables employees to perceive the performance-pay linkage. The individual's performance is followed by a bonus according to a predetermined schedule. Unlike the salary increase, the bonus does not become part of the salary and therefore does not constitute a perennial payment. A bonus is not paid when performance falls below the established standards, because the bonus is intended to reflect the employee's job performance for the period under review.

When bonus replaces the salary-increase, it is necessary to adopt a mechanism to reflect changes in the cost of living. For this purpose some organizations adopt both forms of payment. The salary increase which compensates for changes in the cost of living and in market pay levels is granted to all employees; such adjustments promote external equity. The one-time bonus, based entirely on performance, seeks to achieve individual or personal equity.

The performance-based bonus also offers a radical approach of promoting high performance because it permits pay to vary with performance levels (Lawler and Jenkins, 1992). In this approach, the base pay is set below the market pay rate. The employees' total pay will be a combination of the base pay and the performance-based bonus. This approach provides a powerful performance incentive because it allows the high performers to earn total pay, that is, base plus bonus, which is above the market level; and low performers to earn total pay which is below the market level.

This raises a crucial question: how much lower than the market should the base pay rate be set? Clearly, the managerial and professional employees are likely to tolerate more of their pay being put at risk than the non-managerial employees. To address this fact, the bonus component of total pay could range from 0 to 20 percent at lower pay levels; and 0 to 40 percent at the higher pay levels (Lawler, 1990). However, the specifics of this performance-based bonus approach will depend upon the organization's culture and the preferences of its employees. This approach has begun to be adopted by Canadian organizations (Carlyle, 1994).

THE APPROPRIATE AMOUNT OF MERIT PAY

What size of merit pay will motivate employees to perform effectively on the job? In terms of the expectancy model, the issue of the employee's valence of merit pay, is crucial in employee motivation. An employee will value merit pay when it is instrumental in satisfying his/her salient needs. But if a sizeable merit raise leads to the satisfaction of the salient needs, the result can be a lower valence of merit pay. However, as a recognition of performance, merit pay will be most instrumental in satisfying the employee's self-esteem needs. One can expect that the self-esteem needs of an individual with a high income will be better satisfied with a larger amount of merit pay. As discussed previously, equity or fairness in determining the size of the merit pay should also be considered because it influences the employee's valence of merit pay.

Size of merit pay and motivational impact For merit pay to have a motivational effect, it should make a noticeable difference to the individual (Lawler and Jenkins, 1992). This means that a good performer's merit pay should be significantly greater than that of a poor performer. However, in many organizations the difference in merit pay between good and poor performers is not significant, which is due to the "topping out" problem that results from the use of the *merit increase grid*. Intended primarily as a cost control mechanism, the merit increase grid guidelines recommend a lower merit increase percentage for employees in the higher salary range or grade, and a reduced frequency of within-grade pay increases for employees near the top of the range (Gerhart and Milkovich, 1992).

A factor that influences the motivational impact of the size of merit pay is the extent of openness of the merit pay system. The greater the openness of the system, the greater is the motivational impact of a relatively smaller size of the merit pay. As was noted in the discussion of the effects of secrecy in Chapter 6, the motivational impact of even an above-average merit raise is completely dissipated by the perceptions of inequity that are generated by social comparison based on speculation and rumour.

The size of the merit pay also has a motivational impact in a vicarious sense. Suppose an employee does not receive a merit raise because of poor performance, but is aware of the sizeable merit raises awarded to superior performers. The fact that the organization rewards superior performance by sizeable merit raises can in itself be a significant factor in motivating poor performers to improve their performance.

SUBJECTIVE VERSUS OBJECTIVE MEASURES OF PERFORMANCE

Need for accurate measure of performance   A valid, accurate measure of performance is a crucial element of the performance-based pay system. If the organization intends to reward performance, the performance has to be properly assessed and measured. Such assessment and measurement cannot be a unilateral activity, the judgement of the supervisor alone. The employee's assessment is critical. If the employee feels that the supervisor's assessment does not adequately reflect the performance, the employee will not perceive the outcomes to be equitable. As a result, the employee's valence of the merit raise will drop, and so will the motivational impact of the merit pay system. Hence, it is imperative that the supervisor and the subordinate agree on the assessment of the performance. In reality, this prescription is difficult to follow, primarily because of the nature of the criteria used in measuring performance.

Nature of objective measures of performance   Performance can be measured in terms of objective and subjective criteria. Objective criteria lend themselves to some form of quantitative measure such as output, sales, profits, or scrap rate. These measures have a high degree of validity and are therefore more credible and acceptable to both the supervisor and the subordinates. Of course, even for objective measures, the employee's trust of the supervisor is necessary, particularly in the choice and interpretation of the measures. Because these measures are verifiable, the degree of trust need not be high.

Nature of subjective measures of performance   The subjective measures are the supervisor's judgements of the employee's performance. By their very nature, these measures are not verifiable. Therefore, their acceptance by employees is determined to a large degree by the trustworthiness of the supervisor. Once this credibility has been established, subjective measures contribute to providing a more complete picture of performance, because it is virtually impossible to develop objective quantifiable measures for *all* the behaviours necessary to fulfil the job objectives.

Guide for choice of performance measures   Supervisors often tend to treat objective measures as sacred cows which causes counterproductive results to the organization. For example, it is not uncommon for salespersons to achieve sales targets by neglecting customer service or for a supervisor to achieve the short-term objectives of a department without the proper attention to employees' satisfaction with job content or job context that is necessary for the long-term effectiveness of the department.

Subjective measures allow the supervisor to focus on employee behaviours that are critical to attaining the job objectives. Besides, these measures do not require sophisticated and costly reporting systems. They need competent managers who are willing to "manage" their subordinates, not as mere administrators, but as coaches and mentors deeply committed to providing employees with the guidance, development, and resources they need for effective performance.

It is, therefore, not a question of a choice between objective and subjective criteria. Rather, it is a question of choosing a set of measures, objective and subjective, that adequately capture the job behaviours needed to attain organizational objectives. The performance management process discussed later in this chapter spells out in greater detail the specific activities and requirements that are involved in this process.

THE LENGTH OF THE PAYOUT PERIODS

Rationale underlying frequent payouts This issue requires decisions on the frequency of merit payments. In principle, the frequency should strengthen employee perceptions of the performance-outcomes linkage and increase the saliency of merit pay. Ideally, the reward should immediately follow the performance of the desired behaviour, allowing the employee to see the performance-outcomes linkage. Such immediacy also increases the saliency of the reward and enhances its motivational value. In terms of the behaviour modification approach, the greater frequency of the payout would generally contribute to reinforcing desired behaviours.

Dysfunctional effects of frequent payouts There is, however, the concern that the increased frequency might cause employees to focus on the short-term objectives of the job to the detriment of the long-term objectives. This legitimate concern can be addressed by a reward system that makes rewards contingent upon both the short-term and long-term objectives of the job.

> The National Hockey League reward system illustrates the recognition of short-term and long-term objectives. To win the Stanley Cup is the relatively long-term objective of every team. But the team's chances of reaching that objective get better only when the team does well in the short-term in each game. It has already been shown how the reward system promotes performance behaviours that help the team win each game. When the team is in the Stanley Cup play-offs, the need for teamwork is even more crucial because any player's attempt to perform like a prima donna can ruin the team's chances of success. For the promotion of teamwork, the rewards for winning the Stanley Cup are distributed equally among the team members.

Guidelines on payout frequency decision An important consideration in the decision on payout frequency is the time delay in the availability of performance measures. If the nature of the job is such that there is a time lag before pertinent performance information becomes available, the merit payout will be delayed. This is often the case in managerial jobs where the effectiveness of decisions can be realistically and fairly assessed only at relatively longer intervals. For such jobs the frequency of merit payments will be low. Will the low frequency adversely affect the performance motivation of these employees? Some argue that it will not because such job incumbents are accustomed to delayed rewards. The determining factor in performance motivation, however, is employee perceptions of *when* the performance-outcomes linkage can reasonably be made. So long as employees perceive that the payout intervals are fairly consistent with the time lag in the availability of performance information, the low frequency of merit payments will not affect their performance motivation.

The decision on the frequency of merit payments requires a careful consideration of the nature of the job objectives, short-term and long-term, and the inherent time delay in the availability of performance information.

EMPLOYEE INVOLVEMENT IN DESIGNING AND ADMINISTERING MERIT PAY

Rationale for employee involvement   This option addresses the process issues of secrecy versus openness of the merit pay system and the advantages of employee participation in the design and administration of the merit pay system. Openness in the compensation system contributes to employee motivation in three ways: it engenders employee trust in the system, it promotes employee perceptions of the performance-outcomes linkage, and it provides adequate feedback on performance. These effects of openness in the compensation system are all the more crucial for a performance-based pay system.

Performance-based pay—merits and demerits   The performance-based reward system should be clearly communicated. Employees should know and understand what constitutes job performance, what the expected performance standards are, and how and when the performance will be rewarded. In an open system, employees do not have to rely on speculation and rumours to evaluate whether the merit pay system is functioning as intended. In a well-designed and properly implemented performance-based reward system, employees see that the predetermined or agreed performance levels are equitably rewarded. They also receive feedback on their performance deficiencies.

There are some disadvantages to an open system. When employees see that the performance-based system is not equitably administered, they lose trust in the system and it ceases to have the desired motivational value. The previous chapter examined the arguments against openness in the compensation system and concluded that, on balance, openness was preferred to secrecy. The argument against openness becomes even weaker in the case of performance-based pay. The very notion of rewarding performance implies that employees need to be satisfied that their rewards are equitable relative to their performance and the performance of their peers.

Involving employees in system design It is crucial that employees be involved in compensation design using performance-based pay because of the direct contingencies involved between performance and rewards. Thus, employee involvement in the design and administration of merit pay will have the effect of strengthening employee perceptions of the performance-outcomes linkage and equity of outcomes and the employee will experience a greater satisfaction with the job.

THE ROLE OF PERFORMANCE APPRAISAL IN THE ADMINISTRATION OF PERFORMANCE-BASED REWARDS

- A survey of 405 Canadian organizations found that 93 percent had a performance appraisal system (Carlyle, 1994).

If rewards are to be based on performance, there is a need to evaluate or assess that performance in order to determine the rewards that it deserves. Performance appraisal is an essential part of a performance-based rewards programme. A well-designed performance appraisal system will assure equity and fairness in determining rewards. It will also assure that only those performance behaviours that achieve the organization's objectives are rewarded. Consequently, the performance appraisal system plays an indispensable role in performance-based pay. In view of its importance, the discussion of the performance appraisal system will include not only a description of the major steps of the performance appraisal process but also practical guidelines for the successful conduct of the activities involved in each step and a consideration of some of the essential preconditions that make performance appraisal effective.

THE PERFORMANCE APPRAISAL PROCESS

Step 1 The performance appraisal system should not be a once-a-year ritual that managers plough through reluctantly; it is essentially the on-going, cyclical process of managing employee performance. It begins with the definition of the subordinate's job, unless the job is so simple that there is no doubt about what is the expected job behaviour. In this first step, the manager must *identify* all the important aspects of the job and *clarify* how the job is related to the goals of the organization. One way of identifying job objectives that are concrete and appropriate to organizational goals is to view the recipient of the jobs' products as the "customer" of that job. In this approach, managers assist their employees to identify the customers of their output.

For example, the sales analyst who prepares monthly sales statistics that are routed to the sales manager, the marketing manager, and senior managers sees each recipient as a customer and becomes conscious of the job's responsibility to satisfy the specific needs of the customers. The customer approach enables employees to experience the significance of their tasks and promotes, in varying degrees, identification with the organization's goals. These outcomes are ensured only if the process of job definition is a joint effort of the manager and the employees that leads to an agreed understanding of, and commitment to, the appropriate job behaviours.

Step 2   The second step of the cycle is the *setting of expectations*. The first step spelt out what needs to be done. The second step specifies how well the tasks must be done; it sets the standards by which the job performance will be appraised. Goal-setting theory (Locke and Bryan, 1968), abundantly supported by empirical evidence (Locke *et al.,* 1981), stipulates that employee performance is greatly enhanced when the assigned goals are difficult but attainable and specific but appropriate to the goals of the organization. This step also establishes the performance period, usually six months to a year for non-managerial jobs and two years and more for managerial jobs, the rationale being that it takes longer for performance results to become visible in the latter case than in the former.

With the popularization of Total Quality Management (TQM), there is an increasing recognition that the performance goals and standards, referred to in steps 1 and 2, should cover all the critical aspects of the employee's job beyond the mere quantity and quality of the output or service. Managers should work with employees to include objectives relating to improving the work process and contribution to the work unit.

The process of performance appraisal, despite the most sophisticated attempts to introduce objective procedures, will always remain a subjective process, highly vulnerable to fallible judgements. The participation of employees in the establishment of standards and measures of performance is crucial. The knowledge and expertise of both the supervisor and the employees contribute to performance standards and measures that are reasonable, realistic, and appropriate. This is not to suggest that subordinates, left to themselves, would set unrealistically low standards. In fact, there is considerable evidence that subordinates tend to set unrealistically high goals (Lawler, 1977). The mutual-influence process would, in addition to injecting realism, ensure manager-subordinate agreement and give the subordinates ownership and control which go a long way to generating the trust, acceptance, and commitment so necessary to this highly subjective system (Locke and Latham, 1984).

Illustration of Step 1 and Step 2

As an illustration of these two steps, which constitute the foundation of the appraisal system, consider the job of a salesperson. On the basis of his/her own knowledge and experience and that of his/her salesforce, the sales manager lists all the job behaviours that result in successful sales performance, for example, developing a prospects list, setting up appointments with customers, demonstrating products, customer follow-up, responding to customer complaints/

enquiries, communications with the sales manager, developing budgets, sales reports, training juniors, and initiating new sales approaches. These behaviours are then arranged according to how critical they are to increasing sales. Specific measures such as five customer demonstrations per week, ten new appointments every month, or a sales report by the first of each month are assigned to each behaviour, and become the standards and measures of performance.

The deliberations of the manager and the employee at this stage of the cycle have the potential for generating mistrust and conflict. Preoccupied with productivity, the manager sets the performance goals (expectations) in terms of some measure of productivity. The employee, intent on reaching these goals, performs all the required behaviours only to find his/her efforts thwarted by environmental or other constraints entirely beyond his/her control. Both the manager and the employee will be spared this needless frustration if they recognize the fundamental difference between performance and productivity. Then, in addition to establishing job objectives and measures of performance, the manager will also identify and remove environmental constraints that might interfere with the employee's job performance. If these constraints cannot be removed, the performance standards must be adjusted because these constraints are beyond the control of the employee. Otherwise, it would be unreasonable and unfair to hold the employee responsible for the failure to meet performance goals when such failure is due to work system deficiencies which, as Edwards Deming observed, have not been created by the employee (Gerhart and Milkovich, 1992).

Step 3   The third step of the performance management cycle is *monitoring the performance*. During this phase, the manager provides informal ongoing feedback. When managers function as coaches, they seek to help employees grow and reach desired performance levels. Coaching involves knowing how well employees are performing relative to performance standards in terms of specific, measurable behaviours and discussing areas for improvement. The coach gives praise for work well done and offers constructive criticism when appropriate. In the latter case, the manager cites specific behaviours with specific suggestions on how to correct the performance problems.

Performance standards can never be etched in stone; their validity always assumes a relatively stable environment. The manager who functions like a coach will be sensitive to changing environmental factors and will make suitable adjustments to performance standards. Perhaps the shortfall in performance is due to a deficiency in the employee in certain skills. The coaching approach will cause the manager to be immediately aware of such deficiencies and provide remedial measures. In their coaching stance, managers are careful to create an open, relaxed atmosphere that encourages employees to seek guidance in sorting out priorities or in resolving problems.

Step 4 The fourth step is the *formal appraisal review*, at the end of the predetermined performance period. During this review managers record their assessment of the individual's performance. This phase usually poses the greatest problem for managers as it demands that they play two apparently conflicting roles: coach and judge. The most frequently recommended approach to this phase is termed the problem-solving approach because it focuses on the removal of obstacles to good performance. This approach encourages a joint discussion between the manager and the subordinate.

The mutual exchange of information provides a clearer picture of the individual's job performance and the context in which the job was carried out. As a result, subordinates' trust in the fairness of the process increases because they are now certain that the manager does indeed have all the information needed for a reasonable assessment. Furthermore, the exchange provides an opportunity for discussing the short-term and long-term career objectives of subordinates as well as their training and development needs. The problem-solving approach creates a climate of mutual trust, is non-threatening, and makes the appraisal review the ideal event for discussing and setting goals for the next performance period. In this approach, managers function as both coach and judge, but the emphasis is on their mentoring role as they seek to nurture subordinates' strengths and minimize the negative effects of their weaknesses, if these cannot be completely eliminated.

Rating instruments

Managers can choose from a wide variety of techniques to rate employees' performance; some organizations combine techniques or use different techniques to rate different categories of employees. The criterion for the choice of technique must be the capacity of the technique to capture employee performance in terms of the predetermined job behaviours. The use of personal traits to appraise performance should be avoided unless these are critical to the performance of the job, in which case the traits should form part of the performance standards. For example, a good salesperson or an employee who is a member of a work team needs the ability to work with others. A bench scientist who works alone may not need that personal trait.

If personal traits are critical to the job, the rating format should encourage the manager not merely to record observations in terms of the presence or absence of the traits, but to illustrate the traits specifically with examples of the job behaviours observed. For instance, if a manager rates a supervisor low on resourcefulness, the supervisor will be helped to improve his/her performance if the manager records an example of a behaviour that reflected a lack of initiative and the consequence of the behaviour for the organization.

The rating instrument is not an end in itself but a means of bringing together in one medium information that supports the problem-solving method. Any displacement of the means-end relationship that results in according to the mechanics of the instrument a more important role than to the process that it is designed to support will not contribute to the effective management of performance.

Effects of well-managed performance appraisal process

If the performance review is to aid in performance management, the assessment recorded should provide information that facilitates equitable compensation decisions and identifies training and development needs. When managers ensure equity in compensation decisions, they unleash the tremendous motivational power of the compensation programme with two positive consequences among the many that follow. First, the correct and desirable performance behaviours are reinforced with a resultant increase in the probability that such behaviours will be repeated in the future. The employees get a clear, direct, and unambiguous message about the type and level of performance behaviours expected from them. Second, the satisfaction that follows equitable compensation increases the value employees place on the rewards they receive from the organization. The empirical evidence is overwhelmingly conclusive that employee motivation is high when rewards are contingent upon performance behaviour and are valued by the employees (Kanungo and Mendonca, 1988).

Identifying training and development needs is a necessary first step to improving performance. It must be followed through with appropriate programmes that remedy specific performance deficiencies or provide opportunities for the acquisition or enhancement of certain skills and abilities. This activity is especially critical to organizations that compete in highly dynamic and rapidly growing industries.

ESSENTIAL PRECONDITIONS FOR EFFECTIVE PERFORMANCE APPRAISAL

Organizational work culture

The four steps of the performance appraisal programme described constitute a process that is essential to an equitable and effective performance-based pay system. However, the success of this process is largely dependent on the organizational climate and internal work culture. In an extensive study of performance appraisal practices in nine very different companies of the General Electric conglomerate and covering 700 manager-subordinate pairs from all levels of management, Lawler, Mohrman, and Resnick (1984) found that organizational climate had a significant impact on how well the performance appraisal process went. "When the climate was one of high trust, support, and openness, [appraisers and subordinates both reported] greater participation and contribution by the subordinate, and a higher degree of trust, openness, and constructiveness during the appraisal interview" (p. 31).

Employees—a vital resource

The assumptions that managers make about their subordinates are at the core of an organizational culture that is conducive to an effective performance appraisal programme. Managers must be convinced that their employees are a vital resource and that most employees welcome an opportunity to use their talents and abilities for the mutual benefit of themselves and the organization. How does an organization promote the idea that employees are its most important resource? Such an idea begins at the top and forms an integral part of the organization's culture, its core beliefs and values.

Management commitment: communication and rewarding managers for employee development

The strong commitment of top management to this view should be unequivocally communicated throughout the organization. A practical approach that works if it is consistently followed is to reward managers for developing their subordinates. Managers do respond to rewards and punishments, but caution is needed in administering them.

For example, when managers coach and develop their employees, they often find a high turnover of these well-trained employees through transfers to better positions in other departments. The managers are still held responsible for meeting departmental goals, although they now have to function with new, inexperienced employees. It is unlikely that these managers will continue to invest the needed time and effort in employee development.

Implicit in the approach of rewarding managers for employee development is the accompanying condition that managers be trained with the necessary skills for implementing the performance appraisal programme. One cannot overemphasize the pivotal role of managers in the success of the performance appraisal program. In one organization that the authors studied, both the managers and employees were dissatisfied with merit pay despite its enormous cost to the organization. The managers complained that merit pay did not generate high performance; the employees perceived it to be inequitable. A closer examination revealed some interesting anomalies.

First, the vast majority of the employees (about 75%) received "superior" or "outstanding" performance ratings, about 20% received "satisfactory" performance ratings, and the performance of only 5% were rated as "not satisfactory". Second, the managers did not see performance appraisals as important and they neither set performance standards nor provided feedback to their subordinates.

Figure 9.1: The Performance Appraisal Process and Its Essential Preconditions

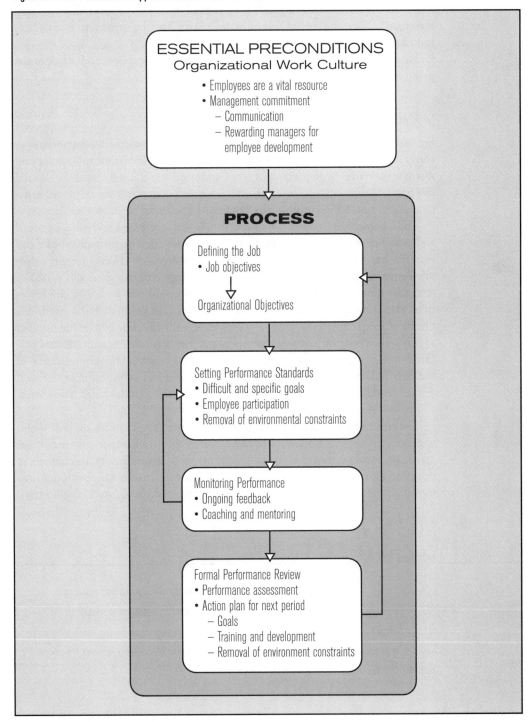

Instead, their performance ratings and the resulting merit pay decisions were based on considerations that were far removed from job performance: "playing favourites"; "not displeasing subordinates"; "avoiding the inconvenience of having to explain and justify merit pay decisions".

Figure 9.1 summarizes the performance appraisal process and its essential preconditions.

SUMMARY

Performance-based rewards are an indispensable element of an organization's compensation system. Through these rewards, the organization can attract and retain achievement-oriented employees, and motivate them towards the desired job performance behaviours. These rewards also contribute to employee satisfaction by increasing employee perceptions of personal or individual equity.

This chapter explored the concept of performance-based rewards in general and performance-based pay in particular. A well-designed performance-based pay plan ties pay to performance, minimizes the negative side-effects of high performance, promotes positive consequences, encourages cooperation, and generally enhances the acceptance of performance-based rewards. In addition, employees must value money. In order to develop such a plan, the organization must decide on the strategic issues: the level of aggregation, individual or group; the number of plans; the mode of payment; the size of the payment; the measurement of performance; the frequency of payment; and the process issues of communication of the plan and employee involvement in the design and administration of the plan. These critical decisions will form employee perceptions of the performance-outcomes linkage and the fairness or equity of the plan.

The effectiveness of a performance-based pay plan also depends on how well it is managed. The performance appraisal process plays an important role in the management of performance-based pay. It not only assures equity and fairness in determining the rewards, but it also provides a mechanism for rewarding only those behaviours that contribute to the attainment of the organization's objectives.

℘ KEY TERMS

effort	*performance appraisal process*
job performance	*performance-based rewards*
level of aggregation	*productivity*
objective measures of performance	*subjective measures of performance*
payout frequency	

REVIEW AND DISCUSSION QUESTIONS

1. Define job performance. How is job performance different from effort and productivity?

2. "Performance-based rewards enable an organization to achieve a variety of objectives in the management of its human resources." Do you agree? Why or why not?

3. "Our performance-based rewards not only do absolutely nothing to increase performance, but they have also proved to promote dysfunctional behaviours." Discuss this comment in the light of the conditions that facilitate the effectiveness of performance-based rewards.

4. What factors should you consider in deciding whether a performance-based pay plan should be on an individual or a group (i.e., work unit, department, entire organization) basis? Explain your reasons for your choice of these factors.

5. Most organizations prefer that merit pay be in the form of a one-time bonus, whereas most employees prefer it to be in the form of a salary increase. Which form of payment is likely to be more effective? Why?

6. In measuring performance, some advocate a strictly objective measure. Others claim that all measures are ultimately subjective. Still others believe that both objective and subjective measures are needed. Which position do you take? Why?

7. It has been argued that for a merit pay programme to be effective, employees must be involved not only in its design but also in its administration. Do you subscribe to this argument? Why? If you agree only partially, state your position and defend it.

8. Refer to the case Star Wars in Chapter 5. From the little information given, explore what you think might be deficient in SATCO's merit system. What changes would you recommend? Why?

9. Review the major steps and the essential preconditions of the performance appraisal process described in the chapter. Do you think any one step is more important or critical to an effective performance appraisal than the others? Why or why not?

CASE

Carpenter Creations Limited

Carpenter Creations is a furniture manufacturer. Started in 1983 by Brian Carpenter, a master cabinet-maker, as a custom-furniture operation, Carpenter Creations has since added an assembly-line operation for certain items. The organizational structure of Carpenter Creations is as follows:

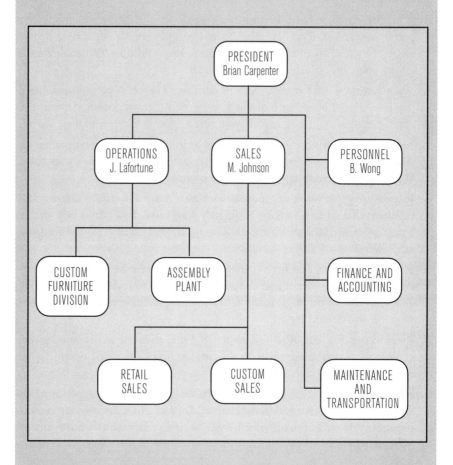

In addition to his technical expertise, Brian brought a strong entrepreneurial ability to the business. He is also a perfectionist, and this characteristic, along with his emphasis on creativity, has attracted some of the best cabinet-makers and carpenters to the custom furniture division, which enjoys a reputation for excellence in the industry. A demanding employer, Brian believes in rewarding outstanding performance. Accordingly, he has operated a performance-based pay system from the inception of the company.

For the past two years, Brian has been concerned that profits have declined despite an increase in sales. Discussions with department managers have uncovered the additional problem of employee dissatisfaction, particularly in the assembly plant. Brian is furious. He can't understand; Carpenter Creations has been the only firm in the industry to operate such a generous reward system.

Betty Wong, the new personnel manager, who has been with the company for just two months, suspects that the performance-based system is the cause of the trouble. She has succeeded in persuading Brian to subject the system to a comprehensive review.

On the basis of his review of the documentation and discussions with managers and some employees, Betty has come up with the following facts and observations relating to the performance-based pay system.

1. At the start of the company, the system was communicated by Brian to the cabinet-makers, each of whom worked independently on the custom-furniture jobs assigned to them. The mutual respect that existed between the cabinet-makers and Brian resulted in a free exchange of ideas on the system, and any suitable modifications, where necessary, were agreed upon.

2. In the assembly plant, information on the system was supposed to have been communicated by the department manager and the group supervisors. The assembly employees were unionized; the union was indifferent to the system. As is typical of an assembly operation, the measurement of any individual's contribution to the end product was difficult. In administering the system, the supervisor exercised his judgement in rewarding performance. Good performers have been socially ostracized; production slowed down during peak periods. Employee complaints resulting in grievance actions unrelated to the system have been unusually high. Supervisors have responded with tighter controls.

3. A salesperson operates relatively independently in his/her territory with responsibility for both custom sales and retail sales. In the sales department, the system pays a commission that is related to the dollar value of sales. Custom sales is a high-ticket item with a low profit margin; retail sales is low-priced but has a high profit margin.

4. In the other departments (personnel, finance and accounting, maintenance and transportation), the system rewards performance on the basis of a subjective evaluation by the supervisor. There are no complaints against the system, but the employees are not particularly enthusiastic about it.

5. The budget for the system is developed as follows:

    For the operating divisions—as a percentage of total production

    For the sales department—as a percentage of sales dollars

    For the other departments—as a percentage of the net profit of the company

    Management, employees, and even the union, agree that the formula for developing the budget is satisfactory. However, only the president and the department managers know the amount of the budget. There is also secrecy with respect to the amount paid to each individual.

Before Betty prepares her report to the President, she seeks your advice on

1. The strengths and weaknesses of the performance-based pay system in relation to
   - the design of the system
   - the implementation of the system;

2. The questions and issues he should explore that will help him to clarify what is critical to an effective performance-based pay system;

3. Specific recommendations for improving the system.

Incentive Systems:

Individual and

Organization-Wide Plans:

Personal Equity II

OVERVIEW

This chapter examines individual and organization-wide incentive plans. It also discusses in some detail strategic and process issues and the conditions that contribute to or hinder the effectiveness of these plans..

 LEARNING OBJECTIVES

- ▶ To understand the rationale underlying the piece-rate, standard-hour, and sales commissions and bonuses plans.

- ▶ To identify and explain the conditions that favour individual incentive plans.

- ▶ To identify and explain the content of the strategic and process issues that must be addressed in the design and management of gain-sharing plans.

- ▶ To understand and describe the Scanlon Plan, the Rucker Plan, and the Improshare Plan.

- ▶ To identify and explain the conditions that favour gain-sharing plans.

- ▶ To understand the purpose of profit sharing plans and the conditions which must exist in order for such plans to be effective.

- ▶ To understand the purpose of stock-based plans.

- ▶ To describe the main features of the different form of stock-based plans.

INTRODUCTION

In incentive plans, monetary rewards are designed to vary with some predetermined measure of performance such as increasing output, improving quality, reducing costs, increasing market share, improving customer service, and reducing absenteeism. Successful incentive plans enable the organization to motivate its employees to make the incremental effort to produce more, better, and efficiently. Table 10.1 depicts the individual and organization-wide incentive plans discussed in this chapter.

Table 10.1: Types of Incentive Plans

Individual Incentive Plans

Piece-rate plans	Standard-hour plans	Sales Commission & Bonus plans	Gain-sharing plans
Taylor plan	Halsey method	Base salary only	Scanlon plan
Merrick plan	Rowan plan	Commission only	Rucker plan
	Gantt plan	Base + Commission	Improshare plan
		Base + Bonus	

Organization-wide Incentive Plans

Profit-sharing plans	Stock-based plans
"First dollar" of profit	Stock Option plan
Profit above a threshold	Stock Grants
	• Performance Share/Unit plan
	• Restricted Stock plan
	• Phantom Stock plan
	Stock Purchase plan

INDIVIDUAL INCENTIVE PLANS

Basic characteristic

The basic characteristic of individual incentive plans is that the worker has control over the operation or the process involved in the job, and benefits from the increased productivity. In some plans, the worker receives the entire incremental gains that result from the increased worker productivity. In others, the incremental gains are shared between the worker and the organization. The rationale for this sharing is that the organization has contributed to the gains through the additional resources it has provided.

Types of plans

As seen in Table 10.1, individual incentive plans fall into three groups: (1) piece-work or piece-rate incentive plans; (2) standard-hour plans; and (3) sales commission/bonus plans.

PIECE-RATE PLANS

Piece-rate incentives, still in use today, can be traced back to the practices that prevailed among craftsmen in ancient times. They were paid for a product that conformed to the desired specifications. Today, the piece-rate is determined by taking into account the external market rate for the job as well as a careful analysis of the job, supported by engineered time studies.

For example

Suppose the market rate (or the union-negotiated rate) for an assembler of components is $12/hour, and the job analysis reveals that an "average employee" can assemble six units of acceptable quality per hour.

The piece-rate for the job will be calculated thus:
$$\frac{\text{Market Rate/hour}}{\text{Estimated Average Output/hour}} = \frac{\$12}{6} = \underline{\$2/\text{unit or piece}}$$

Therefore, an employee who has produced 60 units on one day will earn an income of $120.00 (60 units x $2/unit). The employee's earnings increases with the employee's output.

The assumption underlying "average employee" is that the employee possesses the average knowledge, skills, and ability required by the job, and works at a normal pace using the specified method. The computation also makes allowances for fatigue and delay factors.

Some specific variations of piece-rate plans

The Taylor Plan, also known as the differential piece-rate plan, truly incorporates the contingent-rewards concept. It sets a relatively high, but equitable, task or production standard. The piece-rate for output at or above the established standard is higher than the piece-rate for output below the established standard. The differential can vary between 20 and 30 per cent.

The Merrick Plan, also known as the multiple piece-rate plan has three piece-rates. The highest piece-rate is for output above the predetermined production standard, which is usually set at a high but equitable level. The next highest piece-rate is for output between 83 and 100 per cent of the production standard. The lowest piece-rate is for output below 83 per cent of the production standard (Schwinger, 1975). Both the Taylor and Merrick plans provide powerful incentives for employees to produce at or above the production standard. However, the Merrick Plan is designed to accommodate new employees who need encouragement as they settle into their jobs.

Standard-Hour Plan

Under this plan, workers qualify for an incentive payment when performance exceeds a standard expressed in relation to time.

For example:

Suppose that in the above piece-rate example, the average assembler can produce 6 units/hour. Based on this average, the "weekly standard output" will be 240 units (i.e., 6 units/hour x 8 hour-day x 5 day-week). Since the rate per hour is $12.00 and it takes 40 hours (i.e., 8 hour-day x 5 day-week) to produce this "weekly standard output", the regular (or standard) pay will be $480.00 per week (i.e., 40 hours x $12/hour).

Let us assume that an assembler produces 300 units in a week, that is, 60 units over the standard (i.e., 300 units—240 units). The 60 units represent 10 standard hours (i.e., 60 units/6 units per hour), which indicates that the assembler has done 50 hours of work in a 40-hour week—an efficiency of 125 per cent. Consequently, according to the standard hour plan, the assembler would qualify for an incentive of 25 per cent over and above the base or standard pay. The incentive computation will be:

Base or standard pay	= $480/week
25% efficiency incentive	= $120
Total earnings	= $600

The efficiency of 25 per cent can also be viewed as a saving of 10 hours of production time, an output that would have taken 50 standard hours has been produced in 40 hours. The savings of 10 hours qualifies for an incentive payment of 10 hours x $12/hour = $120.

Some specific variations of the Standard Hour Plan

Under the **Halsey 50-50 Method**, workers receive a guaranteed hourly wage and a bonus that is based on the time saved. Workers are required, to share this bonus with the company, usually on a 50-50 basis. For example, a worker completes a task in six hours instead of the standard time of eight hours — a saving of two hours. The worker will receive payment for only one hour, because the other hour is shared with the company.

The Rowan Plan operates similarly to the Halsey method. The major difference lies in the manner in which the time saving is shared. In the Rowan Plan unlike the Halsey Plan, the worker's share is directly determined by the extent of the saving in relation to the standard time. Suppose the worker completes in six hours a task that has a standard time of eight hours. The worker will receive a bonus of 25 per cent—$[(8 - 6)/8]$ of his/her hourly wage. If the time saving is four hours, the bonus increases to 50 per cent. Under the Rowan Plan, the worker's bonus increases with the increase in the time saved.

The Gantt Plan sets a high standard time; workers who complete the task in less than or equal to the standard time receive earnings equal to 120 per cent of the time saved. Unlike the Halsey and Rowan plans, the time saved is not shared between workers and the company. Further, workers who do not meet the standard receive a guaranteed base wage.

SALES COMMISSIONS AND BONUSES

Types of plans

In this variation of the piece-rate plan designed exclusively for sales people, the employee is paid a percentage of the sales (defined as gross or net sales). Generally, the commission plan structure will provide a minimum base earnings, and vary the commission percentages at an increasing rate for higher sales levels. The base salary-incentive mix gives rise to plans such as base salary only, commission only, base salary plus commission, and base salary plus bonus (Colletti and Cichelli, 1991).

Sales Plan Type	Content
Base salary only	Although no other compensation is offered, exceptional sales effort might be recognized through special sales contests.
Commission only	Total compensation is derived directly from the established commission schedule. Salespersons receive regular income in the form of a draw against expected commission. The draw is adjusted against the actual commissions earned.
Base salary plus commission	The commission is over and above the guaranteed base salary. The salary commission mix varies with the nature of the product, territory, sales support, and similar considerations.
Base salary plus bonus	The bonus is over and above the guaranteed base salary. The bonus is usually on task-and-bonus basis; it is earned only when the established sales quota is met.

Critical design features

Sales plan objective and organizational objectives The specific objectives a plan seeks to achieve may be maintaining or increasing market share and developing new accounts. Salespersons generally tend to perform those behaviours which are rewarded by the incentive plan, and ignore those which are not. Therefore, the incentive plan design should ensure that it promotes objectives which are consistent with the organization's objectives. Suppose that promoting a new product is strategically more important than promoting the older product. If selling the new product requires more sales effort relative to the older product, the sales plan incentive should be weighted more in favour of the new product.

Designing incentive components The factors in the selling situation which affect the base salary-incentive mix are the sales support, sales effort, and the length of the sales cycle. These factors are affected by the nature of the products and the assigned territories. For example, the customers' perceptions of the company's credibility and its products can help or hinder the salesperson from achieving the sales quota.

When the sales force is on its own without any support by way of advertising campaigns or sales aids the task of the salespeople is that much more arduous and deserves to be compensated by a higher sales commission. But as the organization develops a better quality product, improves pricing strategies, and makes a strong marketing and sales support effort, the task is not that difficult. Thus, as the sales person's performance is the major factor that influences the sale, the sales commission should be high; when the salesperson's performance is not critical to the sale, the commission should be low.

Incentive plans should also not reward salespersons for "windfall" or dropping sales which, by their very nature, cannot be attributed to the salesperson's performance. Such can be the case when sales increase dramatically because of a strike in a competitor's plant or due to a favourable foreign exchange situation, or when sales are impacted negatively because of circumstances beyond the salesperson's control.

The factors which affect the incentive mix are summarized on page 215.

Incentive activation threshold

Implicit in the types of incentive plans discussed above is the issue of the sale circumstances when the incentive component is activated.

Under the piece-rate system or the reward-as-you-achieve approach, every sale is rewarded with a commission even though the predetermined sales quota has not been attained. The piece-rate system works best with difficult sales targets. The reward-as-you-achieve approach induces employees to strive for the entire goal because they know that even if they fail, their efforts will not go unrewarded. In other words, they will be rewarded for whatever they have achieved.

Sales jobs	Incentive mix
Minimal effort & little sales support; e.g., to existing customers who routinely reorder or long sales cycle.	Base salary only
Considerable effort & little sales support, e.g., new product; new customers; short sales cycle.	Commission only; or base salary & commission with higher commission as sales effort increases and sales support decreases.
Mature stage of product life cycle; difficult sales territory; multiple performance behaviours.	Base salary plus bonus, with bonus tied to sales performance and related behaviours.

Source: Colletti and Cichelli, 1991

Under the task-and-bonus system, the reward (bonus) is paid only when the employee meets or exceeds the predetermined quota. The task-and-bonus approach is not appropriate for difficult goals. The all-or-nothing concept underlying the task-and-bonus approach does not induce employees to strive for a difficult goal, because they know that should they fail, their efforts will go completely uncompensated. The task-and-bonus approach seems to be appropriate for relatively easy goals. The ease of attaining the goal tends to increase salespeoples' confidence of earning the bonus and as a result serves as an inducement to strive for the goal.

What then is the appropriate incentive activation threshold? As Freedman (1986) observes: "Whatever threshold will make 85% to 90% of the sales force active players in the sales compensation game is the proper threshold to use. If a threshold is set so high that it excludes most of the sales force, it will not motivate the overall sales effort effectively. After all, an incremental dollar of sales is worth the same profit increment whether it comes from an average achiever or a superior one; if the sales incentive plan inspires only superior achievers, it may well be counterproductive" (p. 46).

CONDITIONS THAT FAVOUR OR HINDER THE EFFECTIVENESS OF INDIVIDUAL INCENTIVE PLANS

The preceding discussion identified the salient features and the mechanics involved in the implementation of individual incentive plans. Mechanics alone, despite their mathematical sophistication, do not ensure a plan's effectiveness. For this reason we need to consider the conditions that facilitate or hinder the plan's effectiveness.

CONDITIONS THAT FAVOUR THE EFFECTIVENESS OF INDIVIDUAL INCENTIVE PLANS

Effect of plan on organization's objectives

An incentive plan programme must ensure that the performance behaviours which it seeks to promote and influence do indeed lead to attaining the objectives of the job and of the organization. For example, increasing competition among Canadian banks and trust companies has increased the pressure to resort to incentives in order to promote the sale of financial products such as credit cards, term deposits and so on. However, the likely dysfunctional effects of incentives on overall organizational objectives is being recognized. As a spokesperson for the Bank of Nova Scotia recently observed: "If incentives are given around one particular type of product, you may get staff recommending that product even though that's not what the customer really needs" (Blackwell, 1995, p.13).

Incentive plans are intended to increase output and profits with practically no increase in fixed costs. However it is not uncommon for increases in output (whether of a product or a service) are achieved at the expense of quality. Not infrequently, the high output is achieved at the cost of the inefficient use of physical and financial resources. For example, the plan might focus on competition, instead of cooperation between departments that are interdependent.

The employee's ability to perform

The employee's (E⇨P) expectancy in respect to the performance targets must be high; otherwise, the employees' motivational force to put in the effort to perform will be low. An awareness of this criterion will enable the organization to identify training needs and institute appropriate actions such as empowerment (Conger and Kanungo, 1988) to enhance the employees' belief that they have the capability to achieve the performance targets.

Establish and communicate the performance-reward linkage

The performance-outcomes linkage must be clearly established and communicated. There are two aspects to this condition: (1) the performance standard is within the employee's control; and (2) employees understand and accept the plan.

Performance standard within employee control Employees cannot be expected to suffer a loss of reduction of earnings because of situations beyond their control. For example, an employee's output might suffer because of the failure of another department or employee to properly maintain the machines or to supply materials of the required specifications. In other situations, the job might be machine-paced, and delay an employee's completion of a task. The development of the standards of incentive plans should allow for such unexpected situations, which are beyond the employee's control. When performance objectives are not under the employee's control, the resulting inequity will cause the employee not to value the outcomes.

Employee understanding and acceptance of the plan   The terms, computation formulae, and mode of administration should be understood and accepted by employees. For example, decisions about the establishment of work standards involve a variety of interpretations relating to the definitions of the typical worker, normal work pace, and defined work method; as well as allowances for personal, fatigue, and delay factors. There can be honest differences of opinion on these issues not only between workers and management but also between workers themselves. Any attempt at secrecy or even a reluctance to disclose information will create doubts that can undermine the high level of employee trust indispensable for the plan's success.

For this reason, employees should be involved in the plan design. The net effect of this process is increased trust in the plan, and both workers and management function as co-partners in its design and administration. In unionized organizations, it is imperative to involve the union and obtain its commitment as well. When the union is involved, both the union and management have an opportunity to jointly address their mutual concerns right from the beginning. The involvement also promotes trust between the union and management, and paves the way for the development of the harmonious relationship that is essential for the success of incentive plans.

Provide modification mechanism

The plan design should include a mechanism for modifying it in the event that changed circumstances make such modification necessary. Often a change is necessitated because of the improper development of standards in the first place, or because changes in production or operating processes render the plan inappropriate. When modifications become necessary, employees must fully understand the need for the changes. Otherwise, employees may conclude these changes are arbitrary on the part of management and undertaken to cut rates or increase standards. Employee involvement in the process from the design stage will ensure that the needed changes are implemented with the collaboration of employees.

The worker's extra effort should lead to extra earnings

Implicit in incentive plans is the concept that the worker's extra effort should lead to extra earnings. Hence, the plan's design should ensure that workers in all jobs covered by the plan have the opportunity to earn incentive pay in direct proportion to their increased productivity. Ceilings on incentive pay will be viewed by employees as unjust and inequitable so long as the high earnings correspond with the increases in production. Incentive plans often include a guaranteed minimum wage in order to provide for differences in employee abilities. To ensure the motivational effect of the standard rate, a considerable spread should be maintained between the minimum and the standard rate.

Performance is measurable

When the employee's earnings are related to job performance, the measures of performance should be clear, unambiguous, and capable of measurement. Vagueness in measurement will seriously affect the (P⇨O) linkage, and also give rise to employee perceptions of inequity or unfairness. Individual incentive plans are effective when earnings are computed regularly, preferably on a daily basis, although the payment is on a weekly basis. Such regular, periodic computation and payments avoid ambiguity or vagueness in the measurements.

Employees should value money

Money is valued for its instrumentality to satisfy needs, among other reasons. As the needs are satisfied, the importance of money, and hence its value, decreases—unless money begins to serve as a source of recognition and thus satisfies self-esteem needs. Unless workers value money, incentive plans will not work.

Also, incentive plans affect individuals differently, depending upon whether they are intrinsically or extrinsically oriented. Employees who have a high need for achievement—the n-ach types—will strive to produce more if they believe they are likely to be successful. The n-ach individual is motivated by the satisfaction derived from performance—the feelings of personal accomplishment. An n-ach individual will not strive for a higher level of performance even though it carries a far greater reward if the individual believes that he/she does not have a reasonably moderate chance of success. For the n-ach individual, the increase in performance is not motivated by the incentive plan as such.

On the other hand, for low n-ach types, incentive plans can contribute to an increase in performance and to satisfaction from receiving incentive payments.

CONDITIONS THAT HINDER THE EFFECTIVENESS OF INDIVIDUAL INCENTIVE PLANS

The effectiveness of individual incentive plans can be affected by several conditions; for example: restriction of output; encouragement of competition; and higher accident rates.

Output restriction

Output restriction generally results when there is considerable mistrust between employees and management. Such mistrust fosters the belief that high productivity will lead to rate changes, an increase in standards (quotas), or lay-offs resulting from a high inventory and the inability of the company's marketing efforts to absorb the extra high production. Employees respond to the likely occurrence of these negative outcomes by restricting production. Their efforts in this direction are assisted by social pressures among their peers that operate to socially ostracize high performers.

Encouraging competition

Individual incentives have the potential to promote dysfunctional behaviours. By their very nature, individual incentive plans encourage the individual to focus on his/her self-interest. This is a recipe for disaster when jobs are inter-dependent and call for the norm of cooperation to take precedence over the norm of competition.

Higher accident rates

It is also not uncommon to see higher accident rates in situations where individual incentive plans operate, especially when the task standard is set too high. The desire to increase earnings often causes employees to cut corners, ignore safety regulations, and expose themselves to a higher level of risk. In addition, there are severe adverse effects on workers' health, morale, and efficiency. For these consequences to be avoided, incentive systems should have a guaranteed minimum wage—with a sufficient spread between the guaranteed minimum rate and the incentive plan's standard rate.

ORGANIZATION-WIDE INCENTIVE PLANS

One of the fundamentals of the compensation system is that its design should support the organization's strategies and objectives. Ordinarily, the individual incentive systems should reflect organizational performance provided that these reinforce individual job behaviours directed at achieving organizational objectives. However, not all jobs make a direct contribution to overall organizational performance.

Furthermore, except in small organizations, the nature of the inter-dependent relationships among jobs and functions, make it extremely difficult to assess the impact of an individual's performance. For these reasons, the individual-level performance-based pay or bonus systems are insufficient, and might even prove to be dysfunctional. For example, these systems might promote competition when cooperation is critical, or might not make it possible for the organization to vary its compensation costs in order to maintain its competitiveness. Therefore, organizations need to measure and reward performance at a higher level of aggregation, the work group, the division, or the organization as a whole.

Figure 10.1 Individual Incentive Plan: Context, Design Elements, and Moderating Characteristics

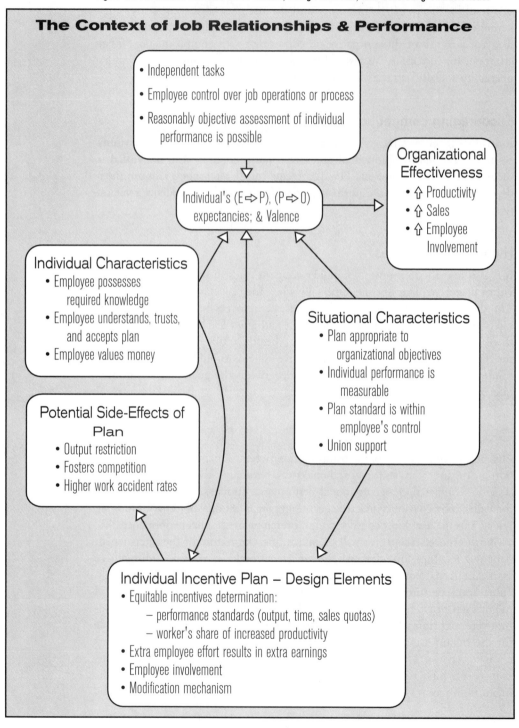

Historically, organizational performance as reflected by results such as profits, return on equity, stock value, and so on constituted the basis of executive compensation and not of the non-managerial employees. This was so because the "line of sight" from executive performance to such end results is strong, relative to that of non-managerial employees. However, with the intense competition in today's global market, there is a greater realization that organizations need to tap the talents and energies of all its employees. For this purpose, the variable pay concept—linking pay to organizational performance—is sought to be extended to employees at all organizational levels.

The compensation approaches that incorporate the "variable pay" concept are gain-sharing plans, profit sharing plans and stock-based plans. The examples which illustrate Canadian practices in these areas are, unless otherwise stated, drawn from a Conference Board of Canada survey by Booth (1990). This survey, referred to in this chapter as the "Canadian Survey" covers 122 organizations from seven industry sectors: energy, utilities, chemical, financial services, general manufacturing, natural resources, electronics, transportation, communication, and wholesale and retail trade; the combined total workforce in these organizations is about 1.1 million employees of which 38 percent are unionized.

GAIN-SHARING PLANS

Objective   The objective of gain-sharing plans is similar to that of individual plans—namely, to increase production (or some other desirable organizational objective) by providing employees with the opportunity to increase their earnings when they contribute to organizational objectives. About 16 percent of the organizations in the Canadian Survey had introduced a productivity gain-sharing plan. The success of these plans in meeting their objectives was rated as 3.5 (1=low, 5=high).

Rationale for group performance based plans

The rationale for the group approach is based on the following considerations:

1. The nature of the production process does not permit the individual to see a strong link between his/her efforts and the output.

2. The interdependent operations involved in the process require the cooperative effort of all employees. Group-based performance plans promote teamwork and cooperation within the group and between groups. Congruence in labour-management objectives have also improved when gain-sharing has been implemented (Lawler and Jenkins, 1992).

3. The group plan is the only alternative when individual performance measures are not available or when individual performance is difficult to measure with the required degree of objectivity.

4. Group plans enable employees to experience non-financial rewards, such as the satisfaction of their social needs.

5. Because employee involvement is critical to the design and implementation of group plans, the negative side-effects of individual incentive plans are generally absent.

Critical design issues

The critical design issues relate to the process of design, the development of a standard, the costs to be covered, the sharing of gains, the frequency of bonus payments, the process to manage change/modifications, and the participative system inherent in the plan (Lawler and Jenkins, 1992). Each of these will now be considered.

What design process is appropriate?

This issue addresses the question: What process will be used in setting up the plan? The options are top-down, participative, and third-party involvement.

The top-down approach: This approach is not appropriate because it does not involve the employees. Because of the high level of aggregation, employees will not see the performance-outcomes linkage, nor will they have a basis on which to decide whether rewards are determined in a fair and equitable manner. The importance of employees' understanding of the plan is well-illustrated by the dissatisfaction reported to have been felt by a major bank's employees when they discovered that bonuses under their new bonus plan were 20% lower at the same time that the bank reported record profits of $986 million. "It could well be legit but I think the reason for some disgruntlement is that no one sees the national business plan (at the branch level)...So you just have to take it on faith that everything has to be cut down by 21 percent (but) it's hard for me to understand how one could be short of any reasonably attainable business plan at the same time as we cranked out 986 million smackers" (Partridge, 1995, p.B3).

The participative approach The organization-wide gainsharing plan has its roots in the management philosophy that all employees play a vital role in the success of the organization. As Max De Pree, C.E.O. of Herman Miller, Inc., observed: "Participative ownership offers Herman Miller a competitive edge" (1989). This philosophy recognizes that every single employee can contribute to the overall effectiveness and continued survival of the organization. For this reason, the participative approach has been found to be more appropriate. The increased input, trust, and understanding that result from employee involvement and participation will lead to a greater acceptance of the plan and to the increased cooperation that is necessary for its successful implementation.

Third-party involvement Involvement by a third party (an outside consultant) can be helpful in advising on the technical aspects of the plan so long as the final decisions are made within the organization with the full participation of the employees.

What are the issues in developing a performance standard?

In determining the bonus, an organization can use the standard of costs or profits. Any improvement over the standard will be shared. To establish a standard, the organization must consider whether to use historical data or engineered or estimated data. When historical data are used, an average of the previous five or so years is generally considered. The difficulty with historical data is the implied assumption that the past is an accurate indicator of the future. This assumption does not appear to be realistic for organizations operating in turbulent environments, where technology and markets are changing. Also, historical data are not feasible for a new company. Engineered or estimated data work is fine if a high level of trust exists between employees and management, and if the expertise of the estimator is credible.

What costs are included in a performance standard?

The Scanlon Plan, the most popular plan, uses labour costs as a proportion of sales. Thus, any improvement in the labour-costs-to-sales ratio is distributed as a bonus. A focus on labour costs has the advantage that these costs are directly under the control of employees. The formula can be kept simple and easy for all to understand. Both considerations strengthen the performance-outcomes linkage and increase the valence of outcomes.

However, such a focus on labour costs tends to be unrealistic in that it ignores costs for material and utilities. Although the addition of these costs makes the plan more realistic, it still suffers from two major difficulties. First, employees may not be in a position to control these costs. Second, as more costs are included, the plan grows more complex and difficult to understand and hence less acceptable to employees as being fair and equitable.

The practices of Holiday Inn, Honeywell, and Thompson-Ramo-Woolridge, Inc (TRW) demonstrate that these difficulties are not insurmountable. Holiday Inn uses revenue and quality of service. Honeywell and TRW use total cost in relation to the bid price. When total cost is below the bid price, that difference is shared three-ways: with the customer, the company, and the employees (Lawler, 1990).

How are gains to be shared?

The response to this question involves decisions on the following:

- the proportion according to which the gains are shared between the company and the employees;
- the proportion according to which the employees' share is distributed among the various categories, for example, office versus factory employees and management versus non-management employees;
- how the share is distributed to each employee: on the basis of salary? on the basis of the employee's performance as assessed by a performance appraisal?

The plans described later in the chapter illustrate these decisions.

What will the payment frequency be?

Will the payout be monthly, quarterly, or annually? Most plans pay out monthly, but the entire amount is not distributed. A portion is kept in a reserve fund to provide for unforeseen exigencies; the fund is held in trust for the employees. The plans of some companies that operate on a seasonal basis pay out at the end of the season to better reflect the performance in that season. The more frequent the payment is, the more visible is the connection between employee efforts and rewards and, therefore, the more effective the reward is.

Should there be a mechanism for managing plan changes?

This issue is critical, particularly for organizations that operate in a changing environment. Major changes in the fields of technology, product mix, markets, products, and so forth will affect the plan standards and formula either adversely or favourably for either the employees or the company. The plan should provide for a mechanism and a process that will identify and initiate changes to the plan.

How will the participative process be maintained?

The participative process is critical to the successful operation of the plan. The experience of Herman Miller, Donnelly Mirrors, Lincoln Electric, Nucor Corporation—to name just a few corporations that have successfully used gain-sharing plans—suggests that gain-sharing plans are more than a mere device to increase productivity; they represent a way of life. Some organizations have adopted a parallel structure, a steering committee that includes representatives of employees and management from all levels and functions as well as representatives of the union. Other organizations have used the suggestion system with special awards for suggestions that have proved to be effective.

TYPES OF GAIN-SHARING PLANS

This section describes three of the more popular organization-wide gain-sharing plans—the Scanlon Plan, the Rucker Plan, and the Improshare Plan. The description focuses on how these plans address the critical issues of the design and implementation process, the bonus formula, distribution scheme, and change management. The discussion also includes a brief assessment of the plans.

SCANLON PLAN
Purpose

In the mid-1930s Joseph Scanlon of the United Steelworkers of America developed the Scanlon plan to promote labour-management cooperation because he was convinced that the efficiency of organizations depended upon such cooperation. Scanlon believed that both employees and the organization would benefit if employees' suggestions for efficient operations were implemented and rewarded. Today, the Scanlon Plan is promoted as a "total system" that seeks to achieve, through a participative and cooperative process, both organizational effectiveness and employee development. The plan covers all employees.

Design and Implementation Process

From its inception, the plan introduced a participative process. Each department has a production committee comprised of representatives of workers and management. The committee seeks ways and means to improve productivity, quality, and methods of operations. In addition, the plan provides for an organization-wide screening committee composed of top management and worker representatives. The screening committee administers the plan, decides on employee suggestions, and is generally the forum for reviewing the impact of major business trends on the organization. The basic objective of the committee is to share the maximum information about the company and its operations with the employees, and to genuinely seek their ideas and efforts to make the organization effective.

Bonus Formula and Distribution Scheme

The bonus formula attempts to assess improvements in productivity through the ratio of total payroll to the sales value of production. This relationship tends to be fairly stable in many organizations. The sales value of production is obtained by adjusting net sales for inventory and goods-in-process. The data relating to labour costs and the sales value of production are analyzed and a base period is selected, so that the formula provides a ratio that truly reflects the relationship of these variables in the organization. Projected labour costs are determined by applying the ratio to the current sales value of production. Current (actual) labour costs are then compared with projected labour costs; the excess of projected labour costs over actual labour costs represents an improvement in productivity, and constitutes the bonus pool.

The bonus pool, usually calculated on a monthly basis, is distributed as follows:

- The first 25 per cent is set aside as a reserve fund for situations when actual labour costs exceed projected labour costs.
- The balance (75 per cent) in the bonus pool is shared between the employees and the company, 75 per cent of the balance to the employees and 25 per cent to the company.
- At the end of the year, the balance in the reserve fund is also shared by the employees and the company on the same 75 per cent/25 per cent basis.

Each employee's share is proportionate to that employee's share of the total payroll.

Example

The ABC Company determined that the data of the previous two years reflected with reasonable accuracy the relationship of its payroll costs to its sales value of production. It used the averages of the previous two years to compute the base or standard ratio:

$$\frac{\text{Average Payroll Costs of Previous Two Years}}{\text{Average Sales Value of Production of Previous Two Years}}$$

$$= \frac{\$\ 5{,}000{,}000}{\$12{,}000{,}000} = 41.7\%$$

Suppose for the first month of the plan period the actual payroll was $300,000 and the sales value of production was $900,000. According to the standard ratio, projected payroll costs for the current sales value of production will be:

($900,000 x .417) = $375,300

The savings for the month, which constitute the bonus pool, will be

(Projected Payroll Costs – Actual Payroll Costs) = Bonus Pool

($375,000 – $300,000)   = $75,000

This bonus pool will be distributed as follows:

Reserve Fund: (25% x 75,000) = $18,750

Bonus Pool Balance (available for distribution):

(75,000 – 18,750) = $56,250

Company Share of Bonus Pool Balance:

(25% x 56,250) = $14,062.50

Employees' Share of Bonus Pool Balance:

(75% x 56,250) = $42,187.50

If Emilia Donato's monthly salary is .007 of ABC Company's payroll, her share of the bonus for the first month will be:

(42,187.50 x .007) = $295.31

Managing Change

Gain-sharing plans need a structure and a process for modifying the plan in response to changes in such factors as product mix, technology, market, and economic environment. In the Scanlon Plan, the committees closely monitor the standard ratio and introduce the necessary changes. The Plan's adaptability is also well-illustrated by the 30 year's experience of Herman Miller, Inc. which modified the plan as conditions changed (Frost, Greenwood and Associates, 1982).

An Assessment of the Scanlon Plan

The Scanlon Plan has produced positive results: cost-saving suggestions; a committed and cooperative workforce with a much greater focus on the economics, goals, and operations of the business; improved labour-management relations; and high levels of employee satisfaction. Critical to the success of the plan is the precondition of trust between labour and management. Also critical to the plan's success is the attitude of middle managers who see employee involvement as a threat to their traditional authority and decision-making role.

RUCKER PLAN

Purpose

The Rucker Plan was developed by Allan Rucker of Eddy-Rucker-Nickels, a firm of consultants. Like the Scanlon Plan, the Rucker Plan is an organization-wide gain-sharing plan with the underlying mission to promote harmonious employee-management relations. Unlike the Scanlon Plan, it has been adopted mostly by non-unionized companies.

Design and Implementation Process

The Rucker Plan also has a structure of committees composed of employee and management representatives. These committees evaluate employee suggestions for improving productivity. The committees also coordinate the various processes relating to the plan.

Bonus Formula and Distribution Scheme

Productivity improvements in the Rucker Plan are assessed by a ratio that indicates the production value added for each dollar of labour costs in relation to the sales value of production. It is claimed that a reasonably stable relationship exists between total labour costs and the sales value of production (Lawler, 1986a). The production value added for each dollar of labour costs is computed by subtracting from the sales value of production the cost of raw materials, supplies, and items related to the services used up in the production and delivery of the product.

Data from accounting and production records for a base period are used to determine the percentage of the sales dollar that can be attributed to labour. That percentage is then used to compute the standard productivity ratio. The productivity ratio is applied to the current total labour costs to project the standard production value for this level of labour costs, which is also referred to as the projected (or expected) sales value of production. The excess of the current (actual) sales value of production over the projected sales value of production represents an improvement in productivity, and constitutes the bonus pool.

The bonus pool is distributed to employees on the basis of labour's contribution to production value; the remainder goes to the company. Usually, about 25 per cent of labour's share is withheld in a reserve fund to cover situations when the current value of production is less than the projected (or standard) sales value of production. However, at the end of the year, any balance in the reserve fund is paid out to the employees.

Example

The ABC Company determined that the data of the previous two years were typical of its operations. It therefore decided to use the averages of these years to compute the productivity ratio. On the basis of these data, the company estimates that the cost of raw materials, supplies, and items related to the services used up in the production and delivery of the product constitutes 60 per cent of the sales dollar; therefore, 40 per cent of the sales dollar is attributable to labour.

The Productivity Ratio will be:

$$\frac{100}{\text{Value Added Attributed to Labour}}$$

$$= \frac{100}{40} = 2.5$$

Suppose the actual payroll for the first month of the plan period was $300,000 and the sales value of production was $900,000. According to the standard productivity ratio, the projected sales value of production will be:

$300,000 \times 2.5 = \$750,000$

The savings for the month, which constitute the bonus pool, will be

Actual Sales Value – Projected Sales Value
 of Production   of Production
 = $900,000   – $750,000
 = $150,000

The bonus pool will be distributed as follows:

Company Share: (60% × 150,000) = $90,000

Employees' Share: (40% × 150,000) = $60,000

Reserve Fund (25% of Employees' Share): (25% x 60,000) = $15,000
Immediate Payout to Employees: (60,000 – 15,000) x $45,000

If Emilia Donato's monthly salary constitutes .007 of ABC's total payroll, her share of the bonus for the first month will be:
(45,000 x .007) = $315

Managing Change

The committee structure attends to the study and modification of the standard productivity ratio as necessitated by significant changes in such factors as technology and work methods.

An Assessment of the Rucker Plan

The plan's inclusion of other costs in the computation of the bonus makes it particularly suitable for organizations where these costs are significant components of the cost structure. But, there might be a downside to this positive feature if it leads to complex computations. However, this problem could be overcome by improved communication to help make the plan more understandable to employees.

Unlike the Scanlon Plan, not much has been published on the effectiveness of the Rucker Plan. From the structure and the process of the plan it can be inferred that the results will not differ greatly from those of the Scanlon Plan. In fact, the proponents of the plan claim that "... the reward aspect of the gain-sharing program is only one-third of the program: the other two, equally important, are feedback of results to employees (and further information sharing) and involvement/participation of employees in productivity-increasing activities" (Wallace and Fay, 1988, 262).

IMPROSHARE PLAN

Purpose

Developed in the mid-1970s by Mitchell Fein, the Improshare Plan was initially designed for the sole purpose of improving productivity through industrial engineering work measurement principles. Today, the plan incorporates a participative management approach. Its underlying philosophy is that employees and management have a common interest in jointly improving productivity and sharing equally in the gains from such improvement.

Design and Implementation Process

Since the plan uses industrial engineering work measurement principles, the design process is dependent on the experts who develop the engineered or estimated data. Employee participation will therefore be low compared with what it is in the Scanlon and Rucker plans. However, organizations that now adopt the plan tend to adopt it along with other high-involvement strategies such as quality control circles. The focus of these organizations, it would appear, is also on encouraging participative management (Lawler, 1986a).

Bonus Formula and Distribution Scheme

The bonus formula measures productivity by the use of engineered time standards as expressed by the number of direct labour hours required to produce one unit of the product during the established base period. This time standard is then applied to the production output in the base period to arrive at the estimated total labour hours required for that output. A ratio of the actual labour hours worked on the base-period output to the estimated total labour hours required provides the base productivity factor, which is used to derive the Improshare standard hours. The Improshare standard hours are then used as the base for computing the bonus.

If the actual labour hours of the plan period are less than the Improshare hours, employees qualify for a bonus. The output data for the bonus computations include only products of acceptable quality. The bonus share of each employee is related to the employee's base salary.

Example

The ABC Company determines that the monthly production of the previous two years is typical, and decides to use the average 2,000 units produced over the past two years as the base. The engineered estimate of the direct labour hours required to produce each unit is 8 hours. Therefore, the estimated total labour hours required to produce the 2,000 units would be (2,000 x 8 h) = 16,000 hours. The company has 100 employees who worked a 40-hour work week to produce the 2,000 units a month. The actual labour hours worked would be (100 x 40 x 4) = 16,000 hours.

Hence the Base Productivity Factor of the company would be:

$$\frac{\text{Actual Labour Hours Worked}}{\text{Estimated Total Labour Hours Required}}$$
$$= \frac{16,000}{16,000} = 1.00$$

The Improshare Standard is:
Base Productivity Factor x Engineered Direct Labour Hours
= (1.00) (8 h) x 8 hours

In the first month of the plan period, 2,200 units were produced by 100 employees working a total of 16,000 hours. The Improshare Earned

Hours for this production are:
(Units Produced) x (Improshare Standard Hours)
(2,200 x 8)
= 17,600 hours

The Hours Gained were:
(Improshare Earned Hours – Actual Earned Hours)
(17,600 – 16,000)
= 1,600 hours

The bonus hours gained are shared 50/50 between the employees and the company. Therefore, the employee share of the bonus hours gained will be (1,600 x .50) x 800 hours.

The Employees' Bonus will be
$$\frac{\text{Bonus Hours Gained}}{\text{Actual Earned Hours}} = \frac{800}{16,000} = 5\% \text{ for each employee}$$

Thus, Emilia Donato will receive in the first month of the plan period an Improshare bonus amounting to 5 per cent of her salary for that month. *Source:* Aft (1985)

Managing Change

Improshare has a well-designed mechanism for change, which is triggered when improvements in productivity exceed 160 per cent, and also when it can be demonstrated that these improvements are attributable to changes in technology or equipment (Henderson, 1989).

An Assessment of the Improshare Plan

The use of engineered or estimated data to establish base standards makes the Improshare Plan suitable for new organizations. It is also suitable for organizations whose past production experience is not a reasonably reliable indicator of future operations and therefore cannot be used to develop base standards that equitably assess and reward productivity improvements.

CONDITIONS THAT FAVOUR GAIN-SHARING PLANS

These conditions can be grouped into two sets of characteristics: the social system characteristics and the situational characteristics. Both sets of characteristics function to facilitate or hinder the effectiveness of the gain-sharing plan, according to their impact on the employee's effort-to-performance expectancy, performance-to-outcomes expectancy, and valence of outcomes.

Social system characteristics

The major social system characteristics are that employees possess the requisite knowledge, skills, and abilities, understand the plan and value money. In addition, high trust should exist between employees and management.

Situational characteristics

The situational characteristics are the capacity of market to absorb the increased output; the employee overtime history; the availability of relatively objective performance measures; the performance standard/goal is within the employees' control; commitment and leadership from management; and, in unionized organization, the plan is supported by the union. The earlier discussion on "conditions that favour the effectiveness of individual incentive plans" has addressed the characteristics of the availability of objective performance measures, employee control of performance standard/goal, and union support.

This discussion will, focus on the capacity of the market to absorb the increased output, overtime history, and commitment and leadership from management.

Market's capacity to absorb increased output   The almost immediate result of a gain-sharing plan is improvement in productivity. If the increased output cannot be absorbed by the market, no revenue will flow to provide for the plan payments. On the contrary, improved productivity might even lead to lay-offs.

Organization's overtime history   If there were considerable paid overtime before the plan was installed, employee earnings from the plan should at least equal the amount of overtime that was previously being earned. Otherwise, employees may resort to actions that will restrict output, defeating the purpose of the plan.

Management commitment to plan   The most important condition is that of commitment and leadership from top management and a willingness to be open and honest with employees on all matters relating to the operations that have an impact on the bonus determination and pay-out. Management's commitment to the plan will also be demonstrated by its willingness to respond to employees' requests for the support and training that will enable them to improve their effectiveness. Any indifference to such requests will affect the plan operations.

Figure 10.2 summarizes the context, elements, and conditions of an effective gain-sharing plan. It highlights the major context in terms of the interdependent relationships among jobs and functions. It identifies the critical design elements, and the social system and situational characteristics which moderate the plans effectiveness in enhancing the elements which generate employee motivation. The increased employee motivation would then lead to organizational effectiveness in terms of productivity, employee innovation and involvement.

Figure 10.2: Organization-wide Incentive Plan: Context, Design Elements, and Moderating Characteristics

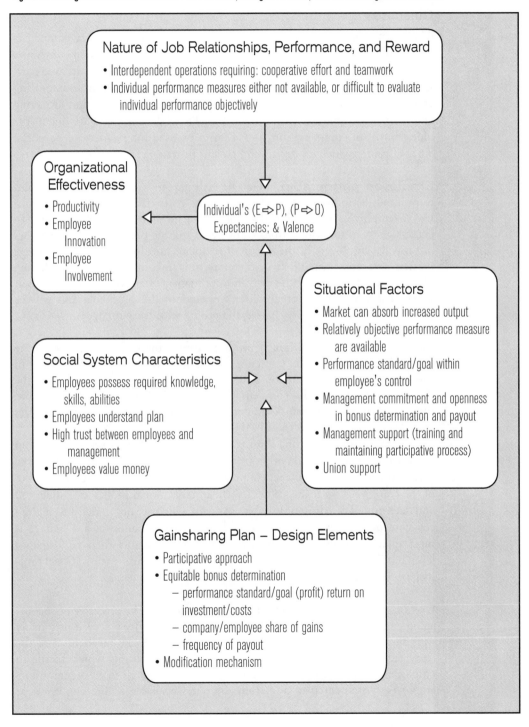

PROFIT SHARING PLANS
Objectives

The profit sharing plan is a reward strategy which links employee compensation to the economic performance of the organization. A survey of companies with profit sharing plans revealed objectives such as promoting employee partnership, providing group incentive, encouraging employee thrift and ensuring employee security, providing variable income beyond base pay, and attracting and retaining employees (Knowles, 1954). Profit sharing plans are one of the oldest forms of compensation, and seem to be used for a variety of purposes. They also vary widely in design and payout provisions.

Employee partnership   Like gainsharing plans, profit sharing plans aim to promote "employee partnership". But this "partnership" is intended to convey to employees the feeling that they are part of the organization and to encourage them to be loyal to it. Unlike gain-sharing plans, profit sharing does not involve employees in the design of the plans nor does it seek to encourage participative management. It is, therefore, not uncommon for profit sharing plans to be introduced at the discretion of management, based solely on their judgement whether the organization's operations are profitable and will be profitable enough to justify sharing the profits with the employees.

Group incentive   Although profit sharing plans seek to create a culture which allow employees to experience a sense of partnership, its effectiveness in this regard is limited by the top-down approach and more significantly, by the discretionary nature of this compensation. When the basis of profit sharing and the computational mechanics are not disclosed, it is less likely that employees truly see themselves as partners in the organization.

In some instances, profit sharing plans are intended to serve as a group incentive. The effectiveness of profit sharing as an incentive depends upon the extent to which the payouts reflect the performance which is under the control of the employees. In reality, however, the organizational profits are influenced and determined by a host of variables many of which are not under the employees' control. The extremely foggy or blurred performance-reward linkage is most apparent when employees maintain or even enhance their performance level, but do not receive the commensurate payout because organizational profits have fallen or are not at the level expected by management.

Encouraging employee thrift and security   The objective of encouraging employee thrift and the resulting employee security is served reasonably well by profit sharing plans. This is achieved through the mechanism of the "deferred" plan. In such a plan, some or all of the profits which accrue to employees are placed in a deferred fund. It is often linked to an organization's employee retirement plan and, thus, becomes available to the employees at retirement. The deferred plan may incorporate provisions for employee vesting rights—employees' rights to the accrued profits in the deferred fund commences only when they stay with the company for a prescribed period of time. Should employees leave before the prescribed period of time, they lose their accrued profits in the deferred fund. With this vesting rights provisions, the deferred plan also serves as a means for employee retention.

Variable pay; employee attraction and retention   The two closely tied objectives for which profit sharing plans seem best suited are providing variable income and attracting and retaining employees. Profit sharing plans enable organizations to vary employee income beyond the base pay, so that the total pay is made up of a fixed and a variable component. The fixed component is the base pay that is generally set below the market pay rate; the variable component is determined by the organization's profitability. Such a pay structure allows the organization to vary its total pay costs according to the organizations ability to pay. Thus, as profits rise, the variable pay component rises, but so does the organization's capacity to afford the higher pay costs. On the other hand, as profits fall, the variable pay component also falls which is consistent with the fact that the lower profits have diminished the organization's capacity to pay.

The variable pay concept is particularly attractive to the organization in cyclical businesses because it contributes to maintaining its cost competitiveness. If organizations do not adopt the variable pay concept, layoffs would be the alternative means to cope with the labour costs that the organization's profitability cannot afford. As Lawler (1990) observes: "with profit sharing, it is possible to reduce costs significantly without reducing the number of employees or adopting work sharing... As is the case in Japan, profit sharing can allow an organization to make a much stronger commitment to employee stability and help it gain the advantages inherent in having a stable work force" (p.126). Profit sharing is also instrumental in attracting and retaining employees because they receive a much higher total pay when the organization prospers.

How does the variable pay concept affect employees when the organization's profitability performance deteriorates? The answer depends upon the relative profitability performance of the competitors. If all the organizations in the industry have a similar low performance level, the employees' perception of external equity relative to competitive organizations will remain unchanged. Employees will experience external inequity only when their organization's profitability performance is low relative to others in the industry. For most employees there is no "line of sight" from their performance to the organization's profits. In other words, they do not perceive a reasonably strong performance-profits linkage.

Critical design issues

Degree of pay variability   The "line of sight" issue is the major reason why the motivational value of profit sharing plans is limited, relative to that of gainsharing. For this reason, the degree of variability is rarely uniform for all employee groups. Thus, variable pay usually constitutes a greater portion of the total pay of managerial employees because the nature of their jobs allows them a better line of sight from their performance to the organization's profits. This is not the case with non-managerial employees whose jobs do not give them the same line-of-sight.

Therefore, the variable pay component needs to be a much smaller portion of their total pay. Lawler (1990) suggests a 30% to 40% variable pay component for employees at the upper levels of the organization whose performance have a greater impact on profits and 0% to 15% for employees at the lower levels of the organization.

Activation threshold   Although the line of sight in profit sharing plans is weak, relative to gain-sharing plans, the motivational impact of profit sharing plans can be enhanced through proper design and communication. An important design element is that the plan's payout commences as soon as profits are made, based on the "first dollar" of profit rather than based on profits in excess of a threshold, usually a predetermined profit level.

Communication   The plan should be clearly communicated together with the profitability objectives and how these relate to the overall organizational mission. Employees should also be kept informed periodically of the organization's performance. In addition to facilitating the employees' understanding and acceptance of the plan, it also educates employees in the economics and financial condition of the business. The Canadian Survey found that profit sharing plans extended to over 75 percent of all employees; of all the incentive plans, it was assessed as the most successful in meeting plan objectives—a success rating of 4 (1=low, 5=high). Furthermore, it was also seen as instrumental in promoting employee awareness of and identification with organization's goals and objectives.

The plan serves to provide the bigger picture of the business—its mission, objectives, and goals; as well it makes clear the role of the various work units in the generation of profits. In this way, employees have an opportunity to view their jobs in their proper perspective, to acquire a better understanding of how their jobs directly or indirectly affect the profitability of the organization.

STOCK-BASED PLANS

Types of plans and participation eligibility

The stock-based plan is the third form of plans designed to make compensation reflect organizational performance. These can be grouped into three categories: stock option plans, stock grant plans, and stock purchase plans. Historically, these plans were usually restricted to executive and senior management employees because a line of sight was believed to extend from their job performance to organizational performance as reflected in stock values. In recent times, however, some of these plans have been extended to employees at lower organizational levels. For example, the Pepsico Groups offered stock options to all its employees (Levine, 1990).

Nevertheless, the participation eligibility for stock options and stock grants are almost always restricted to executives and senior management. As the findings of the Canadian Survey show, the eligibility for these plans extended to 95 percent of all executives, 35 to 48 percent of management and professional, and 1 percent of other employees. However, the same survey found a dramatic change in the eligibility for the stock purchase plans—it extends to about 82 to 92 percent of all employees.

Do these plans motivate employees to higher performance levels? Do these plans truly reward organizational performance? We address these questions as we explore each plan.

THE STOCK OPTION PLAN

Content and mechanics

A relatively popular plan for senior executives, the stock option plan offers employees the right to buy a fixed amount of stock at a price that is set when the stock option is offered. The gain to the employee results if the option is exercised when the stock value rises. They buy at a lower price than the market and can profit by selling their shares at the prevailing higher market price. Until the option is exercised, there is no cash outlay by the employees. In the stock option plan, the executives' interests are linked to the future value of the stock. It serves as an inducement for executives to make sound decisions which emphasize the long-term effectiveness and growth of the organization. To this extent, the plan encourages executives to identify with the stockholders' interests.

Plan effectiveness

It needs to be recognized that the motivational value derived from the performance-stock value linkage is limited because the linkage is not as strong as the performance-profits linkage in profit sharing. The holder of stock options have no control over the stock value which invariably depends on the vagaries of the stock market. This loss of control might be further exacerbated when the stock option is of a company in which the holder is not employed—such as the parent holding company. The Canadian Survey found that the success of stock option plans in meeting their stated objectives was rated as 3.0 (1=low, 5=high), the lowest success rating among the long-term incentive plans.

Although the stock option plan is intended to reflect organizational performance, it often happens that its design is considerably influenced by tax laws which raise the question whether the plan might not be more of a mechanism for tax and estate planning.

THE STOCK GRANTS PLAN
Types, eligibility, effects

There are various ways in which organizations grant stock to employees in order to motivate performance or membership behaviours. The Canadian Survey found that:

- 23 percent of Canadian organizations offered stock grants;
- participation eligibility was restricted to 96 percent of executives, 48 percent of management and professionals, and 1 percent of other employees;
- the success of this plan in meeting its objectives was rated as 3.5 (1=low, 5=high).

The reason why the Stock Grants Plan is rated as more successful than the Stock Options Plan is because its value is not determined solely by market factors. It can be designed to better reflect an individual's performance. The additional advantage to employees is that in all forms of stock grants, they are not required to incur a cash outlay to acquire the stock.

The Stock Grants Plan is particularly well-suited for privately-owned companies (Booth, 1987). The forms of stock grants which we shall explore are the performance share/unit plan, the restricted stock plan, and the phantom stock plan.

The performance share/unit plan: content and effects

Under this plan, eligible employees receive "performance units" based on the organization's performance. The performance relates to the attainment of specific objectives, for example, the rate of earnings per share. Thus, the higher the rate of earnings per share, the larger the number of "performance units" that are awarded according to a predetermined schedule for different levels of earnings per share.

The description, so far, would suggest that it is a bonus plan linked to a performance objective. However, under the plan, the bonus is computed in terms of "performance units" but paid out in stocks, more often in a combination of cash and stock according to a conversion mechanism built into the plan. Relative to other plans, the motivational impact on performance is the greatest in the performance share/unit plan, because the performance criteria—earnings per share—is more within the employee's control than are the factors which determine the stock value.

The Restricted Stock Plan: Content and effects

Under this plan, the stock grants represent a bonus to management or key employees in order to attract or retain them in the company. The benefits to the employees consist of stock dividends, if any, and capital appreciation. To attract the employee, the stock grant is made up-front when the employee joins the company. To retain the employee, the plan imposes restrictive conditions which prevent employees from selling the stock within a certain time period, or until the organization meets certain predetermined objectives.

The stock grants are an incentive to employees to contribute to the organization's effectiveness and, thereby, benefit themselves as well through the resulting increases in dividends and stock value. The motivational value for enhanced performance will depend upon the employees' perception of the degree to which their performance can influence the stock value. However, the restriction on the sale of stock will likely motivate the employees to remain with the company. The tax implications would also need to be considered.

The Phantom Stock Plan: Content and effects

In this plan, there is no grant of actual stock to the eligible employees. Instead, they receive fictitious shares based on a system of units which correspond to a certain number of shares. The value of the units is based on the market price of the shares at the time the unit is awarded. Each unit has a specified maturity term, one, three, or five years. When the unit matures, the unit holder is paid a sum of money computed according to a predetermined formula. Usually, the formula is based on two factors: the market price of the stock, and the attainment of a specified performance objective. In addition to the capital appreciation that may occur at maturity, the unit holder is entitled to dividend payouts on the number of shares equivalent to the units that are held.

THE STOCK PURCHASE PLAN
Content and effects

This plan enables employees to acquire company stock at a price that is lower than the market price. The company may assist employees by providing loans for such acquisitions. Organizations with profit sharing plans may give the employees' share of the profits in the form of stocks. As stated earlier, the stock purchase plan is gaining popularity in Canada. The plan is used by 51% of Canadian organizations and the eligibility for participation extends to over 80% of all employees. The plan's success in meeting its objectives is rated 3.5 (1=low, 5=high).

In terms of organizational performance, the motivational value is generated when the plan is based on profit sharing only to the extent that the line of sight exists from employee performance to the company's profits. It also depends upon the extent to which employees perceive that appreciation of the stock value is linked to their performance. If the stock value is determined mainly by the state of the financial markets or influenced by economic or political factors, the plan's motivational value will be weak.

Nevertheless, employees may still value the plan because of the potential for dividends and capital appreciation. Financing the stock acquisition by a company loan that is repaid through payroll deductions also serves as a vehicle for increased personal savings and, possibly, some tax advantages—features generally valued by the employees.

The stock purchase plan can also serve two other purposes: as a vehicle to raise capital and as a precautionary measure against a potential hostile takeover of the company.

Variable Pay: some concluding observations

The plans we have considered—gain-sharing, profit sharing, and stock-based— are all designed to introduce variability into the compensation package. The objective of variable pay in Canadian organizations is three-fold: (a) to improve business performance; (b) to keep compensation competitive; and (c) to control labour costs. A survey of leading Canadian organizations revealed that nearly 60 percent of employees were likely to have a variable component in their compensation package (Carlyle, 1994).

The concept of variable pay is consistent with the effective reward management model discussed in the text. However, its success in meeting organizationally desired objectives will depend on the degree to which the variable pay plan design and management decisions are based on strategic and process issues.

SUMMARY

This chapter reviewed the major types of individual and organization-wide incentive plans designed primarily to motivate the attainment of a predetermined end result at individual and organization-wide levels. Individual incentive plans examined were the piece-rate, the standard-hour, and sales commissions and bonuses. There are several variations of these plans, but the underlying rationale is essentially the same—to motivate the attainment of a predetermined end result. The piece-rate plan is activated by the production of the targeted output. The standard-hour plan rewards improvements in efficiency above the established standard. Sales commissions and bonuses operate more like the piece-rate plan. The effectiveness of these plans depends not only on the plan mechanics and formula, but also on such critical process issues as the setting of specific and realistically difficult goals, employee involvement, change mechanisms, provision for circumstances beyond the employee's control, and supervisor-worker relations characterized by a high degree of trust.

The organization-wide incentive plans that were discussed were gain-sharing plans, profit sharing plans, and stock-based plans. The effectiveness of these plans also depends on a similar set of conditions. However, special attention should be paid to decisions on critical strategic and process issues in the design and management of group gain-sharing plans. These issues are the design process, bonus determination and distribution, the modifications management process, and the commitment and leadership of management.

KEY TERMS

gain-sharing plan

group incentive plan

Improshare plan

line of sight

performance-profits linkage

performance-stock value linkage

performance share/unit plan

phantom stock

piece-rate incentives

profit-sharing plan

Rucker plan

standard-hour plan

stock option

the task-and-bonus approach

variable pay

REVIEW AND DISCUSSION QUESTIONS

1. Identify the similarities and differences between

   a) the Taylor Plan and the Merrick Plan

   b) the Halsey, Rowan, and Gantt plans

2. The discussion in the chapter has identified seven conditions that contribute to the effectiveness of individual incentive plans. Why are these conditions critical to the effectiveness of the plans?

3. Review the descriptions of the Scanlon, Rucker, and Improshare plans. Which one of these plans has best addressed critical design and implementation issues?

4. What are some of the conditions which favour gain-sharing plans?

5. After Will Walters had obtained his M.B.A., he joined the family toy manufacturing business, Funcrafts Limited, as the assistant plant manager. He was perplexed to find that the Flying Frisbee Toy assembly line had for some time produced a constant 250 kits a day. Further enquiry revealed that

although no targets were ever set, the employees were questioned whenever production fell below 250 kits. He learnt from a student he employed last summer under a federal Challenge grant that production routinely slowed down after lunch and picked up later so that the 250 kits were produced just before closing time. Will is thinking of an incentive plan and seeks your advice on (a) the factors he should consider, and (b) the type of plan—individual or group.

6. What are the objectives of profit sharing plans?

7. Distinguish between: the stock option plan, the stock grants plan, and the stock purchase plan.

8. Compare and contrast gain-sharing plans, profit sharing plans, and stock-based plans on the degree to which: (a) each plan incorporates the objective of variable pay; (b) each plan is likely to be successful in meeting organizational objectives; and (c) the reasons why these might or not be successful in meeting organizational objectives.

CASE

The Elusive Reward

Sharon Rogers became an account representative for a company that produced software packages. An established supplier to large business organizations, the company planned to enter a new market—small businesses.

Larger organizations accepted the products because their employees were familiar with the concepts involved. Employees of smaller businesses did not fully understand or appreciate the concepts underlying the products. Though Sharon's task was formidable, she felt confident that she could manage because she was assured that the customer service department would provide the necessary technical support by developing related sales and user-training materials. Also, the orientation programme for new users included a comprehensive four-day sales seminar that helped bring her academic knowledge and training (a McGill B. Com. with concentration in Management Information Systems) into a proper business focus.

Sharon was assigned a sales quota of $250,000 for the first year—one-half of the average sales quota for an account representative in the established large-business market. She had not anticipated that the quota would be so high considering the nature of the product and the market.

Sharon found the starting salary of $25,000 to be low, but had accepted the job because of the generous bonus plan applicable to those who met the quota. This was Sharon's first full-time job. In her summer jobs, she always opted for challenging assignments and completed them quite successfully.

The report for the first quarter showed that Sharon's sales were far below the targeted figures. Although she had performed all the required behaviours, such as prospecting, demonstrating, and follow-up, these just did not translate into sales. Naturally, she was concerned that at her present rate of sales she might not make her annual quota.

It was now abundantly clear to her that her customers, the small businesses, did not fully appreciate the potential of her products. She proposed a package of new sales materials to favourably influence the customer acceptance of the products. Action on the proposal was delayed because of objections from the controller's office: the costs involved had not been budgeted.

For three months, Sharon's enthusiasm for the job was one long roller-coaster ride. She felt good about her job and took pride in her work, but she felt dejected when her efforts were not successful and wondered whether the attractive bonus package would ever be a reality. She even began to experience nagging doubts about her ability to do the job.

Three more months went by and the situation became even more bleak for Sharon. Her sales figures did not improve, although she continued to perform her tasks as well as, if not better than any other account rep. Her frustrations were aggravated by the failure of the customer service department to develop new sales materials. She discovered that each support (staff) function in the company is a profit centre, evaluated on the basis of its contribution to the activity that brings in the largest profit. Such a practice rewards the customer service department for paying attention to clients from the large-business sector and to ignore those in the small businesses.

Source: Based on Hurwich and Moynahan (1984).

Discussion Questions

1. What is the likely effect of the bonus plan on Sharon Rogers?
2. Evaluate the bonus plan in the light of the conditions that contribute to the effectiveness of incentive plans.
3. What changes (short-term and long-term) to the bonus plan would you recommend in this case? Why?

Action Plan for Pay Strategy for Organizations

APPENDIX

A recent survey of "...almost 550,000 employees found that business is restructuring reward systems to make increased performance the only way for employees to receive real increases in compensation" (*Human Resource Management in Canada*, 1995, 151.2). This focus on pay-for-performance is one of the fundamental thrusts of this text. The preceding chapters have discussed the strategic, structural, and process issues in the different forms of pay-for-performance, merit pay, bonus, gain-sharing, and profit sharing. This Appendix brings together these ideas in an action plan format which outlines the total pay strategy that is appropriate to support the two distinct business strategies—the defender-type strategy and the prospector-type strategy. As will be seen from the outline, performance-based pay is essential to both business strategies. The major distinguishing features would be the use of job-based or person-based pay and the process issues—in particular, a participative or non-participative approach. Stock-based plans are not included in this outline because of the variety of ways in which stock-based plans can be utilized to reflect organizational performance, and because these plans tend to be restricted more to the executive employee group.

TOTAL PAY STRATEGY FOR THE DEFENDER-TYPE ORGANIZATION

Characteristics of Defender-type strategy

- A relatively stable market with incremental change in product and technology.
- Competes primarily through quality, price, and service. Hence, the need to be cost-efficient requires a pay strategy which rewards individual/group performance and also varies total pay costs with organizational performance.

Pay Structure

Design total pay to include fixed and variable components, thus:

- Fixed Component
  - Set base pay below rate of business competitors;
  - Adjust base pay periodically to reflect market changes.
  - Determine base pay using the job-content-based job evaluation system.
  - Since human resource policies include promotion from within, staffing is mainly at the entry level jobs. Therefore, the principal focus is on internal equity.

- Variable Component
  - Organization-wide level:
  - Implement profit sharing plan that reflects organizational performance, and:
    - a) pays out as soon as the organization makes a profit; and
    - b) incorporates a higher variable component of total pay for employees whose jobs have a strong line of sight from performance to profits.
  - Major operating unit or divisional level:
    - Implement gain-sharing plan that focuses on cost reductions.
    - Individual level:
    - Install a performance management process which provides for on-going review and feedback.
    - Recognize individual performance through one-time bonus system.
    - In work areas with independent jobs, determine bonus on group's performance and then distribute on individual performance basis, preferably through peer evaluation.
- Process
- Involve employees in the design of:
  - the performance management process;
  - the job evaluation system;
  - market surveys; and
  - gain-sharing plan.
- Communicate information on pay ranges, costs, organizational strategies to enhance profitability, and organizational performance data.
- Decision making is centralized except when multiple divisions exist.

TOTAL PAY STRATEGY FOR PROSPECTOR-TYPE ORGANIZATION

Characteristics of Prospector-type strategy

- A high degree of change in products, technology, and markets.
- Competes primarily on innovation and quality.
- Employee involvement is generally high. Hence, the need for a pay strategy which is performance-based, fosters growth and learning, and an entrepreneurial culture.

PAY STRUCTURE

Design total pay to include fixed and variable components, thus:

- Fixed Component
  - Set base pay below rate of business competitors.

– Adjust base pay periodically to reflect market changes.
– Determine base pay using the person-based pay system.
– The principal focus is on external equity.

Variable Component

- Organization-wide level:
  - Implement profit sharing plan that reflects organizational performance, and:
    a) pays out as soon as the organization makes a profit; and
    b) incorporates a higher variable component of total pay for employees whose jobs have a strong line of sight from performance to profits.
  - Major operating unit or divisional level:
    • Implement gain-sharing plan that focuses on cost reductions and contributes to teamwork and cooperation.
  - Individual level:
    • Install a performance management process which provides for on-going review and feedback.
    • Recognize individual performance through a one-time bonus system.
    • Where self-regulating work teams exist, determine bonus on team's performance; let the team decide on distribution to its members.
    • To promote innovation, institute "special" recognition award either on an individual or group basis.

Process

- Involve employees in the design of:
  - performance management process;
  - pay-for-skills/knowledge system;
  - market surveys;
  - gain-sharing plans.
- Communicate information on costs, organizational strategies to enhance profitability, and organizational performance data.
- Provide training opportunities to facilitate skills/knowledge acquisition.
- Foster decentralized decision making.

Job Analysis and
Job Evaluation:
Internal Equity I

OVERVIEW

This chapter discusses the techniques and processes that ensure the incorporation of internal equity in the compensation system. The primary thrust of the chapter is job evaluation (its techniques, methods, and processes), which enables the organization to develop a job structure. The effectiveness of the job evaluation programme is dependent on job descriptions that accurately reflect the content and contribution of the job. Hence, the chapter will also discuss the methods of job analysis, which generates the information used to develop job descriptions and job specifications.

 LEARNING OBJECTIVES
- ► To define internal equity.
- ► To identify the sources of the value of a job.
- ► To understand why internal equity plays a predominant role in the design of a compensation system.
- ► To define job analysis, and to explain its important link to the job evaluation programme.
- ► To describe job analysis methods and to discuss their advantages and disadvantages.
- ► To identify the basic contents of a job description statement.
- ► To define job evaluation, and to understand its role in the compensation system.

▶ To describe the methods of job evaluation, and to discuss their advantages and disadvantages.

▶ To understand that the job evaluation process has a decisive impact on internal equity.

▶ To develop strategies for employee involvement in the job evaluation process.

INTRODUCTION

The concept of equity or fairness lies at the heart of the compensation system. Previous chapters—more specifically Chapter 5—explored the elements and the process that contribute to employees' perceptions of the equity or fairness of a reward. There are three types of equity: personal (or individual), internal, and external. Chapters 9 and 10 discussed the methods and processes by which a compensation system can ensure personal equity. This chapter focuses on internal equity. The questions to be addressed are: What is internal equity? What role does it play in the design of a compensation system? What tools (techniques, methods) and processes are used in order to ensure the internal equity of a compensation system?

INTERNAL EQUITY 4Q/

What is Internal Equity?

"Internal Equity is a fairness criterion that requires employers to set wage rates for jobs within companies that correspond to the relative internal value of each job" (Wallace and Fay 1988, p. 17). Neither employers nor employees quarrel with this definition *per se*. It raises several questions, though: What precisely is meant by the value of a job? What is the source or basis of this value? There are a variety of views on job value. According to some of these views, the value of a job should reflect (a) the sociocultural values of a society; (b) the value of the product or service it creates; (c) the investment in education, training, and experience required for the job; and (d) the position of the job in the organizational hierarchy.

In practice, organizations have traditionally focused on the *requirements* and the *contribution* of the job in determining its value. Job requirements or specifications refer to the knowledge, skills, ability, experience, and effort required on the job. For example, a job that requires its holder to have a college degree will, other things being equal, have a higher job value than a job that requires only a high school diploma. The job requirement of the former is judged to be greater than that of the latter.

The contribution of the job refers to its contribution to the economic value of the product or service, or its contribution to the attainment of the objectives of the work unit or of the organization, expressed in terms of profits, production, or some similar measure. In an oil-exploration company, a geologist would ordinarily be considered to be contributing more to the organizational objectives than the company's accountant. As a result, the geologist's job will be viewed as having more value, even though the investment in professional education and training for both jobs may be similar.

The Role of Internal Equity in the Design of a Compensation System

A consideration of two cases will help to explore this question. In case 1, similar jobs in Company A are not paid similar wages; some jobs are paid more than others. In case 2, the jobs in company A are paid less than similar jobs in company B. In which of the two cases will inequity be perceived to be greater? Greater inequity will be experienced in case 1 than in case 2, primarily because in case 1, employees believe that they have a better knowledge of the situation and conditions in their own organization and hence feel more confident in assessing the outcomes/inputs ratios—their own as well as those of the reference source — with relatively greater accuracy. This is not to say that external equity—the condition of case 2—is not important. External equity, which is discussed in Chapter 13, is also crucial to the design of a compensation system. In fact, wages in the external labour market considerably influence an organization's pay structure and policies.

However, the major limitation to using the external labour market as the frame of reference in designing a compensation system is the issue of comparability. One aspect of this issue is: How comparable are the data of wage surveys collected from other organizations? The answer depends upon how identical the jobs in a company are in comparison with the jobs in the surveyed organizations. Usually the jobs, although having the same or similar titles, are different, in terms of both the job content and the job's contribution to organizational objectives. As discussed in the previous section, both job content and contribution are significant factors in determining the value of a job to the organization.

Another aspect of comparability (or lack of it) is that the survey data are an assortment of wages from companies participating in the survey. "Assortment" is emphasized because the wages of each company result from that company's decisions, which are based on such considerations as business strategies, industry practices, and the number of employees in a specific job category. The wage data will also incorporate the company's decisions on cost-of-hiring adjustments, merit pay based on performance, and seniority considerations. If some of the participating companies in the survey are unionized, their wage structure will reflect the dynamic of their unique labour-management relations.

In view of the preceding discussion, it is clear that internal equity will play a predominant role in the design of the compensation system. The major compensation item that is particularly affected by internal equity is base pay. When employees perceive internal inequity in base pay, they experience a drop in valence because equity of outcomes is a determinant of valence. As expectancy theory predicts, a drop in valence results in a lower motivational force. Consequently, base pay will not have the intended motivational impact. The resulting loss to the organization can be severe when it is recalled that an organization's investment in base pay constitutes a substantial portion of its financial resources. Furthermore, a demotivated workforce cannot guarantee the effective utilization of the physical and material resources of the organization. The decision to ensure internal equity is, in effect, a strategic decision that contributes to the efficient and effective utilization of the physical, financial, and human resources of the organization.

Tools and Processes for Ensuring Internal Equity

The primary process for determining the value of a job relative to the other jobs in the organization is *job evaluation*. To evaluate a job, one must have adequate data about the value of the job and about the similarities and differences upon which pay differentials are constructed. The collection of these data is done through the process of *job analysis*. This chapter first reviews the different methods of job analysis and then discusses the methods and processes of job evaluation systems. Some organizations decide on a job evaluation system, so that the job analysis which follows yields the data required to evaluate the jobs. Traditionally, however, job analysis has preceded job evaluation because the data collected from job analysis is used for several purposes besides job evaluation. Some of these purposes are:

1. developing job descriptions and job specifications for recruitment and selection;
2. identifying the critical job behaviours and objectives for performance appraisals;
3. developing training programmes;
4. developing career paths and providing the counselling inherent in career planning programmes;
5. identifying job tasks and work-flow processes for designing or redesigning a job.

JOB ANALYSIS
What is Job Analysis?

Job analysis is the process of collecting information about a job. This process is conducted systematically with a view to gathering information about a job's tasks, duties, responsibilities, working conditions, desirable behaviours, and competencies (Lange, 1991). Stated differently, the process attempts to collect data on:

1. what is done on the job—the tasks and operations involved;

2. how the job is done—the behaviours that must be demonstrated on the job;

3. under what conditions the job is done—the physical and social environments in which the job has to be done;

4. and the knowledge, skills, and abilities (KSAs) needed by the employee to do the job.

The data that result from a job analysis are presented in the form of a job description, which also includes a statement of job specification. This statement spells out the knowledge, skills, and abilities needed for the job.

THE PROCEDURE AND THE METHODS OF JOB ANALYSIS PROCEDURE 4Q

The job analysis process is successful in collecting the necessary information when there is unbiased input from those employees directly involved in the performance of the job, namely, the job incumbent and the supervisor. So that trust and willingness can be generated, certain preparatory steps are necessary. First, all employees must be informed of the plans to conduct a job analysis programme. The communication must include the reasons for such a programme and an assurance that the job incumbent will have an opportunity to review and react to the data collected about his/her job before such data are translated into a definitive description of the job. The communication should also seek employees' cooperation and active participation in the programme. In a unionized organization, it is essential to seek the cooperation and involvement of the union.

Second, job analysts should prepare themselves to see the job in its proper perspective, and to understand its nature. Preparation includes a review of the existing job descriptions and of the organization chart which show the job's location and relationships. A tour of the work site gives the analyst a good idea of the working conditions and the social and technical context of the job. Third, a decision must be made on the choice of the job analysis method. The analyst can pick from a variety of methods. The following subsections review the procedure, and the merits and demerits of some of the following methods: interview, questionnaire, observation, and diary/log.

Methods 3Q

Interview   The job analyst interviews both the job incumbent and the supervisor. If the target job has a large number of positions, it is more productive to interview a knowledgeable employee selected by the employees to represent them. The interview should focus on job information relating to the major tasks (their importance and frequency of performance) and the tools, equipment, machines, and related material and financial resources of the job. In addition, the worker may be asked to provide information on two specific categories of tasks: (1) tasks the employee is now performing, but which the employees believes are not appropriate or efficient for him/her to be performing; (2) tasks not now being performed by the employee, but which the employee believes would contribute to enhanced performance if they were part of the job. Answers to these two questions will be invaluable when job redesign is considered.

The interview method, which is time-consuming and expensive, is most useful for managerial and professional jobs. For other jobs, the interview is effective when it is necessary to clarify the data acquired through other job analysis methods. For the successful use of the interview method, job analysts recognize the necessity of a structured interview format, competence in communication skills and interview techniques, and a sound knowledge of the work flow. They also recognize that they must have the complete trust of the job incumbent if they are to obtain data that are accurate and valid. Before writing up the job description, the collected data should be reviewed with the job incumbent and the supervisor.

Observation This method is probably the oldest job analysis method. Frederick Taylor's scientific management movement had its beginnings in observation, which was later performed with a stop watch. In this method, the analyst observes a complete work cycle of the job, and records the tasks and behaviours that are performed. The collected data are then reviewed by both the incumbent and the supervisor. The effectiveness of this method depends upon the observation of a complete work cycle of a job, which is not feasible for most jobs. Hence, the usefulness of the method is limited to certain factory and clerical jobs where the work cycle is short and repetitive.

Questionnaire In this method, the job incumbent responds to a questionnaire that calls for brief responses. The questions generally relate to the nature of the work tasks/behaviours performed, the tools and the machinery used, working conditions, job challenges, requirements, and principal accountabilities. Depending upon the verbal capabilities of the respondent, a few open-ended questions are useful. The scale is a useful device for obtaining for each job task or behaviour described in the question the frequency of its performance and its degree of importance.

The questionnaire method has the advantage of being inexpensive, and its standardized format facilitates mathematical analysis. The job incumbent's participation, relative to the other methods, is greater. Such participation is conducive to a greater acceptance of the findings by the incumbent. The method is not without its share of problems, notably those related to the verbal abilities of the employee, such as the ability to read, understand, and respond to the questions. The questionnaire method is generally not suitable for employees with minimal reading or writing skills. In addition, the analyst must watch for responses that exaggerate the responsibilities and the complexities of the tasks in an attempt to depict the job as being more valuable than it really is. To probe such responses, the interview method may be used as a follow-up.

Diary/Log 3A The job incumbent is requested to keep a record of the activities/tasks as they are performed weekly, monthly, or quarterly. The analyst then reviews these records to get a picture of the job. Such a record is useful provided the analyst can be sure that it is a faithful description of the activities/tasks performed on that job. The job incumbent needs to be diligent and self-disciplined to maintain a continuous and reasonably accurate record of the job tasks and activities. For this reason, this method is considered appropriate primarily for professionals and managers. Even in these jobs, the analyst is well advised to supplement the information through interviews and questionnaires.

Job Description and Job Specifications Q4 Q5(i - v)

The data gathered from job analysis are used to develop a job description, a document that informs the employee in clear, precise, and understandable terms what his/her job is and what he/she is expected to do. In other words, this document describes the job that must be done and specifies the qualifications (knowledge, skills, abilities, experience) the holder must possess to do the job. The job description usually contains the following sections:

1. Identification: includes information relating to job title, pay grade, location, and so forth.

2. Summary: spells out the major functions/activities that enable the reader to identify and differentiate these functions/activities from those of other jobs. Generally, the summary includes the major responsibilities of the job. A set of about four to seven responsibilities is sufficient to describe a job adequately.

3. Responsibilities: identifies the primary reasons for the existence of the job. Stated differently, if these responsibilities are not carried out at an acceptable level, the consequences to the work unit will be serious enough to require remedial action from management. Responsibilities may be ranked by sequence of occurrence or by importance. For each responsibility there should be listed a set of duties that describes not only what is done but also why and how it is done. A set of about three to seven duties is usually sufficient to describe a responsibility. The duties establish the foundation for the setting of job specifications and performance standards.

4. Accountabilities: describes the major results expected in the satisfactory performance of the responsibilities, and may also stipulate responsibility for the different resources assigned to the job.

5. Specifications: provides the qualifications (knowledge, skill, ability, experience) the incumbent should bring to the job for performance at the accept-

able level. In addition, the specifications section details information on the context of the job, for example, supervisory controls and working conditions. This section contributes significant information for decisions in the job evaluation process. Sometimes, this portion of the information is spelt out in a separate document entitled Job Specifications.

Source: Henderson, 1989

The job description serves the needs of manpower planning, recruitment and selection, training and development, career planning, job design, and compensation. Because job description is the principal source of job information, it is the critical starting point for the job evaluation process. Errors and biases that lead to an inadequate or incorrect job description will result in an incorrect value for the job. In fact, as will be seen in the next chapter, job description is a major source of gender bias, which produces pay inequity.

JOB EVALUATION

What is Job Evaluation?

Job evaluation is the process of determining the value of a job within an organization relative to all the other jobs in that organization. The job value becomes the foundation for establishing pay differentials among the jobs in the organization.

Methods of Job Evaluation Q7

There are basically four methods of job evaluation: *ranking, classification, point method*, and *factor comparison method*. This section discusses each method separately in terms of its procedure, its advantages and disadvantages, and the conditions under which it could be considered to be most effective. The section concludes with a discussion of the similarities in, and differences between, these methods.

Ranking (Q)

Main Features   In this method, jobs are ranked according to their value from the most valuable to the least valuable. What is the basis of the ranking? The job as a whole is considered, using some factor that is believed to be a valid source of value. In practice, however, the "factor" is one person's judgement of what is believed to be of value to the organization.

The rank ordering of jobs can be done by simple ranking, alternation ranking, and paired comparisons. In simple ranking, the jobs are ranked from the most valuable to the least valuable on the basis of some criterion. In alternation ranking, the most valuable job is selected, removed from the list of jobs to be considered, and placed at the top of the job structure. Of the remaining jobs, the least valuable job is selected, removed from the list of jobs to be considered, and placed at the bottom of the job structure. The next most valuable job is then selected, and then the next least valuable. The alternation process of selecting the next most valuable and then the next least valuable continues until all the jobs have been selected and placed in the job structure.

In the paired-comparison method, each job is compared with every other job and a judgement is made on which of the jobs in the pair that is being compared has a higher ranking. The job that receives the greatest number of "higher ranking" judgements is the most valuable job in the job structure. The other jobs are then arranged below this most valuable job according to the number of "higher ranking" judgements received in the paired comparison.

Advantages and Disadvantages The advantages of ranking are that it is simple, inexpensive, and practical. Ranking is suitable for small organizations, which do not have a wide variety of jobs and where the number of jobs is not large. The jobs are usually well known in a small organization, and there is an implicit recognition of which are the more valuable jobs. Ranking has several disadvantages. First, the evaluator's knowledge of all the jobs must be more than superficial. Even then, rank order is not an accurate measure of worth, because the evaluator can easily be influenced by his/her knowledge of the person who holds the job. As a result, the rank assigned might be a judgement of the job incumbent rather than of the value of the job itself. Second, the differentials between the ranks occupied by the jobs are presumed to be equal; often, they are not.

Classification

Main Features The job classification method involves placing jobs in pre-established classes. Each class bears a description relating to such factors as education, responsibility, level of difficulty, and public contact. The classes are then arranged in ascending order from the most simple to the most complex in terms of the factors used to describe the classes.

For example, suppose an evaluator decides to develop a classification system using the factors of nature of work (in terms of simple vs. complex, and easy vs. difficult), responsibility for subordinates (exercising vs. not exercising supervision), and customer contact. In this classification, the lowest class will be:

Simple, easy work; does not exercise responsibility for subordinates; no customer contact.

The highest class will be:

Complex, very difficult work; exercises responsibility for subordinates; maintains contact with customers.

The other classes will fall in between the lowest and the highest classes and will contain varying amounts of these three factors such that the next higher level class has relatively more of one or two of these factors. The highest class has the most of each factor.

The evaluator then reviews the description of the job that is to be evaluated, and places the job into the class that best matches the job description. The job structure is the order of the jobs as given by their place in the classes. The job value is determined by the job's placement in the predetermined series of classes. When the classification system is used, a separate classification is developed for the different occupations that exist in the organization, for example, managerial, professional, clerical, operational.

Advantages and Disadvantages Classification is an improvement over the ranking method in that the evaluation judgement is based on a set of criteria that are clearly, logically, and coherently established. Within each occupation, the classification generally reflects the hierarchy that is implicitly accepted by employees in that occupation. Another advantage is that the hierarchy given by the classification system for each occupation becomes the basis of a career ladder for the jobs in that occupation.

There are several disadvantages to the classification method of job evaluation. To begin with, there is the difficulty of developing the classes—more specifically, the description or definition of each class. The descriptions of the classes are arranged logically in a gradually ascending order from the most simple to the most complex in terms of the factors used. The classification system has difficulty coping with the fact that there is a need to balance the factors in order to ensure that, in the ultimate analysis, jobs of equal total value are treated as such. The classification method also has the problem of "forced fit". This occurs when a job that more properly belongs between two established classes has to be forced into one of these two classes because the in-between class does not exist in the classification system.

The very nature of the classification method requires each occupational group to have its own classification system. This creates an insurmountable problem when interoccupational comparison becomes necessary. Very few persons in an organization are knowledgeable, wise, and impartial enough to know what each occupational class or group contributes to the attainment of the organizational goals and objectives, much less to measure the relative contributions and importance of the responsibilities and duties of each occupational group. This difficulty with the classification method takes on a more serious dimension when the issue of equal pay for work of equal value needs to be addressed. As will be discussed in Chapter 12, pay equity laws in Canada mandate that the pay rates of female-dominated jobs be the same as those of male-dominated jobs when these jobs are equal in value. The determination of whether equal pay for work of equal value exists in an organization necessitates a single job evaluation system for all occupational groups.

The Point Method Q 12(b)

Also known as the *point rating* and *point factor* methods, the point method is the most widely used method of job evaluation. It evaluates a job by reference to an evaluation system that assigns point values to a set of compensable factors. A job is evaluated on each factor and the appropriate points are assigned. The total value of the job is determined by adding up the points assigned to each compensable factor. Before we go into the details of this method, we need to explore two concepts which are critical ingredients of the method: compensable factors and benchmark or key jobs.

Compensable Factors—Main Features and Purpose Compensable factors are those characteristics of a job that are believed to be important for the organization. Therefore, the organization will be willing to pay for them. Their presence in the job gives the job its value. Table 11.2 lists the compensable factors used in one job evaluation system known as the Factor Evaluation System (FES) developed by the U.S. government in the mid-1970s. In this system, there is a total of nine compensable factors: knowledge required by the position, supervisory controls, guidelines, complexity, scope and effect, personal contact, purpose of contact, physical demands, and work environment. An organization that adopts the FES job evaluation system is saying that it regards these nine factors to be important determinants of the values of its jobs. As will be seen later in this chapter, not all nine factors are of equal importance; they are weighted differently. In general, however, the more of these factors a job has, the greater will be its value and consequently, its pay.

In order for the proper value differentials to be developed among the jobs of an organization, the compensable factors must be common to all jobs, and they must be describable and quantifiable. However, the more "common" a factor is to a wide variety of jobs in the organization, the more abstract it will tend to be. As a result, only with difficulty will it be described and quantified adequately enough to be of use in a job evaluation system. The more specific a factor, the more it can be described and measured in order to capture the unique characteristics of a job. At the same time, the specific factor will have limited usefulness because its description will be too narrow to cover a wide variety of the jobs. Hence, it will not be applicable to all the jobs in the organization.

The compensable factor needs to be both "abstract" (common) and "specific." To reconcile these apparently conflicting needs, job evaluation systems have had recourse to expressing the factor in terms of universal factors and degrees (or levels). The universal factor is relatively abstract (for example, the factor of knowledge and skill) and hence can be applicable to a wide variety of jobs. The degrees (or levels) further define the universal factor and indicate the specific amount of the factor that is required in the performance of the job.

Table 11.2: Factor Evaluation System Factors, Weights, and Levels

Factor	Value of Factor as Percentage of Total Points for Factor	Number of (Weight of Factor)	Levels	Points for Each Level
Knowledge required by the position	1,850	41.3%	9	50, 200, 350, 550, 750, 950, 1250, 1550, 1850
Supervisory control	650	14.5%	5	25, 125, 275, 450, 650
Guidelines	650	14.5%	5	25, 125, 275, 450, 650
Complexity	450	10.0%	6	25, 75, 150, 225, 325, 450
Scope and effect	450	10.0%	6	25, 75, 150, 225, 325, 450
Personal contact	110	2.5%	4	10, 25, 60, 110
Purpose of contact	220	4.9%	4	20, 50, 120, 220
Physical demand	50	1.1%	3	5, 20, 50
Work environment	50	1.1%	3	5, 20, 50
Total	4,480	99.9%		

Source: Richard Henderson, *Compensation Management: Rewarding Performance*, 6th ed., ©1994, p. 200. Reprinted by permission of Prentice-Hall, Englewood Cliffs, New Jersey.

As an example of the use of factors and degrees, consider the first factor of the Factor Evaluation System: "knowledge required by the position". This factor appears to be universal, that is, broad enough to cover all the jobs in the organization. But it is too broad to permit a meaningful differentiation between jobs. For this reason, the FES describes the content envisaged by the universal factor of "knowledge required by the position" as:

> The nature and extent of information or facts which the workers must understand to do acceptable work (e.g., steps, procedures, practices, rules, policies, theories, principles, and concepts) and the nature and extent of the skills needed to apply those knowledges. To be used as a basis for selecting a level under this factor, a knowledge must be required and applied. (Henderson and Wolfe, 1985, 108)

The description is much more specific, yet it is not specific enough to capture the differences between jobs whose knowledge requirements can range from the very simple to the very complex. To further differentiate on this factor, the FES has developed degrees or levels of the subfactor. As can be seen in Table 11.2, the factor "knowledge required by the position" has nine levels. For illustrative purposes, only the first and ninth levels are reproduced.

Level 1-1
Knowledge of simple, routine, or repetitive tasks or operations which typically includes following step-by-step instructions and requires little or no previous training or experience. (Henderson and Wolfe, 1985, 108)

Level 1-9
Mastery of a professional field to generate and develop new hypotheses and theories. (Henderson and Wolfe, 1985, 109).

Level 1 and level 9 define the two ends of the broad spectrum of the factor. Levels 3 to 8 define the variations in knowledge as the levels proceed from the simple to the complex. Degrees or levels are the most specific, and for this reason, each level may require a description that fills several paragraphs.

Compensable Factors Number, Definition, and Importance The total number of compensable factors varies according to the system used. An effective system should have at least the following four factors: *skill, effort, responsibility,* and *working conditions.*

It is important to note that compensable factors are not what the job incumbent may possess. Rather, these are characteristics required for the job to be done. For illustrative purposes, the definitions used by the federal government are briefly listed below:

> **Skill** Intellectual or physical skill required for job performance. How these skills were acquired will not be considered when employees are compared on this factor.
> **Effort** The expenditure of intellectual or physical effort required in job performance.
> **Responsibility** The extent of employer's reliance on employee for performance of job duties, and the employee's accountability to employer for assigned resources.
> **Working conditions** Conditions of the work environment such as physical (e.g., sound, temperature, health hazards, etc.)and psychological (e.g., mental stress).

Source: Weiner and Gunderson, 1990

Therefore, a job-content-based evaluation system will use the compensable factors and completely disregard the job incumbent, either the additional knowledge, skills, and abilities the individual may possess, or the individual's performance level. The focus in the job-content-based evaluation system—unlike that in the person-based job evaluation system referred to in Chapter 7 and discussed in some detail later in this chapter—is only on the knowledge, skills, and abilities that are determined in the job specifications as necessary for the job. For this reason, they must be supported by data developed from a well-conducted job analysis programme.

Compensable factors are important to job evaluation because they allow the process of job evaluation to be consistent, uniform, and objective. They also contribute to an increased understanding of the process. When a job is assigned a value, the compensable factors enable one to probe the reason and to be satisfied that the process is based on some objective criteria. Of course, understanding is increased only if the system is not too complicated, a point that will be considered again in discussing the administrative requirements of the job evaluation programme.

Benchmark or Key Jobs—Main Features and Purpose

Benchmark or key jobs are those jobs in the organization that serve as reference points that provide some indication of the values of other jobs. The contents of key jobs do not change as drastically as the contents of non-key jobs. Because of this stability, the contents of key jobs are well known, and usually there is considerable agreement between employees and management about the nature and contents of these jobs. Moreover, there is general agreement about the pay rates of these jobs and the pay differentials that exist among the key jobs. Another important characteristic of key jobs is that such jobs (i.e., with these contents) exist in a fairly large number of organizations; hence, the external labour market regards them as reference points for wage determination.

Procedure of the Point Method

The following is a procedure for developing and implementing a point method job evaluation system. The Factor Evaluation System (FES), outlined in Table 11.2, is an example of the point method; this system is used to illustrate the different steps of the procedure.

1. Decide on the compensable factors, keeping in mind the characteristics of compensable factors. The FES has chosen nine factors (see Table 11.2). The number and the type of factors should fit the needs of the organization, that is, enable the organization to properly identify the similarities in, and the differences between, jobs.

2. Decide on the maximum number of points in the entire system. There is no specific number to use. The number chosen should be easy to work with and large enough to allow for differentiations between and within factors. The FES has a total of 4,480 points.

3. Decide on the weights to be assigned to each factor. The weight is influenced by a judgmental assessment of how important each factor is to the organization. As a practical measure, percentages can be used initially so that all the

weights add up to 100 per cent. Allocate the points to the factors on the basis of the weights. Table 11.2 shows the weights of each factor and the points allocated on the basis of these weights out of the total 4,480 points.

4. Define each factor in detail by using a scale of degrees (levels). There is no optimal number of degrees and all factors need not have the same number of degrees. The primary consideration is the spread from the simplest level to the most complex level of the factor; the greater the extent of this spread, the greater the number of degrees.

    Generally, the factor that has the greatest assigned weight will have more degrees than the factor with a lesser assigned weight. Thus, in Table 11.2, "knowledge required by the position" has been assigned the highest weight (41.3 per cent) and it also has the highest number of levels (nine). Distribute the points to the degrees in each factor. In Table 11.2, the last column shows the points assigned for each of the nine levels; the lowest level has 50 points; the highest level has 1,850 points. The range seems justified on the basis of the description of these two levels (1-1 and 1-9) presented earlier.

5. Validate this system by applying it to the key jobs. To do this, evaluate the key jobs on each factor and determine the total point value of the key jobs. Assess the validity of the values by checking for consistency between the differentials as determined by the job evaluation system and the differentials that are known to exist between the key jobs. The nature of key jobs is such that the differentials are well known and accepted in the organization.

    If an inconsistency is detected (i.e., the job values obtained do not reflect the known and accepted differentials between key jobs), review the judgements made on each factor of the job evaluation system. It might also be that the content of a key job has undergone a change to the extent that it can no longer be considered a key job. If this is so, the job should be excluded from this validation process.

6. After the system has been validated, use it to evaluate the other jobs in the organization.

7. Develop a job structure, by arranging the jobs in the descending order of their point values. Review for any obvious discrepancies or inconsistencies. Investigating and resolving these inconsistencies may require a review of the judgements that were made on each factor of the job evaluation system. Sometimes, the review will raise questions about the adequacy of the information provided by the job analysis and the job description that preceded the job evaluation programme.

8. Provide an appeal process that gives employees the opportunity to have the results for their jobs reviewed and explained to them. This step will be discussed later in the chapter.

The Point Method—Advantages and Disadvantages Q13

The point method has several advantages. It has an objective basis inasmuch as the judgements are made rationally by reference to compensable factors that are job related and are weighted and defined in a manner that is acceptable to both employees and management. The mechanism and the process of the point method is conducive to greater reliability and consistency in judgements. The point values of the job structure provide differences in value between jobs and also indicate the magnitude of the differences. For example, if job A has 200 points and job B has 400 points, the point method permits the reasonable inference that job B is two times more valuable than job A. The point method allows the job structure to be converted into a pay structure. However, since it is constructed without reference to the external labour market, it is free from the pay-rate fluctuations of the external market. Once developed, the point method is easy to use.

The disadvantages are that it is time consuming and expensive to develop and that one can sometimes be faced with the situation of having to "force fit" a job into the predetermined fixed factor levels. However, such force-fitting is not as serious as in the classification method, because the system of levels for each factor permits the development of a range (scale) that suits the needs of the organization. Also, the subsequent adjustments of these levels are relatively easier in the point method. Nevertheless, an important question remains: In view of the fixed factors and fixed scales, can it be validly assumed that all the jobs have the same relationships relative to these factors? Also, the results must be validated by employee perceptions with regard to the equity of the results. Employee perceptions of the validity of the method, including its process, are critical, and some suggestions to ensure employee perceptions of equity are discussed later in the chapter.

The Factor Comparison Method Q12(a)

Main Features This method was developed by Eugene Benge in 1926 to respond to a need for a job evaluation system that could adequately evaluate a wide diversity of jobs (Benge, 1984). In this approach, the key jobs are compared to identify their relative differences in value. The comparison is first based on the ranking of key jobs on each of the chosen compensable factors. The ranking indicates the importance (value) of the job on each factor. The jobs are also compared on the basis of the allocation or apportionment of the market rate of each key job to the compensable factors. The two comparisons together provide a basis for developing a "key scale with anchor points", which is then used to evaluate the other jobs in the organization and to compute their pay rates.

Advantages and Disadvantages Q13 The factor comparison method has several advantages. Like the point method, it makes explicit the compensable factors it uses as the criteria for evaluating jobs. By using the wage rates of benchmark jobs, it has the unique capability of linking external market pay rates to internal work-related factors. And because the method uses a scale of degrees of worth for each compensable factor, it can determine the dollar value of each job.

The major disadvantage of the method is that it is too complex and is often difficult to explain to the employees, especially because of the high degree of subjectivity involved in the allocation of pay rates across the compensable factors. The factor comparison method is the least popular job evaluation method; fewer than 11 per cent of organizations use it (Wallace and Fay, 1988). Since key-job pay rates are used as a critical feature in the method, there is the unstated assumption that these jobs themselves are free from wage inequities that might otherwise contaminate the process. This assumption may not be realistic.

The advantage of the method's unique capability to provide a linkage to the market can also become a serious disadvantage, especially in a dynamic economy when wage fluctuations are high. In such an environment, constant changes in the market will necessitate a continuous updating of job and wage structures. Furthermore, it is unacceptable for pay equity purposes. "This is because it relies on current salaries. Since pay equity is being carried out to ascertain if the salaries associated with female dominated job classes are undervalued, the job evaluation system assessing this cannot be based on these same salaries" (Weiner and Gunderson, 1990, p.26).

The factor comparison method provides the conceptual foundations and the framework for the Hays System (Bellak, 1984), a customized job evaluation system used by a large number of organizations worldwide.

The Four Methods: Similarities and Differences

In both the ranking and the factor comparison methods one whole job is compared with another whole job. The difference is that the ranking method does not use a specific criterion to make this job-versus-job comparison. The factor comparison method uses well-defined compensable factors. The classification and point methods are similar in that both compare the job not with another job, but with a set of standards. The difference is that the standards of the classification method are not defined in as great detail as they are in the point method. Also, the classification method does not provide a quantitative measure of the value of the job and the nature of the differentials between the key jobs. The point method provides a numerical measure of the value of the job that also expresses the relative worth of the differentials between the key jobs.

In terms of simplicity, the ranking method is the most simple and the factor comparison method is the most complex. The other methods fall in between. The point method has the highest acceptance rate because it is relatively easier to understand and also because the subjective judgements involved tend to be minimized by the use of detailed factor levels. The ranking and factor comparison methods have the lowest acceptance among employees. On the consideration of cost, the ranking method is the least expensive, followed by the classification method. The point and factor comparison methods tend to be expensive, particularly because of the developmental work that is involved.

On balance, the point method emerges as the best of the four methods.

ADMINISTERING THE JOB EVALUATION PROGRAMME

From the discussion so far, it is clear that despite any claims of objectivity that might be made, there is considerable subjectivity in the judgements that are required in all four methods. Even the most acceptable point method calls for judgements at practically every stage from the development of the point system right up to its application in evaluating jobs.

To begin with, the point method uses the data collected from job analysis. The entire process of job analysis involves a variety of subjective judgements. In fact, the litigation generated by pay equity legislation has uncovered a variety of gender biases in the development and interpretation of job description documents. Decisions on the choice of compensable factors are fraught with subjective judgements; so are decisions on the weights assigned to the factors and to the definition of the levels of each factor. The application of the system to specific jobs is essentially an exercise in subjective judgements. The sophisticated, quantitative techniques, used to improve objectivity, "...usually have the effect of masking the soft and subjective side of their assumptions and creating a false sense of objectivity" (Korukonda, 1996, p.81).

The purpose of the job evaluation system is to ensure internal equity. Given the high degree of subjectivity in even the best method available, the need for trust on the part of the employees affected is crucial. Otherwise, their acceptance will be seriously compromised and they will not perceive the results to be equitable. The eventual consequence of employee perceptions of inequity with regard to the huge expenditure of base pay is that this deployment of resources will not have the desired motivational effect. Not only will the dollars expended on base pay be wasted, but also the effort put in by demotivated employees may be far too feeble to achieve the organizational objectives. Hence, a sound administration of the job evaluation programme should include efforts and strategies to ensure the employee perception that, although the job evaluation process has several subjective features, the organization is doing its utmost to see that judgements are made in a manner that is as rational and bias-free as possible.

The primary strategy in a sound job evaluation administration programme is *involving* employees right from the inception of the programme. If the organization is unionized, the union should be brought on board from the beginning. A usual way to ensure employee participation is to establish a job evaluation committee with representatives of employees and management, entrusting this committee with the entire programme. The training of committee members is crucial; this training should include any technical training that is necessary as well as the development of interpersonal skills. The latter skills will enable committee members to cope effectively with the differences and disagreements that are inevitable in the deliberations of a committee.

The other critical strategy is to provide a mechanism and a process for appeal. Such a structure and process will help to rectify genuine mistakes and will give the committee an opportunity to get feedback on their work and to gain acceptance for the job structure. More importantly, the existence of such a structure and process gives the employees adequate participation and control over the process, thus helping to assure them of equity in the process.

Although the preceding remarks focus on employee involvement in job evaluation, a similar philosophy of employee involvement in the job analysis process is necessary. As stated earlier, the data from job analysis are the basis for job evaluation. Employees' perceptions of equity will be enhanced when they can see that they also have an input into the collection of data on their jobs.

DEVELOPING A JOB STRUCTURE

The end product of a job evaluation process is a job structure, which arranges all the jobs in a descending order of the total job evaluation points. When a job evaluation system uses compensable factors, the job structure also displays the points assigned to the compensable factors for each job. The job structure can be viewed as the organization's snapshot or statement of job values. The job structure not only shows the similarities in, and the differences between, jobs, but it also becomes the indispensable basis for the development of the pay structure. As such, it is the foundation of internal equity. Given the necessity for the organization to ensure internal equity, no effort should be spared to make sure that the processes of job analysis and job evaluation are conducted with care, competence, and integrity.

SUMMARY

Internal equity requires that pay rates reflect the relative value of jobs in terms of their content and contribution to the organization. Job analysis and job evaluation are the two processes used to determine the value of jobs. Job analysis generates the data on the job's content and contribution, and job evaluation processes this information to identify the similarities in, and differences between, jobs and to determine the values of jobs. The chapter discussed the procedures, as well as the advantages and disadvantages, of the four conventional methods of job analysis: interview, questionnaire, observation, and diary or log; and also the structured, quantitative method of the Position Analysis

Questionnaire (PAQ). Although each method is useful under its own appropriate set of circumstances, these methods may be used more effectively in combination. The chapter also discussed the format for a job description, which puts together in a meaningful manner the data generated by job analysis and becomes the primary source of information for decisions in the job evaluation process.

The chapter identified the purposes of a job evaluation system, and examined the procedures, as well as the advantages and disadvantages, of job evaluation methods: ranking, classification, point method, and factor comparison method. The point method and the factor comparison method use compensable factors, which give them a more objective basis for determining job value. Of these two methods, the point method is the most popular with organizations that use formal job evaluation systems. The chapter concluded with a discussion of the need to involve employees in both job analysis and job evaluation, and with some strategies for employee involvement. A critical element of internal equity is employee perceptions, and employee involvement is absolutely indispensable for ensuring that these perceptions correspond with reality.

KEY TERMS

benchmark (or key) jobs

classification method

compensable factors

factor comparison method

job analysis

job description

job evaluation

job specifications

job structure

job value

point method

position analysis questionnaire (PAQ)

ranking method

REVIEW AND DISCUSSION QUESTIONS

1. Define internal equity. What role does internal equity play in the design of a compensation system?

2. What is job analysis? In what specific way does job analysis serve the design and management of the compensation system?

3. What considerations should be kept in mind when choosing a job analysis method?

4. Some job analysts prefer the interview method, others prefer the questionnaire method, and still others prefer both. Explore the advantages and disadvantages of these methods, and explain how job analysts might use both methods.

5. The job evaluation programme can be said to be one of the pillars that support the compensation structure. Do you agree? Why?

6. Compare and contrast the four job evaluation methods.

7. "Given the high degree of subjectivity in even the best method available, the need for high trust on the part of the employees affected is crucial." What strategies would you propose to ensure that employees accept the conclusions of the job evaluation programme?

Determining the Appropriateness of Job Analysis Methods

EXERCISE
11.1

Objective

To acquire an understanding of which job analysis method is appropriate to collect the job content data.

Procedure

1. The class is divided into groups of five or six participants.

2. Working individually, each participant reviews the preparatory steps and the job analysis methods listed in the worksheet (Table 11.1.1) and decides on the appropriateness of these for the jobs listed in the adjoining columns.

   The decision can be indicated by a check mark in the job column; do this separately for each job. A preparatory step/a job analysis method may be used for more than one job if it is judged to be appropriate, but be prepared to justify all decisions.

3. Share your individual decision with your group. As a group, arrive at a consensus. Make sure the group spokesperson records the group consensus, together with the reasons for any irreconcilable differences.

4. Each group reports its decisions.

5. Discussion will follow each presentation. In exploring the appropriateness of a job analysis method, consider the characteristics of the method and the ultimate objectives of job analysis.

Table 11.1.1: Worksheet for Determining the Appropriateness of Job Analysis Methods

Preparatory Steps and Job Analysis Methods	Manager	Labaoratory scientist	Automobile mechanic	Travelling salesperson	Administrative assistant	Assembly-line operator
Communication						
Review of organization chart						
Review of existing job descriptions						
Tour of job location						
Interview methods						
• Interviewing supervisor						
• Interviewing job holder						
Observation method						
Questionnaire method						
Diary/log method						

EXERCISE
11.2

11.2 Job Evaluation

Objective

To experience some of the activities of job evaluation, and to become aware of the importance of the process issues involved in a job evaluation programme.

Procedure

1. The class is divided into groups of five to six participants. Each group functions as a job evaluation committee of the Tinkerman Corporation (see Chapter 1). The task of the committee is to evaluate two jobs (see the job descriptions in Table 11.2.1) using the job evaluation system (see Table 11.2.2). The job evaluation system consists of four compensable factors: knowledge, decision making, responsibility for contacts, and supervision. For the purpose of this exercise, the committee will evaluate the jobs on only one factor, knowledge.

2. Working individually, each participant studies the job evaluation manual and, consistent with its guidelines, determines the points to assign to the two jobs; do this one job at a time.

3. Share your decisions with your group. As a group, arrive at a consensus. Make sure the group spokesperson records the reasons for any differences that cannot be reconciled.

4. On completion of the job evaluation activity, the group discusses the following questions:

   a) Reflecting on the group discussions, identify the basis or reasons for the initial differences in the points assigned to the job.

   b) How were the differences reconciled?

   c) If you were in charge of the job evaluation programme, what process would you use to form a job evaluation committee? What guidelines would you propose for the committee to follow?

   d) What are some of the other administrative and process issues that you will consider?

   e) Were you satisfied with the job descriptions? What further information would you seek? What method(s) would be most appropriate for obtaining this information?

Table 11.2.1: Job Descriptions—Job A and Job B

JOB A

Writes, tests, and implements new programs. Corrects and modifies existing programs. Develops the information required to create a new application. Analyses the collected information and suggests definition and design of the application. Plans the project on the basis of workload requirements. Develops the database requirements for the planned application. Prepares documentation and trains users on the new application. Involves the computer operations team to maintain and handle the new application.

Knowledge: Computer programming and processing techniques; computer theory and practices; management information systems.

JOB B

Performs accounting work in accordance with generally accepted accounting principles, including cost accounting activities. Maintains financial and statistical records, including petty cash. Prepares budget variation reports and bank reconciliation statements. Reviews revenue projections and operating costs. Provides information on financial procedures and accounting requirements. Trains and supervises subordinates.

Knowledge: Principles, procedures, and practices of general and cost accounting; computerized accounting procedures; legal requirements; office systems and practices.

Table 11.2.2: Job Evaluation Plan

The plan combines point rating (an analytical, quantitative method of determining the relative value of positions) and factor comparison (a method that requires factor-to-factor comparisons on each position). All methods of job evaluation require the exercise of judgement and the orderly collection and analysis of information in order that consistent judgements can be made. This method facilitates discussion and the resolution of differences in determining the relative worth of jobs.

Point Values

The maximum point value assigned to each factor reflects its relative importance. Point values have also been assigned to the degrees of the factors. The minimum point values for knowledge, decision making, and responsibility for contacts are one-fifth of the maximum value, except for supervision.

FACTOR	Minimum Points	Maximum Points	Weight
Knowledge	70	350	35%
Decision making	70	350	35%
Responsibility for contacts	30	150	15%
Supervision	––	150	15%
	170	1,000	100%

Factors

The combined factors do not describe all aspects of positions. They deal only with those characteristics that are useful in determining the relative value of positions. Four factors are used in this plan. All the factors have more than one dimension and have been defined in terms of two or three related elements.

Knowledge	Education Experience
Decision making	Scope for decisions Impact of decisions
Responsibility for contacts	Nature of contacts Persons contacted
Supervision	Level of employees supervised Number supervised

Knowledge

Rating Scale – Education and Experience

This factor is used to measure the amount of education and related practical experience required to perform the duties of the position.

Education

Refers to the level of academic or other formal training required to provide the basis for the development of the skill and the knowledge needed in the position.

Experience

Refers to the minimum related administrative knowledge and skill needed to carry out the duties of the position.

Notes to Evaluating Committee

In selecting the degree of the *experience* element, consideration is to be given to the length of time needed to develop the specialized knowledge and the general administrative knowledge required to carry out the duties of the position. General administrative knowledge is gained through experience in such responsibilities as:

- formulating ideas and expressing them orally or in written form.

- carrying out studies and preparing reports on specific aspects of existing or proposed activities.

- making critical analysis of methods and procedures with a view to recommending improvements.

- planning programmes or work to meet the requirements of the department or organization served and the plans of action developed to achieve them.

- performing advisory duties that require a knowledge of objectives of the organization served and the measures evolved to achieve them.

- supervising and directing staff.

In selecting the degree of the *education* element, the second degree is to be assigned to positions where there is a clear requirement for specialized formal training beyond completion of secondary school education, for example, two to three year programmes at the community college level.

The third degree is to be assigned if there is a clear requirement for a general university degree with a particular field specialization of courses of similar length and difficulty leading to membership in required associations, for example, R.I.A., C.G.A., etc.

The fourth degree of the *education* element is to be assigned when the duties of the position:

1. require university graduation in a specialized field, or

2. require understanding and appreciation of the principles and concepts of two or more specialized fields for which knowledge is normally acquired through university training and which are directly associated with the duties performed, or

3. require systematic study and analysis of complicated general problems and their solution by the application of specialized knowledge acquired through extensive post-secondary school study or training rather than through experience.

(In positions with duties that are in categories 2 or 3, the incumbents will not necessarily be university graduates.)

Knowledge Rating Scale — Education and Experience

Education Requirement
If specialized experience is a requirement, add 25 points.

Experience Requirement	A Secondary School	B Specialized Community College Training	C Post Community College Specialized Training of General Degree	D Degree that Provides Training in Required Job Skills
1 Up to and including 2 years	45	65	90	120
2 Up to and including 4 years	65	90	120	170
3 Up to and including 6 years	90	120	170	235
4 More than 6 years	120	170	235	325

Source: Department of Human Resources, McGill University.

Pay Equity Legislation:

Internal Equity II

OVERVIEW

The previous chapter examined internal equity as it ought to exist in the compensation system so that all employees perceive the system to be fair and equitable. This chapter looks at internal equity as mandated by pay equity laws in Canada. Specifically, the chapter reviews such salient features of pay equity laws as applicability, enforcement mechanisms, and implementation procedures. It also reviews pay equity laws in the light of the principles of moral justice.

LEARNING OBJECTIVES

▶ To define and distinguish the three meanings of *pay equity.*

▶ To identify the major differences in the pay equity laws in Canada.

▶ To describe the mechanisms and processes involved in the development of a pay equity plan.

▶ To understand the sources of gender bias in job analysis and job evaluation procedures, and to develop strategies for eliminating or reducing gender bias.

▶ To understand the moral foundation of equity, and to explain, in the context of pay equity, the concept of equity as a natural right.

▶ To understand the effects of pay equity laws in the light of the principles of moral justice.

INTRODUCTION

Pay equity, or Comparable Worth, as it is referred to in the United States, has been hailed as an idea whose time has come—at least in Canada, where ten out of 13 jurisdictions have enacted laws that prohibit pay distinctions between male and female jobs of equal or comparable value. Advocates of pay equity see it as a historic vindication of women's rights as they struggle for equality in the workplace. Critics have assailed it as "...one of the more aggressive elitist visions of modern life that has surfaced in recent decades" (Berger, 1984, p.71). The issue has obviously provoked strong reactions. This chapter will attempt to steer clear of polemics, and explore pay equity as a human rights issue that transcends gender discrimination. Specifically, the chapter will first consider the salient features of pay equity laws in Canada, including some of the procedural issues in their implementation. It then examines the psychological concepts of equity and its philosophical underpinnings and, in the light of these principles, examine the basis and effects of pay equity laws. The appendix to the chapter briefly reviews the pay equity issue in the United States.

THE SALIENT FEATURES OF PAY EQUITY LEGISLATION

This section will first consider the legal definition of pay equity and briefly review the history of pay equity legislation in Canada. Then the chapter will examine the salient features of pay equity laws and discuss the procedural issues relating to compliance with these laws.

WHAT IS PAY EQUITY?

Equal pay for equal work

The concept of pay equity has evolved over time. Pay equity was originally understood as "equal pay for equal work". Employees, whether male or female, who do identical jobs should be paid the same. For example, a female teacher in an elementary school should be paid the same salary as a male teacher. Pay differentials should only be for reasons of performance, experience, and seniority. The concept of equal pay for equal work was generally accepted in the workplace—although some employers accepted the principle in theory, yet paid men a higher pay rate than women because of their belief that the earnings of a man were the principal source of income for the family.

Equal pay for similar or substantially similar work

Husbands and wives becoming joint income providers for the family, the influence of the feminist movement, and the increasing participation of women in the workforce has brought about a re-definition of pay equity. It began to be seen as "equal pay for similar or substantially similar work". According to this definition, employees who do similar work, whether they are male or female, should be paid the same. Thus, the job of cleaner, predominantly held by women, was seen to be similar to the job of janitor, predominantly held by men, and should therefore be paid the same as the job of janitor.

Equal pay for work of equal value

This change in the definition of pay equity was only a transitional phase to the present understanding of pay equity, which is "equal pay for work of equal value". According to this concept, employees, whether they are male or female, who do different work but whose work is of equal value to the organization should be paid the same. For example, if it can be demonstrated that the job of clerk IV and the job of construction supervisor are of equal value to their employer, these jobs should be paid the same.

Pay equity laws in Canada incorporate the definition "equal pay for work of equal value". With the exception of Quebec, these laws have an exclusive gender-based focus—to redress the pay inequities experienced by employees in female-dominated jobs when compared to employees in male-dominated jobs of equal value. The laws limit the applicability of this definition only to situations of inequity that are experienced by female employees in female-dominated jobs. This restricted use of the concept is a major limitation of Canadian pay equity laws, except those of the province of Quebec which address pay discrimination experienced by **all** employees.

THE HISTORY OF PAY EQUITY LEGISLATION IN CANADA

In 1951, Ontario enacted the Ontario Female Employees Fair Remuneration Act, which mandated that all female employees who do work that is "substantially similar" to that of male employees should be paid the same as the male employees. In 1972, Canada signed the International Labour Organization Convention of "equal pay for work of equivalent value". Quebec incorporated this convention into its Charter of Human Rights and Freedoms in 1976 (see Boivin and Deom, 1995, for a history of pay equity in Quebec). The federal government included the concept in the Canadian Human Rights Act in 1977. After a short lull, from 1977 to 1990, a spate of pay equity laws followed: Manitoba (1985); Yukon (1986); Ontario (1987); Prince Edward Island, Nova Scotia, and Newfoundland (1988); New Brunswick (1989); and British Columbia and the Northwest Territories (1990). Legislation or formal initiative in pay equity areas exists in all Canadian jurisdictions except Alberta and Saskatchewan (Gunderson, 1995).

SELECTED PROVISIONS OF PAY EQUITY LAWS

All pay equity laws, except those of Quebec, have essentially the same objective—to redress the pay inequities experienced by employees in a female-dominated job when the pay rate of this job is lower than that of a male-dominated job of equal value. There are differences, however, in the way that different jurisdictions seek to achieve this objective.

Private vs. public sector coverage

There are differences in the applicability or coverage of these laws. Some of the laws apply only to employees of the government that has enacted the law. Other laws extend coverage to employees of municipalities, school boards, universities, and crown corporations. Pay equity legislation is potentially applicable to private sector organizations in the federal jurisdiction, Ontario, and Quebec. In practice, however, it is only in Ontario that private sector jobs are affected. Both in Quebec and in the federal jurisdiction, pay equity legislation has been applied largely to public sector crown corporations and regulated industries (Boivin and Deom, 1995; Gunderson, 1995).

Proactive vs. complaints based enforcement

There are differences in the way that pay equity is enforced from jurisdiction to jurisdiction. In some, the pay equity redress process is activated only after an aggrieved employee files a complaint; in others, proactive legislation activates the process. Proactive legislation exists in Manitoba, Ontario, New Brunswick, Nova Scotia, and Prince Edward Island. It requires a pay equity plan to be in place regardless of prior complaints or evidence of discrimination. In Newfoundland and British Columbia, proactive initiative through collective bargaining is practised. The federal jurisdiction and Quebec require a complaint before any action is initiated, and therefore have a less stringent pay equity policy (Boivin and Deom, 1995). It may be pointed out that although Quebec's pay equity law does not have a gender-based focus and its enforcement is complaint-driven, the beneficiaries of this law have been mainly women's groups. In an attempt to remedy this situation, the Quebec Human Rights Commission has recommended that Quebec should become more proactive in its enforcement in both the public and private sectors (Bula, 1992).

Gender predominance The third area of differences in pay equity laws relates to the issue of gender predominance. The main thrust of pay equity laws is to redress the pay inequities that result when female-dominated jobs and male-dominated jobs are of equal value, but the former are paid at a lower rate than the latter. A criterion is needed for determining which jobs are female-dominated and which jobs are male-dominated. Some pay equity laws stipulate that a job is dominated by a gender when the employees of that gender constitute 70 per cent of the total incumbents of that job in the organization; other laws place the criterion at 60 per cent. According to the Ontario and New Brunswick laws, a job is female-dominated when 60 per cent of its incumbents are women; a job is male-dominated when 70 per cent of its incumbents are men. The Yukon has not specified any criterion for determining the gender predominance of a job.

Limits on cost to organization

The fourth difference is the limit placed on the cost to the employer of correcting pay inequities. Pay equity laws that require employers to be proactive in identifying and redressing pay inequities generally stipulate limits on payroll costs that result from pay adjustments. For example, in Ontario, such costs need not exceed one percent of the employer's payroll. The exception is Nova Scotia, which requires proactive enforcement but does not specify a limit to the cost of pay adjustments for correcting inequities. The pay equity laws that have a complaint-driven enforcement mechanism have not specified a limit to the cost of pay adjustments that result from pay inequities. As Weiner and Gunderson (1990) suggest, a limit on costs for the complaint-driven mechanism is not necessary, because the case-by-case approach is less likely to place a severe financial burden on the employer in any one year. On the other hand, the proactive approach to enforcement requires a pay equity plan that identifies at one time all the necessary pay adjustments, and making all those adjustments can be a heavy financial burden for an organization in one year.

Implementation through legislation vs. collective bargaining

Pay equity issues are resolved either through legislative acts or through collective bargaining. Collective bargaining of pay equity issues with government employees is practised in Newfoundland and British Columbia. In Quebec, pay equity actions are initiated through negotiation and complaints. Negotiations are undertaken under pressure from unions and sometimes collective bargaining agreements may be questioned on the basis of complaints filed with the Human Rights Commission (Boivin and Deom, 1995).

Table 12.1 summarises the provisions of pay equity laws in Canada in respect of coverage, enforcement, gender predominance, the limits on the cost of resolving inequities, and implementation.

TABLE 12.1

A SUMMARY OF SELECTED PROVISIONS OF PAY EQUITY LAWS IN CANADA

Coverage:	Public sector	Covered by all laws
	Municipalities, school boards, universities	Covered by all laws, except New Brunswick
	Crown corporations	Covered by all laws, except the Yukon
	Private sector	Covered only by Federal, Quebec, Ontario, and the Northwest Territories
Enforcement:	Complaint-driven	Federal, Quebec, the Yukon
	Proactive	Nova Scotia, New Brunswick, Manitoba
	Both	Prince Edward Island, Ontario
Gender predominance:	70% F; 70% M	Federal, Manitoba
	60% F; 70% M	Ontario, New Brunswick, Quebec
	60% F; 60% M	Prince Edward Island, Nova Scotia, Newfoundland
	Not specified	Yukon
Cost limits for resolving inequities:	Case-by-case basis	Federal, Quebec, Yukon
	1% of payroll/year	Manitoba, Prince Edward Island, New Brunswick, Ontario, Newfoundland
	No limit specified	Nova Scotia
Implementation:	Collective bargaining	Newfoundland, British Columbia
	Legislation	Ontario, Manitoba, Prince Edward Island, Nova Scotia, New Brunswick

Source: Adapted from Ontario Pay Equity Commission (1994); Gunderson (1995).

THE PAY EQUITY PLAN

The pay equity laws of each jurisdiction stipulate their own implementation mechanisms and processes. The Pay Equity Act of Ontario is the most comprehensive in terms of its coverage; it is applicable to both the public and private sectors. Ontario's law also provides for both forms of enforcement mechanisms, the complaint-driven as well as the proactive. Furthermore, it would appear that the Ontario model might become increasingly more attractive in Canada. Therefore, it may be instructive to describe the implementation mechanism of Ontario's Pay Equity Act in order to illustrate a systematic process for correcting pay inequities. The description that follows is based on Ontario's pay equity guidelines (Pay Equity Commission, 1989b). The implementation specifics vary according to organization size, and on whether it is in the public or private sector. However, the critical implementation steps are as follows:

1. The organization must determine the number of pay equity plans it must implement. Each establishment of the organization in a given geographic region must have at least one plan. This implies that there may be regional pay differentials. More than one plan may be necessary when there are separate bargaining units in an establishment.

2. The organization determines the extent and the form of employee involvement in the process. For unionized organizations, the Pay Equity Act envisages a negotiated process. Non-unionized organizations are free to involve their employees. Failure to involve employees can seriously undermine the effectiveness of the implementation process.

3. The organization determines the female job classes and the male job classes. A female job class (also referred to as a female-dominated job class) is one in which 60 per cent of the job incumbents are female. A male job class (also referred to as a male-dominated job class) is one in which 70 per cent of the job incumbents are male.

4. The organization selects a gender-neutral system for determining the job classes that are of equal value. The criteria used for the comparison should include skill, effort, responsibility, and working conditions—refer to Chapter 11 for the definition of these factors provided by the federal government guidelines.

    Essentially, this step refers to a job evaluation system that is free of gender bias. Of the job evaluation systems described in Chapter 11, the point method is generally the preferred system. Certain decisions in the operation of this method (i.e., in the job analysis and job evaluation processes) may introduce gender bias. This concern is dealt with in the next section.

5. The organization applies the job evaluation system and determines the female and male job classes that are comparable. The Pay Equity Act has specified a sequential comparison process for this purpose.

6. The pay rate of the female job class is then compared with the pay rate of the comparable male job class. The pay rate, for this purpose, includes the employer's paid contribution to benefits and perquisites.

7. The necessary pay adjustments are then determined. Pay adjustments result only when the pay rate of the female job class is lower than the pay rate of its comparable male job class. When the pay rate of the female job class is found to be higher than the pay rate of its comparable male job class, the Pay Equity Act does not require that the pay rate of the male job class be adjusted upward. Furthermore, when pay adjustments are made, all employees in the female job class, male as well as female, are eligible for these adjustments.

8. The major items of information generated in the previous steps are communicated to employees through the posting in the workplace of a pay equity plan, developed in a prescribed format. The posting of the plan gives employees an opportunity to review it and to file their objections. In non-unionized organizations, the objections should be filed within 90 days of the posting of the plan. In unionized organizations, the agreement of the union constitutes the approval of the plan by the employees.

9. After the objections have been appropriately dealt with, the organization proceeds to making the pay adjustments. As indicated earlier, the total cost to the employer is a minimum of one per cent of the previous year's payroll, until equity is achieved.

All the above implementation steps fall under four generic categories:

- the identification of male-and female-dominated job classes;
- the evaluation of jobs according to gender-neutral job-evaluation procedures;
- the comparison of pay to job evaluation results showing the relationship between the two as reflected in the estimation of the pay lines; and
- the pay adjustment (Gunderson, 1995).

The impact of the Pay Equity Plan Gunderson (1995) estimates that pay equity in Canada and the U.S. has resulted in average wage increases of approximately 20 percent or $4,000 per recipient, amounting to four to eight percent of payroll for the public sector. Besides the impact on wages, pay equity can affect employment of minority groups, wage differentials within minority and female workforce, occupational segregation and labour participation decisions.

Problems in Pay Equity Plan implementation The Ontario experience with pay equity raises two major problems. First, how to make comparisons of female and male job classes when there are no male comparator groups, particularly in organizations or establishments that employ only females. Bill 102, effective July 1993 proposed two steps to resolve this issue. The proportional value method (which involves making pay adjustments of such female-dominated jobs for which comparable male-dominated jobs could be found) can be used for both public and private sectors. If this is not feasible, proxy comparisons (which involves identifying a comparable male-dominated job in another establishment of the same employer) can be used for the public sector only. However, the Omnibus Bill of the Conservative government rescinded the proxy method, which was phased out on January 1, 1997.

The second problem faced by the Ontario Pay Equity Tribunal has to do with the question: What constitutes a gender-neutral job-evaluation plan? This issue is discussed in the following section.

THE ISSUE OF GENDER BIAS IN JOB ANALYSIS AND JOB EVALUATION

The discussion in Chapter 11 underscored the fact that the mechanics and procedures in job analysis and job evaluation involve a considerable degree of subjectivity, which leaves room for bias that spoils the process. This section examines the sources of gender bias in job analysis and job evaluation, and some strategies for minimizing gender bias in these processes.

Gender Bias in Job Analysis

Perceptual errors and biases The first major source of gender bias in job analysis derives from perceptual errors and biases that occur in the collection of data and the writing up of job descriptions. The human perceptual process does not function like a video camera that documents events faithfully. Rather, it is a subjective process influenced not only by the properties and characteristics of objective reality but also by the observer's personality, past learning, motivation, and expectations. In these subjective elements lies the potential for inaccuracies and biases as a person observes, selects, organises, and interprets reality. The job analyst is obviously susceptible to these biases.

For example, in collecting data on the job of a secretary, the major focus might be on the typing activity, which is more salient because it is more audible and visible. As a result, activities that are not as conspicuous (e.g., planning, organising, screening the manager's telephone calls and visitors) are either ignored or assigned less importance. When these activities are ignored or are not properly emphasized in the job description, they do not receive the credit they deserve in the job evaluation process.

The expectations of the job analyst can also result in a misleading job description. When this bias operates, the job analyst will see what he/she expects to see. A good example of this bias is the influence of job titles. To the job analyst, the job title provides the first and immediate source of information on the job. Reliance on this information alone can lead to an erroneous emphasis in the job description if the job content has, in fact, undergone change.

Sociocultural influences The second major source of gender bias in job analysis results from sociocultural factors. The different ways in which men and women have been socialised can influence the ways in which they describe their jobs. For example, women are expected to be "self-effacing", and men, "self-enhancing". Consequently, when women are asked to describe their jobs, they are likely to do so in a modest manner, and their manner will influence the importance assigned to the job in the job evaluation process. A similar phenomenon has been observed with regard to workers from non-western cultures; they are reluctant to "market" themselves and their legitimate accomplishments.

Measures to address gender bias in job analysis

Use multiple sources of information   For example, review the organization chart and existing job descriptions, tour the job site to observe working conditions, and study the social and technical context of the job.

Use standardised data collection format   Without a standardised format to collect and describe data, the choice of what is critical in a job is left to the discretion of the analyst. Both the type and the extent of job details tend to be recorded in an inconsistent manner. Such an approach can result in inadequate or incorrect descriptions of jobs, particularly of female jobs, because many of these jobs are not as specific in terms of job tasks as blue-collar manufacturing jobs.

Gender Bias in Job Evaluation

The source of gender bias in job evaluation systems that use the point method comes mainly from the choice, the weights, and the definition of compensable factors. Perceptual errors and biases creep in when the point method is used, but not as extensively as when the ranking or classification method is used. Most of the traditional job evaluation systems were designed and developed for blue-collar jobs, which are predominantly held by males. Further, the interpretation of the definition of compensable factors was in the context of manufacturing operations. The examples used in the following discussion are drawn from the November 1989 *Newsletter* published by Ontario's Pay Equity Commission (Pay Equity Commission, 1989a).

Compensable factors—choice and definition   The first reason for gender bias is that both the choice and the definition of compensable factors ignore the nature of the tasks and activities of female jobs. For example, the compensable factor of responsibility is usually defined to mean responsibility for things like equipment, machinery, products, finances. In most female jobs (teacher, nurse) the primary responsibility is for people. When this substantive difference is ignored by the job evaluation system, the system operates to the disadvantage of female job incumbents.

Second, the definition of the compensable factor may not be wide enough to capture adequately the specific characteristics of female jobs. For example, the factor of working conditions might include a definition such as "standard office conditions". Most female jobs, clerical and secretarial, are performed inside a building in an office. However, conditions in an office are not necessarily standard for all office jobs. The manager's office environment might be pleasant, but his/her secretary's environment might be exposed to dust, dirt, distractions from people and traffic, and noise from telephones and machines. The job analyst may assume that the "standard office conditions" are pleasant and free from the toxic fumes and temperature extremes of the factory and may therefore not give such conditions much weight in terms of job evaluation points. As a result, predominately female office jobs may not earn many points under the working conditions factor when compared with male-dominated blue-collar jobs.

Perceptual bias The perceptual bias of stereotype creeps in when the requirements of the job are assessed in terms of the preconceived attributes of the female. Weiner and Gunderson (1990) provide interesting examples of the inconsistent manner in which the stereotypes operate. Because men are believed to be physically stronger than women, it is assumed that male jobs will require the exertion of physical effort. Therefore, male jobs get credit for the physical effort needed on a job whereas female jobs do not, although the jobs of nurses involve the exertion of such physical effort as the lifting of patients and prolonged standing. On the other hand, the female-dominated job of institutional supervisor of a home for the mentally retarded was not given credit for the mental and physical effort involved in the job because it was believed that the work of caring for children is "natural to women" and therefore does not need to be compensated.

Addressing gender bias in job evaluation

The basic strategy that an organization should use in addressing the issue of gender bias in job evaluation is to adopt a single job evaluation system. The compensable factors should be chosen, weighted, and defined with one objective—to adequately tap the content and contribution of female as well as male jobs. Some factors may favour male jobs and other factors may favour female jobs (Weiner and Gunderson, 1990). For example, in the factor of skill, the subfactor of knowledge of machinery, and tools will favour male jobs; the subfactor of typing and keyboarding will favour female jobs. Similarly, in the factor of working conditions, the subfactor of physical hazards will favour male jobs and the subfactor of monotony will favour female jobs. As was discussed in Chapter 11, the organization should also ensure proper attention to the process issues that guarantee employee involvement.

MORAL FOUNDATION OF EQUITY AND LESSONS FROM THE CANADIAN EXPERIENCE

This section deals with some of the neglected issues in pay equity laws in the context of the moral foundation of pay equity and the psychological underpinnings of equity.

MORAL FOUNDATION OF EQUITY

Human beings seem to grow up with a sense of fairness, or equity. We all want to be treated fairly even though we ourselves might often fail to accord the same treatment to others. There may be cultural differences in the content or mode of determining equity, but the fact that the notion of equity exists is not in doubt. Is this sense of equity merely a matter of temperament, or the result of the socialization process, or does it reflect one of the fundamental qualities of the nature of the human being? To explore the substantive basis of equity, we need to examine the underlying assumptions which people make when they say that they are being treated fairly or unfairly in an exchange relationship. At the very root of all equity-related perceptions is the individual's belief, well-founded or baseless, that he/she has certain rights in that relationship. Equity is experienced when these perceived rights are respected; when these rights are not respected, the individual experiences inequity.

Individuals develop their awareness and understanding of their rights from a variety of sources. The most visible source of rights are the laws of the land. There is another category of rights—moral rights. These are not contained in a legislative statute, but are rights which are referred to as "natural rights", "human rights", or the "rights of man". The justification of human rights is that they flow from the very nature of "man" (in the generic sense). As Jacques Maritain observed: "The human person possesses rights because of the very fact that it is a person, a whole, a master of itself and its acts, and which consequently is not merely a means to an end, but an end, which must be treated as such" (Cranston, 1987, p.16). The beliefs and values in the non-western traditions also reflect these basic natural rights.

Pay equity relates to the "natural aspiration of justice in the human heart" (W.A. White, cited in Webster's Dictionary, 1981, p.1228), and does not need to be justified by an appeal to a legislative pronouncement. What are the specific principles of distributive justice which pay equity law must satisfy?

Principles of Distributive Justice

The individual's experience of fairness or unfairness is essentially a psychological experience. Therefore, our understanding of the principles of distributive justice, which are intended to ensure fairness, is greatly enhanced when we discuss them in the context of the underlying psychological processes. The psychological explanations of the principles of distributive justice can be categorized in terms of whether the principle incorporates a single or multiple norms.

The single norm perspective It was presented by Homans (1961) who used the concept of distributive justice to analyze social behaviour. He argued that individuals would experience fairness in an exchange relationship if the outcomes were proportional to their investments. Adams (1965) refined this argument in his theory of "Injustice in Social Exchange" and depicted a specific process of how individuals experience inequity and the motivational consequences of such an experience. According to this theory, feelings of equity or inequity are generated by the individual's perceptions of his/her outcomes-inputs ratio and the outcomes-inputs ratio of the person with whom the individual compares himself/herself. When the ratios are perceived to be equal, the individual regards the outcomes to be equitable and is, accordingly, satisfied with them. On the other hand, when these ratios are perceived to be unequal, the individual regards the outcomes to be inequitable or unfair and is dissatisfied with them.

Adams' equity theory explains both the favourable and unfavourable inequities experienced by individuals in the workplace, and posits the different methods individuals might choose to reduce the inequities. Such methods are altering their inputs and outcomes, cognitively distorting their or other's inputs and outcomes, acting on or changing the reference source, or leaving the field. Since pay is the individual's major outcome at the workplace, equity theory becomes critical in understanding and predicting the individual's work behaviour as a consequence of the favourable or unfavourable impact of pay equity laws on the individual's earnings. This formulation of the principle of distributive justice is clearly based on the single norm of "equity". The validity and utility of equity theory particularly in relation to pay is amply supported by numerous studies (Carrell and Dittrich, 1978; Wall and Nolan, 1986; Mowday, 1987; Huseman, Hatfield, and Miles, 1987).

The multi-norm perspective This prescribes that several norms are needed to ensure distributive justice. The number of such norms range from four (Deutsch, 1975, 1985) to 18 (Lerner and Whitehead, 1980; Lerner and Meindl, 1981). Despite the large number, only three norms—"equity", "equality", "need"—have been studied extensively. These norms have been found to be appropriate for most types of resource allocations and contexts. Thus, according to Deutsch (1975, 1985), "equity" will be the dominant principle of distributive justice in the economically-oriented context, "equality" in the social-relations context, and "need" in the personal development and welfare-oriented context.

Which norm is appropriate for pay equity laws? In the context of pay equity laws, the norm of "need" does not become an appropriate principle of distributive justice. It is not denied that the "needs" of workers, be they male or female, single or married, might well justify higher wages. But, if need rather than the "value of work" becomes the norm, we are moving away from the concept of pay equity or comparable worth, and towards socialism. Since socialism is not the avowed objective of pay equity, the norm of "equity", and to a lesser extent, the norm of "equality" become the appropriate principles of distributive justice. The earlier discussion of Equity Theory provides the justification for the norm of "equity".

The norm of "equality" cannot be given the same dominant position because it has two aspects: equality of opportunity and equality of results. By equality of opportunity, we mean that artificial barriers such as race, colour, creed, gender, ethnic origin, etc., should not prevent individuals from attaining their lawful hopes and aspirations. Such artificial barriers create disadvantages for individuals for the sole reasons that they are members of a group. In this situation, "...the state is asked, indeed required, not to abstain but to intervene to protect individuals from discrimination based on a group affiliation.... The reason in human rights we do not treat all individuals the same is because not all individuals have suffered historic generic exclusion because of group membership. Where assumptive barriers have impeded the fairness of the competition for some individuals, they should be removed, even if this means treating some people differently" (Abella, 1991, p.22). Equality of opportunity, therefore, becomes a critical principle to evaluate pay equity laws. It is a standard that helps determine whether pay equity laws respect the right to equality of opportunity of individuals and groups.

Equality of results, on the other hand, "...demands that each person be treated as a component of an organic society; the parts must be rearranged and rewarded so the entire organization will be just" (Paul, 1989, p.121-122). Such an approach will obviously require continuous interference with the individual's freedom of action much like the practices in a centralised, command economy.

For the reasons discussed, we shall adopt the norms of "equity" and "equality of opportunity" as the principles of distributive justice with which to evaluate the pay equity laws described in the earlier sections of this chapter.

PAY EQUITY LAWS—LESSONS FROM THE CANADIAN EXPERIENCE

The legislated pay equity programs in the Canadian jurisdictions are at different stages of implementation. For example, in Ontario, firms employing between ten and 49 employees had until January 1994 to begin wage adjustments (Robb, 1988). The Ontario business community is probably reconciled to these programs for two reasons: (1) the programs have been phased in gradually, and communicated well with guidelines that detail the implementation process in simple and clear terms, including toll-free pay equity hotlines for follow-up clarifications; and (2) organizations see that the annual cost of pay adjustments will not be more than 1% of their payroll. The unions generally support the pay equity laws, but are concerned about their impact on collective bargaining and established union principles, and prefer that the laws not be exclusively gender-based (Weiner and Gunderson, 1990). The federal government, on the other hand, is beginning to feel the pinch of the costs of adjustments as was demonstrated by its recent refusal to accept the Federal court's decrees on pay adjustments which might be as high as $1.5 billion (*Toronto Sun*, 1996). As discussed earlier, the Quebec government was committed to introducing a pay equity law similar to the one in Ontario, but, according to media reports in May 1996, the economic climate does not seem to be hospitable to such a law at this time.

What can the Canadian pay equity experience contribute to the serious discussion of the issue of comparable worth in North America and elsewhere? Interestingly enough, the lessons from the Canadian experience involve issues that were part of the comparable worth debate in the United States long before pay equity laws were enacted in Canada. The Canadian experience provides empirical insights to issues that, until now, might have been viewed mainly in academic terms.

ISSUES NEGLECTED BY PAY EQUITY LAWS

Restricted coverage

The laws do not cover groups—e.g., visible minorities, native peoples, the handicapped—designated as "protected" groups under Canada's employment equity policy. These groups might also experience pay inequity (Howard, 1995). We illustrate this point with reference to the experience of visible minorities in Canada. Numerous studies have documented the systemic employment discrimination against visible minorities (Jain, 1984; Canadian Recruiters Guild, 1988). As an example of the pay inequity experienced by visible minorities, we cite the findings of the 1986 Canadian census which provides striking evidence of the pay inequity experienced by Canadians of South Asian origin relative to the Canadian population. The average annual income of South Asian Canadian males was $23,279 versus the Canadian male average income of $25,991—an earnings gap of 10 percent. The average annual income of South Asian Canadian females was $12,247 versus the Canadian female average income of $14,809—an earnings gap of 17 percent (Statistics Canada, 1989a; 1989b).

To assess fully the inequity underlying these wage gaps it is necessary to view these gaps in the context of South Asian Canadians' education, labour force participation rate, and occupation relative to the Canadian population. A study of the comparative data on these dimensions found that 21 percent of South Asian Canadian adults were university graduates versus 10 percent of Canadian adults, the labour force participation rate of South Asian Canadians was 78 percent versus the Canadian average of 66 percent, and 18 percent of South Asian Canadian males were in professional occupations compared to 13 percent of Canadian males (White and Nanda, 1989). Because of their better education, higher labour participation rate, and higher proportion of professional occupations relative to the Canadian population, the principles of fairness and justice would dictate that the average annual earnings of South Asian Canadians should not be less than that of the Canadians but that it should be substantially more than the Canadian average.

Role of the labour market

The determination of pay inequity of female job classes specifically excludes the role of the labour market. "The wages for male jobs found in the market are assumed to be accurate, and are used as the salary to which female-dominated jobs of equal value must be raised" (Weiner and Gunderson, 1990, p.76). The rationale for the exclusion is that the market is riddled with discrimination. The evidence that is most frequently cited is identical to that cited by the comparable worth proponents in the United States—e.g., the wage gap, sex-segregation in the marketplace, and undervaluation of women's jobs. Several American and Canadian studies have found that factors such as level of schooling, duration of work force experience, number of hours worked, and marital status contribute to narrowing the female-male wage gap to about 10% (O'Neill, 1984; Weiler, 1986; Brown, 1991).

Supporters of pay equity attribute this residual gap to discrimination in the marketplace. Opponents, on the other hand, argue that it can be explained by difficult to quantify factors such as women's expectations of their family responsibilities and job preferences. This latter argument acquires significance in the light of the findings of a 1994 Statistics Canada report on the earnings of men and women that there is practically no wage gap between single women and single men of comparable age and education.

The arguments that discrimination resulted in sex-segregation and under-valuation of women's jobs in the marketplace are not too persuasive. In the past, women made educational and job choices that allowed them the flexibility to balance family responsibilities and the job (Polachek, 1975). A frequently cited example of undervaluation of women's jobs is the case of the wages of the secretary's job declining when women began to replace men as secretaries. Paul (1989) cites a study which suggests that the wages declined not because the job was undervalued but because the job content had undergone a change.

The preceding discussion on whether the labour market discriminates against female job classes in setting pay will remain inconclusive. This is because the type, nature, and context of the innumerable variables involved do not permit studies and investigations whose findings will be acceptable to all. However, suppose we assume that the market does indeed discriminate. The question remains: Is it prudent to replace it with the job evaluation system approach that the laws now require? The answer to this question depends upon the answer to two other questions: Does a job have an "intrinsic" value to the employer that is expressed by the pay assigned to it? Can this intrinsic value be objectively measured? Canadian pay equity laws have apparently answered in the affirmative to both these questions.

Nevertheless, one must express serious concern with respect to the proposition that pay should reflect only the intrinsic value of the job. The value of a job to an organization is determined by both its value-in-use, as well as its value-in-exchange. The value-in-use is assessed internally in the context of the organization's objectives through the job evaluation system. Value-in-exchange is the "price" of the job and is a function of the supply and demand of labour Adam Smith (1950) cautioned us not to confuse these two meanings of value.

In this context, Gold (1983) cites Ehrenberg who estimated that the price to mow a lawn was about $4.00 an hour and the price for a baby-sitter was about $1.50 an hour, and added: "It's strange, when you think about it, because your children are a lot more important to you than your lawn" (p.60). It is rather a simple case of demand and supply which determines the price of each job regardless of whether it happens to be a male- or a female-dominated job. The market system is not perfect, but it is the best mechanism we currently have to allocate resources efficiently in our society in relative freedom. The requirements of pay equity interfere with the free operation of the market to determine pay and allocate human resources.

The consequences of such interference is best illustrated in a scenario by Gold (1983). Suppose a job evaluation system gives equal points to the jobs of the High School Math Teacher and the Home Economics Teacher; suppose also that the former is a male-dominated job and the latter is a female-dominated job. Now, let us assume that a job develops in the training department of a business organization which is ideally suited for the Math teachers. The organization attracts them with higher pay Under Pay Equity, this action creates consequences for both the business organization and the school. If the trainer's job in the business organization is male-dominated, the pay rate of the comparable female jobs in that organization will also have to be raised. The school, on the other hand, might also have to raise the pay of the math teachers to retain them and, when it does this, pay equity will require that the pay rate of the comparable female-dominated jobs also be raised. Thus, in both situations, pay equity results in inefficient resource allocations, because it increases the pay rates of those jobs where the supply of labour would allow them to be filled at lower rates.

Undue reliance on the job evaluation system

There are also serious concerns when the job evaluation system is intended as a replacement of the labour market. First, there is the arduous task of developing a job evaluation system whose compensable factors are weighted and defined in a sufficiently abstract manner to cover the variety of jobs and, at the same time, are specific enough to capture the unique features and characteristics of each job. The difficulty inherent in the process is well illustrated by the reported inability of Ontario's community colleges and the union which represents the colleges' 7000 employees to agree on a "gender-neutral" job classification system, despite several years of negotiation (Human Resource Management in Canada, 1992). Second, even after a job evaluation plan that is acceptable to the employer and the employees is developed, it would be difficult to convert the job values derived from the plan into dollars if the labour market forces are ignored (Gunderson and Riddell, 1991).

Third, despite the claim to the contrary, the market expresses the free choices of millions of average individuals. Reliance on job evaluation is no guarantee of objectivity in judgements and accuracy in determining the value of a job. Job evaluation is largely a process involving subjective judgements about the choices of compensable factors, weighting of these factors, definition of sub-factors, and assigning point values to jobs on the basis of job descriptions that are also the product of a subjective process.

As noted in the previous chapter, quantitative techniques, however sophisticated, can create a false sense of objectivity (Korukonda, 1996). It is not uncommon for two professional job evaluation experts armed with their own perfectly acceptable job evaluation systems to come up with quite different values for the same job (Seligman, 1984). In a US study (Burr, 1986), the job rankings that were derived on the basis of comparable worth job evaluations differed substantially for the same jobs across four states. The appeal process to review complaints of assigned job values is also an entirely subjective process.

Employer's rights ignored

In addition to the various consequences of ignoring the labour market in pay determination one cannot lose sight of the impact on the rights of employers. Pay equity laws deny employers the right to freely negotiate wages with their employees freely. Such denial constitutes a restriction on their freedom of action in the exercise of their trade, business, or profession. Private sector employers in Ontario are additionally inflicted with pay equity adjustment costs that place them at a competitive disadvantage with their competitors outside the province.

Can pay equity be reconciled with the reality of the labour market?

In order to reconcile the essence of pay equity with the reality of the labour market, it is necessary that pay equity laws be based on the principles of equity and justice. Pay equity laws ought to require that organizations develop a job evaluation system whose mechanism and process best capture the job aspects that are of significant value to the organization regardless of the gender, race, ethnic origin, and so forth of the job incumbents. Pay equity laws should also permit the pay determination process to incorporate the realities of the labour market.

To meet these overall objectives of pay equity laws, it is imperative that employees from all levels, functions, and occupational groups be encouraged to participate directly, or through their representatives, in every phase of the design and implementation of the pay determination mechanisms and processes. Such employee involvement would include their input into decisions on job evaluation systems. It would also include employee involvement in the salary surveys. This approach includes the employer's commitment to the program, as well as the allocation of resources for training that equips participants with the technical expertise and interpersonal skills necessary to ensure the effectiveness of the process.

The major role of the Pay Equity Commission ought to be one of providing directive principles of pay equity and encouragement and support to employers and employees to arrive at mutually acceptable solutions. Some of the specific areas of critical support to organizations would be the dissemination of research findings on the available job evaluation systems and related issues. In addition, the agencies of the Pay Equity Commission can adopt a proactive stance in providing training to employer-employee groups involved in each organization, and offer them process consultation skills. Genuine participation and involvement gives employees ownership and control of the process and enhances their acceptance of the outcomes as fair and equitable. In a study of self-imposed pay equity programs—employer and employees working through mutually acceptable solutions, versus pay equity programs imposed by legislation in Minnesota—it was found that the former were successful with high levels of employee satisfaction with the program; "...the mandatory effort to put pay on a rational basis at the local level in Minnesota has caused chaos in implementation" (Azavedo and Roth, 1990, p.534).

The issue is not one of scientific and mathematical precision, but of internal equity: do employees perceive that the job values have been arrived at by a process they understand and believe to be fair? The jobs with the same values—regardless of whether these are male or female jobs—can then be treated as "jobs of equal value" and paid the same. There is, however, one exception. How is the impact of the labour market needs considered? Suppose the supply and demand forces of the labour market require some jobs to be paid more. In these cases, their pay rates should be revised without, at the same time, increasing the pay rates of the other jobs of equal value. When the forces of demand and supply put an upward pressure on the wages of some jobs and the organization cannot do without these job incumbents, it is evident that the organization has a need for these employees and must pay them more because this is the only way of hiring these employees who are essential to attaining the organization's objectives. Employees understand such actions to be consistent with the compensation management principle of external equity.

SUMMARY

This chapter reviewed the meaning of the concept of pay equity from "equal pay for equal work" through "equal pay for similar work" to its present statutory definition of "equal pay for work of equal value". After a thumbnail sketch of the history of pay equity legislation in Canada, the chapter examined the salient features of pay equity legislation. Most laws cover public-sector employees. Ontario's law is the most comprehensive—its coverage also extends to private-sector employees. Enforcement mechanisms are either complaint-driven or proactive. Some jurisdictions, such as Ontario, include both mechanisms and prescribe a format for a pay equity plan. The gender-predominance criterion for determining female-dominated and male-dominated job classes ranges from 60 to 70 per cent, and most jurisdictions limit the cost of pay equity adjustments to 1 per cent of the total payroll. The chapter identified in the job analysis and job evaluation processes the sources of gender bias that can cause pay inequities for incumbents in female-dominated jobs, and suggested strategies for eliminating or reducing this bias.

The issues neglected by pay equity laws were explored with reference to the moral foundations and the psychological underpinnings of pay equity.

KEY TERMS

complaint-driven enforcement	pay equity
gender bias in job evaluation	equity
equal pay for equal work	proactive enforcement
male-dominated job class	female-dominated job class
equal pay for similar work	value-in-exchange
moral rights	gender bias in job analysis
equal pay for work of equal value	value-in-use

REVIEW AND DISCUSSION QUESTIONS

1. Explain the differences in the following concepts: "equal pay for equal work", "equal pay for similar work", and "equal pay for work of equal value".

2. Explain how the basic natural rights of an individual constitute the firm foundation of equity.

3. Which of the job evaluation methods discussed in Chapter 11 provides the best approach for achieving the objectives of pay equity? Why?

4. Using examples from your own (and others') observations and experiences (including case reports), discuss the sources of gender biases in job analysis and job evaluation procedures.

The Pay Equity Debate

Objective

To explore the pros and cons of pay equity.

Procedure

1. Divide the class into groups of four to five participants.
2. Assign to half the groups the role of advocates of pay equity and to the other half the role of critics of pay equity.
3. Each group discusses the arguments relating to its assigned role. See Statement A for some of the typical arguments.
4. Class debate: Teams of advocates and critics, composed of a representative from each of the groups, debate the pros and cons of pay equity.

Statement A

Advocates of pay equity argue as follows:

- Sex discrimination in the labour market is the major reason why women workers earn less than men, as evidenced by the following decisions of the Canadian Human Rights Commission (1984):
- Female nurses in federal penitentiaries in the Atlantic Region were paid less than male technicians although they performed the same tasks and were better qualified;
- The predominantly female clerical and factory workers at the Atomic Energy of Canada's Glace Bay plant in Nova Scotia performed job tasks that were equal in value to those of the male workers at the plant, but the women workers were paid less than the men.
- Federal government librarians (predominantly female) were paid less than historical researchers (predominantly male) for work of equal value.
- The jobs of male paramedics and female nurses and X-ray technicians at Canadian National Railways involve work that is equal in value, but the paramedics are paid more than the nurses and X-ray technicians.

- Gender bias in job analysis and job evaluation procedures operates to produce a lower pay for female jobs.
- The sexist socialization process inherent in our societies is the principal cause of occupational segregation that results in lower labour market pay rates for predominantly female jobs.

Critics respond as follows:

- The earnings gap is not due to discrimination in the labour market but to occupational segregation, which is largely the result of free choice exercised by women.
- The dollar value of a job is not determined by the intrinsic worth of the job but by the forces of the marketplace. Failure to recognize this reality could eventually jeopardise the competitiveness of Canadian businesses.
- "As long as women are free to become plumbers and prefer to become secretaries instead, they have no right to demand plumbers' pay for secretaries' work" (Gold 1983, 94).

Pay Equity in the United States

APPENDIX

C. Pendleton, former chair of the U.S. Commission on Civil Rights described the notion of "comparable worth" as "the craziest idea since Looney Tunes" (cited in Agarwal, 1990). But, the proponents of "comparable worth", as pay equity is referred to in the US, do not trust the labour market to fairly determine the wages of female-dominated jobs. They argue that the market is riddled with discrimination against women's jobs and its use will only serve to perpetuate the inequities that women experience. As evidence, they cite the wage gap (women earning 60 cents for every dollar earned by men), sex-segregation in jobs which they claim is caused by the oppressive socialization practices that direct women into the lower-paid jobs, and the deliberate undervaluation of women's jobs simply because these jobs are held by women (Paul, 1989).

To remedy this grievous injustice, the supporters of comparable worth, predominantly women's rights groups, advocate that female-dominated jobs be paid the same rate as that of the male-dominated jobs of equal value. To achieve this objective, they demand that the market mechanism of setting wages be totally replaced by a system which sets wages according to the "intrinsic worth" of jobs determined objectively by professional job evaluators. Such an approach, they argue, allows entirely dissimilar jobs to be matched on the basis of the points assigned by the job evaluation experts. Jobs, be they male or female-dominated, with the same point values can then be paid the same, thereby eliminating the pay inequities which the labour market now inflicts on women.

The supporters of comparable worth have worked hard to enlist the government's support for their cause without too much success. US Federal laws such as The Equal Pay Act (1963) and Title VII of the Civil Rights Act (1964), interpret pay in terms of "equal pay for equal work" rather than "equal pay for work of equal value". The jurisprudence, so far, has clearly recognized and accepted the role of the labour market system in determining wages (Paul, 1989; Wiener and Gunderson, 1990). The initiatives of the Democratically-controlled Congress were thwarted by the Republican-controlled Senate, which even prevented a resolution to study the comparable worth issue from being passed; the Federal agencies—the Justice Department, the US Civil Rights Commission, and the Equal Employment Opportunity Commission, have also decided against the view that Title VII of the Civil Rights Act (1964) can be construed to incorporate the concept of comparable worth (Paul, 1989).

Essentially, several fundamental questions on comparable worth have remained unanswered: Does the gender wage-gap provide the irrefutable evidence of labour market's discrimination against women's jobs? Does a job have an "intrinsic" value? Are there "objective" ways of determining this intrinsic value? Do professionals and experts agree on both these questions relating to "intrinsic" value? What are the adverse consequences of completely setting aside the role of labour markets in wage determination—on the economy? on employment prospects for women? on wages of blue-collar workers (males and females)? These are also the questions which have been found to be problematical for full implementation of the pay equity laws in France and the United Kingdom.

Nevertheless, at the state level, government actions indicate that the notion of comparable worth has gradually begun to influence the pay systems of the public sector (Kovach and Millspaugh, 1990). According to Paul, "the National Committee on Pay Equity estimated that, by the end of 1986, thirteen states would have begun the process of distributing pay-equity adjustments while thirty-four other states would be moving in the same direction.... The report concluded that ten of the states had a written pay equity or comparable worth policy, while twenty-eight states in all had conducted some type of comparable worth study" (Paul, 1989, p.92). Critics of comparable worth point out that governments can afford comparable worth because, unlike private organizations, they can "...finance their mistakes by taxation without having to worry about consumer loyalty" (Levin, 1987, p.148).

It is understandable, therefore, that both the proponents and opponents of pay equity are keeping a close watch on the Canadian experience in pay equity described in this chapter.

CHAPTER 13

Salary Surveys and

Pay Structure:

External Equity

OVERVIEW

The focus of this chapter is on designing a pay structure that reflects the differentials in the job values inherent in the job structure. It covers the sources of pay rates and the issues and methods involved in salary surveys, which provide the major input in developing a pay structure. It also examines the procedures of designing a pay structure and related issues.

 LEARNING OBJECTIVES

▶ To identify the internal and external factors that influence the setting of pay rates.

▶ To define the relevant external labour market and to identify its dimensions.

▶ To explain the purpose of a salary survey and to identify its contents.

▶ To describe the processes and methods of conducting a salary survey.

▶ To discuss the advantages and disadvantages to the organization of conducting its own survey compared with acquiring market data from third-party surveys.

▶ To understand typical procedures in the analyses of survey data.

▶ To identify the major pay level policies, and to discuss the rationale and criteria for the choice of a pay level policy.

▶ To describe the procedural steps in pricing a job structure.

▶ To discuss the basic approaches to constructing a pay structure.

▶ To describe the procedural steps in the construction of pay grades and ranges, and to explain the purpose of pay ranges.

▶ To explain the reasons for salary cases that fall outside the salary structure, and to recommend appropriate salary administration policies for dealing with these cases.

INTRODUCTION

The pay structure assigns dollar values to jobs based on the differentials in job values. For a pay structure to be developed, three decisions are necessary: a decision on the sources or bases for pay rates; a decision on the collection of pay data; and a decision on the architectural features of the pay structure—its pay grades and pay ranges. We first discuss the considerations that underlie these decisions, and then the salary administration policies for dealing with individual salary cases that fall outside established pay grades.

THE SOURCES OR DETERMINANTS OF PAY RATES

How do organizations establish the dollar values or the prices of jobs? The major determinants of pay rates are the organization's ability to pay and the pay rates in the external labour market.

Organization's ability to pay   Because salaries and wages constitute a substantial portion of operating costs, an organization views the pay structure largely in terms of its effects on cost structure. Hence, the ability of the organization to bear the cost becomes the critical determinant in job pricing. Business strategies and product life cycle stages provide the compensation specialist not only with an overall sense of direction, but also with information on the likely availability of resources and the optimal allocation of these resources. Organizations whose operations are highly labour-intensive are relatively more sensitive to labour costs, and this sensitivity becomes an important determinant in the pricing of jobs. Pay rates high enough to deprive an organization of its competitive edge can seriously affect its survival.

External labour market   In order to attract and retain qualified and productive employees, organizations compete with one another, and this competition translates into the demand for labour in the external labour market. The availability of people with the required knowledge, skills, and abilities constitutes the supply of labour in the external market. The interaction of demand and supply establishes pay rates in the labour market. When employees in an organization find that their pay rates do not compare favourably with pay rates in the external labour market, they will experience external inequity. And when they do, the organization's ability to attract and retain employees is seriously impaired.

THE RELEVANT EXTERNAL LABOUR MARKET

The pay data from the external labour market are collected through salary surveys. Before proceeding to consider the methods and techniques used in salary surveys, it is necessary to discuss the issues involved in choosing the relevant labour market.

Issues in choice of relevant labour market

Organizations with similar employee needs Traditionally, organizations treated the industry as the relevant external labour market. The high mobility of employees in some jobs across industries has forced compensation specialists to reconsider the traditional focus on industry-relevant comparisons alone. An organization's relevant external labour market is any other organization in any geographic area from which the organization's employees are drawn and to which its employees are likely to move. Exit interviews, conducted systematically and with tact, can be a good source of information about companies that have succeeded in attracting employees away from the organization.

Geographic area and nature of jobs A review of an organization's present workforce in an occupational group might reveal that its employees are drawn from a certain geographic area, say a radius of 30 kilometres. This fact would suggest the geographic boundary of the organization's labour market for that occupational group. The geographic boundary varies according to the nature of the jobs or of the occupational groups. For instance, for office, production, and maintenance employees, the boundary might be a local market within a radius of 30 to 40 kilometres; for professionals and managers, the boundary might well extend beyond the regional to the national international geographic area. A good example of the latter is the oil exploration industry, which draws professionals from an international pool.

Organization size and industry The size of the organization and, more particularly, the nature of its industry bear considerably upon the organization's capacity to pay. An organization aims to be competitive not only to attract and retain employees but also to manage its costs in such a manner that it does not surrender its competitive edge. As will be discussed later, these considerations are also critical when actual survey data are analysed to determine what is the *typical* market rate for a job. For instance, the pay rate of a company that employs only one engineer could not be considered the typical rate for a company that employs 20 engineers, because the cost impact of pay decisions is obviously different for the two companies.

SALARY SURVEYS

After a decision has been made on the external labour market that is relevant and appropriate to the organization, data are collected from the market through salary surveys. This section examines what a salary survey is, and what methods and techniques are used in collecting pay data.

WHAT IS A SALARY SURVEY?

Definition and purpose   Just as job evaluation is an essential and useful tool for ensuring internal equity, the salary survey is an essential and useful tool for ensuring external equity. The salary survey provides information on the typical or "going" pay rate for a job. As discussed earlier, different labour markets exist for different jobs in an organization. Therefore, although a typical or going rate is spoken of, in reality there are a variety of rates, as revealed by not just one survey but by different surveys that cover the appropriate labour markets. The survey provides the organization with the data to develop a pay structure consistent with its pay level policy, that is, to lead, lag behind, or meet the market.

Type of salary data collected   Generally, the data collected depends upon the nature of the jobs being surveyed. Usually, the major items include job title; average or median pay rate; the number of employees in the job; the pay grade (i.e., minimum, midpoint, maximum); the highest and lowest actual pay; starting pay rate; and the compa-ratio (i.e., the relationship of actual pay to pay grade's midpoint). The usefulness of this data is discussed later.

SALARY SURVEY APPROACHES AND METHODS

There are basically two approaches to salary surveys: (1) the organization conducts its own surveys, or (2) the organization acquires surveys conducted by third parties.

Conducting Own Survey

Some organizations conduct their own surveys because they can focus on the external labour market that is relevant to them and can thus obtain the data that best meets their needs. The assumption here is that the organization has the competence and resources to undertake this task efficiently and effectively.

Critical conditions for successful conduct of survey

Choice of companies   This is also known as the determination of the survey sample. The general guideline in this decision is to include companies from which the organization draws its employees and to which its employees will likely go. The companies will be different for the different employee groups—managerial, professional, production, maintenance, office, and technical. The analysis of the relevant labour markets for these groups will help identify such characteristics as industry, size, and geographic area which should be considered in determining the composition of the survey sample.

Type of jobs The jobs that should be covered by the survey are benchmark jobs from the different occupational categories and salary levels. It is also useful to include entry-level jobs, and those jobs that pose particular problems to the organization due to difficulty in attracting qualified applicants, or an unusually high turnover rate.

Number of jobs Theoretically, the greater the number of jobs that are included in the survey, the more comprehensive the survey data will be. In practice, if too many jobs are included, the survey data is adversely affected for two reasons. One, the survey return rate may be reduced because participating companies might resent the effort required to respond to a large number of jobs. Even if the return rate is satisfactory, participating companies may fail to make the effort required and, as a result, provide incomplete or inaccurate information. Hence, it is prudent to include only those jobs that are absolutely essential; the suggested number is about 25 to 30 percent of the jobs in the organization (Wallace and Fay, 1988).

Confidentiality of data The successful conduct of a survey depends also on the willingness of the companies to participate in the survey. Companies are generally more willing to participate if they can be assured of the confidentiality of the information they provide, and if they can have access to the information generated by the survey. In the interest of confidentiality, the data are shared in a manner that does not reveal the data of the individual companies participating in the survey.

Survey methods The survey methods for obtaining data that are relevant and comparable are (1) the key job matching method, (2) the occupational survey method, and (3) the job evaluation method (Henderson, 1989). The procedure for each method is briefly outlined.

The Key Job Matching Method The organization identifies the key jobs and selects one from each job category or class series and from each organizational level. The key jobs selected represent the different organizational functions and levels. A brief job summary of each job is written up and sent to the organizations selected to participate in the survey, along with a request for the following information on similar jobs in their organizations: rates of pay, pay ranges (minimum, mid-point, maximum in each range), the number of employees in each range, and the job evaluation method used.

This method has limitations when the job has unique features that aggravate the task of matching. The negative effects of this limitation can be minimized by requesting that the respondent organizations review the job descriptions and assess the job match on a scale of poor to perfect match.

The Occupational Survey Method The organization sends the participants a job summary of each of its occupational groups—accounting, operating, engineering, and so forth. The participating organizations are requested to identify their comparable occupational groups and to furnish information for each group relating to the pay range (minimum, midpoint, maximum) for each class, and the number of employees in each class.

The advantage of this method is that the respondent reports on objective data because it is not required to match jobs but simply to report the data that exist for the occupational groups in its company. This method has been found to elicit information on many more jobs than has been received under the key job matching method. However, there still remains the critical task of forming judgements on the comparability of the occupational groups on which the data are received.

The Job Evaluation Method In this method, the organization sends to the survey participants a list of its benchmark jobs and their corresponding job evaluation points. The participants are asked to identify similar jobs with the identical job evaluation points in their companies and to provide for these jobs the pay information, that is, the pay ranges (minimum, midpoint, maximum) and the number of employees in each range.

This method appears to be the best in that the matching issue is the least problematical. Nevertheless, even in identical job evaluation methods, the subjectivity that is inherent in the job evaluation process can still produce substantial differences in the resulting job evaluation points.

Acquiring Surveys of Third Parties

Organizations that do not have the resources to conduct their own surveys acquire the surveys conducted by such third parties as governments, professional associations, and private consultants.

Surveys of government agencies The data from these surveys are often not useful, because the labour markets covered may not be relevant or appropriate. Also, there is the problem of obsolescence resulting from the time lag between the collection and the publication of the data.

Surveys of professional associations The data from these surveys are useful so long as the problems of job match can be overcome. Some professional associations provide data that are used in the development of *maturity curves*. These are graphical representations of the salary data of the members of a professional group (e.g., engineers) arranged on the basis of years of experience or years since receiving a degree. Generally, the data in maturity curves show pay levels to increase initially, but it levels off in later years depending upon the effect of technical obsolescence. An organization can use maturity curves as a frame of reference for determining its relative position in the labour market.

Surveys by private consultants These surveys have advantages and disadvantages. On the one hand, these are not time-consuming and are relatively inexpensive provided the organization is a participant in the survey. The large number of participants contribute statistical soundness. The data are generally well summarized.

On the other hand, the participating organizations do not get to select the jobs they might be interested in, and are unable to identify the data of the individual respondent organizations that have contributed to the survey. Such identification is useful in determining the job match. The participating organizations do not get to control what data are collected and often find themselves inundated by both relevant and irrelevant data.

Employee Involvement in Salary Survey process

Whether an organization conducts its own survey or acquires third party surveys, the ultimate objective of a survey is to generate information demonstrating that external equity exists in the compensation system. If the compensation system is found to be inequitable relative to the external labour market, the survey information provides a rational and systematic basis for restoring external equity. The key to employees' perceptions of external equity is their trust in both the process and the information it generates. Employees can have legitimate concerns about the comparability of the companies, the jobs, and the data relating to pay.

An important way of addressing these concerns is to involve employees in the salary survey process from the very beginning, including the selection of the jobs and the companies to be surveyed, as well as the choice of the survey methods. The effectiveness of compensation techniques, to the extent that they impinge on employee perceptions of equity, is greatly enhanced by involving employees in their design and implementation.

TECHNIQUES OF DATA COLLECTION

The major preoccupation of salary survey methods is to assure the job match and the resulting comparability of data. Once the method has been decided upon, a decision is made on the choice of techniques for collecting data. Data can be collected by means of telephone, mailed questionnaires, personal interviews, and a conference of the participants.

The telephone is useful when the job can be easily identified by the respondents and the survey is not too extensive, both in terms of the number of jobs and the detail of the data that is needed. The telephone technique permits an immediate check for the job match and the comparability of data.

The mailed questionnaire is the most popular technique used in collecting survey data. Although it can be quite efficient, returns can be poor especially when the survey instrument is a lengthy questionnaire.

The personal interview is the most favoured technique if the respondent is willing to take the time for it. It readily resolves the question of job match and, as a result, enhances the comparability of the data. It also relieves the respondent of the clerical work that is entailed in the questionnaire technique.

A conference of all the participants works well if the participating organizations share common interests and problems. It has all the advantages of the personal interview as far as resolving the questions of job match and data comparability is concerned. The effective use of a conference is often impeded by a lack of common interests and by the logistics of getting together at a mutually convenient time and location.

A CRITIQUE OF SALARY SURVEYS

Reluctance to participate in surveys   Even though surveys are a useful tool for ensuring external equity, organizations appear to be reluctant to participate in them. Some companies complain that there are too many requests for surveys; for example, one firm received about one hundred requests to participate in a salary survey in a single year.

The issue of usefulness   The statistical analysis needed to make the data useful is severely hampered by poor comparability, many restraints on information disclosure, an inadequate sample size, and poorly designed questionnaires that are full of ambiguous questions.

Impact on economy   Surveys tend to encourage the "leapfrogging" effect. As organizations work towards catching up with the market, they may eventually fuel inflationary pressures in the economy.

A response to the criticisms   While these criticisms cannot be completely ignored, the fact remains that salary surveys are needed to provide the linkage between internal and external equity. In the ultimate analysis, pay contributes to inflation only when it is not commensurate with productivity. The more appropriate compensation strategy for combating inflation is a greater focus on performance-based pay that is equitably designed and managed. The response to these criticisms is not to discard salary surveys but to make greater efforts to improve job match and comparability.

ANALYSIS OF SURVEY DATA

The objective of a survey is to provide data that enable the organization to develop a pay structure that is consistent with external equity. This objective imposes the obligation of using only the data of market jobs that best match the organization's jobs. Survey data should therefore be subjected to a rigorous review to make sure that they are accurate and that only these data selected fairly reflect the labour market rates of survey jobs. There are typical analytical procedures for reviewing the survey data. This discussion of the procedures refers to "ABC's job(s)" to mean the job(s) of the organization that is conducting the survey, and the term "market job(s)" refers to the corresponding job(s) in the organization's external market.

Determining the job match How good is the match between ABC's jobs and the market jobs? To answer this question for each job, ABC compares its job descriptions with those of the market jobs. If the comparison indicates that the match is acceptable, the jobs are comparable, and there is no need to adjust the survey data. If the match is not acceptable, the jobs are not comparable and the survey data must be adjusted. The data are adjusted through the technique of "survey levelling" (Milkovich and Newman, 1996), which in effect reduces both jobs to a level playing field to facilitate comparison. According to this technique, the survey data are multiplied by a factor to bring them in line with ABC's job value.

> For example:
>
> Suppose the analysis suggests that ABC's job A has slightly less value than the market job; say the value of ABC's job is about 85 per cent of the value of the market job. The survey data will be multiplied by .85. If the market job pay is $30,000, and ABC's job is determined to be 85 per cent of the value of the market job, the market pay rate of ABC's job will likely be ($30,000 x 85 per cent) = $25,500.

Extent of dispersion in the survey data After having assessed the comparability of the jobs, ABC analyses the pay data. Not all companies pay the same rate. Each company's pay rate reflects the company's assessment of the relative content and contribution of all the jobs in the company. The pay rate also reflects other factors, such as the pay level policy, employee performance, the age and the tenure of employees, and the number of employees in the job. ABC can expect pay rates to vary among companies, but does need to know the extent of the variation or the dispersion of the data. Widely dispersed data indicate companies with considerable differences in pay level policies. The dispersion is measured by the spread between the highest and lowest pay rates.

For example:

Suppose the data for job A show the lowest average salary to be $28,000 and the highest average salary to be $36,000. The ratio of $28,000 to $36,000, which is .78, indicates the dispersion, and vice versa.

Distribution of the pay rates Another statistical procedure for analysing the data is the distribution of the pay rates. A normal distribution suggests a certain degree of consistency in the data; hence, the data are useful. A distribution that is not normal suggests inconsistencies in the data, which may indicate variations in pay level policies. The frequency distribution also makes it possible to identify the extreme values.

For example:

12 companies provided information on the average salary for job A:

Company	$
1	28,000
2	29,200
3	31,000
4	29,500
5	30,500
6	31,070
7	31,000
8	30,000
9	36,000
10	28,300
11	28,500
12	30,600

The average salary of job A in all companies except company 9 is in the range of $28,000-31,070. Company 9 is outside the range with an average salary of $36,000. Should ABC retain this extreme value? Does it reflect the market rate for job A?

To address these questions, ABC must probe the average salaries of the other survey jobs in company 9. If the average salaries of the other survey jobs are also high, ABC can conclude that company 9 does not reflect the market rate for job A.

On the other hand, if the average salaries of the other jobs in company 9 are not high, its salaries might well reflect the market rates.

The extreme difference in the salaries for job A might be that this job in company 9 does not match job A in the other companies, nor does it match ABC's job A. However, before ABC decides to eliminate company 9 from the data, it should review its job description of job A to verify the job match.

If there is a good match, ABC should retain the data from company 9 and reconsider the data from the other companies as far as job A is concerned. If the job match between ABC's job A and company 9's job A is poor, ABC should eliminate the data of company 9.

Choice and weighting of data   The analysis of the survey data also involves judgements on the choice of the available data. Should ABC choose the mean or the median pay rates? Given that the mean is the arithmetical average of the payrates and the median is the point at or below which exactly 50% of the cases fall, should ABC weight the mean or the median by the number of employees in the job? Generally, the mean is chosen, but when its value is distorted by extreme values, the median is the preferred statistical measure of central tendency. Whichever measure is chosen, it is advisable to weight it by the number of the employees in the job in order to get a truer picture of the market rate.

To conclude: The different procedures that have been described enable the compensation specialist to include only those companies whose pay rates are more likely to reflect the market rate for the surveyed jobs. After such decisions have been made about the data for all the surveyed jobs, the compensation specialist will have prepared the ground for the next series of procedures that are necessary for the design of the pay structure.

DESIGNING THE PAY STRUCTURE

There are three major steps in the design of a pay structure. First, the organization decides on a pay level policy. Second, the pricing of the job structure is made consistent with the pay level policy. This is achieved through statistical procedures that relate the data from the relevant external labour market to the organization's job structure. Finally, the organization constructs a pay structure—pay grades and pay ranges.

PAY LEVEL POLICY

Objective of pay level policy decisions

The objective of all the decisions and activities that lead to a pay structure is to maintain the relationship between internal equity (as expressed in the job structure) and external equity (as expressed in the data from the relevant external labour market). This pay relationship can be established at a variety of levels.

Choice and rationale of pay level policy

The first decision is to choose to establish the pay structure in one of the following levels: (1) *above the level* that exists in the market; (2) *at the level* that exists in the market; or (3) *below the level* that exists in the market. That is, the organization decides to lead, to match, or to lag the market.

The second decision is to determine more specifically by how much the pay structure will be above or below the market. The compensation specialist has the option of combinations: paying above the market for part of the year and then paying below the market for the rest of the year (i.e., lead/lag); paying below the market for part of the year and then paying above the market for the rest of the year (i.e., lag/lead); matching the market first and then leading later in the year (i.e., match/lead), and vice versa.

Decisions on the organization's market position are strategic and should merit a place in the organization's compensation philosophy (as discussed in Chapter 7). The rationale for a choice of position—lead, match, or lag behind the market—is provided by the organization's compensation objectives.

Effects of "lead-the-market" pay level policy

Increase of pay valence If the organization wants to be certain that it will attract and retain employees with a high level of competence and ability, it will follow a lead policy. Why are employees attracted by a lead policy? Higher pay creates a higher valence because, other things being equal, a greater amount of pay is more instrumental in satisfying needs. Generally such a policy will contribute to high pay satisfaction provided that the processes of the compensation system that ensure internal equity in pay determination are functioning properly.

Communicates that employees are a valued resource By leading the market in the pay level, the organization is saying that it wants the best workforce and is suggesting that its employees are its most valued resource. Through rigorous selection procedures, the organization makes sure that only the best are hired, and employees feel that they belong to an elite group. The desire to be members of an elite group is a powerful force that attracts employees, and it also has a substantial influence on the retention of employees.

High labour costs The organization must reckon, however, with high labour costs that result from a lead policy. Some organizations are able to withstand the effects of high costs because of increases in labour productivity and, more particularly, because of the competitive edge they gain as a result of the innovation and creativity of their employees. The mere fact of paying high salaries does not, of course, guarantee high labour productivity nor does it automatically lead to innovation. Sometimes, the fit between high pay levels and the organizations cost structure is ignored. This can occur when organizations that can afford the higher pay levels extend these to the companies they acquire even though the latter's cost structure cannot afford the burden of these pay levels.

When energy companies "...have taken over or developed chemical operations, they have paid oil industry wages to managers and technical people in their chemical operations...In many cases, this has made their chemical operations non-competitive because chemical companies—particularly independent ones—have paid historically lower wages than energy companies...This problem has been even more severe when energy companies have gone into such unrelated businesses as office products, land development, and department stores" (Lawler, 1990, p. 190). Other organizations are able to contain labour costs because of efficiencies in their cost structure, or because they are able to pass on these costs to consumers without jeopardizing their competitive position.

Effects of "lag-the-market" pay level policy

Alternative strategies to attract and retain employees The preceding discussion suggests that organizations that follow a lag policy will have difficulty in attracting and retaining competent employees. Although this would appear to be the case, one cannot generalize due to the many factors that go into the decision to join and to stay on in an organization. Many organizations offer reward items other than pay to attract the employees they need.

For example, Spar Aerospace Limited in the suburbs of Montreal attracts exceptionally brilliant and competent scientists and engineers because of the challenging work the company provides, which is on the cutting edge of space technology. University faculties attract competent researchers because they offer opportunities to work with people who have established themselves in a particular area of study. Other organizations attract employees by their location—sylvan surroundings, a peaceful and safe neighbourhood, proximity to a good school.

In the matter of retention, satisfaction or dissatisfaction with pay is not the only reason employees stay with or leave an organization. Environmental factors (such as family responsibilities and the availability of jobs) compel employees to stay on even though they may be dissatisfied with pay. Although pay is an important item, it is only one element of the compensation mix of base pay, incentives, and benefits. Organizations have been successful with a compensation mix that is determined by their product life cycle and business strategies.

Effective labour cost control A lag policy can also serve to implement a pay strategy that ties pay levels to organizational performance. "Implementing such a policy requires the use of variable compensation, typically in the form of incentive pay or profit sharing" (Lawler, 1990, p.193). In such a pay strategy, the base pay is set below the pay rates of the organization's business competitors. But, the employees are also entitled to incentive pay or profit sharing. Thus, the employee's total pay varies with the organization's performance, and this organizational performance-pay linkage produces several effects.

First, it enables employees to earn incomes well above the market. The high performing employees prefer this approach and, as a result, it operates to attract and retain this type of employee. The organization will succeed in retaining such employees even in an economic downturn because all its business competitors will be similarly affected. Second, since it varies total labour costs with organizational performance, the organization's cost competitiveness is maintained. The underlying assumption in this discussion of the organizational performance-based pay strategy is that the variable component (incentive pay, profit sharing, and the related process issues) are designed and managed properly, as discussed in Chapter 10.

Effects of "match-the-market" pay level policy

Competitive in external labour market   Organizations adopt the policy of matching the market because they wish to be competitive in the external labour market in order to attract and retain the workforce they need. A match policy will generally not have the high labour costs associated with a lead policy. Ultimately, however, the effectiveness of this policy will depend on the composition of the organization's compensation mix, which will be influenced by the organization's business strategies and the life cycle stages of its products.

Other considerations in choice of pay level policy

A significant question that is often raised is: Should the choice of the pay policy differ for the different job categories or organizational levels? For example, should managerial job pay levels be set above the market, whereas those of non-managerial employees be set below or equal to the market? The only justification for such differentiation is the needs of the business, whether it offers the business a competitive advantage. However, such advantages should be viewed in terms of their negative consequences such as divisiveness and low employee morale. For these reasons, this pay strategy is inappropriate in organizations which seek to promote a culture of employee involvement and participative management.

The choice of a pay level policy is a critical strategic issue in compensation. The organization's business strategies, the economics of the relevant external labour market, and the impact of labour costs on the total cost structure of the organization must be considered in developing a compensation mix of base pay, incentives, and benefits that will help achieve the objectives of the organization's compensation system. Therefore, the decision of the pay level policy cannot be divorced from the decision on the compensation mix.

PRICING THE JOB STRUCTURE

Objective   The procedure of pricing the job structure is an attempt to relate the survey data of the relevant external labour market to the organization's job structure, in accordance with its pay level policy. The resulting pay structure will express the internal equity of the job structure in terms of the relevant external labour market.

This procedure would be relatively simple if the jobs that existed in the organization also existed in the market because, in that case, all that would be necessary would be to determine the market rates for these jobs and, depending upon the pay level policy, apply those rates to the jobs in the organization.

In reality, however, this simple procedure is not applicable, because the jobs in the market are rarely identical to the jobs in the organization. It is therefore necessary to use key or benchmark jobs to function as the medium through which the job structure is related to the market by means of the statistical procedure of regression analysis.

Major procedural steps   The major steps in this procedure are as follows:

1. **Job match—organization's and surveyed jobs**   The job descriptions of the organization's jobs are carefully compared with the job descriptions of the surveyed jobs to assess the match of these jobs. The jobs with a good and acceptable match are referred to as key or benchmark jobs. At least three key or benchmark jobs are needed if regression analysis is to provide good results.

2. **Collecting job evaluation points and survey pay rates of matched jobs**   The job evaluation points for each benchmark job are collected from the job structure, and its pay rate, from the survey data. Collecting the job evaluation points is straightforward, because each job in the job structure has only one value. This is not the case with pay rates. The survey generally provides data on a variety of pay rates for each job, for example, the average actual pay rate expressed as the mean or the median pay rate; the lowest actual pay rate, the highest actual pay rate, and the pay range in terms of the minimum, the midpoint, and the maximum.

   Which pay rate should an organization choose? The decision will depend on the organization's pay level policy. If the policy is to lead the market, the pay rate above the average market rate is chosen, and an adjustment is made to reflect the percentage by which the pay structure will be above that pay rate. If the policy is to match the market, then a measure such as the mean or the median pay rate, which reflects the market average, is chosen. If the policy is to lag the market, then the lowest pay rate is chosen.

3. **Conduct regression analysis**   To describe this statistical procedure, let us assume that the pay level policy is to match the market. In this case, the regression analysis is conducted using the job evaluation points of the benchmark jobs and the average pay rates of these jobs in the market. The output of the regression analysis is the regression model in the form of

$$y = a + bx$$

where

y is the predicted salary;

a is a constant, the value of y when the job evaluation points equal 0;

b is the slope, the rate by which the value of y will change with a change in the job evaluation points;

x is the job evaluation points of the job for which the salary is to be predicted.

The regression analysis will also provide two other extremely important measures: the correlation coefficient and the standard error of the estimate.

- The correlation coefficient indicates how good the "fit" of the data is. A correlation coefficient of less than .9 would indicate a poor fit and a need to review the comparability of the data and the decisions on the job match.

- The standard error provides a measure of the error that is likely when the regression model is used. This measure should not exceed 1.5 to 2 per cent (Wallace and Fay, 1988).

Pricing the job structure—an illustration Suppose that the Edmonton Manufacturing Company (EMC) has 25 jobs. After comparing these jobs with 40 jobs from the survey data, EMC comes up with the following six benchmark jobs. The job evaluation points of these jobs from the company's job structure and the market median pay of these jobs are as indicated below.

Job	Job Evaluation	Market Median
	Points	Pay ($)
A	470	1,315.47
B	270	1,194.15
C	260	941.32
D	190	906.95
E	170	742.69
F	170	832.86

The output of the regression model with these data will be $y = 548.29 + 1.73\ (x)$ with a correlation coefficient of .9 and a standard error of .43.

The regression model is acceptable in terms of both the correlation coefficient and the standard error. It can then be used to compute the pay of all the jobs (not of the individuals who hold these jobs) in the company. Consider the following two cases:

Case I

The pay of job A, a benchmark job with 470 job evaluation points, will be:

$$\text{Pay} = 548.29 + 1.73 \text{ (job evaluation points)}$$
$$= 548.29 + 1.73 \text{ (470)}$$
$$= 1{,}361.39$$

Case II

The pay of job J, a non-benchmark job with 155 job evaluation points, will be:

$$\text{Pay} = 548.29 + 1.73 \text{ (job evaluation points)}$$
$$= 548.29 + 1.73 \text{ (155)}$$
$$= 816.44$$

The statistical procedure has helped to relate the job structure to the relevant external labour market and provided the means of converting the job structure into the pay structure. The specific manner in which this is done is discussed in the next section.

CONSTRUCTING THE PAY STRUCTURE: PAY GRADES AND PAY RANGES

Approaches to pay structure

There are three approaches to constructing a pay structure: (1) treating each job evaluation point as a pay grade; (2) grouping jobs into pay grades; and (3) broadbanding.

Treating each job evaluation point as a pay grade

This approach takes the job structure as it is and, using the regression model, converts the job evaluation points of each job into a dollar value that represents the pay of that job. Under this approach, every job with different job evaluation points will be treated differently and will, in effect, become a separate pay grade. Thus, there will be as many pay grades as there are jobs with different job evaluation points. This approach is logical and is consistent with the theory that if jobs have different point values, they are necessarily different jobs and should therefore be paid differently.

In practice, this approach has many difficulties. The difference between job A and job B might be a mere 5 points. However, there may not be grounds to conclude that these jobs are so substantially different from each other that they warrant different salaries. The job evaluation process has not reached a stage of precision where a job can be said to deserve exactly 300 points. The point values assigned are judgements in a process filled with many subjective judgements that are always subject to a revision that will result in a few points more or less for the job. Hence, this approach opens the door to constant reviews.

One of the realities of the workplace is that jobs undergo minor modifications that slightly change their value. According to this approach, any pay change, however small, becomes necessary for any minor modification in a job, and the implementation of the compensation system becomes an administrative nightmare.

Grouping jobs into pay grades

The second approach is to group jobs into pay grades, with each grade consisting of jobs within a certain range of point values.

Procedural steps for constructing pay grades The example of the Edmonton Manufacturing Company will be used again to illustrate the mechanics of constructing pay grades. Suppose that the job structure in this company shows a range of job evaluation points from a low of 50 points to a high of 650 points. The procedural steps are as follows:

1. Subtract the lowest from the highest (650–50) and obtain a range, which in this example is 600 points.

2. Decide on the optimum number of pay grades. Generally, the number of pay grades has been found to be related to the categories of employees (Henderson, 1989), thus:

Employee Category	Number of Pay Grades
Non-Exempt	12 - 16
Exempt	10 - 15
Senior Management	8 - 10

Assume that seven pay grades is believed to be the optimum number for the Edmonton Manufacturing Corporation.

3. Given the range of 600 points and the optimum number of 7, the grade interval of 100 points is convenient and reasonable.

4. Convert the midpoint of the interval of job evaluation points of each grade (i.e., 50, 150, 250, 350, 450, 550, 650) into dollars by using the regression model: $y = 548.29 + 1.73\ (x)$.

From these procedures is obtained the following table: it shows the pay grades, the interval of the job evaluation points within each pay grade, and the midpoint of the pay grade, which was derived from the regression model.

Pay Grade	Job Evaluation	Midpoint
	Points	
1	1 – 100	634.79
2	101 – 200	807.79
3	201 – 300	980.79
4	301 – 400	1,153.79
5	401 – 500	1,326.79
6	501 – 600	1,499.79
7	601 – 700	1,672.79

5. The pay structure is completed constructing the pay ranges, which are the height or spread of each pay grade. The range provides the minimum and maximum of each pay grade, and it varies according to the needs of the organization for the different categories of employees. Some suggested ranges are as follows (Henderson, 1989):

Employee Category	% Spread
Non-Exempt: Labour and Trades	up to 25%
Non-Exempt: Clerical, Technical, Paraprofessionals	15 – 40%
Exempt: First-Level Management, Administrators, Professionals	30 – 50%
Exempt: Middle and Senior Management	40 – 100%

The pay ranges of the Edmonton Manufacturing Company are displayed below. On the assumption that the jobs are mainly clerical and technical, the ranges have been constructed using a spread of 15 to 40 per cent.

Pay Grade	% Spread	Minimum	Midpoint	Maximum
1	15%	590.50	634.79	679.08
2	18%	741.09	807.79	874.49
3	22%	883.59	980.79	1,077.99
4	25%	1,025.59	1,153.79	1,281.99
5	30%	1,153.73	1,326.79	1,499.85
6	35%	1,276.42	1,499.79	1,723.16
7	40%	1,393.99	1,672.79	1,951.59

Note: The grade minimum and maximum are computed as follows:

Minimum: Divide the midpoint by one and one-half of the percentage spread assigned to the pay grade.

E.g., Pay grade 1 minimum = 634.79 ÷ 1.075 = 590.50

Or,

$$\frac{634.79}{1 + (.15/2)} = 590.50$$

Maximum: Add to the midpoint the difference between the midpoint and the minimum.

E.g., Pay grade 1 maximum = [634.79 + (634.79 - 590.50)]

Pay ranges— means to recognize differences between employees in same pay grade   The differences between employees whose jobs are in the same pay grade may be due to *experience, specialized training*, or *performance*. Many organizations also use the pay range to recognize *seniority*. The pay ranges, then, must be tailored to the needs of the organization.

Generally, pay grades at the lower end of the pay structure have smaller spreads. Jobs in these pay grades are usually entry level jobs, and organizations do not expect their employees to stay too long in these jobs; either they will be promoted to jobs in higher pay grades or they will be terminated. Therefore, these pay grades do not need a large spread. Further up in the pay structure, the opportunities for promotion are limited, and employees stay relatively longer in these jobs. The larger spread of the ranges in these pay grades permits the organization to recognize the outstanding performance of employees who cannot be, or do not wish to be, promoted.

Considerable judgement—based on the accumulated experience of the desirable length of stay in the same job, on the opportunities for promotion, and on the organization's policy on performance-based pay and seniority pay—goes into the decision about how small or large the spread of the pay ranges should be.

Alternative ways to recognize the differences between employees whose jobs are in the same pay grade Organizations can give cash payments separate from base pay. If this is done, the pay grade need not be used and pay ranges are not necessary. There is the need to make periodic adjustments for cost of living, which can be done by multiplying the regression model by the amount of the adjustment that is necessary. But organizations have traditionally used the pay structure to recognize the differences mentioned.

There is, however, an increasing trend not to use the pay structure to recognize performance; instead, bonus payments are given when the required level of performance is demonstrated. When merit pay for performance is given through an increase in the base pay, it becomes a perpetual payment that recurs in future years even when performance drops. Organizations that give merit pay through a salary increase do not reduce the salary in later years when the employee's performance has dropped. To avoid this kind of situation, organizations are adopting the practice of bonus payments.

The bonus approach is also useful in two situations which pay ranges cannot address. First is the situation in which employees have received merit salary increases that are well-justified by their high performance levels and, as a result, have reached the top of the pay range. They maintain their high performance levels but because they are at the maximum, they will not receive further salary increases. The only way for such employees to receive salary increases is a promotion to jobs in the next pay grade. If promotion opportunities are limited as in the case in advances to jobs in the higher pay grades, their motivation to perform and even to remain in the organization can be adversely affected. Thus, a performance-based bonus is an effective alternative in these cases.

The other situation where the bonus approach is useful is in the case of new hires who are usually placed at or below the minimum of the pay grade of their jobs. If the new employees are exceptionally good performers, they may find that their salary change as determined by pay grade increments does not adequately reflect their performance. Of course, these employees may qualify for promotions to jobs in the higher pay grades, but such promotion opportunities might not be readily available. In these cases, a bonus, in addition to the pay grade increase, would help to better reflect their performance. Such a bonus should be specific to the performance period under review and does not become part of the salary.

Advantages of pay grades When jobs are grouped into pay grades, all the jobs with points within the interval of the pay grade receive the same pay. Thus, the table on page 315 shows in step 4 that a job that has 205 points and another job that has 295 points will both receive the same base pay. The base pay change will occur only when the employee is promoted to a job in the next pay grade. This approach overcomes most of the administrative difficulties associated with the first approach—that is, of treating each evaluation point as a pay grade. There may still be requests for a review of job evaluation points from employees whose jobs are near the point value that begins the next pay grade.

For example in step 4 in the table, an employee in a job that has 395 points might press for a review in the hope that the job will merit 401 points, and thus fall into the next pay grade. This approach also provides meaningful differences in pay rates when an employee moves from a job in a lower pay grade to a job in the next higher pay grade.

Broadbanding

Broadbanding is another approach to constructing pay grades. This technique takes further the traditional idea of pay grades which group together jobs within a predetermined range of job evaluation points. Traditionally, each pay grade consists of a relatively narrow interval of job evaluation points which gives rise to several pay grades. The broadbanding technique has a larger interval of job evaluation points. The effect of the larger job evaluation points interval of each pay grade is to collapse several pay grades into one or two bands. Each band has its own minimum and a maximum pay.

For example, through "broadbanding" the 14 pay grades of General Electric's nonexecutive salaried employee group was collapsed into four bands (Abosch, Gilbert, and Dempsey, 1994). One study reports considerable interest in broadbanding in Canada. Of the 374 respondent organizations, 10 percent have implemented broadbanding and 39 percent are considering it (Carlyle, 1994).

Because broadbanding takes in a larger number of jobs within one pay band, job responsibilities can now be defined more broadly. It is, therefore, suitable for flatter organizational structures which need flexible job descriptions and skill or competency-based pay. In the traditional multi-pay grade structure, a move into a job in the next higher pay grade is automatically accompanied by a pay increase. Broadbanding eliminates such automatic pay increases because the move is into jobs in the same pay band. The pay increase will be based only on the individual's experience and competency in the new job. It thus allows for relatively freer career movement across jobs. On the down side, broadbanding could lead to increased costs. Also, in broadbanding managers tend to exercise greater discretion in salary decisions. It, therefore, increases the potential for employee inequity as a result of arbitrary salary decisions or inconsistency in these decisions.

PAY STRUCTURE AND SALARY ADMINISTRATION POLICIES

Need for policies to deal with unusual situations

A well-designed pay structure maintains the right balance between internal and external equity consistent with the organization's compensation philosophy. There are, however, situations where the individual's salary is outside the established pay ranges, either below the minimum or above the maximum of a pay grade. Often, a large number of employees will be bunched close to or at the top of a pay grade. In these situations, the motivating potential of the pay structure is not fully realized. This section examines the reasons for these situations and considers the appropriate salary administration policies for coping with these situations.

Individual's salary is below the minimum of the pay grade

This situation is caused by a new employee or the "capping" policy of the organization. When new employees do not have the experience required for the job, they may be placed on probation and started below the minimum of the grade. As soon as the employees successfully complete their probationary period, their pay rate is raised and falls into the regular pay structure.

Under the capping policy, the organization limits the salary increase to a certain amount that an employee can receive at any one time. A promotion can involve a movement from a lower pay grade to the minimum of the next higher pay grade, which can result in a substantial salary increase. The capping policy will reduce the increase to the established limit and, as a consequence, the individual's salary will fall below the minimum of the next higher pay grade. The primary reason for the capping policy is cost control. If the individual's performance continues to be satisfactory, the next salary review will place the individual in the regular pay grade.

Individual's salary is above the maximum of the pay grade

There are three reasons for this situation. One reason is that employees have been receiving substantial seniority increases, which have placed them beyond the maximum of the pay grade. These increases were intended as rewards for their long tenure. Either there were no opportunities for promotion or they were probably incapable of being promoted to jobs in the higher pay grades. Employees in this situation are generally near retirement.

The second reason is that an employee's outstanding performance has justified the merit increases that placed him or her above the maximum of the pay grade. Here, too, there were probably no promotion opportunities, or the employee's present knowledge, skills, and abilities were not adequate for higher level jobs. If the latter is the case, then serious thought should be given to the development of this employee.

The third reason is the existence of a problematic situation. The employee's salary is above the maximum of the pay grade, most probably because of a demotion from a job in a higher pay grade to a job in a lower pay grade with the salary remaining unchanged. Another reason might be inflated merit increases, which were not justified by the individual's performance. Individuals in these situations are noted with a "red circle"; their pay rates are also referred to as "flagged" or "personal out-of-line differentials". The appropriate salary administration strategy in this situation is to freeze or to reduce the individual's salary. Most organizations freeze the salary until upward revisions in the pay structure bring the salary into the regular pay range.

A large number of employees at the top of a pay grade This situation, referred to as "running out of range", might occur in a relatively old organization where employees of about the same age started at the same time. Limited growth opportunities might also have restricted their upward movement in the pay structure. These employees are good performers, but further increases will push them out of the pay grade. On the other hand, they will be demotivated when they find that their good performance, which brought them to the top of the pay grade, now has become an obstacle to further increases.

There are long-term and short-term strategies for dealing with this situation. The long-term solution is an employee development programme to prepare them to move to jobs in the higher pay grades. In the short-term their motivation can be maintained through cash bonuses, which do not affect the pay structure.

The pay rate of a job falls outside the job's pay grade This situation is termed as the case of the "shadow range"; it applies to a job rather than an individual. In this case, there is a shortage of labour for a particular job. The excess demand relative to supply of labour pushes up the market pay rates of this job, and the organization finds itself having to pay this job more than its internal job value. Hence, the pay rate falls outside the pay grade in which the organization's job structure has placed it. Unlike the red circle case, the shadow range situation does not pay the individual more than he/she is worth. Rather, the organization's job evaluation system gives the job a lower value than the market.

An organization might be tempted to resolve this case by revising its assessment of the job's value and placing it in a higher pay grade. This is a satisfactory solution only if the job's value really justifies the higher pay grade. If it does not, then this solution will disturb the internal equity of the compensation system. A better approach is to keep the job outside the pay grade, because the market labour shortage might be a temporary phenomenon. If it is not a temporary phenomenon, the job's evaluation should be thoroughly reviewed. Perhaps there are features of the job that are captured by the external labour market but escape the organization's job evaluation process.

To conclude The pay structure, like any other compensation technique, method, and structure, should be viewed as a means to an end. As discussed in previous chapters, the compensation system should support the business objectives and strategies of the organization. If the pay structure is treated as an end in itself, the decisions relating to it are sure to become dysfunctional and will not contribute to the effectiveness of the organization. Adjustments to the pay structure should be understood and managed in the perspective of the compensation system as a potent instrument for achieving both the effectiveness of the organization as well as the satisfaction of the employees.

SUMMARY

This chapter dealt with the issues, procedures, techniques, and methods through which organizations strive to blend internal and external equity in the compensation system. It examined the relevant external labour market accessed by salary surveys, as an important source of pay rates. The chapter then described the methods and processes of conducting a salary survey, and considered the advantages and disadvantages to the organization of conducting its own salary survey as compared with acquiring survey data from third parties. The chapter also examined typical analytical procedures for ensuring that the survey data are relevant and comparable for the user's situation and needs.

The chapter discussed the rationale and the criteria for the choice of a pay level policy, which determines the organization's position *vis-à-vis* the market. The chapter then described the procedural steps for pricing the job structure, namely, determining the job match, choosing the comparable companies and the pay data, and developing the organization's pay line through regression analysis. The chapter examined the purpose of pay grades and pay ranges, and described the procedure for constructing them.

Finally, the chapter discussed the appropriate salary administration policies for dealing with individual salary cases that fall outside the pay grades.

KEY TERMS

pricing the job structure	*salary surveys*
red circle situation	*occupational survey method*
job evaluation survey method	*shadow range situation*
relevant external labour market	*pay grades*
job match	*pay level policies*
runnning out of range situation	*survey levelling*
key job matching survey method	*third-party surveys*

_ℛ_ REVIEW AND DISCUSSION QUESTIONS

1. What are the internal and external factors that influence the setting of pay rates?

2. Explain the purpose of salary surveys. What are the critical questions that should be included in a salary survey?

3. What are the advantages and disadvantages of an organization conducting its own survey as compared with acquiring the data from third-party surveys?

4. "Survey data should be subjected to a rigorous review to make sure that they are accurate and that only the data selected fairly reflects the labour market rates of survey jobs". Explain the analytical procedures to be used in reviewing and selecting the survey data.

5. Discuss the rationale and the criteria for the choice of a pay level policy.

6. In the following graph:

   • Case *1, the salary is above the pay grade.

   • Case *2, the salary is below the pay grade.

   • Case *3, several salaries are clustered at the top of the grade.

Explain the possible reasons for each of these situations. What actions would you propose for dealing with these situations?

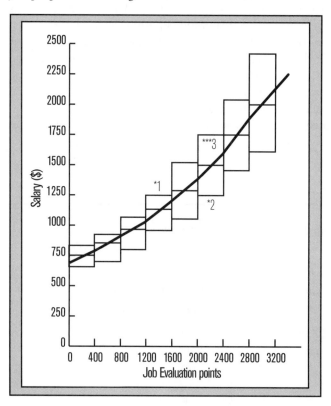

Figure 13.1 Job Evaluation Points

Constructing the Pay Structure

Objective

To construct the salary structure of the clerical and administrative staff of Beaverbrook Community College.

Data

All activities that need to be done prior to this phase (for example, developing the job structure, conducting the salary survey) have been completed. In addition, Beaverbrook's manager of salary administration compared Beaverbrook jobs with those obtained from the salary survey and came up with five benchmark jobs. She also decided to use the market median pay of these jobs because she believes that it better reflects the market pay rates, and is also consistent with Beaverbrook's pay level policy of matching the market. The benchmark jobs and their corresponding job evaluation points and median pay follows.

Job Title	Job Evaluation Points	Market Median Pay ($)
Porter	220	772.47
Typist	390	1,013.79
Clerk	690	900.73
Secretary	9,101	213.58
Assistant Accountant	2,245	1,328.81

Procedure

1. Using the above data points, conduct a regression analysis to obtain the regression model in the form of $y = a + bx$. Most statistical software packages will let you do this on your personal computer.

2. Construct pay grades and pay ranges. Refer to the procedural steps illustrated in the chapter.

Discussion

1. Review the correlation coefficient. Is it satisfactory? If it is, identify the specific actions/judgements of the compensation specialist that might have contributed to an acceptable correlation coefficient. If it is not, indicate what aspects you would look at to improve it.

2. The compensation specialist believes that by choosing the market median

pay rates, she is implementing a pay level policy of matching the market. In which sense is she matching the market, and in which sense is she not matching the market?

3. Compare your decisions on the number and the interval of points in the pay grade with the decisions of the other participants in this exercise. Discuss the reasons for the similarities and the differences.

4. Compare your decisions on the height or spread of each pay range with the decisions of the other participants. Discuss the reasons for the similarities and the differences.

Employee
Benefits
Programmes

OVERVIEW

This chapter explores the wide variety of benefits offered to employees. Some of these benefits are legally mandatory, and others are either the result of union-management negotiations or are provided at the discretion of the employer. The chapter also examines the emerging flexible benefits approach and discusses guidelines for the design of a benefits programme.

LEARNING OBJECTIVES

► To identify the objective of a benefits programme.

► To understand the purpose, eligibility conditions, benefits, and financing arrangements of the various benefits programmes, namely, income protection programmes, reimbursed time off, and employee services and perquisites.

► To understand the rationale of the flexible benefits approach and to distinguish it from the traditional standardized benefits programme.

► To determine the essential criteria for the effective design of a benefits programme.

EMPLOYEE BENEFITS PROGRAMMES
Benefits—a significant element of compensation costs

It was remarked in Chapter 1 that employee benefits have increased both in variety and cost. In 1953-54, these programmes constituted 15 per cent of the gross annual payroll. A Conference Board of Canada survey (Carlyle, 1994) found that in 1992, the total benefit costs averaged 26.9%, with some respondent organizations reporting costs as high as 52% of the gross annual payroll. Furthermore, this survey indicated that some of the cost control measures they have taken are reduced coverage, increased employee contributions, and increased deductibles. Organizations are concerned to manage these costs effectively so that both the organization and its employees derive the greatest benefit from these programmes.

What is an employee benefits programme?

It is a planned offering of benefits designed as a component of the organization's reward system to attract and retain employees, to maintain employee morale and motivate performance, and to comply with legal requirements. An employee benefits programme also offers the organization significant tax advantages. The variety of benefits organizations offer can be grouped into three major categories: income protection programmes, reimbursed time off, and employee services and perquisites.

Origin of benefits programmes

Many of the programmes now taken for granted are of relatively recent origin. Prior to World War II, employee benefits were restricted to work-accident compensation and employee housing. The latter was quite common for companies situated in remote locations. The beginnings of the present array of benefits can be traced to developments during World War II. Anticipating that shortages of personnel and materials during the war would inevitably fuel inflation and jeopardize the war effort, the government introduced wage and price controls, which prevented companies from offering higher wages to compete for a limited labour pool. Companies could use deferred benefits, which did not involve a substantial current cash outlay, to retain and attract employees.

Some employee benefits programmes that have become a regular part of the compensation system of most organizations are now described.

INCOME PROTECTION PROGRAMMES
Types of income protection programmes

These programmes protect employees when their income is disrupted because they have lost their job, because they are unable to work due to illness, disability, or a work accident, or because of retirement. Two types of programmes are designed to achieve these objectives. The first type is the universal coverage programmes mainly funded by the federal government, such as Old Age Security (OAS) and the Guaranteed Income Supplement (GIS). Neither employers nor employees are required to finance these universal benefits, which are funded from government revenues. The second type is programmes that require contributions by the employer and the employees. This chapter will focus on these programmes. Some of these programmes—Employment Insurance, Canada/Quebec Pension Plan, and Workers' Compensation—are required by law. Most of the larger organizations provide additional protection for their employees through private pension plans and group insurance programmes.

Employment Insurance (EI)

Objective and salient features The Unemployment Insurance (UI) programme was introduced in 1940 to provide income protection in the event of unemployment due to the loss of a job or a lay-off. The program has been amended now and then to improve its effectiveness. For instance, recently the old UI system has been replaced by a new EI (Employment Insurance) system. On April 18, 1996, the House of Commons Standing Committee on Human Resources Development proposed some adjustments to Bill C-12 (Employment Insurance). The new EI system came into force on July 1, 1996 and replaced the old UI Act and the National Training Act. It is intended to strengthen work incentives by offering not only basic income support to unemployed Canadians, but also providing them a better chance to return to the job market. EI does not cover employees who are on strike or have been locked out. The fundamental objective of EI is to provide temporary income support in order that the individual who is available for and able to work can locate a job that suits his/her knowledge, skills, and abilities. All part-time work is counted for determining eligibility for benefits. Furthermore, EI enables the unemployed to get information and advisory services from the National Employment Service to find job and training possibilities.

The EI programme is administered by the federal government, and both employers and employees contribute to its funding. The premiums are tax deductible and the benefits are treated as taxable income.

Starting January 1, 1997, the EI income benefit is based on a minimum number of hours worked rather than weeks. The hour-based system of entitlement to benefits motivates both full-time and part-time workers to work longer hours during any given "qualifying period". Besides the income benefit, there is a family income supplement for the claimants which is determined by the number of children in the family. Unemployed individuals qualify for EI benefits if they have contributed during the "qualifying period", and after a "waiting period" stipulated in the EI Act. How long one can draw these benefits depends on how long one has worked and the unemployment rate in the region. In most cases, 55% of one's insured earnings up to a maximum of $413 per week is received as EI benefit. EI also pays special benefits to employees who are sick, injured, in quarantine, or on maternity leave. For details on EI benefits one may refer to the publication on Employment Insurance by the Minister of Supply and Services, Canada, 1996.

Some employers—notably in the automobile industry—provide supplemental unemployment benefits (SUB) to their laid-off workers. Under SUB, the laid-off worker receives 95 per cent of his/her income—an attractive inducement to ride the lay-off period and return to the former employer. The SUB is an effective strategy for guaranteeing that the organization will not lose its skilled and trained workers in the event of temporary layoffs.

Workers' Compensation

Objective and salient features This benefit is provided by the Workers' Compensation Act that exists in each province and territory of Canada. Essentially, the programme covers employee injury, disability, or death caused by a work-related accident. The programme is administered by the Workers' Compensation Commission of each province and territory, and funding is through a premium collected from the employer. The rate of premium depends upon the risk factor associated with the industry. Law and accounting firms, considered to be non-hazardous workplaces, will pay a much lower premium compared with companies in the high-risk mining industry. The premium is levied on the total annual payroll, and pooled into a fund of the industry group, which is then utilized to settle claims from employees in that industry group.

This is essentially a no-fault insurance, because employee claims are settled by the Workers' Compensation Commission on the basis of an established schedule of the injury and its corresponding compensation. The liability of the employer or of the employees is not considered. However, there is now a trend to assess premiums on the basis of a company's safety record. Companies with a good safety record will be assessed a relatively lower premium. The objective here is to encourage companies to improve or maintain safe working conditions in the workplace.

Canada/Quebec Pension Plan (CPP/QPP)

Objective and salient features Introduced on January 1, 1966, the Canada Pension Plan and the Quebec Pension Plan have essentially the same features and are portable across Canada. Both plans are administered by the government and funded entirely by a payroll tax on a portion of the total employee earnings stipulated in the regulations. This tax is then shared equally between the employer and the employee. Self-employed individuals pay the entire payroll tax. The contributions are compulsory for all employees and self-employed individuals between the ages of 18 and 65.

The plans cover retirement benefits at age 65, which amount to 25 per cent of the Average Pensionable Earnings. An individual whose disability prevents him/her from earning an income is entitled to a disability pension for the duration of the disability. When the individual reaches age 65, the disability pension is replaced by the retirement pension. Other benefits included in the plans are a death benefit and a benefit to the surviving spouse and dependent children of eligible age.

Contributions to the plans are tax deductible, and pension benefits are treated as taxable income.

Private Pension Plans

Types Some companies have established private pension plans to provide their employees with additional retirement benefits. These plans are tailored to suit the needs of the employees and the organization. The plans vary depending on the amount of employer and employee contributions that are necessary in order to obtain the desired level of pension benefits. With regard to the contributions, an important consideration is whether the plan should be contributory or non-contributory. In a contributory plan, the employees contribute to the pension fund; in a non-contributory plan, the pension fund is financed solely by the employer. One advantage of a contributory plan is that employee contributions increase the pool of funds and a correspondingly lower level of financing is required from the company. The other advantage is that employee contributions lead to greater employee interest in the plan. The major disadvantage is that the employer does not have complete freedom and autonomy in the management of the pension fund.

Benefit determination In most plans, the pension income at retirement is determined by two factors: (1) the percentage for each year of service, and (2) the average earnings of the years before retirement—usually the best five years. For example, the basic pension calculation formula for the plan of Quebec Civil Service employees is as follows (CARRA, 1990):

	Number of		Average		Basic
2% x	years service (max. 35)	X	pensionable salary for 5 best-paid years	=	annual pension

In pension plans where the pension benefit is predetermined, the amount of employee contribution to the pension fund is generally fixed. But the amount of the employer's contribution depends upon the actuarial assessment of the amount needed to meet the objective of the plan, that is, the annual pension benefits that must be paid as they become due. The fixed, predetermined benefit imposes upon the employer the obligation of generating the necessary funds to pay the pension benefits.

In other plans, both employer and employee make fixed contributions to the pension fund and this fund is invested. In these plans, the employee's pension benefit is not predetermined but depends entirely upon how well the fund's investments have performed. For the organization, a fixed contribution clearly defines its cost commitment. For the employee, there is considerable uncertainty with regard to the benefit that will be received.

Eligibility conditions and commencement of benefits In designing the pension plan, some of the other decisions relate to eligibility conditions and the date when pension benefits become due. In eligibility conditions, the issue is whether the employee is eligible to join the plan when he/she starts work or on the satisfactory completion of the probationary period. The pension benefit ordinarily commences at the "normal" retirement age stipulated in the plan. Most pension plans allow early retirement, and therefore the early drawing of pension benefits, but most do so with a penalty that reduces the pension. For example, the three largest pension plans administered by the Quebec Government's Commission reduce the pension by a rate of .5 per cent per month of the period between the date of the early retirement and the normal retirement date (CARRA, 1990).

The plan may also allow employees to retire at a date later than the normal retirement date. In such a case, the employee's pension benefits begin as soon as he/she reaches the normal retirement age, and the employee ceases to contribute to the pension fund from this date. Alternatively, the employee does not draw pension benefits on reaching the normal retirement age and continues to contribute to the pension fund. The plan then allows the employee to draw a higher pension benefit when he/she actually retires. The options allowed by the plan for late retirement will depend on the organization's policy on whether it wishes to encourage employees to stay beyond the normal retirement.

Vesting rights and portability Another critical issue in pension plans is the employee's vesting rights. These are the rights of an employee to the contribution that the employer has made to the pension fund on his/her behalf. The vesting rights determine when and under what circumstances an employee has the right to benefit from the employer's contributions. This issue assumes importance in the event the employee leaves the company before retirement. In such an event, the employee has full rights to the contributions he/she has made to the pension fund. However, the rights to the employer's contributions depend upon the vesting provisions of the plan. The vesting provisions are often an effective leverage for retaining an employee. The laws of most provinces confer vesting rights when the employee meets two conditions: he or she is 45 years old and has completed ten years of service with that employer.

There is an increasing interest in the issue of portability, the right to carry to the pension fund of a new employer the contributions accumulated in the pension fund of a previous employer. For example, the McGill University Pension

Plan has reciprocal transfer agreements with several universities and government plans in Quebec and across Canada. Portability privileges enable the consolidation of contributions which then have the potential of a higher pension benefit.

Contributions to a pension fund are tax deductible up to certain maximum limits, and the pension benefit is considered as taxable income.

Group Insurance Programmes

Advantages of group insurance programmes Many organizations find group insurance to be a relatively economic way of offering employees the benefit of income protection. Lower administrative costs to the insurance carrier, combined with tax advantages for the employer, make these programmes quite attractive. In addition to the cost savings, the pooling of risks inherent in group insurance programmes allows uninsurable employees to be covered. It also allows the coverage of employees in high-risk occupations. Premium rates for individual insurance policies for these employees would be prohibitive. Group insurance programmes offer income protection in the event of disability or death.

Group disability insurance plan Under the group disability insurance plan, employees are protected against income disruption resulting from long-term disability that is not attributable to their occupation. Separate coverage for non-occupational disability is necessary for two reasons. First, the Workers' Compensation programme discussed earlier covers only work-related disability. Second, non-occupational disability coverage is a useful supplement to the low disability pension benefit received under the CPP/QPP. The amount of the disability benefit depends upon the policy negotiated with the insurers and can vary from 66 2/3 per cent to 80 per cent of the employee's salary. The benefits under long term disability plans generally begin after a waiting period ranging from 120 to 180 days and end when the employee returns to work or reaches retirement age.

Group life insurance plans Group life insurance provides a sum of money to the employee's survivors in the event of death. It is usually a term life insurance contract which requires the insurer to pay the insurance benefit (i.e., the amount insured) only in the event of death. Since term life insurance does not include an investment component, the premiums are considerably lower than for whole life or similar life insurance policies. Group life insurance policies may include a survivors' benefit plan. Under such a plan, the beneficiary who receives a lump-sum payment on the death of the employee may opt to convert this into a continuing monthly income to provide for the employee's survivors. Some benefit packages also include a "dependants' life insurance". Under this plan, the amount insured is payable on the death of the insured dependent to the employee, the employee's spouse, or the dependant's legal heirs.

Group life and disability insurance programmes may be sold by insurance companies as a package that includes health insurance. The health insurance component, as described later, covers prescription drugs, private hospital rooms, ambulance services, dental care, and so forth. Most group life and disability insurance plans are contributory; the employee pays some or all of the premiums.

Group Insurance plans—major design issues The major design issue in group insurance programmes is whether employees should contribute (contributory plan) or whether these plans should be financed entirely by the employer. When employees contribute to the plan, they add resources that enable the plan to provide a much higher level of benefits. The process involved in a contributory plan results in better employee appreciation of the costs. The process also makes employees more willing to cooperate in the cost control of the plan. In a non-contributory plan, the employer has greater control over the administration of the plan.

In most cases, the group insurance programme is for the employees of a single organization. However, several employers in an industry can pool together to buy a group insurance policy, as is the case in the construction and small retail sectors. In the construction industry, workers change employers as projects come to an end; a small retailer does not have the numbers to profit from a group insurance policy (McPherson and Wallace, 1985).

Reimbursed TIme Off

Types Time off includes all the work breaks the employee is permitted: lunch and coffee/tea/smoke breaks, annual vacations, national/religious holidays, personal holidays, sick leave, maternity/paternity and adoption leave, and jury duty. Some of these benefits are mandated by law. A good reference source for these is Labour Canada's annual publication *Labour Standards in Canada* (Labour Canada, 1986). Other benefits are either negotiated with the union or provided at the discretion of the employer.

Annual vacation Most Canadian jurisdictions stipulate a minimum paid annual vacation of two weeks. However, many organizations offer more than the minimum. The vacation entitlement is related to years of service. Generally, it is four weeks for 9 to 12 years of service, and five weeks for 15 to 20 years of service. Some collective agreements provide for four weeks for 6 to 9 years. In some organizations, employees with more than 25 years of service receive six to seven weeks of paid vacation. Annual vacations are intended to satisfy the employee's need for a prolonged period of rest and recreation.

Public holidays The number of paid public holidays that are legally required varies in the different jurisdictions. The common holidays observed in most provinces include New Year's Day, Good Friday, Victoria Day, Canada Day, Labour Day, Thanksgiving Day, Christmas Day, and Boxing Day. Additional holidays may be observed in each province, for example, Saint Jean-Baptiste Day in Quebec. Employees who are required to work on these days are entitled to premium pay varying from 2 to 2 1/2 times the regular pay.

Personal days Paid "personal days" is another form of reimbursed time off in many organizations. The entitlement varies from two to five days and is intended to give employees an opportunity to meet personal, family, and social obligations. In some organizations, flex time arrangements become a useful alternative for meeting some of these obligations.

Most organizations offer paid sick leave programmes, but the entitlements and conditions differ considerably. Some allow up to ten days of sick leave a year, which can neither be accumulated nor cashed in if unused. Other organizations permit accumulation of the unused sick leave which can be availed of at a later date or cashed in at retirement.

To prevent the abuse of this benefit, some organizations require a medical certificate to support the request for this leave. Often organizations buy insurance policies to cover the costs of this benefit.

Maternity leave Maternity leave is now a legal entitlement in almost all Canadian jurisdictions. Paternity leave, on the other hand, is a legal entitlement only in the federal jurisdiction and in some provinces such as Saskatchewan. Some of the larger organizations provide paternity and adoption leave. During these types of leave the employee retains all rights and benefits, including the accrual of seniority rights.

Time off for jury duty and sabbaticals It is legally obligatory for organizations to provide time off for employees who are called to perform jury duty. Many organizations pay for such leaves of absence. Sabbaticals or educational leaves for managers are becoming increasingly popular in many organizations. The Polaroid Corporation has an innovative time-off programme called the "rehearsal retirement" programme (McGrath 1988). Any employee can take advantage of this programme, but it is mostly used by those near retirement. Under this programme, an employee can take time off for three months to explore such options as hobbies, starting his/her own business, volunteer work, and relocating. At the end of the three months or even before that the employee can return to his/her job. Alternatively, if the employee has discovered a viable option, he/she is free to retire immediately to work on this new interest. Rehearsal retirement not only provides retirement options but also counselling and the opportunity to make the transition into retirement smooth and graceful.

Employee Services or Perquisites

Types There is an infinite variety of employee services or perquisites. Some of the more common employee services or perquisites are health insurance plans, educational assistance, subsidized cafeterias, recreational facilities and programmes, parking privileges, discounts on company products, and credit unions.

Private health insurance plans—salient features These are intended to supplement government funded medicare benefits to provide for costs not covered by government plans. Typically, these health insurance plans cover supplementary hospital and medical costs, health costs outside Canada, prescription drugs, private duty nursing and emergency ambulance services, vision and hearing care, and dental care. In most organizations, these plans are contributory, although there are wide variations in the sharing of the premiums between the organization and the employees.

Cost control is maintained through deductibles, co-insurance, and benefit maximum. The higher the deductible, the lower the cost of the premiums. For a family plan, such a deductible is about $25 per year; the employee bears the first $25 of the claims he/she has submitted in a year. In co-insurance, the employee is reimbursed only about 80 per cent of the claim; the non-reimbursed amount is borne by the employee. The third cost-control mechanism, benefit maximum, stipulates that the total claims paid in a year shall not be above a specified maximum.

Educational assistance program The components of the educational assistance programme vary in different organizations. Some organizations reimburse tuition fees and the cost of course materials. Others also provide time off and tuition loans for employees who pursue a programme of study. Sometimes the assistance is limited to job-related study programmes and includes paid time off. In some organizations, educational assistance is also extended to employees' dependants.

Other perquisites Subsidized cafeterias are quite common in large organizations. So are recreational facilities and programmes, including hockey, bowling, and softball teams. Often the recreational programme takes the form of subsidized memberships in fitness clubs. Discounts on company products are popular in organizations that manufacture or market consumer goods and services. For example, retail store employees can buy products at special discounts; similarly, financial institutions provide their employees with mortgage loans at reduced interest rates. Large organizations also provide facilities for employee credit unions. The convenient feature of this service is the payroll deduction, which is also used for savings and stock purchase plans.

Managers and executives have their own set of perquisites or "perks", which include a company car, club memberships, the payment of a spouse's travel expenses when the spouse accompanies the employee on company business, or tickets to the theatre and related cultural events.

Emerging employee services and benefits Some emerging employee services and benefits are employee assistance programmes (EAPs), child care, and flex time.

Although the focus of **employee assistance programmes** is primarily on alcohol and drug rehabilitation, EAPs now also include employee counselling on stress, burn-out, and related conditions.

With the increasing participation of women in the workforce, **child-care** services are now a much-sought-after benefit. Some organizations provide child-care facilities at the workplace. These are run either by the company itself or by an independent organization. On-site child-care facilities give user-employees much peace of mind. They have also proved to be beneficial to the employer in terms of reduced absenteeism and turnover, and as a competitive advantage in hiring (Paull, 1986). In other organizations, this benefit takes the form of an allowance to help employees defray their child-care costs.

Flex time gives employees the freedom to determine the time when they will begin and end the work day, provided they put in the required total hours of the work day. It is understood that the exercise of freedom in this programme is subject to supervisory approval to ensure the efficient and effective fulfilment of job objectives. Hence, the flex-time system often stipulates a period of "core hours" during which all employees should be present. Outside of the core hours, employees can schedule their own starting and quitting times. In some companies, employees maintain the same schedule for a week or more. In other companies, a greater variation is allowed.

Flex time promotes favourable employee attitudes (job satisfaction and organizational commitment). Employees now have larger blocks of time available for leisure or for personal, family, and social obligations, and the absenteeism that was previously necessary to meet these personal needs is eliminated. Flex time also gives employees greater control over their jobs. Often the logistics of flex-time scheduling require that employees learn the other jobs in the work unit to ensure its uninterrupted operation. As a result, flex time can lead to job enrichment. The effects of flex time on performance range from no change to positive effects (Pierce et al., 1989).

Establishment of narrow core hours would contribute to the success of flex time, but the feasibility of narrow core hours depends upon the processes and the operations of the work unit. The flex-time system cannot succeed without employee involvement in its design and implementation. The effect of flex time is, to some extent, a move towards employee self-management. Therefore, its success will also depend upon the cooperation and support of middle management. Flex time is not suitable for work units in which the work process or technology creates interdependent jobs. Some of the other disadvantages of flex time are increased administration costs and the administrative difficulties that arise when the flex-time schedule conflicts with legislation relating to overtime pay and rest periods.

THE FLEXIBLE BENEFITS APPROACH

The rationale for flexible benefits Traditionally, organizations have offered their employees a standardized benefits program. This approach is still used in most organizations. However, several factors are making organizations question the wisdom of this approach. There are questions about whether the benefits programme addresses the needs and preferences of the employees. For example, older employees have greater preferences for pensions; employees with children prefer health insurance plans. Moreover, a standardized benefits programme often duplicates the coverage for employees whose spouses have similar coverage with their employers. If employees do not value the programme, the organization is not effectively deploying the enormous resources it invests in the standardized benefits programme. For these reasons the flexible benefit or the cafeteria-style approach is gaining popularity. A relatively recent survey of 405 Canadian organizations found that 18 percent have introduced flexible benefit plans and 22 percent are planning to do so (Carlyle, 1994).

Salient features Under a flexible benefits programme, the organization decides on a "core" coverage, which includes the absolute minimum for life insurance, medical, disability, pensions, vacations, and so forth. These are compulsory for all employees. In addition, the organization offers a "flexible dollar allowance" which employees can utilize to acquire more life insurance or medical or disability or other benefits according to their needs and preferences. By trading in other benefits, employees can increase the flexible dollar allowance. For example, employees of Noranda Inc. can trade their vacation time for additional life insurance or long-term disability benefits. Employees of Canadian General Tower have similar flexibility (Gibb-Clark, 1991). Employees can even cash the unused portion of the flexible dollar allowance.

There are concerns that employees might trade away such critical benefits as life insurance and leave their families unprotected. The compulsory core coverage of the flexible benefits approach can and should be designed to provide the needed safeguards. Noranda Inc. places restrictions on the trade of vacation time, making a minimum of vacation time obligatory for all employees; this minimum depends upon the employee's vacation entitlement as well as the minimum vacation required by law.

Advantages The flexible benefits approach has the advantage of meeting individual needs and preferences. It also gives employees a better understanding and appreciation of the benefits, leading to a more effective utilization of the programme. Increased autonomy in the choice of benefits results in a more positive attitude towards the organization; this positive attitude can influence retention behaviour.

Disadvantages The major disadvantages relate to costs. The costs of benefits generally tend to be about 5 per cent higher than in the traditional approach. (*The Globe and Mail*, June 24, 1991). There are the costs of installing and implementing the system. Finally, there is the potential that inequity may arise when the increased costs of one benefit plan require that more resources be allocated to it than to the other plans. On balance, however, the advantages outweigh the disadvantages.

GUIDELINES IN DESIGNING THE BENEFITS PROGRAMME

Critical to an effective design of a benefits programme is to ensure that it meets the test of saliency, valence, and contingency.

Saliency Employees will perceive benefits to be salient when these benefits are properly communicated. Benefits can be communicated through booklets, meetings, and personalized statements. Booklets that summarize the key features and provide details in a readable format are the most effective means of communicating the benefits programme. Employees retain these as a reference source for consolation when needed. Meetings help to further clarify the information in the booklets and to answer questions that may arise. Personalized benefit statements, which highlight the benefits that have accrued to the employee as well as projected future benefits, are effective in increasing the saliency of the benefits and can serve to influence retention behaviour.

The key to increasing saliency is to present the information so that it is easy to understand, and to include information on the content and the mechanics of the plan. Employees should also be informed of the process to modify the plan. If these things are done, the employee is not confronted with any surprises as he/she begins to take advantage of the benefit.

Valence Benefits should be valued by employees. In this respect, the flexible benefits or cafeteria-style benefits programme is a much better approach than the traditional standardized benefits programme. The freedom of the employee to choose those benefits that meet his/her needs and preferences is a critical feature that increases the valence of the benefits. Employee participation in the design and implementation of the benefits programme will also help to increase saliency and valence. The valence of a compensation item is also determined by employee perceptions of internal and external equity. Employee involvement from the very inception of the design process, including the benefits survey process, will contribute to feelings of the fairness and equity of the programme.

Contingency The benefits programme should be contingent on the desired work behaviour that can be appropriately related to the benefit item. This consideration should be reflected in the design of the programme. For example, the discussion of absenteeism in Chapter 8 illustrated how a sick leave benefits programme could be dysfunctional in producing unintended, undesirable behaviours. For many benefits, the primary contingent work behaviour is that of retention.

Exit interviews can be useful in assessing the effectiveness of the benefits programme in influencing retention behaviour. The action programme discussed in the next chapter can be used to identify those items of the benefits programme that are deficient in this respect; the action programme also proposes specific measures for improving the effectiveness of such items.

SUMMARY

This chapter explored the various benefits programmes offered by organizations. The discussion focused on three major categories: income protection programmes, reimbursed time off, and employee services and perquisites. The typical programmes in each category were discussed in terms of objective, eligibility conditions, benefit provisions, financing arrangements, and advantages and disadvantages. Some of these programmes are mandated by law, and others are either negotiated between union and management or provided at the discretion of the employer. The discussion of flexible benefits or cafeteria-style benefits showed that such a benefits programme has several advantages over the standardized benefits programme currently offered by most organizations. In conclusion, it was noted that a benefit can be said to be effectively designed only when it is perceived by employees to be salient, valent, and contingent on the desired work behaviour.

KEY TERMS

employee benefits programme
employee services and perquisites
flexible benefits programme

income protection programme
reimbursed time off
standardized benefits programme

REVIEW AND DISCUSSION QUESTIONS

1. Refer to the benefit items in the income protection programmes, reimbursed time off, and employee services and perquisites categories. Which compensation objective(s) would be served by each benefit item? Why?

2. Distinguish between the traditional standardized benefits programme and the emerging flexible benefits approach. What are the factors that weigh in favour of the flexible benefits approach?

3. What are the key design and administration issues in the following benefits programmes?

- Pension plan

- Group insurance (life and disability) plan

- Dental insurance plan

4. Although there are a variety of employee benefits, each benefit should meet certain essential criteria if it is to be effective. What are the criteria? Why are they essential?

Evaluating a Benefits Programme

EXERCISE
14.1

Objective

To use the framework of the model of effective reward management to evaluate a benefits programme.

Procedure

1. Prior to this exercise, participants are asked to collect information on employee benefits programmes from organizations of their choice. It is desirable that this information include at least one item from each of the three major categories: income protection programmes, reimbursed time off, and employee services and perquisites.

2. Divide the class into groups of three to four participants.

3. Each group reviews the employee benefits programmes collected by its members. The review should

   a)   evaluate the likely effectiveness of each programme in the light of the guidelines in designing the benefits programme discussed in the chapter; and

   b)   explore what aspects of the programmes they might design and/or implement differently, and the reasons for these changes.

4. Each group then shares its findings with the class. The class discussion that follows at this stage should focus on the reasons for the similarities and differences between employee benefits programmes in different organizations.

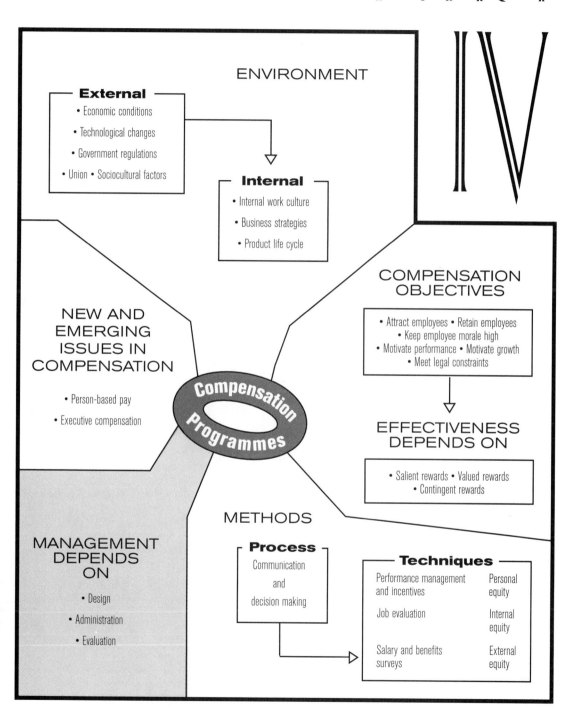

PART

IV

ENVIRONMENT

External
• Economic conditions
• Technological changes
• Government regulations
• Union • Sociocultural factors

Internal
• Internal work culture
• Business strategies
• Product life cycle

COMPENSATION
OBJECTIVES

• Attract employees • Retain employees
• Keep employee morale high
• Motivate performance • Motivate growth
• Meet legal constraints

NEW AND
EMERGING
ISSUES IN
COMPENSATION

• Person-based pay
• Executive compensation

Compensation
Programmes

EFFECTIVENESS
DEPENDS ON

• Salient rewards • Valued rewards
• Contingent rewards

METHODS

MANAGEMENT
DEPENDS
ON

• Design
• Administration
• Evaluation

Process
Communication
and
decision making

Techniques

Performance management and incentives	Personal equity
Job evaluation	Internal equity
Salary and benefits surveys	External equity

CHAPTER 15

Managing the

Compensation

System

OVERVIEW

This chapter discusses the administrative process of the salary budget, which has traditionally been used to manage the compensation system. The chapter's major focus is on a managerial action plan to evaluate the effectiveness of compensation systems.

 LEARNING OBJECTIVES

► To understand the meaning of *compa-ratio* and to discuss the usefulness of the compa-ratio in evaluating the impact of salary decisions.

► To describe the *top-down* and *bottom-up* approaches to developing a salary budget.

► To understand the rationale underlying the action programme for evaluating the effectiveness of the compensation system.

► To describe the procedural steps of the action programme and to understand the purpose of each step.

► To understand the analytical procedures used in the action programme.

► To develop competence in analysing the results of the diagnostic procedure of the action programme and in recommending the appropriate corrective actions envisaged in the programme.

INTRODUCTION

Managing the compensation system involves the administrative process of the salary budget. Equally important is the systematic and rational evaluation of the compensation system to determine whether the system is achieving its objectives. We first discuss the salary budget process, and then an action plan to assess the compensation system.

THE SALARY BUDGET PROCESS

The major compensation decision in the budget relates to the overall salary increase an organization can afford. In other words, the budget is the organization's salary level policy statement for the budget year. Before the approaches to developing a salary budget are considered, it is helpful to consider the concept of the compa-ratio, a useful device for providing meaningful information on the impact of salary decisions.

Compa-ratio

The compa-ratio is an indicator of how the salary of the individual or group relates to the midpoint of the relevant pay grade. Is the salary below, at, or above the pay grade's midpoint?

Compa-ratio formula to assess individual's salary When the compa-ratio is used to assess decisions on the salary of the individual employee, the formula is

$$\text{Compa-ratio} = \frac{\text{Salary of the employee}}{\text{Midpoint of the pay grade}}$$

Compa-ratios above or below one indicate that the individual's salary is above or below the midpoint of the pay grade. The significance of the compa-ratio depends upon the meaning assigned to the midpoint. The pay grade midpoint can be viewed as an average benchmark for salary decision criteria such as performance, tenure, and experience. The manager can assess whether the individual's salary compa-ratio reflects the individual's job performance, tenure, or experience, and then can initiate measures to address the inequities.

Compa-ratio formula to assess group's salaries The compa-ratio can similarly be used to assess salary decisions of a group of employees in the same pay grade. The formula for this purpose will be

$$\text{Compa-ratio} = \frac{\text{Average of salaries paid}}{\text{Midpoint of the pay grade}}$$

In addition, the compa-ratio will alert the manager to movement within and across pay grades. For example, a compa-ratio considerably lower than one indicates relatively high turnover or new employees. A compa-ratio considerably higher than one indicates that a large number of employees are bunched at the top of the pay grade and suggests that not much movement is occurring across pay grades.

The compa-ratio is also used to develop salary budgets.

Approaches to developing salary budgets

There are two approaches to developing the salary budget: the top-down and the bottom-up.

The Top-Down Approach

The top-down approach to salary budgeting is based on the compa-ratio. The organization decides a specific compa-ratio of its total salaries paid to the total midpoints of the pay grades for the budget year. From this targeted compa-ratio, the salary budget is derived.

In the top-down approach, top management decides on the salary budget for the entire organization. The budget forecast is based on four factors: (1) the organization's pay structure policy relative to the market; (2) the estimated change in the market rates expected in the budget year; (3) the organization's employee pay policy for the budget year; and (4) the organization's experience factor relative to salary budget forecasts. Chapter 13 discussed the major pay structure policies, namely, to meet, lead, or lag behind the market. The following example illustrates how these factors contribute to the development of the salary budget.

Example

For the budget year, the relevant data for Edmonton Manufacturing Company (EMC) is as follows:

- EMC's employee pay policy for the budget year is to meet the market at the end of the year;
- The market is expected to increase by 9 per cent;
- The total of the midpoints of the pay grades of EMC employees at the start of the budget year is $102,550.
- The organization's experience factor is the ratio of the budgeted or targeted compa-ratio and the actual compa-ratio at year end. The new hires, promotions, separations (voluntary and involuntary), and retirements account for the difference between the budgeted and the actual compa-ratios. The experience factor of 102 per cent for the prebudget year is considered to be typical and therefore suitable for incorporation in the budget year salary forecast.

The EMC salary budget process for the budget year incorporates these data in the following three steps:

Step 1: Establish EMC's target compa-ratio for the budget year This step considers EMC's pay structure policy relative to the market, the increase in the market rate for the budget year, and EMC's employee pay policy for the budget year. The midpoints of the pay structure approximate the market. Because the market rate is projected to increase by 9 per cent and EMC's pay objective is to meet the market, the target compa-ratio for the budget year will be 109 percent.

Step 2: Moderate the target compa-ratio by the experience factor The target compa-ratio is multiplied by the experience factor to obtain the revised target compa-ratio: 109% x 102% = 111.18%

Step 3: Compute EMC's salary budget for the budget year The salary budget is derived from the compa-ratio:

$$\text{Compa-ratio} = \frac{\text{Total budgeted salaries}}{\text{Total midpoints of the pay grades}}$$

$$111.18\% = \frac{x}{\$102{,}550}$$

Solving for x gives the salary budget of $114,015.09.

The Bottom-Up Approach

In the bottom-up approach, the salary budgeting process builds on the work unit's manpower plan, which is based on the projected business activities and the estimated human resource flows—new hires, promotions, and separations (voluntary and involuntary)—of the unit. The manager develops salary projections for each employee on the basis of his/her anticipated decisions relative to issues that require salary changes. Some of these issues are cost-of-living adjustment, merit increase, seniority increase, promotion, and adjustments for temporary transfers.

In making these adjustments, the manager is guided by the organization's policies. For example: (a) the starting salaries of new hires should be 5 per cent below the minimum of the pay grade and adjusted upward to the minimum on successful completion of the probationary period; (b) all salary increases resulting from promotion to a job in a higher pay grade should be capped at $5,000. Following these adjustments, the revised salaries of all the employees are added up and become the projected salary budget of the work unit. The projected salary budgets of all the work units are consolidated to form the salary budget of the organization.

EVALUATING THE EFFECTIVENESS OF THE COMPENSATION SYSTEM

"When you pay your employees, do you get a fair return for your investment?" "How do you know?" If these questions are posed to today's managers, the chances are that they will consider them to be irrelevant or regard them as mysteries too obscure to resolve. Yet, these managers routinely subject their organization's capital and operating costs to an array of rigorous analyses to determine whether the target rates of return are being obtained. They will also ensure that the variances are studied and investigated, and an appropriate plan of action is initiated for achieving the desired goals.

Logically, the compensation package should be subjected to the same cost-benefit analysis. In absolute dollars, the compensation package involves a considerable cash outflow. In relative terms, too, the cash outflow is significant—often more than 50 per cent of the total costs of the organization and, in many service industries and public-sector organizations, as high as 80 per cent. Why then do managers treat compensation costs differently? The answer to this question can be traced to managers' understanding of how pay and benefits affect work motivation.

There was a time when business and industry designed compensation programmes to pay only for what was produced. Such programmes—pioneered by Frederick Taylor, the father of scientific management—were widespread from around the turn of the century until World War II. As was discussed in Chapter 4, these programmes were based on the belief that money was a prime motivator of people's work efforts. In such a context, managers could properly be expected to assess whether their compensation programmes motivated employees to the extent and in the direction established by the organization.

However, after World War II, the belief that money was a prime motivator of performance was seriously challenged. By the 1960s, behavioural scientists with humanistic orientations, notably Herzberg and McGregor, began to argue that people do not work mainly for money but for ego-need gratification and self-fulfilment. If pay and benefits do not motivate performance, then it is only logical for managers to shrug off these rewards as an expense—an expense that is necessary but is not specifically designed to influence and improve work behaviour. Hence, the management of these rewards, despite the outlay involved, does not become a major concern of managers.

However, an examination (Chapter 4) of the intrinsic-extrinsic dichotomy in rewards management found that the theory is conceptually flawed, and that the empirical findings contradict its motivational assumptions. The theory also ignores the fact that a reward, intrinsic or extrinsic, will influence and improve work behaviour as long as it is valued by the recipient and received as a consequence of that behaviour. This fact has been recognized by the expectancy theory model, which offers a better explanation of work behaviour and also provides the compensation specialist with a sound theoretical framework for designing the reward system and evaluating its effectiveness (Chapter 5).

In this text, the discussion of the design of the compensation system has been consistently rooted in the constructs of the expectancy model. Whatever has been considered—the design of base pay, merit pay, incentives and gain-sharing, benefits, or even the non-economic elements of the compensation system such as job design—the basic question pervading the design process has been this: Will the employee perceive the item as *salient, valued,* and *contingent on the desired behaviour?* The constructs of expectancy theory provide the basis of a diagnostic procedure for evaluating the effectiveness of the compensation system.

This diagnostic procedure can be used to evaluate each item of the compensation programme and to recommend design changes that will improve its effectiveness. Because this diagnostic procedure is inextricably linked to compensation system design, it is more appropriately designated an action programme for designing and administering the reward system, and for evaluating its effectiveness. Discussion of the action programme will first focus on its rationale and procedural steps, and then on its use, as illustrated in a study of the effectiveness of the reward system in a Canadian corporation.

AN ACTION PROGRAMME
Rationale

The rationale underlying the action programme is as follows:

1. In designing its compensation programme, the organization intends that each component of the programme will elicit a specific set of behaviours from its employees to further the overall goals of the organization.

2. The intended set of behaviours will be realized only to the extent that each component of the programme is perceived by the employee as salient, valuable, and contingent on producing the intended set of behaviours.

3. The critical test of the effectiveness of the compensation programme is a comparison of the intended set of behaviours for each component of the programme with employee perceptions of that component in terms of valence, contingency, and saliency.

Procedural Steps

The procedural steps of the action programme are presented schematically in Figure 15.1.

Figure 15.1: Managerial Action Programme for Assessing and Designing a Reward System

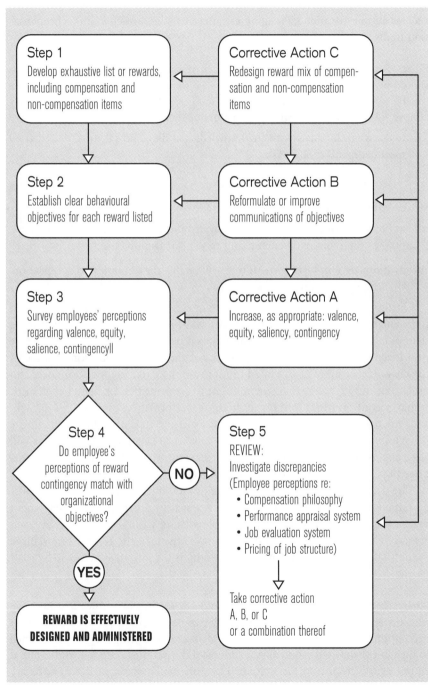

Step 1: Develop a list of all the rewards the organization offers its employees. The list should include rewards that involve cash payments and benefits (the economic compensation items) and those that do not involve any payments, such as autonomy and challenging assignments (the non-economic compensation items).

Step 2: Decide on the purpose of each reward that is listed. The purpose should be expressed in behavioural terms, so that the realization of the purpose can be objectively assessed. Experience suggests that organizations frequently choose from among the following five major behavioural objectives:

a) to attract individuals with the knowledge, ability, and talents demanded by specific organizational tasks;

b) to retain valued, productive employees;

c) to motivate regular attendance and a desired level of performance;

d) to promote attitudes conducive to loyalty and commitment to the organization, to high job involvement, and to job satisfaction; and

e) to stimulate employee growth that will enable the employee to accept more challenging positions.

Objectives such as these become the target behaviours, which are expected to be elicited by the rewards it offers. A reward may be intended to elicit more than one behaviour. If this is so, the targeted behaviours for a reward must be prioritized to clearly reflect the intentions of the organization. For example, if the reward "merit pay" is intended to motivate the retention, performance, and growth of employees, management ought to set priorities for these behaviours. It may accord priorities in terms of high for performance, medium for growth, and low for retention. The priorities spell out the type and the extent of the behaviour that management expects the reward to generate. Management will also state, at this stage, its beliefs about the extent to which the rewards are perceived by employees to be salient and valued.

The decisions made in this step of the programme will clearly state the purpose management has in mind for each reward. In other words, management makes a conscious, deliberate choice of what it wishes to achieve by each reward. Thus, the targets for returns on investment in the reward programme are definitively established. Against these targets the reward system will be evaluated.

Step 3: Conduct a survey of the employees to find out how they perceive each reward. The survey seeks to identify two sets of employee perceptions: (a) perceptions relating to reward saliency, valence, and contingency with reference to the target behaviour; and (b) perceptions of the personal, internal, and external equity of the compensation system. Data on the latter set of perceptions are collected through questions on employee perception of the fairness of compensation policies, practices, and procedures relative to the performance appraisal system, the job evaluation system, and the pricing of the job structure. The first set of perceptions provides feedback on the effectiveness of each reward. Both sets of perceptions aid in the diagnostic investigations of step 4 of the action programme.

For example, suppose management had decided that the primary goal of the reward of promotion is to motivate employees to superior job performance, and this reward is therefore made contingent on superior performance. Also suppose that the survey results indicate that employees perceive promotion to be highly valuable (because it satisfies their strong esteem needs and is perceived as equitable because it is based on a performance appraisal system acceptable to employees), highly salient (because its existence and the conditions for awarding it have been frequently communicated), and based on outstanding performance. The findings suggest that there is complete congruence between the objectives of the organization and the perceptions and expectations of the employees. Consequently, management can conclude that its design and administration of the reward of promotion will be effective in eliciting the behaviour established for it.

On the other hand, suppose the survey results for this same reward indicate just the opposite: promotion is not seen by the workers as valuable, salient, or contingent. In this situation, promotion will be a meaningless reward for employees and will not produce the job behaviour intended for it by management.

Step 4: Examine the findings of the survey and investigate those rewards where the perceptions of employees relative to behaviour-reward contingency, saliency, and valence are different from those established by the organization. Such discrepancies or lack of congruence imply that the reward is not attaining the objective intended for it by management. Clues to the causes of the discrepancies will come from survey results about employee perceptions of reward valence and saliency and about employee perceptions of the fairness of compensation policies and practices.

The following situations, which use the reward of promotion as an example, show how the discrepancies revealed by the survey results could indicate that employees do not perceive promotion to be valuable, or salient, or contingent on performance.

a) *Employees do not perceive promotion to be a valuable reward.* If the results show that this reward is administered in an equitable manner, and the reward saliency is high, there can be two reasons why employees do not value the reward of promotion. The first reason is that employees lack the ability needed in the higher level job; if further investigation find this to be the case, then training is recommended. The second reason is that employees do not have a desire for enhanced self-esteem and are happy with their present jobs; if this is the case, counselling may help, followed by training. Finally, employees may perceive that the reward is administered inequitably and hence will not value it. The remedy in this case is to remove the inequities through corrective measures in the form of performance appraisals and peer evaluations. If the inequities in awarding promotions are not real but are only perceived as such, improved communication and the development of a climate of trust should help.

b) *Employees perceive promotion to be a valuable reward, but the reward saliency is low.* This situation can only be resolved by better and more frequent communication of the performance-based promotion policy.

c) *Employees do not see promotion as contingent on superior performance.* For a reward system to be effective, the contingency link must be clearly and unambiguously communicated in words and, more importantly, in deeds. If employees are not aware of the appropriate contingent behaviour for a specific reward, that reward may influence a different set of behaviours that could be counterproductive to the ones intended by management. For example, suppose the promotion policy makes promotion contingent on superior performance. However, it is common knowledge that, in practice, only employees who socialize or get along well with their supervisors are promoted. In this situation the contingency link between superior performance and promotion will be severed. What is more insidious is that the practice conveys that the way to the top is through indulging in ingratiating or similarly dysfunctional behaviour.

For reasons beyond management's control it may not be feasible to alter employee perceptions of a reward by the recommended action or by another appropriate action. It may also happen that because of legislation or contractual obligations, a particular reward cannot be made contingent on a behaviour intended for it by management. In these circumstances, management will change the behavioural objective to one that reflects the reality of the situation.

Step 5: The final, and most vital, step in the action programme is review. This consists of reformulating the reward package objectives or redesigning the reward system or both on the basis of the diagnosis of the present reward system. Employee perceptions of the personal, internal, and external equity of the compensation system are significant input to the review process. These data will point to the specific policy, technique, and process (i.e., compensation philosophy, performance appraisal, job evaluation, and job structure pricing) that needs to be modified.

These modifications will be the vehicle for corrective actions A, B, and C identified in Figure 15.1. At this stage, a great deal of learning takes place as management reflects on the perceptions and expectations of its employees and their impact on organizational goals. It is also a time for important decisions; it is time for management to respond not in a reactive mode but more in a proactive stance that considers how best the reward system can be creatively employed to cope with the new challenges that constantly confront a dynamic organization. Although review is the final step, it is also an ongoing process that enables management to keep on top of the situation at all times.

As shown in Figure 15.1, the implementation of these steps requires regular monitoring of reward attributes and appropriate response to the feedback. The next section illustrates the entire process involved in the programme.

ILLUSTRATION OF THE ACTION PROGRAMME

A study that used the procedures of the action programme tested the effectiveness of the compensation programme of a group of senior managers of a Canadian corporation.

Methodology

1. For each of the organization's 23 rewards (which included both economic compensation items such as pay and vacation and non-economic compensation items such as participation in decision making, sense of belonging, and challenge) the compensation specialist was asked to indicate

   • the targeted behaviour under the categories of retention, performance, and growth; and

   • the priority accorded to the targeted behaviour in terms of high, medium, and low. The priorities designate the type and the extent of the behaviour that management expects will be generated by the reward. If a particular behaviour was not targeted for a reward, the compensation specialist responded with a "not applicable" for that behaviour. The compensation specialist had the option of assigning equal priorities to the targeted behaviours if such were management's expectations for the reward. The status of the compensation specialist's position in the management hierarchy of this organization qualified him to reflect adequately the organization's priorities for the compensation programme. These are summarized in Table 15.1.

2. Discussions with the compensation specialist revealed that management believed that the employees were fully aware of the rewards and the contingencies involved in earning them. Management also believed that the employees placed a high value on the rewards offered by the organization. The reward system therefore operated on the assumption that each reward was perceived by the employees to be highly salient and valuable. Hence, the values assigned to saliency and valence by management were high.

Table 15.1 Summary of Reward Costs, Organizational Priority for Targeted Behaviours, and Employee Perceptions of Rewards

Reward Item	Cost of Reward as % of Total Compensation Costs	Organizational					Employees' Perceptions				
		Priority for the Targeted Behaviours of			Belief of Reward's		Reward Contingent on			Reward's	
		Retention	Performance	Growth	Saliency	Valence	Retention	Performance	Growth	Saliency	Valence
Company pension	12%	High	Medium	Low	High	High	High	Low	Low	Low	Low
Post-retirement ins.	0.11%	High	Medium	Low	High	High	High	Low	Low	Low	Low
Medicare	0.28%	High	Medium	Low	High	High	Medium	Low	Low	Low	Medium
Term life insurance	0.72%	High	Medium	Low	High	High	Medium	Low	Low	Low	Medium
Dental plan	0.50%	High	Medium	Low	High	High	Medium	Low	Low	Low	Medium
Long-term diasbility	1%	High	Medium	Low	High	High	Low	Low	Low	Low	Medium
Blue Cross plan	0.44%	High	Medium	Low	High	High	Medium	Low	Low	Low	Medium
Health insurance	3%	High	Medium	Low	High	High	Medium	Low	Low	Low	Medium
Pay	77.95%	Medium	High	Low	High	High	Medium	High	High	High	High
Salary increases	4%	Medium	High	Low	High	High	Low	High	High	Low	Medium
Job security	--	High	Medium	Low	High	High	Medium	Medium	Medium	Low	Medium
Personal challenge	--	Low	High	Medium	High	High	Low	High	High	High	High
Job variety	--	Low	High	Medium	High	High	Low	High	High	Low	High
Recognition	--	Low	High	Medium	High	High	Low	High	High	Medium	High
Achieving organizational goals	--	Medium	High	Low	High	High	Medium	High	High	Medium	Medium

Table 15.1 Continued

Reward Item	Cost of Reward as % of Total Compensation Costs	Organizational					Employees' Perceptions				
		Priority for the Targeted Behaviours of			Belief of Reward's		Reward Contingent on			Reward's	
		Retention	Performance	Growth	Saliency	Valence	Retention	Performance	Growth	Saliency	Valence
Personal growth and development	--	Medium	High	Low	High	High	Medium	High	High	High	Medium
Pride in work	--	High	Medium	Low	High	High	Medium	High	High	Low	Medium
Sense of belonging	--	High	Medium	Low	High	High	Medium	Medium	High	Medium	Medium
Participation in decision making	--	Low	Medium	High	High	High	Medium	High	High	High	High
Sick leave	-- NA	High	Medium	Low	High	High	High	Low	Low	Low	Medium
Vacation pay	-- NA	High	Medium	Low	High	High	High	Low	Low	Low	Medium
Free rail transportation	-- NA	Medium	High	Low	High	High	Low	Low	Low	Low	Low
Educational financial aid	-- NA	Low	Medium	High	High	High	Low	Low	Low	Low	Low

3. The employees were surveyed to obtain for each of the 23 rewards, their perceptions about whether the reward was contingent on retention, performance, and growth; was salient; and was valued. The median of employee perceptions was categorized as high, medium, or low for each reward item. The cost of each monetary and in-kind reward item was obtained as a percentage of the total cost of all such rewards. These data are presented in Table 15.1.

Analyses

So that the perceptions of the compensation specialist could be compared with those of the employees for each reward item, it was necessary to reduce them to a common unit of measurement. This was done by calculating two sets of three scores representing the reward's saliency, valence, and contingency. One set of scores was derived from the responses of the compensation specialist and expressed the organization's expectations and beliefs about the reward; the other set of scores was derived from employee perceptions. For saliency and valence scores, the responses of the compensation specialist and the employees, categorized as high, medium, and low, were assigned factor values of 1.00, 0.70, and 0.30 respectively.

For reward contingency, the targeted reward contingency value (TRCV) and the perceived reward contingency value (PRCV) were calculated. The TRCV combines the organizational priorities for the targeted behaviours of a reward. The PRCV combines the employees' perceptions of the contingent behaviours for a reward. For a reward item that involves a direct money or in-kind payment, the targeted and perceived reward contingency values were weighted to reflect the appropriate costs of the reward. The computation of these scores (TRCV and PRCV) is illustrated below.

For Reward Items Involving Direct Money or In-Kind Payments

The computation for this category of rewards is illustrated using the data from Table 15.1 for the reward item company pension.

a) Compute the TRCV by combining the targeted behaviours for company pension with the cost of company pension, expressed as a percentage of the total cost of the compensation package. This is done in two steps:

(1) Assign a factor value to the priority accorded to the targeted behaviours: 1.00 for high, 0.70 medium, and 0.30 for low, and 0.00 for not applicable. For company pension, the assigned factor value will be

Item	Targeted behaviours	Priority accorded	Assigned factor value
Company pension	Retention	High	1.00
	Performance	Medium	0.70
	Growth	Low	0.30

(2) Multiply the cost of company pension by the assigned factor values to obtain the targeted reward contingency value as follows:

Item	% of Total cost	x	Assigned factor value for targeted behaviour	=	Targeted reward contingency value
Company pension					
	12	x	1.00 (for retention)	=	12
	12	x	0.70 (for performance)	=	8
	12	x	0.30 (for growth)	=	4
Targeted reward contingency value (TRCV)				=	24

The TRCV of 24 represents a standard that the organization expects to attain for company pension if employees do in fact perceive this reward to be contingent on the behaviours targeted for it.

b) Compute the *perceived reward contingency* value (PRCV) by combining the perceived behaviours for company pension with the cost of company pension expressed as a percentage of the total compensation costs. This is also done in two steps:

(1) Assign factor values to employee perceptions of the contingent behaviours for each reward item: 1.00 for high, 0.70 for medium, 0.30 for low. For company pension, the assigned factor value will be

Item	Targeted behaviours	Priority accorded	Assigned factor value
Company pension	Retention	High	1.00
	Performance	Low	0.30
	Growth	Low	0.30

(2) Multiply the cost of company pension by the assigned factor values to obtain the perceived reward contingency value, as follows:

Item	% of Total cost	x	Assigned factor value for targeted behaviour	=	Targeted reward contingency value
Company pension					
	12	x	1.00 (for retention)	=	12
	12	x	0.30 (for performance)	=	4
	12	x	0.30 (for growth)	=	4
Targeted reward contingency value (TRCV)				=	20

For Rewards That Do Not Involve Money or In-Kind Payments

The computation of the targeted and perceived reward contingency values (TRCV and PRCV) for this category is illustrated below using the data from Table 15.1 for the reward personal challenge.

a) Compute the TRCV by assigning a factor value to the priority accorded to the targeted behaviours for each reward item: 1.00 for high, 0.70 for medium, 0.30 for low, 0.00 for not applicable. For personal challenge, the assigned factor value will be

Item	Targeted behaviours	Priority accorded	Assigned factor value
Personal challenge	Retention	Low	0.30
	Performance	High	1.00
	Growth	Medium	0.70
Targeted reward contingency value (TRCV)			2.00

b) Compute the PRCV by assigning a factor value to employee perceptions of the contingent behaviours for each reward item: 1.00 for high, 0.70 for medium, 0.30 for low. For personal challenge, the assigned factor value will be

Item	Targeted behaviours	Perceived contingency	Assigned factor value
Personal challenge	Retention	Low	0.30
	Performance	High	1.00
	Growth	High	1.00
Perceived reward contingency value (PRCV)			2.30

Table 15.2 shows the two sets (organization's and employees') of scores for each reward. These reward attributes have a multiplicative, motivational effect on the recipient of the reward, hence, the significance of the product of each set of scores. The product of the organization's set of scores denotes the *intended effectiveness* of each reward; whereas the product of the employees' set of scores denotes the *actual effectiveness* likely to result from employee perceptions of each reward.

Implications of the Results

The theoretical foundation for this diagnostic tool postulates that the targeted set of behaviours will be realized only to the extent that each reward item is perceived by the employees as valuable, salient, and contingent on the targeted behaviours. Therefore, a comparison of the two sets of scores (Table 15.2) helps

Table 15.2 A Comparison of the Intended and the Actual Effectiveness of Rewards

Reward Item	Organizational Score				Employees' Score				Action to Retain/ Modify*
	Targeted Reward, Contingency Value (TRCV) x	Saliency (S) X	Valence (V) =	Intended Effectiveness	Perceived Reward Contingency Value (PRCV) x	Saliency (S) X	Valence (V) =	Actual Effectiveness	
Company pension	24.00	1	1	24.00	20.00	0.3	0.3	1.80	Modify
Post-retirement ins.	0.22	1	1	0.22	0.18	0.3	0.3	0.02	Modify
Medicare	0.56	1	1	0.56	0.36	0.3	0.7	0.08	Modify
Term life insurance	1.44	1	1	1.44	0.94	0.3	0.7	0.20	Modify
Dental plan	1.00	1	1	1.00	0.65	0.3	0.7	0.14	Modify
Long-term disability	2.00	1	1	2.00	0.90	0.3	0.7	0.19	Modify
Blue Cross plan	0.88	1	1	0.88	0.57	0.3	0.7	0.12	Modify
Health insurance	6.00	1	1	6.00	3.90	0.3	0.7	0.82	Modify
Pay	155.90	1	1	155.90	210.47	1	1	210.47	Retain
Salary increase	8.00	1	1	8.00	9.20	0.3	0.7	1.93	Modify
Job security	2.00	1	1	2.00	2.10	0.3	0.7	0.44	Modify
Personal challenge	2.00	1	1	2.00	2.30	1	1	2.30	Retain
Job variety	2.00	1	1	2.00	2.30	0.3	1	0.69	Modify
Recognition	2.00	1	1	2.00	2.30	0.7	1	1.61	Modify
Achieving organizational goals	2.00	1	1	2.00	2.70	0.7	0.7	1.32	Modify
Personal growth and development	2.00	1	1	2.00	2.70	1	0.7	1.89	Modify
Pride in work	2.00	1	1	2.00	2.70	0.3	0.7	0.57	Modify
Sense of belonging	2.00	1	1	2.00	2.40	0.7	0.7	1.18	Modify
Participation in decision making	2.00	1	1	2.00	2.70	1	1	2.70	Retain
Sick leave	2.00	1	1	2.00	1.60	0.3	0.7	0.34	Modify
Vacation pay	2.00	1	1	2.00	1.60	0.3	0.7	0.34	Modify
Free rail transportation	2.00	1	1	2.00	0.90	0.3	0.3	0.08	Modify
Educational financial aid	2.00	1	1	2.00	0.90	0.3	0.3	0.08	Modify

*For illustrative examples, refer to the section Implications of the Results.

identify the relative motivational effectiveness of each reward, highlights the specific reasons why a given reward has reduced effectiveness, and provides clues for appropriate intervention to increase the effectiveness of the reward.

The next sections discuss the implications of the findings in Table 15.2 in respect to the reward items involving direct money and in-kind payments, and then in respect of the reward items that do not involve such money payments.

Rewards Involving Money and In-Kind Payments

In this category of rewards, discussion will focus on company pension and pay. For the reward of company pension, there is a glaring disparity between intended effectiveness (24) and actual effectiveness (1.80). This indicates that the organization is not achieving the targeted rate of return on its investment in the reward of company pension. The TRCV is 24; the PRCV is 20. This suggests that the employees perceive the reward as being contingent on behaviours to an extent less than that anticipated by the organization.

A closer examination of Table 15.1 shows that this disparity in reward contingency can be traced to the targeted behaviour of job performance. The priority accorded to this behaviour by the organization was medium, but employee perceptions that this reward was contingent on performance were low. Employees saw a weak link between deferred pension benefits and present job performance. If the organization still intends that the reward of company pension should have a moderate effect on performance, it should devise some form of *performance-based deferred compensation* that could be seen by the employees as eventually making a significant impact on the pension payout. If such a method is not possible or desirable, the organization must lower the priority accorded to this targeted behaviour.

From Table 15.2 it can be seen that this reward is not highly salient to employees, nor is it highly valued by them. Therefore, the organization should take steps to raise the saliency and valence of company pension. One way to increase a reward's salience is to communicate to employees periodically the salient features of the reward programme. In the case of company pension, information on how improved performance can lead to a *faster accumulation* in the fund, resulting eventually in a much *higher payout*, will increase the valence of company pension.

For the reward of pay, the intended effectiveness (156) is considerably lower than the actual effectiveness (210). This indicates that the organization has exceeded the targeted rates of return on its investment in this reward. Since employees perceive pay to be both highly salient and valued, the primary reasons for the motivational effectiveness of pay can be traced to the reward contingency. The TRCV is 156; the PRCV is 210.47. This suggests that the employees perceive the reward as being contingent on the targeted behaviours to an extent much greater than that anticipated by the organization.

From Table 15.1 it can be seen that employees perceive pay to be moderately contingent on retention and highly contingent on performance (exactly as targeted by the organization), but also as highly contingent on growth, which was not the priority accorded to it by the organization; the organization had accorded growth a low priority. Since pay functions as a powerful motivating influence in promoting the behaviours of retention, performance, and growth, this reward and the manner in which it is administered should be retained.

The other reward items in this category (money and in-kind payments) can be similarly investigated and appropriate plans of action considered.

Rewards Not Involving Money and In-Kind Payments

For this category of rewards, discussion will focus on the rewards of participation in decision making and achieving organizational goals.

The motivating effect of participation in decision making has exceeded the organization's expectations, as can be seen from the actual effectiveness value of 2.7 as against the intended effectiveness value of 2.0. Since both the organization and the employees perceive this reward to be highly salient and valued, the primary reason for the added motivational effectiveness can be traced to the reward contingency. The TRCV is 2, as compared to the PRCV of 2.7. This disparity suggests that the employees perceive this reward to be contingent on the targeted behaviours but to an extent greater than that anticipated by the organization.

From Table 15.1, it can be seen that the employees perceive this reward's contingency to be high on growth, exactly as targeted by the organization. The employees perceive the reward to be also highly contingent on job performance and moderately contingent on retention, whereas the organization had accorded performance a medium priority and retention a low priority. Participation in decision making is an effective reward in generating the behaviours of retention, performance, and growth in the right direction. It should therefore be retained.

For the reward *achieving organizational goals*, there is a disparity between the intended effectiveness (2.0) and the actual effectiveness (1.3). This disparity indicates that the motivational impact of the reward is less than was expected by the organization. The reason for this disparity is not in the reward contingency scores (PRCV of 2.3 as against the TRCV of 2.0), which shows that employees perceive this reward to be contingent on the targeted behaviours to an extent greater than that anticipated by the organization. Rather, the disparity is in employees' perceptions of saliency and valence, which is medium, in contrast to organizational expectations that the reward is highly salient and valuable to the employees. The organization should initiate measures to increase both the saliency and the valence through the effective communication of the potential benefits of this reward.

Rewards that do not involve money or in-kind payments are generally received by employees as they perform the tasks of their job. In such task-related rewards, the reward contingency is automatically perceived as the tasks are performed. Hence, the perceived reward contingency value of these rewards will generally be high. But employee perceptions of the saliency and the valence of these rewards may not be high unless the organization takes specific steps to bring about increases in the saliency and valence. Any interventions in task-related rewards call for actions to increase employee perceptions of the saliency and valence of these rewards.

All the other rewards in this category can be similarly investigated and action plans initiated to modify the reward—its design and/or its administration—suitably.

Conclusion

An organization's investment in its employee compensation programme is always at a level that cries out for innovative approaches that will ensure a reasonably fair return. The action programme is an approach that transforms the manager's role from that of a passive, helpless observer of enormous compensation expenditures to an active, confident manager who makes deliberate, conscious decisions on behavioural objectives for each reward item. By using the action programme, the manager can evaluate the effectiveness of the reward system by subjecting it to the same rigorous analysis that is routinely employed on other operating costs.

The programme also serves as a diagnostic tool. As the manager probes a reward item whose targeted objective is not being realized, the data provided by the analysis will reveal specific reasons why the objective is not being realized. The survey instrument utilized in the study, which was discussed in the preceding illustration of the "action program", focused on identifying the reward's effectiveness in respect to saliency, valence and contingency. Although this data is critical, the investigation and analysis is greatly enhanced when the instrument includes questions on employee perceptions of (a) the equity of each reward item and (b) the compensation policies, procedures and practices.

Figure 15.2 is an example of questions designed to capture employee perceptions regarding: compensation philosophy (Questions 1 and 2); performance appraisal system (Questions 3 to 9); job evaluation system (Questions 10 to 12); and salary survey practices (Questions 13 to 16). Responses to these questions reveal information which enables managers to assess the impact of specific practices on reward saliency, valence and contingency.

Figure 15.2: A Survey of Compensation Policies, Procedures and Practices

Listed below are some compensation policies, procedures, and practices. Indicate against each the extent to which you believe it exists in your organization and the manner in which it is implemented. Please indicate your response by circling the corresponding numerical value.

	Strongly Agree			Strongly Disagree		
1. My organization has a compensation philosophy.	1	2	3	4	5	6

		Strongly Agree				Strongly Disagree	
2.	The compensation philosophy has been communicated to me.	1	2	3	4	5	6
3.	My performance is periodically evaluated.	1	2	3	4	5	6
4.	I am aware of the criteria on which my performance is evaluated.	1	2	3	4	5	6
5.	Generally my supervisor does not consult me in determining the job objectives on which I will be evaluated.	1	2	3	4	5	6
6.	My supervisor is in constant dialogue with me coaching me to achieve my job objectives.	1	2	3	4	5	6
7.	My assessment of my performance is generally in agreement with my supervisor's assessment of my performance.	1	2	3	4	5	6
8.	My performance plays an important role in determining the rewards I will receive.	1	2	3	4	5	6
9.	Although I put in more time and effort and generally achieve more of the job objectives than my peers, I am paid the same as my peers.	1	2	3	4	5	6
10.	Compared to other similar jobs in the organization, the salary of my job is not equitable.	1	2	3	4	5	6
11.	I understand the mechanics (system and procedure) used to evaluate the worth of my job to the organization.	1	2	3	4	5	6
12.	There is a process which I can use to correct any inequity or unfairness which I may notice in my job evaluation.	1	2	3	4	5	6
13.	I am aware that salary surveys are conducted in my company.	1	2	3	4	5	6
14.	I am aware of the type of data collected in salary surveys.	1	2	3	4	5	6
15.	Employees have input into the salary survey process through their representatives on the compensation committee.	1	2	3	4	5	6
16.	When salaries are adjusted, the nature and form of adjustment is explained to me.	1	2	3	4	5	6

For example, suppose the study shows that an employee's valence is low for the reward item of "merit pay". Suppose, further, that employees perceive "merit pay" to be unfairly administered. In this situation, employee responses to Questions # 3 to 9, Figure 15.2, should provide the reasons for employee perceptions that "merit pay" is unfairly administered and, hence, their low valence for it. These responses also indicate specific aspects of the policies and practices relating to "merit pay" which needs to be modified in order to ensure its effectiveness. We see that the assessment of the compensation system's practices, as illustrated by Figure 15.2, provides a basis for appropriate remedial interventions. The weighting procedure of each reward by its relative cost is a useful mechanism in helping managers to focus their efforts on those rewards for which the cost-benefit consideration is the most significant.

The action programme can be implemented with relatively little effort and expense. However, its successful implementation presupposes three essential conditions. First, management must accept its responsibility to obtain a fair return on its compensation expenditures. Second, management must be committed to designing and administering the reward system in a manner which ensures that employees clearly perceive the rewards to be valuable, salient, and contingent on the targeted behaviours. Third, management must be willing to review the reward system continuously and to modify it, as necessary, in the light of organizational goals and employee perceptions relative to valence, saliency, and contingency.

Most organizations today believe that the employee compensation programme is an investment in its most valuable resource. Implementing the action programme will bring the organization a step closer to realizing the tremendous potential of that investment.

SUMMARY

This chapter considered the traditional administrative process of the salary budget, and an action plan to evaluate the effectiveness of the compensation system. The procedures involved in the top-down and the bottom-up approaches to developing a salary budget were described. Then, an action programme to evaluate the effectiveness of the reward items was considered in detail.

As shown in the description of the action programme and illustrated by data from its use in a Canadian corporation, the programme not only identifies ineffective reward items but also proposes specific remedial measures for improving their effectiveness. It must be emphasized that the programme's success depends upon management's recognition that enormous compensation expenditures are an investment rather than an expense. Furthermore, management must be committed to managing the reward system in a manner which ensures that employees clearly perceive the rewards to be valued, salient, and contingent on the targeted behaviours.

KEY TERMS ꙮ

action programme for evaluating
    employee compensation
actual effectiveness of rewards
bottom-up approach to budgeting
compa-ratio
intended effectiveness of rewards

perceived reward contingency value
    (PRCV)
targeted reward contingency value
    (TRCV)
top-down approach to budgeting

REVIEW AND DISCUSSION QUESTIONS ꙮ

1. The following table provides information on tenure, performance rating, and compa-ratio of the seven clerks in the sales department of Omega Products Limited.

Name	Gender	Performance Rating (1=low; 5=high)	Tenure (years)	Compa-ratio
Suzy	Female	5	3	.95
Frank	Male	2	3	1.10
Richard	Male	3	8	1.20
Joann	Female	4	5	.85
Harry	Male	4	6	1.23
Chantal	Female	5	7	.90
Angela	Female	5	9	.80

What might these compa-ratios mean? What areas would you wish to probe further? Why?

2. Which approach to budgeting salaries—top-down or bottom-up—would you prefer? Why?

3. Explain the underlying rationale of the action programme for evaluating the effectiveness of the compensation system.

4. Would the action programme be suitable for all organizations? Why or why not?

CASE

Getting the Motivational Bang from the Compensation Bucks

The young, dynamic president of the Canadian Transportation Company is rather uneasy about the costs of the compensation package—about 70 per cent of the total operating costs. It is not that she grudges the bill. In fact, she takes pride in being the leader in innovative compensation practices in the industry. But she wants to get her money's worth. All business expenditures (except for compensation) are rigorously reviewed to determine whether the targeted rates of return are achieved, and appropriate corrective actions are initiated. Mindful of this concern, the compensation specialist administered the diagnostic instrument of the action programme (described in the chapter) to the middle managers. Tables 15.1.1, 15.1.2, and 15.1.3 show the findings for four reward items. The compensation specialist seeks your advice, specifically:

- to interpret these findings and to explain their significance relative to the effectiveness or ineffectiveness of these items;
- to propose concrete remedial actions, where necessary.

TABLE 15.1.1. Summary of Organizational Priority for Targeted Behaviours and Employee Perceptions of Rewards

| Reward Items | Organizational Priority for Targeted Behaviour | | | | | Employee Perceptions or Reward | | | | |
| | Reward Contingent on: | | | Saliency | Valence | Reward Contingent on: | | | Saliency | Valence |
	Retention	Performance	Growth			Retention	Performance	Growth		
Merit Pay	high	high	medium	high	high	medium	medium	medium	medium	medium
Vacation	high	low	low	high	high	medium	low	low	medium	high
Educational Assistance	medium	medium	high	high	high	low	low	low	low	medium
Interesting Work	high	high	high	high	high	high	high	high	high	high

TABLE 15.1.2
Employees' Responses to the Question Whether the Rewards are Fairly Administered or Not

Reward Item	Fairly	Administered Unfairly	Undecided
Merit pay	50%	33%	17%
Vacations	100%	—	—
Educational assistance	67%	11%	22%
Interesting work	78%	5%	17%

TABLE 15.1.3
Employees' Responses to the Questions on Performance Appraisals Policies and Practices

QUESTIONS	RESPONSE (on 6 point scale) Strongly Disagree = 1 Strongly Agree = 6
My performance is periodically evaluated	5
I am aware of the criteria on which my performance is evaluated	2
My supervisor consults with me in determining the job objectives on which I will be evaluated	3
My supervisor is in constant dialogue with me, coaching me to achieve my job objectives	2
My assessment of my performance is generally in agreement with my supervisor's assessment of my performance	2
My performance plays an important role in determining the rewards I will receive	3
Although I put in more time and effort and generally achieve more of the job objectives than my peers, yet I am paid the same as my peers	5

PART V

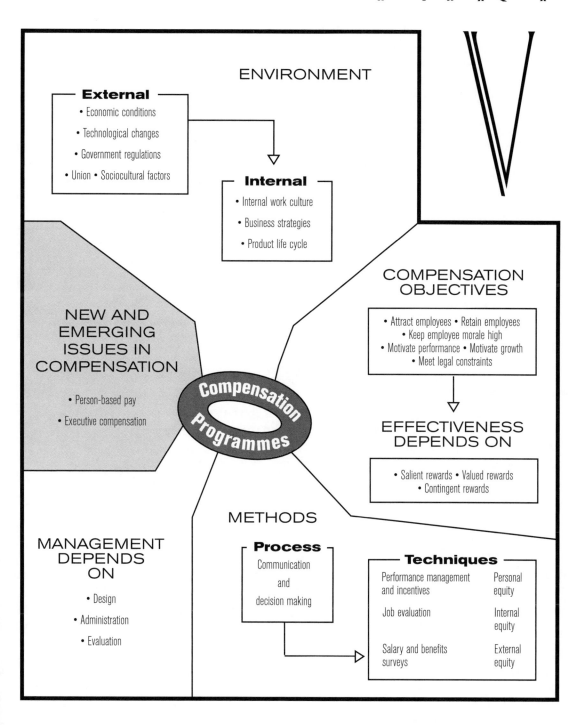

ENVIRONMENT

External
- Economic conditions
- Technological changes
- Government regulations
- Union • Sociocultural factors

Internal
- Internal work culture
- Business strategies
- Product life cycle

NEW AND EMERGING ISSUES IN COMPENSATION
- Person-based pay
- Executive compensation

Compensation Programmes

COMPENSATION OBJECTIVES
- Attract employees • Retain employees
- Keep employee morale high
- Motivate performance • Motivate growth
- Meet legal constraints

EFFECTIVENESS DEPENDS ON
- Salient rewards • Valued rewards
- Contingent rewards

MANAGEMENT DEPENDS ON
- Design
- Administration
- Evaluation

METHODS

Process
Communication and decision making

Techniques

Performance management and incentives	Personal equity
Job evaluation	Internal equity
Salary and benefits surveys	External equity

CHAPTER 16

New and Emerging Issues in Compensation

OVERVIEW

The chapter focuses on three new and emerging issues in compensation management: person-based pay; issues in executive compensation; and reward system design and management in the sociocultural context of developing countries.

LEARNING OBJECTIVES

▶ To define *person-based pay* and to distinguish it from *job-based pay*.

▶ To understand the different forms of person-based pay.

▶ To apply the concept of person-based pay to the design and implementation of multi-skilling or pay-for-skills.

▶ To discuss the advantages and disadvantages of person-based pay and to identify the conditions that favour it.

▶ To describe the components of executive compensation.

▶ To understand the basic considerations involved in the determination of each component of executive compensation.

▶ To understand the process issues in the design of executive compensation.

▶ To describe the components of the compensation package of the Canadian Members of Parliament.

▶ To understand how the major procedural steps in the evaluation of parliamentarians' compensation are consistent with the basic concepts of the effective reward management model.

▶   To describe the impact of the sociocultural environment of developing countries on reward design and management.

▶   To understand the organizational interventions and managerial strategies for the design and management of a reward system with the right cultural fit.

PERSON-BASED PAY

Limitations of the job-content-based evaluation system

Chapter 11 discussed the job-content-based job evaluation system traditionally used by organizations in designing the compensation system. The effectiveness of this approach has been questioned for several reasons (Lawler and Jenkins, 1992). Its focus on job descriptions and responsibility levels that reflect hierarchical relationships reinforces traditional bureaucratic management. The job-content-based job evaluation system measures the worth of employees in terms of their jobs—what they do in terms of the demands of the job rather than what they can do in terms of skills repertoire. Since the job value employee's pay is largely based on the content of the job description, employees often "dress up" their job description to increase the value of their job. As well, the job evaluation system becomes an end in itself, instead of a means of supporting the organization's business objectives and strategies. Today's turbulent business environment demands a compensation system that motivates people to learn, grow and develop; that rewards them as they acquire more skills and become more flexible; and that promotes employee involvement and commitment.

An emerging alternative approach to compensation system design, is person-based pay (Lawler and Jenkins, 1992). A Conference Board of Canada study (Booth, 1990) found that about 16% of the respondent organizations had used person-based pay and "...that their experience with this alternative form of pay has been positive" (p.21). This section explores person-based pay in terms of definition, different forms, design mechanics, merits, and challenges.

Definition

In the person-based pay approach employees' pay is determined by the skills or knowledge they possess even though they may not use all the skills and knowledge on the job. Person-based pay is also referred to as multi-skilling or as a knowledge-based pay (KNP) system.

Forms of person-based pay

Of the different forms or types of skill and knowledge acquisition which person-based pay can foster we focus on three types of skills: horizontal skills; in-depth skills; and upwardly vertical skills (Lawler, 1990).

Horizontal Skills The form of person-based pay that fosters the acquisition of horizontal skills can be used in both manufacturing and non-manufacturing jobs. However, it is used more frequently in manufacturing jobs. The employee's pay increases as he or she acquires the skills needed for all the related jobs in an integrated production process.

> Manufacturing jobs—an example The person-based pay system of the Shell Canada Chemical Company plant in Sarnia, Ontario provides a good illustration of the horizontal skills type of person-based pay. On entry to the Sarnia plant, the employee's salary is $1,124. After satisfactory completion of the basic training as determined by appropriate tests and measures, the employee receives a raise. The employee can earn future raises by progressively acquiring proficiency in the job knowledge clusters and competency in the four modules of the specialty skill that is established for that raise. Thus, the employee with the top salary of $1,698 will have demonstrated proficiency in the 10 job knowledge clusters, and competency in the 40 modules of such specialty skills as instrumentation, electrical, pipefitting, millwrighting, and so forth.
>
> The expected level of competency is not journey level, but just enough to cope successfully with the relatively less complex situations that frequently crop up. The more complex problems are attended to by the journey-level workers. An employee who has completed all or part of the job knowledge clusters and specialty skill modules would be in a job that does not use all the acquired competencies, but the salary rate of the employee would nevertheless be based on the acquired competencies.

> Non-manufacturing jobs—an example The person-based pay approach can also be used in non-manufacturing jobs. Suppose that the human resource department sees that it can better serve the organization if the specialists acquired the knowledge, skills and abilities in training and development. To achieve this, the staffing manager would receive additional remuneration when he or she acquires the competencies in training and development.

In-depth Skills Person-based pay promotes in-depth skills acquisition when it rewards the acquisition of in-depth knowledge of a job. Its focus might also be increased specialization or expertise in the same job, rather than the acquisition of knowledge of other jobs.

> Manufacturing jobs—an example In manufacturing jobs, an example of in-depth skills acquisition would be to pay the maintenance and repair technicians more as they achieve greater skill levels in their field.

Non-manufacturing jobs—some examples Jobs of research scientists illustrate well this focus on the acquisition of in-depth knowledge and expertise, because such acquisition generally increases the likelihood that individuals will become more innovative and productive in their work. Another illustration of knowledge-based pay is the system used by several public school boards for its teachers.

The Montreal Catholic School Commission, the largest single school board in Canada, pays its teachers on the basis of *scolarité*, the total number of years of schooling. For example, a teacher who holds a bachelor's degree will ordinarily be credited with 16 years of schooling, computed as follows: 11 years for high school, 2 years for CEGEP (the college-level program in Quebec), and 3 years for undergraduate studies. For every additional 30 university credits in a recognized certificate, diploma, or degree programme acquired by the teacher, he/she receives an additional year of schooling, which entitles him/her to a salary raise. However, there are no differences in the teaching job of teachers. It is quite common for multisections—say of Grade 9 Canadian history—to be taught by teachers whose years of schooling ranges from 15 to 20 years.

Upwardly Vertical Skills This type of person-based pay is designed to encourage employees to learn skills and acquire competencies which are ordinarily performed at higher job levels. Generally, these relate to planning, coordinating, directing, and developing interpersonal skills.

Manufacturing jobs—an example In the manufacturing context, these skills are essential when organizations intend to promote autonomous or self-regulating work teams. These teams assume full responsibility for the operations including such activities as hiring, training, and appraising team members; developing production schedules; inventory control; quality control; and problem-solving. The role of the supervisor is generally limited to functioning as a "resource" person in these areas.

Non-manufacturing jobs—an example At the supervisory and middle management levels, the upwardly vertical skills approach would reward the acquisition of knowledge and competencies needed at the next higher management levels.

The Design Mechanics of Person-based Pay

To illustrate the major procedural steps in the design of person-based pay, we draw on the case study of the Pay-for Skills (PFS) plan at the General Mills' Squeeze-it beverage manufacturing facilities. The plant uses a continuous process technology which requires constant monitoring and control for the timely detection of production and quality problems. The objective of the person-based pay system was to equip workers to detect problems even if they are not in their work areas (Ledford, Jr., and Bergel, 1991).

The critical steps in the design mechanics of a skill-based pay are briefly described:

1. Creating Skill Blocks: A "skill block" is a package of critical skills that are used in the work system. At General Mills, the plan decided on four skill blocks; the skills content of each block are specific to the four basic work areas in the production process: materials handling, mixing, filling, and packaging. Within each skill block, three skill levels were identified which resulted in a total of twelve skill levels. The skill levels are then defined in terms of related work criteria.

2. Pricing the Skills Levels: This step involves three basic activities. First, the relevant labour market is surveyed and pay rates data gathered on jobs which are comparable to the lowest and highest skills levels identified in the previous step. Second, the pay rates for the lowest and highest skill levels are established based on the company's pay level policy to lead, lag behind, or be equal to the market. In the person-based system, employees at the lowest skill levels are generally paid the entry level rate that is comparable to the market rate. Employees at other skill levels tend to earn pay rates that are higher than the market rates.

   In fact, a strict comparison between company jobs and market jobs is not possible because jobs with such skill blocks do not exist in the market. For this reason, the organization's pay level policy will tend towards the low end of the market rates. The market rates are surveyed periodically to assure that the differentials between the lowest and highest skill level rates are competitive with market rates. At General Mills, after the highest and lowest skill levels rates are set, the Pay-for-Skills Design Committee assigns pay rates to the other skill levels.

3. Training and Skills Certification: Supervisors and peers are generally involved in the training. At General Mills' Squeeze-it plant, the employees play a significant role in the training and certification of each other.

   An "employee-trainer" is one who is certified for a skill level and has the responsibility to train an employee who desires to acquire that skill level. It is also the responsibility of the employee-trainer to certify that the trainee can perform the skills of that level. The certified employee is then placed or rotated into a work area in order to practice the newly acquired skill. Generally, the trainee is rotated into the position of the employee-trainer who can now be released for training to acquire another skill level.

4. Communication: Although communication appears last in the sequence of procedural steps, it is the thread which holds together the entire system. At General Mills, the employees or team members were kept informed by the

Pay-for-Skills Design Committee through oral and written reports. Before the plan was finalized and presented for management's approval, each team had an opportunity to fully discuss the plan and submit their views to the Design Committee.

It is noteworthy that the plan mechanics are consistent with the fundamental elements which make pay effective: saliency, contingency, and valence.

Merits and Challenges of Person-based Pay

The underlying rationale for multi-skilling and knowledge-based pay systems is that such systems increase employee productivity and satisfaction and make employees more valuable to the organization. Specific merits and challenges of person-based pay system have been identified (Lawler and Jenkins, 1992).

Merits The merits mainly relate to a flexible workforce that has a better understanding of the strategies and operations of the organization. When the workforce is flexible, the production process does not experience the disruptions that might be caused by employee absenteeism. A flexible workforce is better prepared to adapt to technological and production process changes. Because of multi-skilling, employees are better informed and more knowledgeable about their own tasks as well as of those of the work unit. They are also more involved in the problem-solving and decision-making activities of the work unit.

A person-based pay system gives employees an opportunity to get an overview of the entire operation. This is particularly so in the case of self-regulating work teams which are made possible by the acquisition of horizontal and upwardly vertical skills. Jobs in such a system tend to be relatively high on skill variety, task identity, task significance, autonomy, and feedback. Consequently, as discussed in Chapter 6, employees will experience the critical psychological states of meaning, responsibility, and knowledge of work results, producing high internal work motivation. The resulting increased involvement and commitment will also make employees more alert to spot opportunities for innovation in their work unit, which significantly enhances the organization's effectiveness.

Challenges The challenges of the person-based pay are increased labour and training costs, reduced productivity during learning periods, unfulfilled expectations, and skill obsolescence.

Increased labour and training costs These are to a considerable extent offset by increased productivity, a reduced level of staffing, and the substantial benefits that accrue from a flexible, motivated, and committed workforce.

Reduced productivity The issue of reduced productivity during the training period has several aspects. First, production will be affected while the employee is away on training. Second, since the system rewards the acquisition of skills, some employees acquire additional skills without giving themselves the time to develop the high level of competence that can only come from practice. This issue, however, may be more a criticism of the implementation of the person-based pay system than of the system itself. Organizations can address this issue by requiring that employees not be permitted to acquire an additional skill unless they have spent a period of time on the job practising the previously acquired skill, and developing a certain level of competence in it.

Unfulfilled expectations The negative effects of unfulfilled expectations can be quite serious and need to be properly managed. One of these effects is the *topping out* effect (Lawler and Jenkins, 1992). The topping out effect is produced when employees have acquired all the possible skills and are now earning the top pay. The system does not provide an opportunity for further increases in salary. For example, when a Shell Canada Chemical Company employee in Sarnia becomes proficient in the 10 job knowledge clusters and the 40 specialty skill modules, he/she will feel frustrated if there are no opportunities for further salary raises or career progression.

Skills obsolescence Another negative effect occurs when changes in technology render certain skills obsolete. Appropriate strategies to cope with these negative effects are a well-designed career-development plan and a gain-sharing plan. Employees also experience frustration when they do not have opportunities to use their skills which may atrophy as a result. To address this situation, the person-based pay system should develop a sound job rotation programme.

To conclude: On balance, the advantages of a person-based pay system significantly outweigh the disadvantages. However, organizations will be able to reap the full benefits of a person-based pay system only when the beliefs and values of management are consistent with the underlying philosophy of the person-based pay system.

The person-based pay system works best when management genuinely believes that its employees have high growth needs, and that they seek and can handle challenge, autonomy, and responsibility. Management recognizes that in a state of frequent and turbulent changes, the organization can respond effectively to new opportunities and challenges only when its employees are afforded opportunities for growth and development. Hence, the job design will include enriched jobs and autonomous work teams. The person-based pay system is the appropriate reward strategy for organizations with such a participative work culture.

ISSUES IN EXECUTIVE COMPENSATION

INTRODUCTION

- The *Montreal Gazette*, recently reported that university administrators in Quebec were paid six-figure salaries which, in many cases, were higher than the salary of the province's education minister and even of the province's premier. The report also observed that the cuts in education funding did not affect the perks enjoyed by the university administrators (Thompson, 1995).

- Canadian Members of Parliament are entitled to a retiring allowance equal to 30 percent of the average sessional allowance after a 6-year term and it increases by 5 percent for each additional year up to a maximum of 75 percent after 15 years (Martel and Pouliot, 1994).

- In 1994, the highest paid executive in Canada "...took home more than Cdn $40.7 million...a record for executive pay in Canada..." (*Financial Post Daily*, 1995, p.6); that same year, the highest paid executive in the United States made US$25.9 million which is only 13% of the $203 million paid to Disney's CEO in 1993 (Byrne and Bengiorno, 1995).

The public's interest and concern raised by executive compensation is understandable, if for no other reason than the sheer magnitude of the numbers involved. However, as taxpayers, consumers, and shareholders, one has a legitimate curiosity about the basis of such compensation levels. In the UK, an executive's salary is the subject of parliamentary hearings and it is only one-third of the average US executive's salary (Byrne and Bongiorno, 1995). The fundamental issue is whether the compensation be that of university administrator, parliamentarians, or CEOs, reflects the "value" provided to their respective organizations.

As Jensen and Murphy (1990) observed: "The relentless focus on how *much* CEOs are paid diverts public attention from the real problem—*how* CEOs are paid. In most publicly held companies, the compensation of top executives is virtually independent of performance" (p.138). Implicit in the issue of "value" is the issue of equity or fairness—a recurring and dominant issue in compensation. A glaring fact in executive compensation in North America is the wide gap between a CEO's compensation and that of the lowest paid employee. Although figures vary, "... the senior executive in a large corporation is typically paid at least fifty times more than the lowest-paid employee in the same corporation...the top-to-bottom ratio is about nine to one in Japan and perhaps fifteen or sixteen to one in Europe" (Lawler, 1990, p.188).

It is necessary to recognize the difficulties inherent in drawing inferences from media reports because such data can be presented differently in different publications. Baytos (1991) cites the media reports on Heinz CEO's compensation. The total pay varied considerably as presented in four reputable publications ($2.1 million [on an annual basis] in *Fortune*; $9.7 million [over 3-year period] in *Business Week*; $4.9 million in *Forbes*; $3.0 million [on annual basis] in *CEO Magazine*. Also, the reporting in *Fortune, Business Week,* and *Forbes* seemed to suggest that this CEO's compensation level was high; whereas *CEO Magazine* implied that the CEO was underpaid.

Therefore, a meaningful discussion of executive compensation can only take place in the context of a conceptual framework which provides a sound basis for assessment. In terms of the Effective Reward Management model presented in the text, the compensation package design should support the organization's mission and objectives—both short and long-term—and meet the tests of internal, personal, and external equity. The design process should be open and transparent, free of undue political manoeuvring in the choice of survey data and total pay positioning of the company. Keeping these criteria in mind, our discussion will cover the component elements of executive compensation; the design features of each component and the process mechanism in the design and administration of compensation.

Finally, we briefly describe some issues in the compensation of a relatively special group—Canadian Members of Parliament. Its objective is to illustrate the analysis, which is necessary and possible, in order to evaluate the compensation of groups that may not easily lend themselves to such analysis.

COMPONENTS OF EXECUTIVE COMPENSATION

The component elements of executive compensation are base salary, short-term incentives, long-term incentives, benefits, and perquisites. A study of 282 firms in the Toronto Stock Exchange's 300 Index found that on average a CEO's compensation mix was: 46 percent salary, 51 percent incentives, and 3 percent other sources (*Financial Post Daily*, 1995). We shall now discuss how each is determined.

Base Salary

Base salary is determined by the salary structure of the organization. Jobs are evaluated using a job evaluation system, and then priced in accordance with the organization's pay level policy in relation to pay data from salary surveys. Such surveys are generally from comparable organizations, but should also include the competition in order to ensure the organization's cost competitiveness. The point factor system of job evaluation, discussed in Chapter 11, is considered to be the most popular approach (Crystal, 1984). It is important that the job evaluation system is designed to capture the critical components of managerial resourcefulness such as affective, intellectual, and action-oriented competencies (Kanungo and Misra, 1992).

The pay level policies, salary survey procedures, and the process of constructing a salary structure is discussed in Chapter 13. However, in assessing and choosing the salary data, the organizational and job characteristics which should be considered are the level of company's assets, industry, the job reporting level, profit levels, and the number of employees directly supervised and number of subordinate levels. As well, it must consider whether the job entitles the holder to membership of the board of directors (Crystal, 1984).

Generally, the greater the size of assets and the higher the profit levels, the greater is the company's capacity to pay a higher base pay. Also, the greater the number of employees directly reporting to the job and the more subordinate levels under it, the greater the responsibilities and the higher the job's base pay will be. The base pay will also be higher if the job reports directly to the CEO or is entitled to a seat on the board of directors. The type of industry can also make a difference to the base pay data. For example, companies in the energy industry typically tend to pay more than those in the chemical industry. Hence, a consideration of the organizations and jobs represented in the survey data allows for better decisions on the appropriateness of the data to one's organization.

It is necessary to recognize the fact that the relatively high executive compensation in the United States—about the highest in the world—makes it extremely costly for Canadian corporations to attract talent from US firms. In addition to the higher US salary in absolute terms, there is the cost of translating it into Canadian dollars. "Ironically, you can get away with a huge spike in salary for a CEO because he or she has no peer...where you run into problems is when you hire a senior vice-president of marketing who's standing shoulder to shoulder with five other SVPs and making twice what they are" (*Financial Post*, 1995, p. 57).

Unlike other employee groups, executives generally do not receive across-the-board cost of living adjustments. However, the base pay adjustment for cost of living is made through the annual salary increase although such increases are generally made in order to keep the salary competitive.

Short-term incentives

Annual bonus, or short-term incentives, are offered by most organizations. In Canada, cash bonus plans in addition to merit or annual increases exist in about 79% of the organizations and extends to 93% of the executives. The success of the plans in meeting their objectives is rated as 3.5 where 1 is low and 5 is high (Booth, 1990). The eligibility criteria for participating in bonus plans vary.

Good bonus plans are generally designed to reflect performance such as return on equity, return on assets, earnings per share, operating income, net income, development of new products/services and market share. If the organization operates solely within one industry, performance measure should reflect corporate-wide performance. However, if the organization has different, unrelated product divisions, it should adopt a plan which reflects both divisional and corporate performance. The performance criteria can also be varied to make it more appropriate to the life-cycle stage of the division. Thus, the progress of product development is appropriate in the start-up stage, market share and earnings in the growth stage, and cashflow and return on equity in the mature stage (Chingos, 1991).

As discussed in Chapter 10, the risk-reward linkage in variable pay should be greater for employees at the higher organizational levels. Since bonus is a variable component of total pay, its payout design should reflect this risk-reward relationship. Other considerations for determining the fixed-variable mix are responsibility for operating results, the extent to which the performance measure is within the executives' control, whether the results can be measured, and the practices in competitor organizations.

In some bonus plans, a part of the payout might be deferred; the right to the deferred amount vests in the employee only if the employee stays with the company for a stipulated number of years. Such deferral provisions, often referred to as the "golden handcuffs", are intended to promote employee retention.

Long-term incentives

The various forms of long-term incentives are stock option plans, stock grant plans, and stock purchase plans. These have been described in Chapter 10. As a component of total pay, long-term incentives are becoming increasingly larger to the point that, in some cases, they exceed the value of the entire base salary (Crystal, 1984). The major criticism is that these payouts do not reflect corporate performance; instead, they "... represent a transfer of wealth from shareholders to executives" (Jensen and Murphy, 1990, p.139).

In order to remedy this situation Jensen and Murphy (1990) have put forward two policies. First, CEOs should be required to own a substantial percentage of the total stock of the company. This requirement will provide for a greater and meaningful shareholder wealth-executive wealth linkage. Second, a CEO's compensation should be structured in a manner that provides for big rewards for outstanding performance as well as big penalties for mediocre and poor performance. However, in practice, stock options are exercised only when the stock value increases; when the stock value falls, the stock options are not exercised, and the CEOs are not penalized.

Since the values of stock-based incentives depend on stock market fluctuations which are beyond the CEOs control, cash compensation should be linked to performance such as return on equity relative to the performance of comparable companies. Such linkage can also serve to compensate CEOs who hold substantial company stock when its market value decreases despite outstanding company performance. "In some cases, it might even make sense for pay to go up in bad years to serve as a financial *shock absorber* for losses the CEO is taking in the stock market" (Jensen and Murphy, 1990, p.142). Thus, the requirement that CEOs hold substantial company stock creates an incentive for CEOs to attend to the long-term interests of the company. By relating cash compensation to corporate performance relative to comparable companies, the CEO is appropriately rewarded or penalized.

Benefits

Some of the typical benefits received by executives are pensions, life and medical insurance, and "golden parachute" agreements. Although they are similar to those received by other employee groups, these benefits generally tend to be at higher levels since several of these are computed on the individual's salary. The "golden parachute" agreement comes into operation when there is a "change of control" in the company, such as a hostile takeover of the company. In this situation, executives are fired or opt to leave, and these executives are entitled to exercise their rights under the agreement if one exists. Such an agreement provides for the continuation of salary and short-term incentives for periods that may range from two to five years, and, depending upon the agreement, may cease when the executive takes up another job. These agreements are intended to protect the top executives who "...are the most vulnerable ... especially if they fought the takeover and thereby caused the acquiring company to have to pay more than otherwise might have been the case"(Crystal, 1984, p.170).

Perquisites

Executives receive a variety of perquisites, also known as "perks. Examples are, a company car, first-class travel, club memberships, financial, tax, and legal counselling, and liberal expense accounts. Originally, there were two reasons for executive perks. One was symbolic of the executives' status in the organization. The other was the high taxes on cash income. However, the tax advantage is gradually disappearing as tax laws are amended to treat several of these as taxable income. Although the desire for the status symbol continues, one notices an increasing sensitivity of CEOs to the public's adverse reactions to perks as status symbols, particularly in organizations which seek to promote participative management and a high employee-involvement culture. For example, many organizations have discontinued the first-class travel perk, except for long distance travel.

THE PROCESS ISSUES IN EXECUTIVE COMPENSATION

The responsibility for executive compensation rests with the compensation committee set up by the board of directors. Largely because of the publicity generated by the executive compensation disclosure requirements of the

Ontario Securities Commission, an increasing number of boards have set up compensation committees (*Maclean's*, 1995). The members of this committee are selected from among the "independent directors", those who are not eligible to participate in the compensation plans.

When we discussed the issue of base pay, we highlighted the issues of internal and external equity. However, it is necessary to recognize the possibility of self-serving behaviour on the part of CEOs which can distort the committee's decision making. For instance, Crystal (1991) provides interesting experiences of how regardless of the merits of the case, the process can be manipulated to increase the CEO's compensation. Thus, when the CEO's compensation fairly reflects the organization's performance, pay data from organizations with a "lead" pay level policy is used to justify increasing the CEO's salary.

On the other hand, when the CEOs' compensation is high relative to the organization's poor performance, it is argued that the generally low pay levels for executives might lead to a turnover of competent executives. This argument seems to result in compensation increases for all executives, including the CEO. Of course, the issue of the organization's poor performance, despite such competent executives, is conveniently ignored. Perhaps it is believed that were it not for the sound decisions and direction by these competent executives, the organization's performance might have been worse.

However, there are signs that "... boards of directors have indeed been over-hauling pay practices to tie pay to performance as never before...CEOs these days stand to see their pay shrink if they fail to deliver the goods to shareholders" (Byrne and Bongiorno, 1995, p.88). In this process, the very first step is to develop and communicate the organization's compensation philosophy, which will support the organization's mission and objectives. Instead of vague, meaningless generalities such as "to provide highly competitive and excellent compensation", Johnson (1991) advocates that the compensation philosophy statement include specifics in relation to:

- the goal—will it be a 15% return on equity?

- the competitiveness—which organizations?

- pay level policy—at, below, or above the median pay rates?

- what percentile of the median pay rates will be paid at what performance levels?

The compensation philosophy should also be specific on the emphasis on short-term and long-term performance for determining bonuses and incentives. For example, the Booth (1990) survey indicates that respondent organizations preferred a 50/50-split for short-term/long-term incentives, but, in fact, the existing emphasis is 75 percent for short-term and 25 percent for long-term incentives.

Baytos (1991) suggests some ways in which the organization's top human resource professional can assist the compensation committee. First, develop and present competitive pay data in its proper perspective. In other words, show how the organization's performance and pay levels compare with the industry-specific profitability and pay levels. For this purpose, the necessary documentation should be provided and full discussion of the issues encouraged. Second, present a reasonable range of options including the likely costs and consequences of each. Third, although it is helpful to have information about practices in other organizations, it is more important to assess these practices in light of your own organization's compensation philosophy.

The compensation committees of several organizations in Canada use compensation consultants with the skills and expertise and the fortitude to withstand political pressures. "The board wants someone who can go toe-to-toe with the CEO. There's no point in hiring someone who will cave in psychologically to the CEO, who, let's face it, got there because he's aggressive and assertive" (*Maclean's*, 1995, p.50).

The issues of internal and external equity as well as of personal or individual equity are critical to the credibility of the compensation system. Traditionally, considerable secrecy surrounds the compensation system. For this reason, the design and management process, including communication and employee involvement, becomes even more crucial. When senior managers are not involved in the process, it is not uncommon for a manager to "create" significant additional responsibilities for his or her reports to be placed in the higher grade and, thereby, get more pay. "If the manager gets his way, it won't be long before managers in other departments hear of this success story and begin to place their own form of pressure on the compensation group" (Crystal, 1970, p.57).

A compensation system should be perceived by executives to be equitable in order that it may have the desired motivational value. It should, at the same time, support the organization's objectives, and be in the best interests of the shareholders. Designing a compensation system to serve both these ends is indeed a major challenge. Profit sharing plans tend to emphasize relatively short-term objectives which may not be in the best interests of the organization. Furthermore, the accounting criteria, inherent in the determination of profitability, have the potential to be manipulated to show a higher current profit level. The long-term incentive plans also tend to be problematic. These plans might not motivate executives because they do not have control over the market-based performance indicators, or because executives' tolerance for risk is low. On the other hand, these plans might induce executives to make risky decisions which may not be in the best interests of the shareholders (Pennings, 1991).

The lack of congruence between the goals of the shareholders, as represented by the board of directors, and executives, and the resulting conflict between the two is discussed at length in the agency theory literature (refer to review by Eisenhardt, 1989). Briefly stated, agency theory deals with the principal-agent relationship. This relationship results from a contract, expressed or implied, in which the agent (the senior executives) undertakes to operate in the best interests of the principal (the board of directors). In return, the principal undertakes to compensate the agent for all reasonable expenses incurred in the course of the execution of the mandate. The principal-agent relationship is fruitful and harmonious when both share the same goals, and when the principal has the capacity to determine that the agent has operated within the terms of the mandate.

In addition to the lack of goal congruence between shareholders and executives, the other major reason for the conflict, is that the board of directors do not have the same access to information, as executives do. Without such information it becomes difficult for the board to properly evaluate whether executives have performed in the best interests of the shareholders and to reward them accordingly (Eisenhardt, 1989). A closer examination of this conflictual relationship, in the context of the executives' role in the organization, suggests that the underlying reasons for the conflict would not exist if executives performed their proper role of leadership.

Let us consider the role of the CEO. The organization, including its board of directors, expects the CEO to provide leadership which clearly goes beyond maintaining the status quo. The true leadership role entails the assessment of the deficiencies in the status quo and of opportunities for growth. Based on this assessment the leader formulates a vision which benefits and is consistent with the values of the organization's stockholders. However, formulating and articulating the vision is not enough. The leader must demonstrate the competence and expertise and, equally important, the willingness to pursue the vision even at personal sacrifice. These leader behaviours, characteristic of charismatic or transformational leaders, (Conger and Kanungo, 1988b; 1992) effectively address the source of the conflictual relationship.

First, the vision, undoubtedly, incorporates the long-term interests of the organization, constitutes the core of its mission, and becomes the guiding principle for its strategic and operational decisions. Consequently, senior executives should expect their compensation to be based on the extent to which they succeed in leading the organization closer to the realization of its vision. In more concrete terms, the senior executives' compensation should reflect the organization's performance in achieving long-term corporate objectives in strategic areas, as can be determined from the appropriate corporate-level performance indicators.

This approach means a relatively heavy risk-burden on senior executives, but it also means an opportunity to earn higher rewards commensurate with the risks involved. It is also consistent with their strategic positions and the impact of their decisions on the organization's long-term growth and effectiveness. Accepting risks and personal sacrifice are the ingredients of true and effective leadership. When senior executive's compensation design is based on these considerations, the interests of the shareholders and other stockholders are well-served.

Second, we cannot ignore the fact that the executive's leadership role also has ethical dimensions which impose on executives the obligation to subject "...the vision as well as the means to achieve it to the rigorous scrutiny of the purpose that it is intended to serve" (Kanungo and Mendonca, 1996, p.98). As an ethical leader, the executive makes full disclosure of the relevant information on the vision and its purpose which, ultimately, is to serve the interests of all the stakeholders of the organization.

It is worthwhile to recall Deming's remedy to one of management's deadly diseases: "Create constancy of purpose toward improvement of product and service, aiming to become competitive, to stay in business, and to provide jobs" (Gartner and Naughton, 1996, p.303). Thus, the source of the conflictual relationship between executives and board of directors can perhaps be traced to the absence of ethical leadership at senior executive levels, as reflected in their lack of commitment to the organization's vision and purpose.

COMPENSATION ISSUES OF CANADIAN MEMBERS OF PARLIAMENT

Canadian Members of Parliament (hereafter referred to as "MP") are in a sense similar to the executives of the corporation. Their decisions have the potential for great impact over large numbers of people and for long periods of time. Their compensation is not based on actual hours worked. Rather, it is intended to enable them to fulfil a set of obligations and responsibilities. Many parliamentarians have held executive positions which they interrupt during their term of office as MPs, and often return to executive jobs at their previous or higher organizational levels.

Parliamentarians are similar to corporation executives in respect of the tremendous interest which the electorate has in their compensation. Of all the component elements of their compensation package, the pension plan, voted in by themselves, is the subject of much public condemnation. This plan is perceived by the public to offer not only overly generous benefits, but to also permit "double-dipping". This term is used to describe the situation of the individual who, after ceasing to be a MP, is employed by the federal government or its agencies and, as a result, (a) receives the regular compensation of the new job, (b) continues to receive their MP's pension, and (c) is also able to eventually qualify for another pension according to the pension program that exists in the new job.

The President of the Treasury Board commissioned Sobeco Ernst & Young Inc. to study, evaluate, and make appropriate recommendations on MP's compensation package. The topics and related issues discussed in this section is based entirely on a report (Martel and Pouliot, 1994) of that study.

Compensation Package: Elements & Compensation Value

The major elements of the parliamentarians' compensation package are: sessional indemnity and additional allowances when assigned additional responsibilities; expense allowance; travel allowance; pension plan and insurance programs; and career transition provisions.

A compensation element is defined to have "compensation value" when it is not intended for expenses that are incurred and required by the position. In other words, an element has "compensation value" when it becomes a source of income for the recipient. The total compensation of the MPs is determined by adding up the compensation value of each element of the compensation package. The compensation value, in the case of deferred benefits, is the "present value" of such benefits.

Sessional Indemnity and Additional Allowances

All members of parliament are entitled to sessional indemnity of $64,400 per year. It corresponds to the base pay of Member of Parliaments (MP). An additional allowance is paid to some MPs when they hold positions such as Speaker or Cabinet Minister.

Expense Allowance The expense allowance—$21,300 per year—is a non-taxable allowance and MPs are not required to account for it. It is intended to compensate MPs for expenses they incur in order to perform their duties. However, the study found that it is used for expenses such as housing and lodging; donations and miscellaneous contributions; business meals; travelling expenses; social activities; and clothing. All MPs receive the same amount regardless of their place of original residence. Consequently, those whose original residence is not in the Ottawa area might experience inequity relative to those whose original residence is in the Ottawa area.

In fact, the public believes that this expense allowance should be "...considered as the equivalent of a salary of $42,600, i.e., $21,300 x 2, since it is non-taxable" (Martel and Pouliot, 1994, p.10). To reduce the inequity, the report proposed that instead of an allowance, it be designed as a reimbursable item on production of expense vouchers. The proposed change will reflect its original purpose—to pay for job-related expenses. It will also eliminate its potential to become a source of income for some MPs and not for others, and the resulting inequity that it creates.

Travel Allowance The travel allowance is made up of two elements. First, an allowance for accommodation and meals when MPs travel between Ottawa and their constituency provided the distance between the two is more than 100 km. This allowance, payable on production of appropriate expense vouchers, is up to a maximum of $6,000 per year. Since it is a reimbursable item, it has no compensation value. The second element is the transportation costs—air and rail. The air transportation is on a point-system basis which works out to 64 return air trips. There is not much restriction on rail travel.

The design of both items makes it possible for these to be used by the MPs or their family and staff for trips that are related, as well as for trips that are unrelated, to the MPs' duties. In the latter case, it cannot strictly be deemed to be a job-related expense. For this reason, the report attributed compensation value to some portion of the transportation benefit—thus: $4,000 per year for air transportation and $500 per year for rail transportation.

Pension Plan The total value of the pension plan for MPs as computed by the study is equal to 55.1 percent of the sessional indemnity and additional allowances. However, since MPs contribute 11 percent to the plan, the net figure for the purpose of the compensation value is 44.1 percent. Thus, for MPs without additional responsibilities, its compensation value is $28,400—that is, 44.1% of $64,400 (sessional indemnity).

Insurance Programs The insurance program covers life insurance for self, spouse, and each dependent child; health insurance; dental insurance; long term disability insurance; and special risks insurance. The compensation value of the entire insurance program was computed as 6.9% of the sessional indemnity and additional allowances. For MPs with sessional indemnity only, this amounted to $4444, that is, 6.95% of $64,400.

Career Transition Provisions Included in these are severance allowance, resettlement, and moving expenses. Only MPs who have held office for less than 6 years and, are not entitled to the pension plan receive a severance allowance. Its compensation value was computed at $2,576, that is, 4% of $64,400.

The resettlement provisions apply to members who are not re-elected. It consists of reimbursing expenses for career transition support up to a maximum of $9,000. Its compensation value was computed at $450, that is, 0.7 percent of the sessional indemnity of $64,400. Since the moving expenses are reimbursable as actual expenses, no compensation value was assigned to this item.

Process and Basis for Recommendation The total compensation value of the preceding items for a MP without additional allowances was computed at $104,770 per year. Some of the major process steps and basis for determining compensation value is outlined below:

The first step was to identify, analyze and evaluate each element of the compensation package and to derive its compensation value.

The second step was to compare the MPs' total "compensation value" with that paid to comparable positions in the public and private sectors, as well as to legislators in other countries. The choice for comparator groups was based on the following considerations:

a) different interest groups were surveyed to determine which positions in the public and private sectors they deemed to be comparable to the MPs;

b) the types of positions held by MPs before election and after they ceased to be MPs.

As a result, the comparator groups were legislators in other countries (UK, France, Sweden, Australia, USA, Belgium); provincial legislators in Quebec, Ontario, and British Columbia; federal public servants; general managers, school principals; chiefs of police; executive positions in small, medium-sized, and large companies; and self-employed professionals. Also of interest were those positions whose total compensation was at the same level as the MPs, because this provided an opportunity to assess if any similarities in responsibility levels existed between the two.

The study proposed the following guidelines or principles which can serve as the basis for determining MP's compensation. First, the compensation package level should attract and retain capable people and not cause financial hardship to them. Second, all reimbursable expenses should have specific, job-related objectives and take into account legitimate differences among MPs in order to ensure equitable treatment. The design of such expenses should not permit these to become a source of income. Third, the transition of MPs to private life should be facilitated. Fourth, the benefits, including pension plans, should be comparable with the private and public sectors. On the issue of performance-based pay, the report was careful to point out that much more study was necessary in order to ensure that the criteria for such compensation were indeed within the control of the MPs.

The compensation policy should permit MPs as well as Canadians to perceive that the parliamentarians' financial compensation level is fair and equitable. For this purpose, the study proposed an independent representative group of Canadians, including compensation specialists, to review and propose changes to the compensation package and qualifying conditions. This would be a more objective alternative to the present situation where parliamentarians vote for themselves the compensation that they deem to be proper.

The process and guiding principles suggested above illustrate that the principles of "contingency" and "equity" in design and administration of the compensation system are equally applicable to the compensation of unique groups such as MPs.

REWARD MANAGEMENT IN DEVELOPING COUNTRIES

INTRODUCTION

Two developments in Canada—one, in the area of international business, and the other, in the area of immigration—make the design and management of reward systems in developing countries a relevant and important topic. With NAFTA and the recent successes of Team Canada (an initiative of Canadian business corporations which generated business worth billions of dollars in China, India and other countries in Asia), means that more Canadian business organizations will operate in the developing countries. Canada's declining birth-rate has made immigration the critical source for its human resource. Based on the present trends, it is estimated that most of the immigrants will be from Africa, the Near and Far East, and Asia. Consequently, an increase in the cultural diversity of the workforce is inevitable in Canada. The effects of both developments for managers is that they will be called upon to manage in different cultural contexts, either in their organizations in developing countries, or in Canada.

In Chapter 2, we explored the characteristics of the sociocultural environment and the organization's internal work culture and discussed how these impact on the design and management of the reward system. Consequently, the state-of-the-art reward systems, developed in the sociocultural context of North America, will not be effective in other cultural contexts unless these are appropriately modified to fit the characteristics of other cultures.

In the sections which follow we consider the critical features of the sociocultural environment in developing countries with particular reference to those aspects that are likely to facilitate and hinder the adoption of the practices and techniques of an effective reward system. We then propose specific practical managerial strategies to build on the cultural facilitators and to overcome the cultural constraints in order to derive the full benefit of these practices and techniques.

THE SOCIOCULTURAL CHARACTERISTICS OF DEVELOPING COUNTRIES

As indicated in chapter 2, the cultural differences between developed and developing countries in an organizational context can be understood in terms of the four dimensions suggested by Hofstede (1980b). On average, developing countries have been found to be high on Uncertainty Avoidance and Power Distance and low on Individualism and Masculinity (Kanungo and Jaeger, 1990, Jorgensen, 1995). We now discuss how each characteristic (dimension) of the socio-cultural environment is likely to promote or hinder the effectiveness of the reward management practices.

IMPACT OF THE SOCIO-CULTURAL ENVIRONMENT

High Uncertainty Avoidance

Content The relatively high uncertainty avoidance implies an unwillingness to take risks, primarily because of early socialization practices. These practices promote the view that each member of society has a specific, prescribed role which is a function of the person's age, occupation, or family and social status. Any deviation from it is discouraged, and sometimes, penalized. These practices also foster an external locus of control—the belief that the external environment controls them which is a fatalistic approach to life and living.

Effects High uncertainty avoidance is not conducive to performance-based pay which is essentially at-risk pay. Rewards are based on managerial decisions which employees are not expected to question. As a result, the individual's high external locus of control is reinforced, and secrecy is introduced in the reward system which creates inequity perceptions and reduces reward valence. The reluctance to take personal initiatives, implicit in role-bound behaviour, inhibits the use of non-economic rewards such as challenging assignments and job autonomy.

Low Individualism

Content Low individualism implies that family concerns and group attainments take precedence over the individual's work concerns and achievements. Unlike Western cultures, individuals do not see work as an act of self-fulfilment or self-expression, but primarily as a means to fulfil one's family and social obligations. What is also more salient are the personalized relationships generated by the job; employees tend to see job performance as work they do to please their superiors or co-workers who might be their friends or relatives. Thus, even when they perform extremely well, they tend to get satisfaction from "work well recognized", rather than from "work well done".

Effects In a low individualism work culture, contingent rewards will be more effective when based on group, rather than on individual performance. Economic rewards, including a flexible benefits program, that enable them to meet their family obligations will be valued. Employees will also value non-economic rewards that recognize the individual's contribution to significant others in the job context. Employees will be loyal to the organization, and expect a reciprocal loyalty from the organization in terms of rewards based on seniority.

High Power Distance

Content High power distance implies that managers and subordinates accept their respective positions in the organizational hierarchy and operate from these fixed positions. It seems inevitable in the prevailing hierarchical social structures which place a high value on obedience to the holder of the position not on any rational basis but simply by virtue of the authority of the person. Managers do not consider subordinates to be people just like me; neither do the subordinates view their managers as people just like themselves.

Effects It discourages employee participation and involvement in reward design and implementation which is critical to employee's perceptions of the reward's saliency, valence and contingency. Managers expect employees to unquestioningly accept their reward decisions; employees fear to disagree with them. The resulting mistrust adversely affects employee perceptions of the performance-rewards linkage. Also the system tends to emphasize hierarchy-based status symbols and pay differentials which do not truly reflect the job's contribution to organizational objectives.

Low Masculinity

Content Low masculinity implies that the orientation of employees is towards people or personalized relationships rather than job performance. Consequently, the satisfaction of affiliative needs takes precedence over satisfaction derived from achieving job objectives; performing socially approved duties in the interpersonal context takes precedence over job performance.

Effects The norms and values implicit in low masculinity expect that individuals be rewarded for membership behaviours rather than for performance. Low masculinity emphasizes the importance of non-economic rewards that satisfy affiliation needs. Such an emphasis can frustrate the performance management process as work relationships tend to shift away from the job tasks at hand. For example, employees might expect that personal loyalty to the supervisor is a more important behaviour that should be included in the performance evaluation. Also, the job performance feedback might be misconstrued as attacks on the person rather than on job behaviours.

The characteristics of the socio-cultural environment and their impact on effective reward system practices are summarized in Table 16.1.

IMPACT OF THE INTERNAL WORK CULTURE ON REWARD MANAGEMENT

In reviewing the impact of the cultural dimensions on reward management practices, our focus has been on the effects of the socio-cultural environment which form part of the beliefs and values which employees carry with them when they join an organization, and influence the organization's internal work culture. Although the internal work culture of the organization is affected by the socio-cultural environment, it has a more direct impact on the way the reward system is managed in the organization.

As discussed previously in Chapter 2, Kanungo and Jaeger (1990) have categorized the culture determined management values and climate of beliefs and assumptions that characterize the internal work culture, under two broad headings: (a) the descriptive assumptions about human nature, and (b) the prescriptive assumptions about the guiding principles of human conduct. According to this scheme, the internal work culture in developing country organizations will

Table 16.1 Impact of the Soci-Cultural Environment on Reward Design and Management

Socio-Cultural Characteristics (Dimensions)	Manifest Behaviours Attitudes and Dispositions	Impact on Reward System Design and Management
High Uncertainty Avoidance	• Promotes role-bound behaviour; discourages personal initiatives • Fosters high risk-aversion • Inculcates external locus of control	• Inhibits the use of performance-based (at risk) pay and non-economic rewards (e.g. autonomy, challenging assignments) that satisfy high growth needs • Promotes secrecy of the reward system resulting in employee perceptions of inequity of the system

Low Individualism	• Work is not a means of self-fulfilment, but a means to fulfill family and social obligations
	• Group concerns are more salient than task accomplishment
	• Seeks recognition from peers and superiors rather than from task accomplishment
		• Inhibits the use of rewards based on individual performance
		• Facilitates:
		  • group-based contingent rewards
		  • flexible benefits approach that fits employees personal and family needs
		  • non-economic rewards that recognize contribution to significant others in the job context
		• Employee perceptions of reward system's significance is enhanced when it supports the organization's mission to serve a "'higher" purpose rather than just the pursuit of profits
		• Facilitates employee involvement in design of reward system

Low Masculinity	• High focus on personalized rather than contractual relationships
	• Satisfaction of affiliative needs takes precedence over satisfaction from achieving job objectives
	• Expect to be rewarded for loyalty to one's superiors or organization
		• Inhibits the use of performance-based rewards
		• Rewards perceived to be valued are those that
		  • recognize membership behaviours
		  • satisfy affiliation needs

High Power Distance	• Acceptance of hierarchical authority structures and relationships • Expect direction and guidance from superiors, and willing to accept the superior's decisions because of the authority of their office	• Inhibits employee involvement in the design and implementation of reward system techniques and processes • Not conducive to trust and proper performance-rewards linkage that are critical to employee perceptions of reward valence and contingency • Disproportionate focus on status symbols • Wage/salary differentials do not reflect job's contributions to achieving organizational objectives

likely be characterized as follows:

Descriptive Assumptions About Human Nature	Prescriptive Assumptions About Guiding Principles of Human Conduct
- External locus of control	- Reactive stance to task performance
- Limited or fixed potential	- Success is judged on moralism
- Immediate need gratification	- Paternalistic/authoritarian
- Short term perspective	- Context dependent

The impact of the internal work culture on the reward system and related techniques and practices will be as depicted in Figure 2.3 under the "Management Assumptions #2".

ORGANIZATIONAL INTERVENTIONS TO ENSURE CULTURE FIT

Organizations should consider a systematic approach to remove the cultural constraints and build upon those cultural beliefs and values which have the potential to enhance the effectiveness of the reward system in the areas of: compensation philosophy, performance management program, job evaluation system, and wage and salary surveys.

Table 16.2 summarizes the managerial actions in one approach to minimize the cultural constraints and build on the cultural facilitators to ensure the effectiveness of the reward system.

SUMMARY

This chapter considered three new and emerging issues in compensation. First, it discussed person-based pay in terms of the forms of person-based pay, its design mechanics, and its merits and challenges. Second, it explored the issues in the compensation of executives and parliamentarians. The third emerging issue that was examined was the design and management of reward systems to fit the characteristics of sociocultural contexts different from those in North America.

Table 16.2 Proposed Organizational Interventions to Ensure Culture-fit of Reward

		Mode and Effect of Organizational Intervention (ie., overcoming Cultural Constraints; Building on Cultural Facilitators	
Organizational Intervention Relating to Strategic and Process Issues in Reward Design and Implementation	Reward Philosophy	• State reward system as a means of attaining the organization's mission which is expressed in terms of the organization's higher purpose—i.e., having a larger cause or community than the mere pursuit of material gains for the investors. • Performance-based pay linked to group performance • Assurance of training to meet performance objectives • Pay differentials to reflect job value to organization, and pay rates in relevant labour market • Clearly and frequently communicated	EFFECTS • Minimizes the cultural constraints of high uncertainty avoidance, high power distance, and low individualism • Builds on the cultural facilitators of low masculinity and low individualism
	Performance Management Program	• Set specific and difficult goals with clearly defined time targets, and within the employee's competency level, and provide information on the rewards that follow the different performance levels. Where feasible, establish group goals and rewards based on group performance • Express goals in terms of their contribution to attaining the departmental goals and the organization's mission in order that goal attainment becomes a means of satisfying the "relationship or people orientation" • Provide feedback on performance that considers positive and negative features in a constructive and supportive climate, with a discussion of training, and performance improvement suggestions (including necessary organizational resources) which contribute to enhancing the employee's self-efficacy beliefs. Feedback should also emphasize impact of performance on "significant others" • Provide valued rewards that fairly reflect job performance including public recognition that highlights job performance as service to others and fulfilment of personal duty • Manager functions as coach and mentor and strives to involve the employees in the activities and process of performance management	EFFECTS • Gradually minimizes the cultural constraints of high uncertainty avoidance, high power distance, low masculinity, and low indivualism • Avails of the facilitating characteristics of low masculinity, low individualism, and high power distance, that conflict with performance evaluation systems
	Job Evaluation System	• In organizations that use the job-content-based job evaluation system, ensure that the choice and weighting of the compensable factors are relevant to job objectives and the organization's mission • In work units staffed by professionals or semi-autonomous work groups, consider person-based job evaluation system such as knowledge-based or skills-based pay • Involve employees in the design of the job evaluation systems, and provide for an appeal mechanism in the job evaluation administrative process	EFFECTS • Takes advantage of some aspects of high uncertainty avoidance, high power distance, low individualism, and low masculinity, that do not conflict with designing job evaluation systems • Minimizes the constraining effects of some aspects of low masculinity, low individualism, and high power distance that conflict with designing job evaluation systems
	Salary Surveys	• Establish pay policy consistent with the organization's mission and in terms of the relevant external labour market • Communicate pay policy—in particular, its relationship to the critical elements of the organization's business strategies and mission • Conduct salary surveys in a systematic manner, and involve employees in the process	EFFECTS • Minimizes the constraining effects of low masculinity • Involving employees allows managers to take advantage of the facilitating characteristics of low masculinity

_____ ℘ _____ KEY TERMS _____

ethical leadership   level-of-benefit method
horizontal skills   vertically upward skills
in-depth skills
knowledge-based pay

_____ ℘ _____ REVIEW AND DISCUSSION QUESTIONS _____

1. Distinguish between person-based pay and job-based pay.

2. Distinguish between horizontal skills, vertically-upward skills, and in-depth skills.

3. What are the advantages and the disadvantages of person-based pay?

4. What are the major components of executive compensation? Describe the main features of each component element.

5. What are some of the process issues in executive compensation?

6. Explain the nature of the conflict between shareholders and senior executives? How can it be addressed?

7. Discuss the impact of the sociocultural environment on the design and management of rewards in developing countries.

Designing Reward System Consistent With the Sociocultural Environment of Developing Countries

Objective

To identify the impact of the sociocultural environment on reward design and management, and to develop specific strategies to ensure the culture-fit of the reward system.

Procedure

First, do activities 1 to 3 listed below, individually. Then discuss your proposals in your work groups, and arrive at a group consensus, keeping note of the major differences.

1. Refer to the case Roasted Duck Delicacies Limited (RDDL) in Chapter 2. Roasted Duck Delicacies Limited has decided to open RDDL outlets in developing countries.

2. Using Hofstede's dimensions, identify the specific impact of the sociocultural characteristics of developing countries on the design and management of the reward system.

3. Develop specific reward design and implementation strategies which RDDL should consider to overcome the cultural constraints and build on the cultural facilitators.

4. Each group reports on its decisions to the class, and a plenary discussion follows.

References

Abella, Judge Rosalie Silberman.(1991) "Quality and human rights in Canada: Coping with the new Isms." *University Affairs* June-July.

Abosch, Kenan S., Dan Gilbert, and Susan M. Dempsey. (1994) "Contrasting Perspectives—Broadbanding: Approaches of Two Organizations." *ACA Journal* (Spring): 46-53.

Adams, J. S. (1965) "Injustice in Social Exchange." In *Advances in Experimental Social Psychology* Vol. 2, edited by L. Berkowitz. New York: Academic Press.

Agarwal, N. (1990)"Pay Equity in Canada: Current Developments." *The Labor Law Journal* 41:518-525.

Allen, N.J., and J.P. Meyer. (1990) "The measurement and antecedents of affective, continuance and normative commitment to the organization." *Journal of Occupational Psychology* 63:1-18.

Azavedo, R.E., and L. Roth. (1990) "Canadian-United States experience with comparable worth: The view from Minnesota." *The Labor Law Journal* 41:531-534.

Balkin, David B., and Luis R. Gomez-Mejia. (1987) "Towards a Contingency Theory of Compensation Strategy." *Strategic Management Journal* 8:169-82.

Baytos, Lawrence M.(1991) "Board Compensation Committees: Collaboration or Confrontation." *Compensation and Benefits Review* (May-June): 33-38.

Becker, T.E., R.S. Billings, D.M. Eveleth, and N.L. Gilbert. (1996) "Foci and Bases of Employee Commitment: Implications for Job Performance." *Academy of Management Journal* 38:464-482

Beer, Michael, Russell A. Eisenstat, and Biggadike. (1996) "Strategic Change: A New Dimension of Human Resource Management," in Gerald R. Ferris, Sherman D. Rosen, and Darold T. Barnum (eds.) *Handbook of Human Resource Management.* Cambridge, MA: Blackwell Publishers, pp.115-138.

Bellak, Alvin O. (1984) "Specific Job Evaluation Systems: The Hay Guide Chart-Profile Method," in *Handbook of Wage and Salary Administration*, edited by Milton L. Rock. New York: McGraw-Hill.

Benge, Eugene J. (1984) "Specific Job Evaluation Systems: The Factor Method," in *Handbook of Wage and Salary Administration*, edited by Milton L. Rock. New York: McGraw-Hill.

Berger, B. (1984) "Comparable worth at odds with American realities." *Comparable Worth:Issue for the 80's*, Vol. 1. Washington, D.C: United States Commission on Civil Rights.

Boivin, J. and E. Deom. (1995) "Labour Management Relations in Quebec," in M. Gunderson and A. Ponak (eds.) *Union Management Relations in Canada*, 3rd edition. Don Mills, Ontario: Addison-Wesley, 455-493.

Booth, P.L. (1987) *Paying for Performance: The Growing Use of Incentives and Bonus Plans.* Ottawa: Conference Board of Canada.

———. (1990) *Strategic Rewards Management: The Variable Approach to Pay.* Ottawa: Conference Board of Canada.

———. (1993) *Employee Absenteeism : Strategies for promoting attendance-oriented culture.* Ottawa: Conference Board of Canada.

Brown, Grant A. (1991) "The Myth of the Gender Wage Gap." *Women in Management*, Vol.2. London, Ont.: National Centre for Management Research and Development's Women in Management Program.

Bula, Frances. (1992) "Pass Law to Guarantee Pay Equity: Rights Commission." *The Montreal Gazette* (March 7):A3.

Burr, Richard E. (1986) *Are Comparable Worth Systems Truly Comparable?* St.Louis: Center for the Study of American Business.

Byrne, John A., and Lori Bongiorno. (1995) "CEO Pay: Ready for Takeoff." *Business Week* (April 24):88-94.

Canadian Council on Working Life. (1990) "The Cardinal River Story," in CCWL's *A Learning Visit to an Innovative Site* (March) 14-16, 1990. Hinton, Alberta.

CARRA. *See* Commission administrative des regimes de retraite et d'assurances.

Carlyle, Nathalie Borris.(1994) *Compensation Planning Outlook 1995.* Ottawa: Conference Board of Canada.

Carrell, Michael R., and John E. Dittrich. (1978) "Equity Theory: The Recent Literature, Methodological Considerations, and New Directions." *Academy of Management Review* (April):202-210.

Chingos, Peter T.(1991) "Annual Incentive Compensation for Executives" in Milton L. Rock and Lance A. Berger (eds.) *The Compensation Handbook: A State-of-the-art Guide to Compensation Strategy and Design.* New York: McGraw-Hill, Inc., pp.322-338.

Colleti, Jerome A. and Cichelli. (1991) "Increasing Sales-Force Effectiveness Through the Compensation Plan," in Milton L. Rock and Lance A. Berger (eds.) *The Compensation Handbook.* New York, NY: McGraw-Hill, pp.290-303.

Commission administrative des regimes de retraite et d'assurances. (1988) *An Investment for the Future: RREGOP, TPP, CSSP.* Quebec: Services des communications, CARRA.

———. (1990) *My Retirement.* Quebec: Services des communications, CARRA, September.

Conger, J.A., and R.N. Kanungo. (1988) "The Empowerment Process: Integrating Theory and Practice." *The Academy of Management Review* 13:471-82.

———. (1988b) "Behavioral Dimensions of Charismatic Leadership," in J.A. Conger and R.N. Kanungo (eds.) *Charismatic Leadership: The elusive factor in organizational effectiveness.* San Francisco, CA: Jossey-Bass, pp. 78-97.

———. (1992) "Perceived behavioral attributes of charismatic leadership." *Canadian Journal of Behavioral Sciences* 24:86-102.

Craig, A. (1988) "Mainstream Industrial Relations in Canada." In G. Hebert, H. Jain, and N. Meltz (eds.) *The State of the Art of Industrial Relations.* Kingston and Toronto: Queen's University Industrial Relations Centre and University of Toronto Centre for Industrial Relations.

Cranston, Maurice. (1987) "What Are Human Rights?" in *Human Rights and Freedoms in Canada.* Edited by Mark L. Berlin and William F. Pentney. Toronto: Butterworths.

Crystal, Graef S. (1970) *Financial Motivation for Executives.* New York: American Management Association.

———. (1984) *Questions and Answers on Executive Compensation: how to get what you're worth.* Englewood Cliffs, New Jersey: Prentice-Hall, Inc.

———. (1991) *In Search of Excess.* New York: W.W. Norton.

Davis, L. E., and A. B. Cherns. (1975) *The Quality of Working Life.* Vol. 2, *Cases and Commentary.* New York: Free Press.

Deci, E. L. (1972) "The Effects of Contingent and Noncontingent Rewards and Controls on Intrinsic Motivation." *Organizational Behavior and Human Performance* 8:217-29.

Depree, Max. (1989) cited in *Corporate Values: A Statement of Herman Miller Inc.* Zeeland, Michigan: Herman Miller, Inc.

Deutsch, M. (1975) "Equity, equality and need: What determines which value will be used as the basis of distributive justice?" *Journal of Social Issues* 31:137-149.

———. (1985) *Distributive Justice: a social-psychological perspective.* New Haven: Yale University Press.

Dubin, R. (1956) "Industrial Workers' Worlds: A Study of the Central Life Interests of Industrial Workers." *Social Problems* 3:131-42.

Dyer, L., and D. F. Parker. (1976) "Classifying Outcomes in Work Motivation Research: An Examination of the Intrinsic-Extrinsic Dichotomy." *Journal of Applied Psychology* 60:455-58.

Eisenhardt, Kathleen M. (1989) "Agency Theory: An Assessment and Review." *Academy of Management Review* 14(1):57-74.

Elig, B.R. (1981) "Compensation Elements: Market phase determines the mix." *Compensation Review* Third quarter: p.30.

Fein, M. (1974) "Job Enrichment: A Reevaluation." *Sloan Management Review* 15(2): 69-88.

———. (1976) "Motivation for Work," in *Handbook of Work, Organization, and Society.* Edited by Robert Dubin. Chicago: Rand McNally College Publishing Co.

Financial Post, The. (1988) "Day Care Becoming Management Issue: On-Site Centres Latest Addition to Modern Office." (October 18):43.

———. (1995a) "Canadian pay hampers CEO talent hunt." 89(16), April 22/24:57.

———. (1995b) "Average pay packet for CEOs $800,000" 8(128), September 15:6.

Freedman, Robert J. (1986) "How to Develop a Sales Compensation Plan." *Compensation and Benefits Review* (March-April): 41-48.

Freeman, Richard B. and James L. Medoff. (1984) *What do unions do?* New York: Basic Books, Inc.

Frost, Greenwood and Associates. (1982) *The Scanlon Plan Today.* Lansing, Mich.: Scanlon Plan Associates.

Gartner, William B., and James M. Naughton. (1996) "A summary of 'Out of Crisis' by W. Edwards Deming," in J.L. Pierce and J.W. Newstrom (eds.) *The Manager's Bookshelf: A Mosaic of Contemporary Views.* New York, NY: Harper Collins.

Gazette, The (Montreal). (1980) "Absenteeism Is '10 Times Costlier Than Strikes.'" (October 14):54.

Gerhart, Barry, Harvey B. Minkoff, and Ray N. Olsen. (1996) "Employee Compensation: Theory, Practice, and Evidence," in Gerald R. Ferris, Sherman D. Rosen, and Darold T. Barnum (eds.) *Handbook of Human Resource Management*. Cambridge, MA: Blackwell, pp. 528-547.

Gerhart, Barry and George T. Milkovich. (1992)"Employee Compensation: Research and Practice," in Marvin D. Dunnette and Leaetta M. Hough (eds.) *Handbook of Industrial and Organizational Psychology*, 2nd Edition, Vol. 3, Paolo Alto, CA: Consulting Psychologists Press, pp.481-569.

Gibb-Clark, Margot. (1991) "Flexible Benefits Let Employees Tailor Coverage." *The Globe and Mail* (June 24):B4.

———. (1996) "Union shops urged to consult workers." *The Globe and Mail* (January 10):B8.

Gold, Michael Evan. (1983) *A Dialogue on Comparable Worth*. Ithaca, N.Y.: ILR Press, Cornell University.

Gomez-Mejia, L.R. and D.B. Balkin. (1992) *Compensation, Organizational Strategy, and Firm Performance*. Cincinatti: South-Western.

Gray, John. (1996) "Anxiety over potnetial loss of jobs issue at core of civil service strike." *The Globe and Mail* (March 2):A1, A7.

Greenberg, Jerald. (1986)"Determinants of Perceived Fairness of Performance Evaluations." *Journal of Applied Psychology* 71(2):340-42.

Gunderson, Morley and Douglas Hyatt. (1995) "Union Impact on Compensation, Productivity, and Management of the Organization," in Morley Gunderson and Allen Ponak (eds.) *Union-Management Relations in Canada*. Third Edition, Don Mills, Ont: Addison-Wesley Publishers Limited, pp.311-337.

Gunderson, Morley and Allen Ponak. (1995) "Industrial Relations," in Morley Gunderson and Allen Ponak (eds.) *Union-Management Relations in Canada*. Third Edition, Don Mills, Ont: Addison-Wesley Publishers Limited, pp.1-20.

Gunderson, M. (1995) "Gender Discrimination and Pay Equity Legislation," in L.N. Christofides, E.K. Grant, and R. Swidinsky (eds.) *Aspects of Labour Market Behaviour: Essays in Honour of John Vanderkamp*. Toronto: University of Toronto Press, 225-247.

Gunderson, M. and W.C. Riddell. (1991) "Economic issues pertaining to pay equity," in D. M. Saunders (ed.) *New Approaches to Employee Management*. Vol. 2. Greenwich, CT: JAI Press, pp. 115-27.

———. (1993) "Economic Issues Pertaining to Pay Equity," in D.M. Saunders (ed.), *New approaches to employee management* (Vol.2). Greenwich, CT: JAI Press, pp.115-127.

Guzzo, R. A. (1979) "Types of Rewards, Cognitions, and Work Motivation." *Academy of Management Review* 4:75-86.

Hackman, Richard J., and Greg R. Oldham. (1980) *Work Redesign.* Reading, Mass.: Addison-Wesley.

Henderson, R. I. (1989) *Compensation Management—Rewarding Performance.* 5th ed. Englewood Cliffs, N.J.: Prentice-Hall.

Henderson, R. I., and Michael N. Wolfe. (1985) *Workbook for Compensation Management: Rewarding Performance.* Reston, Va.: Reston Publishing Co.

Herman Miller. (1987) *See* "Participative Management at Herman Miller: An Innovative Strategy for Action."

Herzberg, F. (1966) *Work and the Nature of Man.* Cleveland, Ohio: World Publishing.

Herzberg, F., B. Mausner, and B. Snyderman. (1959) *The Motivation to Work.* New York: John Wiley.

Hofstede, G. (1980a) *Culture's Consequences: International Differences in Work-Related Values.* Beverly Hills, Calif.: Sage Publications.

_____. (1980b) "Motivation, Leadership, and Organization: Do American Theories Apply Abroad?" *Organizational Dynamics* 9(1): 42-62.

Hom, Peter W., Fanny Caranikas-Walker, and Gregory E. Prussia. (1992) "A Meta-Analytical Structural Equations Analysis of a Model of Employee Turnover." *Journal of Applied Psychology* 77(6): 890-909.

Homans, G.C. (1961) *Social Behavior: Its Elementary Forms.* New York: Harcourt, Brace and World Inc.

Howard, Ross. (1995) "Study links minority males, wage gap." *The Globe and Mail*, p. A7.

Human Resource Management in Canada. (1991) "Ontario Expands Pay Equity Program." *Report Bulletin* No. 96, Scarborough, Ontario: Prentice Hall.

———. (1992) "Pay equity glacial, union says." *Report Bulletin* 111, Scarborough, Ont: Prentice-Hall.

———. (1995) "Pay for Performance Spreading Downward." *Report Bulletin* 151 (September): 1-16.

Husemann, R.C., J.D. Hatfield, and E.W. Miles. (1987) "A New Perspective on Equity Theory: The Equity Sensitivity Construct." *Academy of Management Review* (12):222-234.

Information Booklet. (1991) "Team Operator Recruitment Process." Shell Canada Brockville Lubricants Plant, pp. 1-11.

Jain, Harish C. (1984) "Racial Discrimination in Employment in Canada: Issues and Policies," in *South Asians in the Canadian Mosaic,* edited by R.N. Kanungo. Montreal: Kala Bharati.

Jensen, Michael C., and Kevin J. Murphy. (1990) "CEO Incentives —It's Not How Much You Pay, But How." *Harvard Business Review* (May-June):138-149.

Johns, Gary. (1980) "Did You Go to Work Today?" *The Montreal Business Report* (Fourth Quarter): 52-56.

Johnson, Alan M. (1991) "Designing Total Compensation Programs," in Milton L. Rock and Lance A. Berger (eds.) *The Compensation Handbook*. New York, NY: Mc Graw-Hill, pp.311-321.

Jorgenson, J. (1995) "Restructuring public enterprise in East Africa: The human resource management dimension," in R.N. Kanungo (ed.) *New Approaches to Employee Management: Employee Management in Developing Countries*. Greenwich, Connecticut: JAI Press, pp.35-36.

Judge, T.A. (1993) "Does affective dispostion moderate the relationship betweeen job satisfaction and voluntary turnover?" *Journal of Applied Psychology* (78):395-401.

Kanfer, R. (1990) "Motivation Theory and Industrial and Organizational Psychology." In M.D. Dunnette and L.M. Hough (eds.) *Handbook of Industrial and Organizational Philosophy.* Palo Alto, CA: Consulting Psychologists, 75-170.

Kanungo, R.N. (1975) "Managerial Job Satisfaction: A Comparison between Anglophones and Francophones," in *Canadian Industrial Relations.* Edited by S.M.A. Hameed. Toronto: Butterworths.

————. (1980) *Biculturalism and Management*. Toronto: Butterworths.

Kanungo, R.N., and J. Hartwick. (1987) "An Alternative to the Intrinsic-Extrinsic Dichotomy of Work Rewards." *Journal of Management* 13:751-66.

Kanungo, R.N., and A.M. Jaeger. (1990) "Introduction: The Need for Indigenous Management in Developing Countries," in *Management in Developing Countries*, edited by A. M. Jaeger and R. N. Kanungo. London: Routledge, pp.1-19.

Kanungo, R.N., and M. Mendonca. (1988) "Evaluating Employee Compensation." *California Management Review* (Fall): 23-29.

————. (1994) *Fundamentals of Organizational Behavior*. Dubuque, Iowa: Kendall/Hunt.

————. (1996) *Ethical Dimensions of Leadership*. Thousand Oaks, CA: Sage Publications.

Kanungo, R.N. and S. Misra. (1988) "The Basis of Involvement in Work and Family Contexts." *International Journal of Psychology* 23:267-282.

Keenan, G. (1996) "Big Three plants keep workers away for a week." *The Globe and Mail* (March 9): B5.

Kiechel, Walter. (1993) "How will we work in the Year 2000?" *Fortune* (May 17):38-52.

Knowles, P.A.(1954) *Profit Sharing Patterns.* Evanston, Ill: Profit Sharing Research Foundation.

Kohn, A. (1994) *Punished by Rewards: The Trouble with Gold Stars, Incentive Plans, Aís, Praise, and Other Bribes.* Boston, MA: Houghton-Mifflin.

Korukonda, Appa Rao. (1996) "Cognitive Processes and Computer Advances in Job Evaluation: Innovation in Reverse?" *Canadian Journal of Administrative Sciences* 13(1):78-82.

Kovach, Kenneth A., and Peter E. Millspaugh. (1990) "Comparable Worth: Canada Legislates Pay Equity." *Academy of Management Executive* 4(2): 92-101.

Lange, Norman R. (1991) "Job Analysis and Documentation," in Milton L. Rock and Lance E. Berger (eds.) *The Compensation Handbook.* New York, NY: McGraw-Hill, pp.49-71.

Lawler, E.E. (1971) *Pay and Organizational Effectiveness.* New York: McGraw-Hill.

———. (1972) "Secrecy and the Need to Know," in *Readings in Managerial Motivation and Compensation,* edited by M. Dunnette, R. House, and H. Tosi. East Lansing: Michigan State University Press.

———. (1977) "Reward Systems." In *Improving Life at Work,* edited by J.R. Hackman and J. L. Shuttle. Santa Monica, Calif.: Goodyear.

———. (1981) *Pay and Organizational Development.* Reading, Mass.: Addison-Wesley.

———. (1986a) *High-Involvement Management.* San Francisco, Calif.: Jossey-Bass.

———. (1986b) "What's Wrong With Point-Factor Job Evaluation." *Compensation and Benefits Review* 18(2): 20-28.

———. (1990) *Strategic Pay: Aligning Organizational Strategies and Pay Systems,* San Francisco, CA: Jossey-Bass Inc.

Lawler, E.E., A.M. Mohrman, and S.M. Resnick. (1984) "Performance Appraisal Revisited." *Organizational Dynamics* (Summer): 20-35.

Lawler, E.E., and G.D. Jenkins. (1976) "Employee Participation in Pay Plan Development." Unpublished technical report to the Department of Labor, Ann Arbor, Michigan, cited in *Pay and Organizational Development,* edited by E.E. Lawler. Reading, Mass.: Addison-Wesley.

Lawler, E.E., and J.R. Hackman. (1969) "The Impact of Employee Participation in the Development of Pay Incentive Plans: A Field Experiment." *Journal of Applied Psychology* 53:467-71.

Lawler, E.E., and Gerald E. Ledford. (1985) "Skill-based Pay: A Concept That's Catching On." *Personnel* (September):54-61.

Ledford, Jr., Gerald E., and Gary Bergel. (1991) "Skill-Based Pay Base Number 1: General Mills." *Compensation and Benefits Review* (March-April):24-38.

Lerner, M.J., and J.R. Meindl. (1981) "Justice and altruism," in J.P. Rushton & R.M. Sorrentino (eds.) *Altruism and Helping Behavior.* Hillsdale, N.J.: Erlbaum.

Lerner, M.J., and L.A. Whitehead (1980) "Procedural justice viewed in the context of justice motive theory," in G. Mikula (ed.), *Justice and Social Interaction.* Bern: Hans Huber.

Levin, Michael E. (1987) *Feminism and Freedom.* New Brunswick, N.J.: Transaction, Inc.

Levine, H.E., (1990) "The Board Speaks Out." *Compensation and Benefits Review* (May-June):18-32.

Lewin, Kurt. (1935) *A Dynamic Theory of Personality.* New York: McGraw-Hill.

Locke, E.A., and J.F. Bryan. (1968) "Goal-Setting as a Determinant of the Effect of Knowledge of Score on Performance." *American Journal of Psychology* 81:398-406.

Locke, E.A., and G.P. Latham. (1984) *Goal-Setting: A Motivational Technique That Works!* Englewood Cliffs, N.J.: Prentice-Hall.

Locke, E.A., K.N. Shaw, L.M. Saari, and G. P. Latham. (1981) "Goal-Setting and Task Performance: 1969-1980." *Psychological Bulletin* 90:125-52.

Luthans, F., and W.E. Reif. (1972) "Does Job Enrichment Really Pay Off?" *California Management Review* 15:30-36.

———. (1973) "Job Enrichment: Long on Theory, Short on Practice." *Organizational Dynamics* 3:30-43.

Maclean's (1995) "Million-dollar grown-ups: executive compensation is on the rise, as profits increase." 108(16)April 17: 48-50.

Makin, K. (1996) "Law Graduates Starving for Work." *The Globe and Mail* (March 9): B5.

Martel, Phillippe and Yvan Pouliot. (1994) *Parliamentarians' Compensation: Report to the President of the Treasury Board.* Montreal: Sobeco Ernst & Young.

Maslow, Abraham H. (1954) *Motivation and Personality.* New York: Harper.

Mathias, P. (1992) "Pricing Canadian Jobs." *The Financial Post* (Jan. 13):S8.

McFarland, Janet. (1996) "Employees at the controls." *The Globe and Mail* (March 5):B8

McGrath, Karen. (1988) "Polaroid Workers Able to Picture Retirement." *The Globe and Mail* (Toronto) (January 28):B1-B2.

McGregor, D. (1966) "The Human Side of Enterprise," in *Leadership and Motivation: Essays of Douglas McGregor,* edited by W.G. Bennis and E.H. Schein with C. McGregor. Cambridge, Mass.: MIT Press.

McMullen, K., N. Leckie, and C. Caron. (1993) *Innovation at Work: The Workplace Technology Survey 1980-91.* Kingston, Ontario: IRC Press, Queen's University

McPherson, David L., and John T. Wallace. (1985) "Employee Benefit Plans," in *Human Resource Management in Canada.* Scarborough, Ont.: Prentice-Hall.

Meyer, John P. (1988) "Organizational Psychology in the 1980s: A Canadian Perspective." *Canadian Psychology* 29(1):19-29.

Miles, Raymond E., and Charles C. Snow. (1984) "Designing Strategic Human Resources Systems." *Organizational Dynamics* 13(1): 36-52.

Milkowich, George T., and Jerry M. Newman. (1996) *Compensation.* Homewood, Ill.: Richard D. Irwin.

Miner, J.B. (1980) *Theories of Organizational Behavior.* Hinsdale, Ill.: Dryden Press.

Monsalve, Marco A. and A. Triplett. (1990) "Maximizing New Technology." *HR Magazine* March:85-87.

Mowday, R.T. (1987) "Equity Theory Predictions of Behavior in Organizations," in R.M. Steers and L.W. Porter (eds.) *Motivation and Work Behavior*, 4th Edition. New York: McGraw Hill.

Murphy, Susan.(1993) *Reward Systems Report: Prepared for A Maritz Client (Generic Version).* Saint Louis, Missouri: Maritz Performance Improvement Company.

Newman, Janice and Tom Chase. (1993) *Readings of the Ecology of Work Conference.* Montreal, Sept. 29-Oct. 1.

O'Neill, June. (1984) "Earnings Differentials: Empirical Evidence and Causes," in Gunter Schmid and Renate Weitzel (eds.) *Sex Discrimination and Equal Opportunity: the labour market and employment policy.* England: Gower Pub. Co. Ltd.

Panchatantra. Translated from the Sanskrit by Arthur W. Ryder (1949). Bombay: Jaico Publishing House.

Partridge, John. (1995) "Bank of Montreal bonus reduced for branch workers." *The Globe and Mail* (December 22):B3.

Paul, Ellen Frankel. (1989) *Equity and Gender.* New Brunswick, N.J.: Transaction Publishers.

Paull, Jay. (1986) "How to Boost Productivity—Put a Nanny on Your Payroll." *Canadian Business* (March): 122-23.

Pay Equity Commission. (1989a) "Assessing the Gender Bias of Your Point Factor Job Evaluation System." *Newsletter* 1(9): 1-7. Toronto: Government of the Province of Ontario.

―――. (1989b) *Pay Equity Implementation Series # 15* (January):15.1-15.7. Toronto: Government of the Province of Ontario.

Pennings, Johannes M.(1991) "Executive Compensation Systems: Pay Follows Strategy or Strategy Follows Pay?" in Milton L.Rock and Lance A. Berger (eds.) *The Compensation Handbook: A State-of-the-Art Guide to Compensation Strategy and Design.* New York: McGraw Hill, pp. 368-382.

Pierce, Jon L., John W. Newstrom, Randall B. Dunham, and Alison E. Barber. (1989) *Alternative Work Schedules.* Toronto: Allyn and Bacon.

Polachek, Solomon William. (1975) "Differences in Expected Post-School Investment as a Determinant of Market Wage Differentials." *International Economic Review* 16:451.

Quinn, James B. (1988) "Strategies for Change," in *The Strategy Process: Concepts, Contexts, and Cases*, edited by James B. Quinn, Henry Mintzberg, and Robert M. James. Englewood Cliffs, N.J.: Prentice-Hall.

Reid, Frank, and Noah Meltz. (1984) "Canada's STC: A Comparison with the California Version," in *Short-Time Compensation: A Formula for Work Sharing*, edited by R. MaCoy and M. V. Morand. New York: Pergamon Press.

Rice, R.W., S.M. Phillips, and D.B. McFarlin. (1990) "Mulitiple discrepancies and pay satisfaction." *Journal of Applied Psychology* (75):386-393.

Robins, Stephen P. (1996) *Organizational Behavior: Concepts, Controversies, Applications.* Englewood Cliffs, NJ: Prentice-Hall.

Roethlisberger, Fritz J. and Willain J. Dickson. (1939) *Management and the Worker.* Cambridge, MA: Harvard University Press.

Rusk, James and Martin Mittelstaedt. (1996) "Key issues settled in strikes by 55,000 Ontario civil servants." *The Globe and Mail* (March 29):A9.

Schein, E. H. (1985) *Organizational Culture and Leadership.* San Francisco: Jossey-Bass.

―――. (1988) "Innovative Cultures and Adaptive Organizations." Working Paper, Sloan School of Management, Massachusetts Institute of Technology, Cambridge, Mass.

Schwinger, P. (1975) *Wage Incentive Systems.* New York: Halsted.

Seligman, Daniel. (1984) "Pay Equity is a Bad Idea." *Fortune* (May 14):133.

Sethia, N. and M. Von Glinow.(1985) "Arriving at Four Cultures by Managing the Reward System," in R. Kilman, M. Faxton, and R.Serpa(eds.), *Gaining Control of the Corporate Culture.* San Francisco, CA: Jossey-Bass, pp. 400-420.

Shapiro, W. Jack, and Mahmoud A. Wahba. (1978) "Pay Satisfaction: Empirical Test of Discrepancy Model." *Management Science* 24(6):612-22.

Simon, H. A. (1957) *Administrative Behavior*. New York: Free Press.

Smith, Adam. ([1796] 1950) *An Inquiry into the Nature and Causes of the Wealth of Nations*. Edited by Edwin Cannan. Vol. 1. London: Methuen.

Sowell, Thomas. (1984) *Civil Rights: Rhetoric or Reality*. New York: William Morrow & Co.

Statistics Canada. (1989a) *The Nation, Total Income: Individuals*. Ottawa: Supply and Services Canada.

———. (1989b) *Dimensions: Profile of Ethnic Groups*. Ottawa: Supply and Services Canada.

———. (1994) *Canada, Jobs and Growth: Building a More Innovative Economy*. Ottawa: Supply and Services Canada.

Staw, B.M. (1984) "Organizational Behavior: A Review and Reformulation of the Field's Outcome Variables." *Annual Review of Psychology* 35:627-66.

Thompson, Elizabeth(1995) "University Chiefs Paid more than Parizeau." *The Montreal Gazette* (December 14):A1.

Tolman. E. C. (1932) *Purposive Behavior in Animals*. New York: Century.

Toronto Sun. (1996) "Pay equity may cost feds $1.5 billion." (February 18):14.

Treece, James B. (1990). "Here Comes GM's Saturn: More Than a Car, It Is GM's Hope for Reinventing Itself." *Business Week* (April 9):56-62.

Vroom, V.H. (1964) *Work and Motivation*. New York: Wiley.

Waldie, Paul. (1993) "Absenteeism costs $15B annually, report says." *Financial Post* (March 25):4.

Wall, V.D., and L.L. Nolan. (1986) "Perceptions of Inequity, Satisfaction, and Conflict in Task-oriented Groups." *Human Relations* November: 1033-1052.

Wallace, Marc J., and Charles H. Fay. (1988). *Compensation Theory and Practice*. Boston: PWS-Kent.

Webster's Third New International Dictionary of the English Language (1981). Springfield, Massachusetts: Merriam.

Weiler, Paul. (1986) "The Wage of Sex: The Uses and Limits of Comparable Worth." *Harvard Law Review* 99:1728-1807.

Weiner, Nan, and Morley Gunderson. (1990) *Pay Equity: Issues, Options and Experiences*. Markham, Ont.: Butterworths.

Index

WE WANT TO HEAR FROM YOU!

By sharing your opinions about *Compensation: Effective Reward Management* 2/e, you will help us ensure that you are getting the most value for your textbook dollars. After you have used the book for a while, please fill out this form. Fold, tape, and mail or fax us toll free @ 1(800)565-6802!

Course name: _____ School name: _____

Your name: _____

1) Did you purchase this book (check all that apply):
   - ❏ From your campus bookstore
   - ❏ From a bookstore off-campus
   - ❏ New   ❏ Used   ❏ For yourself
   - ❏ For yourself and at least one other student

2) Was this text available at the bookstore when you needed it:
   - ❏ Yes   ❏ No

3) How far along are you in this course (put an ✕ where you are now)?

   ❏ _____ ❏ _____ ❏
   Beginning   Midway   Completed

4) How much of this text have you used (put an ✕ where appropriate)?

   ❏ _____ ❏ _____ ❏
   Skimmed   Read Half   Read entire book

5) Have you read the introductory material (ie., the preface)?
   - ❏ Yes   ❏ No   ❏ Parts of it

6) Even if you have only skimmed this text, please rate the following features:

Features:	Very valuable/effective	Somewhat valuable/effective	Not valuable/effective
Value as a reference			
Readability			
Design & illustrations			
Study & review material			
Problems & cases			
Relevant examples			
Overall perception			

7) What do you like most about this book?

_____

_____

_____

What do you like least?

_____

_____

_____

8) Are you a member of a provincial human resources association? Yes _____ No_____

   If yes, which one? _____

9) Do you think that this book will be a useful reference to you in your future career? Yes _____ No_____

   Comments: _____

   _____

10) May we quote you? Yes _____ No_____

    If you would like to receive information on other Wiley management books, please fill in the following information:

    Mailing address: _____ _____
                       (Street)   (Apt. #)

    _____ _____ _____

    (City)   (Province)   (Postal Code)

11) At the end of the semester, what do you intend to do with this text?

    ❑ Keep it   ❑ Sell it   ❑ Unsure

Thank you for your time and feedback!

WILEY

-   (fold here)   -